NATIONAL UNIVERSITY
LIBRARY

D0222336

EDUCATIONAL ADMINISTRATION AND POLICY
Effective Leadership for American Education

JAMES W. GUTHRIE
RODNEY J. REED

University of California at Berkeley

Prentice-Hall, Inc., Englewood Cliffs, New Jersey 07632

Library of Congress Cataloging in Publication Data

Guthrie, James W. (date)
   Educational administration and policy.

   Includes bibliographies and index.
      1. School management and organization—United States.
   2. Education and state—United States.   3. Educational
   law and legislation—United States.   I. Reed, Rodney J.
   II. Title.
   LB2805.G88 1986   379.73   85-9333
   ISBN 0-13-235672-4

Editorial/production supervision
  and interior design: Shirley Stern
Cover design: 20/20 Services, Inc.
Manufacturing buyer: Barbara Kittle

© 1986 by Prentice-Hall, Inc., Englewood Cliffs, New Jersey 07632

All rights reserved. No part of this book may be
reproduced, in any form or by any means,
without permission in writing from the publisher.

Printed in the United States of America

10 9 8 7 6 5 4 3 2 1

ISBN 0-13-235672-4   01

PRENTICE-HALL INTERNATIONAL (UK) LIMITED, *London*
PRENTICE-HALL OF AUSTRALIA PTY. LIMITED, *Sydney*
EDITORA PRENTICE-HALL DO BRASIL, LTDA., *Rio de Janeiro*
PRENTICE-HALL CANADA INC., *Toronto*
PRENTICE-HALL OF INDIA PRIVATE LIMITED, *New Delhi*
PRENTICE-HALL OF JAPAN, INC., *Tokyo*
PRENTICE-HALL OF SOUTHEAST ASIA PTE. LTD., *Singapore*
WHITEHALL BOOKS LIMITED, *Wellington, New Zealand*

We wish to dedicate this book to our children:
Karen, Kip, Kyle, Sarah, Shannon, and Ursula.
We have learned much from them about our schools and ourselves.

CONTENTS

v

PREFACE

The purpose of this book is to assist in the professional preparation of individuals who manage or who plan to manage an educational organization. Such organizations span a spectrum of endeavors. The most common are public elementary and secondary schools. Also included are colleges and universities, state and federal agencies, and professional associations. Nonpublic schools, both proprietary and nonprofit, and units within private sector firms responsible for training employees fall into this category as well.

As diverse as these organizations appear, they share at least one feature: They exist to enhance the knowledge and understanding of those enrolled within them. The knowledge an institution is expected to transmit may be relatively simple in preschool or kindergarten, and escalate to matters of considerable complexity at the postgraduate level. Regardless of the specific purposes or the range of subject matter involved, educational administrators have as their prime professional responsibility the effective management of institutions so as to appropriately fulfill the hopes of the individual students enrolled within them. Administrators must also serve the legitimate purposes of the broader society which supports these learning institutions.

Characteristics of an Effective Administrator

In order to provide the leadership needed to enhance the educational attainment of students and meet societal expectations for educational organizations, an administrator must exhibit knowledge and skill in several crucial dimensions:

Communication. Communication is at the core of those abilities expected of an effective administrator. On occasion, successful communication may involve only the straightforward written or oral transmission of information—just "the facts." On other occasions, it may be important to persuade others of the utility of adopting a particular course of action. At yet other times, an administrator may need to provide inspiration or solace. The purposes of communication may change with the audience being addressed. Speaking before a school board, a college board of trustees, or a legislative hearing may call for a dramatically different presentation than, for example, conveying the results of an annual personnel evaluation to a teacher or explaining a school's code of conduct to a group of entering freshmen. These are all important occasions for communication; however, one's vocabulary, demeanor, and sense of compassion may vary substantially with each.

A major obligation of an administrator is to accomplish the objectives of the organization by motivating and coordinating actions of other people. Thus, whether it be spoken or written, appropriate and effective communication is a *sine qua non* for effective administration. Regrettably, one can seldom achieve perfection in this dimension. The only way to become an effective speaker or writer is to engage in those activities and continually strive to improve. Reading widely is a major asset in this process.

Professional demeanor. The flowery embellishments characterizing personal exchanges in the eighteenth century have given way to the substantially greater informality and straightforward communication of the twentieth. Clearly, attitudes and their expression change over time. What does not change is the necessity for an effective administrator to comport him- or herself in a professional manner. In practical terms, this dictum translates into the intellectual and ethical traits of honesty, deference, courtesy, and compassion. Manners do not make an administrator, but they supply a revealing portrait of one's administrative style. For a variety of reasons, it is easier to display professional behavior to one's superiors in an organization. A better portrait of an administrator is provided by attitudes displayed toward subordinates.

Reflection. Socrates insisted that an "unexamined life is not worth living." Similarly, an administrator cannot hope to become more effective without consciously undertaking systematic self-appraisals of decisions and actions. There is too little known about the world to regard administration as a science. It continues to involve much that is creative, intuitive, and artistic. Consequently, an effective administrator regards decisions and actions as hypotheses to be tested by their results. This testing need not be in the strictest scientific sense. Rather, when faced with practical administrative choices, the position which appears logically, intuitively, or morally correct should be taken. Reflection upon the outcome should inform the next decision of a similar nature. Over time, by being appropriately self-critical, one can amass a repertoire of examined experiences which thereafter provide a vast sense of confidence in effectively directing the activities of organizations.

Growth. The administrator who is completely satisfied with his or her performance is professionally moribund. It is virtually a moral imperative that administrators strive for more efficacious means of satisfying the objectives of their organizations, serving clients, and achieving the public's interests. The need for continued growth may, but need not, involve ambition for higher administrative responsibility. What is crucial is a frame of mind which systematically seeks opportunities to improve one's professional performance. It is conceivable that a manager may have such a constricted assignment that he or she can perform only in a rather mechanical manner. Such a situation is routine and bureaucratic. A professional administrator has clients whose welfare always demands a continued striving for higher levels of service.

Ability to do. Accomplishing purposes is at the heart of the job. "Doing" may involve many steps: defining problems, assembling information, seeking advice, consulting those affected, projecting the consequences of choices, weighing alternatives, and so forth. However, an administrator must ultimately make a decision, must take action. On occasion, boldness is in order. At other times, caution is appropriate. Whatever the circumstances, purposeful action is at the heart of the job. To consistently withdraw into contemplation and avoid making decisions is to defer to inertia and obviate the need for the administrative position.

Education Administration in a Democracy

The five qualities described, characterize managerial effectiveness for any kind of organization, whether it be small or large, public or private. However, there are features of *educational* organizations, particularly public institutions in a democracy, which impose an added obligation upon administrators.

Leaders as models. Among other important expectations, society holds educational organizations responsible for the transmission of values. Schools are not alone in this undertaking. Families, churches, the military, the media, and organizations such as the YMCA, Boy Scouts, and Girl Scouts contribute to the formation of values as do informal agents such as one's peer culture. Educational institutions, particularly those concerned with students on the youthful end of the spectrum, are looked to as one of the major public agencies for inculcating personal ethics and civic virtue. Because of this important and publicly sensitive role, educational administrators need to be not only effective managers and leaders, they must also exhibit high levels of professional behavior in performing their managerial tasks. They are seen as models for those in their charge, and thus professionalism in this setting has an added symbolic value.

Public trust. Administrators in publicly supported and governed educational agencies need to be constantly mindful of the fact that management of the institution is entrusted to them. They do not own the school or agency, and it is unlikely that they have been divinely willed the position. Authority to operate a public educational institution is derived from consent of the citizens. Institutional purposes are a product of public expectations. To act contrary to those purposes is to violate the public's trust, abrogate the social contract, and invite dismissal.

WHAT ADMINISTRATORS NEED TO KNOW

We do not know if good administrators are "born" or "made." We do know that, regardless of their origins, administrators must possess certain knowledge and skills in order to lead and manage effectively. Many personal qualities—sensitivity, insight, humor, energy, moral judgment, poise—we acknowledge as being important for administrators, but their acquisition or enhancement stems from avenues other than the strictly academic.

This book presents information and explanations about two domains which are at once amenable to formal learning and crucial for successful administrative performance. These domains are: (1) the environment in which educational leadership occurs, and (2) the skills professional administrators employ in the conduct of their business. These two areas are not mutually exclusive. Nevertheless, the division is convenient for organizational purposes, and each domain is addressed in this text.

THE PLAN OF THE BOOK

The first part of the book explains the concepts and facts which provide the basis for educational administration and policy formation in the United States. The second part of the book explains the major skill areas important for educational managers and leaders.

Part One

The initial chapter in Part One provides an introduction to educational administration and policy. Important historical events in the development of the profession are explained, and the magnitude of current educational undertakings in the United States is described. This chapter also explains the major values which shape U.S. public policy in general and educational policy in particular. The chapter concludes with an analysis of current major educational policy issues and provides reasoned speculation regarding the future of such matters.

Remaining chapters in this part are aimed at describing the governmental, legal, financial, and organizational operation of America's system of public education. Substantial attention is given to the three major levels—local, state, and federal—involved in establishing policy for and governance of elementary and secondary education. A separate chapter provides a sociological explanation of the organizational dynamics which characterize educational institutions. In addition, Part One contains a chapter explaining important legal concepts undergirding the performance of educational managers. Attention is also given to describing the unusual complexity surrounding the manner in which America finances its schools. This part includes an explanation of curricular and instructional policy issues and describes means by which educational administrators can provide leadership in shaping the content and process of schooling.

Chapters comprising the first part explain the history and evolution of the governmental, legal, financial, organizational, curricular, and instructional policy environment of education. Additionally, attention is given to analytic background for contemporary educational policy issues. The intent is to provide an administrator with an understanding of important past developments, knowledge of current structures, and the ability to decide about future issues.

Part Two

The second part of this book is devoted to an explanation of the most important areas of managerial and leadership skills. These skills enable an administrator to establish direction for an organization, assess alternative tactical approaches for achieving objectives, allocate resources consistent with chosen courses of action, mobilize and motivate employees in the pursuit of objectives, appraise the outcome of a particular strategy, and distribute information regarding results. This part begins with a chapter on the behavior of leaders, and stresses important personal objectives—such as allocating time—upon which managers need to focus. Subsequent chapters describe and analyze skill functions such as planning, budgeting, evaluating, bargaining, communicating with the public, and the use of modern management tools such as computers. The concluding chapter in this part, and for the entire book, offers observations regarding likely future issues for educational administrators and explains the continued necessity for exhibiting strong professional leadership.

WHAT THIS BOOK DOES NOT INTEND

This book aims to enhance the ability of educational managers and leaders. However, by design, it is not intended to accomplish administrative specialization. This is an introductory text for individuals who have recently assumed a beginning administrative position or who aspire to such a position. It provides the information needed to build a base of management know-how. For an individual who may already have assumed an administrative position and who desires to strive for managerial specialization in an area such as school finance, business, personnel, or data processing, this book will not provide sufficient specialized knowledge. However, each of the above topics, plus dozens more, are introduced in this text, and current information and concepts are provided for specialized fields. However, space considerations limit the scope of this material to the provision of introductory information to the general administrator or specialist wishing to keep abreast of the latest information and trends in areas other than the one in which he or she is now already intensely engaged.

HOW TO USE THIS BOOK

Reference

For those interested in using this book for reference purposes, the table of contents and index will guide you to your topic. For practicing administrators anxious to gain an update or appraisal of an administrative topic, we have attempted to facilitate your task by a thorough provision of references and citations to current studies and significant writings. These reference aids are generally provided as footnotes to each chapter.

Instruction

As a text in introductory educational administration and policy courses, this book lends itself to a variety of instructional formats and time schedules. The entire book can be covered within a standard semester by assigning approximately one chapter each week. An effort has been made to render chapters approximately equal in length to facilitate such use.

For institutions utilizing a quarter system, there are at least two alternatives. One is to assign approximately two chapters per week and move through both parts of the text in rather rapid order. A second option (using the text for two quarters) is to utilize Part One on the *Environment of Educational Administration* in an initial quarter and supplement it with topics taken from the references listed at the end of the each chapter. Under this extended two quarter plan, a similar format could be followed with Part Two on *Administrative Skills* in the subsequent quarter.

ACKNOWLEDGEMENTS

A textbook such as this by its nature is comprehensive. Consequently, it is necessary to draw upon the talents of numerous other individuals in bringing it to fruition. The authors are anxious to acknowledge the assistance of those whose names are listed below. However, we are ourselves responsible for weaknesses. Also, in the event there are any individuals whose contributions we have neglected, we wish to offer an apology.

Jacob Adams, Charles Benson, Guy Benveniste, Helen Cagampang, Terry Emmett, William Gerritz, Bernard R. Gifford, Marcia Linn, Pamela Robbins, David Stern, Staten Webster, and Aaron Wildavsky, all of the University of California at Berkeley, were generous in offering ideas, advice, and reactions. Decker Walker and Michael Kirst of Stanford University were particularly helpful in commenting on the chapter on curriculum. David Girard, of Girard and Griffin, was generous in correcting our ideas regarding the law and education. Richard W. Pratt of the California Legislative Analyst Office contributed Chapter Ten.

Walter I. Garms of the University of Rochester, Lawrence C. Pierce of the University of Oregon, John W. Evans of the Educational Testing Service, and Theodore Lobman of the Hewlett Foundation were helpful in contributing ideas on numerous topics. Paul Disario and Donald Davis, of the Oakland and Berkeley public schools respectively, contributed to the chapter on budgeting.

Carol Thomas of the Southwest Regional Laboratory for Educational Research and Development, who served as a research assistant, provided invaluable assistance in identifying and summarizing references.

Justine Davis, Viviane Dutoit, Jennifer Klasky, Norma Needham, Kazuko Nishita, Judy Snow, and Jean Thompson were generous in typing draft after draft of the manuscript. Shirley Stern of Prentice-Hall provided editing assistance with with uncommon ability and heretofore unheard of patience. Susan Willig, Education Editor of Prentice-Hall, gave support and encouragement whenever they were needed. Special thanks to Sarah Guthrie for her work with the index.

James Guthrie wishes to acknowledge a considerable intellectual indebtedness to I. James Quillen and H. Thomas James, both former deans of the Stanford University School of Education, Lee J. Crombach, Stanford Professor Emeritus, and to James A. Kelly, the Executive Director of the Springhill Foundation in Wayzata, Minnesota.

EDUCATION IN THE UNITED STATES

chapter 1

The United States maintains an educational system which is probably more diverse, disparate, decentralized, and dynamic than any other in the world. This system depends little upon national government to make educational policy or to provide financial support for educational institutions. Instead, governmental authority for American education is distributed primarily among the fifty states which, in turn, delegate administrative responsibility to thousands of local school districts. The consequence is fifty systems of public tax-supported lower and higher education in which policy is made by fifty sets of state officials, governors, legislatures, judges, state boards of education, and their counterparts in thousands of local communities. As if this were not sufficiently complex, there is a parallel system of private or nonpublic institutions, generally outside of governmental jurisdiction, for both higher and lower education.

Decentralization has permitted development of a wide array of institutions. Local administrative districts in America vary in size from small one-room schools to huge urban systems, such as New York City, which has almost 1 million students. Some public school districts operate only elementary schools, others only secondary schools; yet others operate both types. There are "community colleges," which offer two years of postsecondary instruction. Beyond this are both colleges and universities ranging in size from small four-year liberal arts institutions to huge university systems. The latter may have one or more campuses offering instruction in a remarkable array of liberal arts courses as well as graduate and professional fields. Here again, almost everything that exists through public financial support is mirrored in the private sector.

Despite such decentralization and diversity, America's educational institutions are unusually comprehensive. Formal education encompasses almost every segment of the population in terms of students' age, interests, and ability levels. In excess of 58 million students are formally enrolled in both lower and higher educational institutions.[1] It is increasingly typical that an American child will begin nursery school or preschool at age three or four. Thereafter, 90 percent of an age cohort will graduate from secondary school and more than 50 percent will attend a postsecondary institution. Literally millions of adults attend vocational and avocational nondegree classes. (This does not take into account those adults attending proprietary (profit-making) schools, generally for vocational training purposes.) Together, these institutions employ approximately 4.5 million individuals working in more than 100,000 buildings. When one considers pupils and employees, and the members of their immediate families, American education directly involves 25 percent of the total population.

Despite the extent to which education is generally pursued, U.S. systems of education are riddled with paradox. Schooling is intended to benefit those who are gifted, handicapped, and all those in between. The old, the young, the elite, as well as the poor are all targets of specific school programs. Education is expected to ensure social cohesion as well as cultural diversity; academic achievement as well as vocational relevance; moral virtue as well as individual self-enhancement. Schools are expected to be free of politics yet responsive to public clients; sensitive to national needs, yet subject to the desires of local citizens; controlled by lay persons while staffed with professionals. All such expectations are to be met in a national climate of values which stresses equality, liberty, and efficiency. More complicated yet, educational policy is the concomitant responsibility of all three levels of government—federal, state, and local. Given this complexity, the wonder is that education works at all in America.

How does such a remarkably diverse social institution operate? What are the publicly held values that shape this system? What is its present structure and financial status? With what major policy problems has the system been confronted within the last quarter century, and with what issues is it likely to be occupied in the near future? These are the topics with which the remainder of this chapter is concerned.

STRUCTURAL FEATURES OF AMERICAN EDUCATION

The decentralization to which we frequently refer has resulted in substantial organizational diversity. There is no single grade configuration which completely dominates American schooling. Nevertheless, nationalizing influences, both formal and

[1] According to the U.S. Department of Education estimates for 1985, the annual operating cost of this "system," both public and nonpublic higher and lower education, approximates $250 billion annually.

informal, have been sufficiently pervasive to account for several modal patterns. We describe these structural features in terms of the sequence of progression—preschool, elementary school, and secondary school—for both public and private schools.

Preschool

Approximately 2.1 million (36 percent) of three- and four-year olds in the United States attend nursery or preschools.[2] Now that it is increasingly the pattern for mothers to work outside the household (70 percent of U.S. women between the ages of 25 and 65 are employed), preschool enrollments can be expected to grow even more.

Public Schooling

Almost 88 percent of elementary and secondary students are enrolled in *public* schools.[3] This American pattern of public school dominance begins to emerge from the onset with kindergarten. In 1981, there were 3.2 million five- and six-year olds, 94 percent of the age cohort, enrolled in a kindergarten class. Most American elementary schools begin with kindergarten and extend through at least grade six. Some elementary schools, depending upon the pattern adopted by their school district board of trustees, may encompass grades seven and eight as well. These two patterns together accounted for 30.25 million students in 1984.

In local school districts adhering to what is described as a 6:3:3 plan (six years of elementary schooling, three years of junior high school, and three years of high school), students enter "junior high school" at the beginning of the seventh grade. Junior high schools were begun as a transition from the self-contained classes of elementary schools to the fully developed departmentalization of senior high schools. In practice, however, junior high schools have almost always become fully departmentalized. Increasing numbers of districts operate "intermediate schools." These typically encompass only grades six through eight (twelve- to fourteen-year-old students). They offer less intensive levels of departmentalized instruction and are seen as a more gradual transition to secondary school. In these instances, students usually attend ninth grade at the local high school, and do not go to a junior high.

In 1984 there were 13.7 million students enrolled in secondary schools. Secondary schools encompass either grades 9-12, where students previously attended either K-8 or K-6, 7-8 schools. Where the junior high school is the dominant pattern, secondary schools contain grades 10-12. Over time and in different geographic regions, the United States has experimented with a wide range of secondary school grade patterns. These, as well as elementary school variations, are displayed in Figure 1.1.

---

[2] These and other enrollment statistics in this chapter are taken from *Current Population Reports* of the U.S. Census Bureau of the U.S. Department of Commerce of 1982 and from 1984 U.S. Department of Education estimates.

[3] The *National Survey of Private Schools* conducted in the fall of 1983 revealed that there were approximately 5 million students enrolled in K–12 grade nonpublic schools. This was approximately 12 percent of the total U.S. K–12 enrollment.

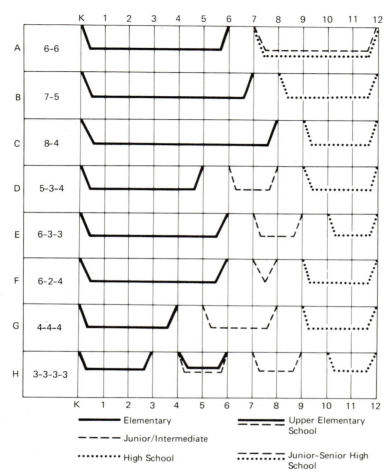

Figure 1.1 **Organizational Patterns for Local Schools. Selected Patterns of School Organization. Adapted from James J. Jones, G. Jackson Salisbury, and Ralph L. Spencer,** *Secondary School Administration* **(New York: McGraw-Hill, 1969), pp. 96–97.**

Nonpublic Schools

Parallel to the public tax-supported lower education system is a private system. These nontax-supported institutions also stretch from preschool through secondary school. By the mid-1980s, nonpublic school enrollments accounted for 12 percent of total U.S. K–12 enrollment. The overwhelming part of the nonpublic system consists of schools operated by Catholic churches. Additionally, other religious denominations operate schools—Lutheran, Seventh Day Adventist, and Jewish prominent among them. The most rapidly growing private elementary schools are so-called "Christian" schools characterized by a rigid discipline code and rather fundamental interpretation of the Protestant Bible.

There also exist nonsectarian private schools. Indeed, many of the most prestigious private schools, "preparatory schools," are of this nature. They specialize in preparing students for entry into top-ranked colleges and universities. They are few in number and enroll a small percentage of students, but they exert disproportionate influence upon school practices because of their longstanding academic traditions and generally elite clientele.

PUBLIC VALUES AND PUBLIC SCHOOL POLICY

United States' school policies and practices are the result of a constant interplay between proponents of three deeply held values—equality, efficiency, and liberty. These values significantly influence public policy generally and education particularly. Government actions regarding national defense, housing, taxation, antitrust regulation, racial desegregation, and literally hundreds of other policy dimensions, including education, are motivated and molded by one or more of these three values.[4]

Equality, liberty, and efficiency are viewed by an overwhelming majority as conditions that government should maximize. These three values are considered "good," "just," and "right." Belief in them has historical roots that are deeply embedded in America's common heritage. This belief permeates the ideology promulgated by political parties, churches, courts, schools, and other social institutions.

Despite widespread public devotion to these values as abstract goals, their ultimate fulfillment is virtually impossible. At their roots, the three desired conditions are inconsistent and antithetical. Exclusive pursuit of one violates or eliminates the others. For example, imagine that government, in an effort to increase equality, nationalized the construction industry and then mandated that housing production be standardized. Presumably all citizens above a specified age would be guaranteed a government-produced home. Only one kind or a few limited variations upon a single type of building would be manufactured. Consequently, all eligible consumers would be provided with identical products and would by definition have equal housing. An added degree of efficiency might be achieved by the high volume of manufacture possible with extraordinarily uniform products. Though unit costs of houses might possibly be reduced, liberty would be sacrificed in the process. The absence of variety in housing would severely restrict or totally prevent choice. In the absence of choice, it logically follows that there is no liberty. Moreover, in time, lack of competition might discourage the search for new production techniques and thus actually impair economic efficiency.

Would the absence of inequality be worth the presumed loss of freedom and efficiency? This question illustrates the trade-offs constantly faced by policy makers. What emerges is that the exclusive pursuit of equality will restrict or eliminate liberty and efficiency. Conversely, complete attention to either liberty or effi-

---

[4] For more on this topic see John W. Gardner, *Excellence, Can We Be Equal and Excellent Too?* (New York: Harper & Row, Pub., 1961).

ciency diminishes the other values. Consequently, efforts to rearrange society so as to maximize one of the three values are constrained by forces designed to preserve the status quo. The dynamic equilibrium among the three values constantly shifts, with the balance at any particular point fixed by a complicated series of political and economic compromises.

It can be argued that liberty is the highest of the three values. Efficiency for its own sake has little meaning. The justification for desiring that an endeavor be undertaken efficiently is to conserve resources that could then be used for other endeavors, thus expanding choice. Similarly, equality *qua* equality appears hollow. Few if any persons desire absolute parity with their peers. Rather, equality of wealth and circumstances can be viewed as a desirable means to the end of greater choice.

Among the eighteenth century leaders of the United States, education was viewed as a means to enable the citizen to participate as an equal in the affairs of government and was thus deemed essential to ensure liberty.[5] It was not until the nineteenth century that education began to assume significance in economic terms. The increasing demands of industrial technology necessitated an educated work force; henceforth, schooling was taken as an important contributor to economic efficiency. By the twentieth century, intensified technological development and economic interdependence made formal preparation the *sine qua non* for an individual's economic and social success. Consequently, education assumed new importance from the standpoint of its role in maximizing equality.

CONTEMPORARY U.S. EDUCATION POLICY ISSUES

The 1954 United States Supreme Court decision in *Brown* v. *Board of Education,* along with the increase in federal government educational programs of the 1960s and the school finance reform efforts of the 1970s, directed a major portion of twentieth century educational policy toward achieving greater equality. Thus we begin our discussion of values and United States' school policy by concentrating on "equality." Subsequently, we will discuss efforts following World War II to achieve greater efficiency and liberty.

Equality

Post-World War II education policy reforms focused upon equality have followed three particular paths: (1) efforts to gain more equal client access to educational services; (2) more equal distribution of state financial resources; and (3) more equal employee access to decision making.

---

[5] See Frederick Rudolf, ed., *Essays on Education in the New Republic* (Cambridge: Harvard University Press, 1969).

Access to Services

The United States Supreme Court's 1954 decision in *Brown* v. *Board of Education*[6] has proven to be among the most significant in the history of the nation. This case not only had the particular consequence of disallowing the previously established constitutional legitimacy of racially segregated school systems, it also unleashed a substantial nationwide movement to redress civil rights grievances in other areas such as voting, housing, and employment. The *Brown* decision and the furor which surrounded subsequent governmental efforts to implement it probably constitute the single most significant policy issue in post World War II American education. By the mid-1980s, school systems in southern states that previously had been racially segregated by law were reasonably well desegregated. Controversy centered more frequently upon northern and western cities where racial segregation of schools assumed more subtle forms, frequently being *de facto* rather than *de jure*. Though school desegregation is no longer preeminent as a policy issue, it remains an important concern three decades after the *Brown* decision.

Handicapped students. Throughout most of U.S. history, severely handicapped individuals have not had equal access to publicly provided educational services. In the early 1970s, two major judicial decisions,[7] relying heavily upon the U.S. Constitution's Fourteenth Amendment "equal protection" clause, required state legislatures to provide equal school access for handicapped individuals. These court decisions facilitated 1975 congressional enactment of the Education for All Handicapped Children Act. This statute provides substantial federal funding to assist state and local school districts in the provision of educational services to handicapped students. The Act is described in greater detail in Chapters Four and Six. We mention it here only to emphasize its significance in the overall context of recent U.S. efforts to enhance equality of educational opportunity.

Bilingual students. Beginning in the 1960s, the United States began to experience a substantial increase in the number of immigrants. Initially, these individuals were mainly from Puerto Rico and Cuba. Subsequently, natives of Mexico and Central America predominated. Following the Vietnamese War, many Indochinese refugees also emigrated to the United States. The situation varied by geographic region: New York City experienced a large influx of Puerto Rican immigrants. Miami became home for tens of thousands of Cuban refugees. San Francisco was the relocation site for many thousands from mainland China, Vietnam, and Latin America. Increasing numbers of school-age children could not speak English or had only a limited grasp of the language. Indeed, by the mid-1980s, 10 percent

[6] *Brown* v. *Board of Education,* 347 U.S. 483, 495 (1954) and 349 U.S. 294 (1955).

[7] *PARC* v. *Commonwealth of Pennsylvania,* 834 F. Sup. C7. 1257 (ED Pa. 1971) 343 F. Sup. 279 (ED Pa. 1972) and *Mills* v. *Board of Education,* 348 F. Sup. 866 (PCC 1972).

of the students in California's schools were either non-English or limited-English speaking.[8]

Court cases, particularly *Lau* v. *Nichols,* proclaimed the legal right of such students to receive effective instruction and equal access to educational services.[9] A federal program was initiated to provide funding to assist in these instructional efforts. Many states also enacted categorical financial aid programs to provide assistance to local school districts for bilingual education. Though few now deny the need to provide bilingual students with appropriate assistance, the form that such aid should take is increasingly debated. The controversial political question is the degree to which bilingual education should assist in sustaining and explaining students' cultural heritage, be it Hispanic, Asian, or any other, versus simply enabling students to learn English as quickly as possible. The problem is exacerbated by relative scarcity of public resources, and is likely to be an intense educational policy issue for the remainder of the twentieth century.

Migrant education.   American agriculture depends to a substantial degree upon the labor of individuals and families willing to move with seasonal crop patterns. The children of such workers were, and to some degree remain, neglected by the school systems into which their parents periodically move. In order to assist local school districts to better educate such students, both the federal government and a number of states have enacted financial categorical aid programs.

Distribution of Resources

Three major efforts have been made since World War II to redistribute financial resources in education in order to provide greater equality of educational opportunity. Two of these efforts, the Elementary and Secondary Education Act and student financial aid programs for postsecondary education, are sponsored by the federal government. The third effort at achieving greater resource equality is the school finance reform movement, which has been a judicially oriented strategy aimed primarily at state-level authorities.

Compensatory education.   In the mid-1960s, President Lyndon B. Johnson launched a social reform campaign known as "The War on Poverty." A significant struggle in this "war" was to compensate selected students for the educational deficit with which they entered school. The outcome was enactment of the 1965 Elementary and Secondary Education Act.[10] This statute was, and continues to be, the federal government's major educational program in terms of resources—annual congressional appropriations exceed $3 billion. Funds are allocated to states, and subsequently to local school districts, based on the number of children in each

[8] See Kevin F. McCarthy, *Immigration and California: Issues for the 1980s* (Santa Monica: The Rand Corporation, 1983).

[9] *Lau* v. *Nichols,* 414 U.S. 563 (1974).

[10] Combined in the Education Consolidation Improvement Act of 1981.

county from low-income households. Funds are used to provide intensified instruction, generally in the elementary grades. This program is explained more fully in Chapter Four.

Postsecondary student aid. The United States has relied upon three major federal government-sponsored programs to assist college students financially. One of these, the Serviceman's Readjustment Act, enacted following World War II, is important historically. It was not, however, primarily an equal opportunity measure in that it was available only to veterans and was based on the length of military service, not financial need. The other two programs, the Guaranteed Student Loan Program (GSLP) and Basic Education Opportunity Grants (BEOG), are designed to assist students based on parents' income level. The BEOG program provides federal funds to postsecondary students to pay schooling costs. The Guaranteed Student Loan Program provides federal subsidies to commercial lending organizations, mainly banks, to defray interest on loans. This provides students with loans at rates lower than would otherwise be the case. Upon graduation, students are responsible for beginning repayment. Administrative arrangements are made between the student, lending institution, and college at which the student is enrolled. There is little direct contact between students and the federal government. These loan programs are intended to ensure that students are not denied access to higher education for lack of family or personal finances.

School finance reform. Since the early part of the twentieth century, school finance revenue generation and distribution arrangements in most states have resulted in unequal taxing burdens and disparate expenditures. In the 1960s, legal scholars constructed a means for questioning the constitutionality, both federal and state, of these financing arrangements. The outcome was disappointing at the federal government level. The U.S. Supreme Court ruled in *Rodriguez* v. *San Antonio* that such unequal state systems were not in violation of the U.S. Constitution.[11] However, state courts thereafter often judged such systems to violate state constitutions.[12] Consequently, the period from 1970 to 1980 was witness to the greatest school finance reform movement in any period of American history. The outcome, though not uniform across states, was substantially greater equality in the provision of school support and tax burden than was previously the case.[13] (This movement and the underlying legal principles are described in detail in Chapter Five.) In that public higher educational institutions are funded directly by the state in most instances, these equal protection cases did not apply to them. The excep-

---

[11] *Rodriguez* v. *San Antonio,* 411 U.S. 1 (1973).

[12] State cases such as *Serrano* v. *Priest,* 18 Cal. 3rd 729.

[13] The effort to obtain greater equality of resource distribution through the judicial process is summarized by Michael W. LaMorte and Jeffrey D. Williams in "Court Decisions and School Finance Reform," a paper delivered at the 1983 annual meeting of the American Education Research Association in Montreal, Canada, April 11, 1983. The actual effects of the reforms are the subject of the entire Spring 1983 issue of the *Journal of School Finance.*

tion to this statement is those community college districts historically aligned with K–12 school districts which continue to utilize property tax revenues as a source of support.

Access to Decisions

Early twentieth century growth in professional school administration, increased size of school districts, both in terms of pupil enrollments and geographic distances, and bureaucratization of large city school districts contributed to the post World War II growth of lower education teacher unions. Particularly in large school systems, teachers increasingly came to view themselves as disenfranchised by their inability to participate in decisions regarding the terms and conditions of employment. An answer to this sense of powerlessness was to organize collectively in order to intervene in the decision-making process by bargaining directly with the school board.

This movement began most visibly in 1955 in New York City and thereafter spread quickly to other east coast cities and eventually to the entire nation. It is now the case that collective bargaining takes place, either sanctioned by statute or informal agreement, in almost every state. By the 1980s, U.S. teachers were unionized in such numbers that the National Education Association (NEA) and its state and local affiliates had more than 1.5 million members and the American Federation of Teachers (AFT) had approximately 300,000 members. (Chapter Twelve addresses this topic in substantial detail.)

Efficiency

Efforts to render schools more productive, to maximize output at a specified resource level, are not unique to the post World War II period under consideration in this chapter. Raymond Callahan[14] and David Tyack[15] have each written insightful descriptions of the "cult of efficiency" that pervaded American education at the beginning of the twentieth century. This earlier effort assumed that adoption of scientific management principles would earn for schools the mantle of legitimacy then accorded private sector business endeavors. More recent efficiency movements have also attempted, in part, to pattern schools after business. In the struggle to make schools "accountable," contemporary reformers, frustrated by the inability of technocratic procedures to increase educational productivity, evolved two additional features—testing and fiscal containment. This section chronologically traces each of the three features of the more recent efficiency movements, beginning with the technical-industrial accountability model.

The 1957 Soviet space success, Sputnik, triggered substantial criticism of America's public schools. Education was tried in the press and quickly found guilty of defrauding the United States of technological supremacy. Congress responded

---

[14] Raymond E. Callahan, *Education and the Cult of Efficiency* (Chicago: University of Chicago Press, 1962).

[15] David B. Tyack, *The One Best System* (Cambridge: Harvard University Press, 1974).

by enacting the 1958 National Defense Education Act, intended to buttress instruction in science, mathematics, and foreign language. Cynics were quick to observe that America's schools were remarkably responsive: A year later, 1959, the United States launched its first successful space capsule. Whatever the objective performance of America's schools at the time, the seeds of public dissatisfaction had been widely sown. Moreover, as the space program began to accomplish even more amazing feats, the question continued to be asked, "How is it we can put a man on the moon while the student on the street cannot read, write, or count satisfactorily?"

Against this backdrop of unfocused public dissatisfaction with school productivity, there appeared the 1966 "Coleman Report" with its widely misinterpreted findings regarding school resources and student achievement. Whereas Coleman and his research colleagues only stated that schools appeared to have little influence on achievement *independent of the social class conditions of individual students,* laymen frequently were quick to assume that this meant schools had no beneficial effect and that added dollars for schools would be wasted.[16]

Technocracy

If student achievement was disappointing, and dollars spent in the conventional pattern had little influence, then the time had come for new strategies. Techniques such as program performance budgeting systems (PPBS), zero based budgeting (ZBB), systems analysis, program evaluation and review techniques (PERT), and management by objectives (MBO) had been honed during World War II, polished in the private sector during the postwar period, and propelled to their greatest prominence with the space program successes of the 1960s. Efficiency proponents were quick to suggest that these and other private sector management techniques, if appropriately applied to schools, could provide answers—by which they meant higher student performance and lower costs. Thus, the latter part of the 1960s and the early portion of the 1970s witnessed numerous efforts to apply technocratic management strategies to public education.[17]

In 1967, the year following publication of the Coleman Report, President Johnson issued an executive order facilitating implementation of program performance budgeting throughout the executive branch of the federal government. America's educational system has long been subject to the rapid adoption and subsequent discarding of fanciful fads, and PPBS was to be no exception. If the Department of Health, Education, and Welfare, including the Office of Education, had to implement program planning budgeting, then surely so should school districts. Also, if it was good enough for the Pentagon and the federal government, then it would just as surely benefit schools. Education publications were quick to trumpet the virtues of the new management techniques. Consulting firms rapidly packaged the

[16] James S. Coleman et al., *Equality of Educational Opportunity* (Washington, D.C.: U.S. Government Printing Office, 1966).

[17] Donald Martin, George E. Overholt, and Wayne J. Urban, *Accountability in American Education: A Critique* (Princeton, N.J.: Princeton Book Company, 1976).

new management tools for sale to local school district superintendents and school boards who, even if they did not know what PPBS and PERT were, certainly knew they needed them. It was difficult to resist such a popular steamroller.

States, frustrated at not being able to dictate increased school output, began to legislatively intrude on school processes. Competency-based teacher education (CBTE) became yet another crest on the accountability wave. Literally dozens of states began requiring that teachers be trained with an eye toward those instructional techniques that were most effective with students. Once they mastered these professional techniques, then they would be licensed to teach and certified as competent. The idea was badly flawed. There exist few scientifically verified instructional skills.[18] Teaching was and continues to be more of an art and a craft than a science. Despite exaggerated claims by many teacher trainers and the impetus given to the idea by federal conferences on the topic, the then-existing scientific base of pedagogy was simply too thin to justify competency-based teacher education, and the idea generally was short-lived.

Testing

For all its publicity, money, and effort, the technocratic accountability movement appeared to have produced little in terms of results by the early 1970s. The scorecard used by the public continued to reflect failure. Standardized test results had been declining since the mid-1960s. The College Entrance Examination Board annually reported that scores on the Scholastic Aptitude Test (SAT) were lower than the preceding year.[19] If new management techniques could not reverse the sorry situation, then what could? One answer to the question was to utilize more tests. The assumption behind the strategy was that by subjecting student performance to the glare of public scrutiny, educators would be induced to work harder or more efficiently.

Beginning in 1964, the federal government contributed to the testing movement by appropriating funds for the National Assessment of Education Progress (NAEP). After the initiation of the NAEP, a number of states began mandating statewide testing programs. Frequently these tests were tied to the awarding of high school graduation certificates. Proficiency standards and areas of minimal competence were important phrases frequently echoed by legislation. By the latter portion of the 1970s, thirty-five states had adopted a form of testing to encourage higher educational productivity. Educators resisted on grounds that tests were insufficient to capture the full range of school purposes and that overuse of examinations would distort the ends of education. A backlash of sorts occurred. The assertion was made that standardized tests were imperfect measures, the results of which were overused and misinterpreted. Several states, New York prime among them, enacted "truth in testing" bills intended to protect the rights of students.

[18] Robert W. Heath and Mark A. Nielson, "The Research Basis for Performance-Based Teacher Education," *Review of Educational Research,* 44, no. 4 (Fall): 463–84, 1974.

[19] H. Thomas James, "Declining Test Scores: The State's Reaction," *Compact,* 9, no. 5 (December): 9–12, 1975.

Despite such criticisms, the public generally continued to believe that tests were accurate measures of school output. A spring 1980 Gallup poll revealed that 75 percent of the public was favorably disposed to testing; an even higher proportion of minority group citizens held such views.[20] By the mid-1980s, the decline in nationally administered test scores finally appeared to have stopped.

Fiscal Containment

School districts have lived with property taxing limitations for more than a century. Conventional school finance plans permit local school boards to maintain taxing discretion only under a mandated ceiling; if the tax rate is to be higher, it necessitates voter approval. Beginning in the 1970s, however, a new strategy began appearing with increasing frequency: state limitations on spending. In 1972, in an effort to avoid a court ruling in the previously described case, *Serrano* v. *Priest,* the California legislature imposed a spending ceiling upon school districts. This spending limit, when coupled with declining enrollments, meant that for the first time, some districts annually found themselves in the position of having the same or smaller total operating budgets than the previous year. Ten other states followed suit in adopting spending ceilings.

Efficiency proponents contended that if schools could not be made more productive, then at least it would be possible to limit the amount of public money wasted. The spending limit wave began to build and spilled over beyond the boundaries of public schooling. By the mid-1970s, a large number of spending limitation campaigns for all local public services had been organized—twenty-five of them succeeded. Several state governments had spending ceilings imposed upon them, and serious sets of proposals were made not only to annually require that federal spending be balanced against revenues, but also to limit federal spending to a specified proportion of the gross national product (GNP).[21]

The fiscal containment movement met with a measure of success. A Rand Corporation survey revealed that total government spending as a function of GNP grew steadily from 1929 to 1975. By that year government spending, including schools, equaled 35 percent of the total value of all goods and services produced in the United States. From 1975 to 1979 this percentage fell to 32.6 percent. Lower education's—that is, K–12's—share of GNP also declined from its 1975 level, from 7 to 5 percent of GNP. As a percent of total government spending, education had fallen from 30 percent in 1956 to 27 percent by 1975 and even lower by 1979.[22]

[20] Spring 1980 Gallup poll on public acceptance of testing reported in the February 1980 issue of *School and Community.*

[21] The 1978 *Congressional Quarterly Almanac* covering the second session of the 95th Congress (*Congressional Quarterly 1979*) contains an extensive description and analysis of the spending limitation proposals at the federal level. Similarly, John Augenblick has summarized state legislative actions in 1978–1979 in an Education Commission of the States Report F 79-4, July 1979.

[22] Anthony H. Pascal and Mark David Menchik, *Fiscal Containment: Who Gains, Who Loses?* (Santa Monica: The Rand Corporation, September, 1979).

Efforts to achieve greater equalization need not directly conflict with reforms aimed at influencing school processes or outputs. At least occasionally, proponents of equality and a more rigorous school curriculum—for example, "back to basics"—can coexist and may even cooperate. However, attempts to achieve greater school efficiency by limiting inputs of school dollars are seldom compatible with equity reforms. School reform is difficult if not impossible in an atmosphere of fiscal containment. Without additional resources, equity necessitates redistribution—taking from some to give to others. Fiscal containment policies militate against surpluses; in their absence equity can come only from redistribution. Altering a state school finance plan to redistribute resources such that there are not simply winners and even bigger winners (or at least winners and those held harmless), but rather winners and losers, invites intense political conflict. It is such conflicts that frequently give birth to proposals for greater liberty or choice.

Liberty

Freedom to choose among alternatives is a long-respected component of American culture, schooling included. Since its colonial inception, America's educational system has been characterized by substantial diversity. Choices have always existed whereby parents and citizens could satisfy their preferences for schooling. In *Pierce* v. *Society of Sisters* (1925), the U.S. Supreme Court affirmed the right of parents to select from among both public and private school alternatives. Even within the public school sector, efforts have consistently been made to ensure that even though schooling was compulsory, schools themselves were nevertheless responsive to clients. Responsiveness was intended for public schools to facilitate choice, to be a proxy for liberty in a system that otherwise held a monopoly position for most parents and students.

Post World War II efforts to ensure or enhance liberty for public schools have taken two primary paths: (1) reforms intended to render public schooling more diverse and more responsive to clients, and (2) proposals to encourage expanded private offering of schooling.

Private Offering

The mid-1950s Supreme Court school desegregation decisions precipitated numerous reactions. One outcome—white efforts to avoid racially desegregated schools—took various forms: violent resistance, civil disobedience, legal subterfuge, delay, and escape. This last of these resulted in the greatest surge in nonpublic school enrollments in the twentieth century. By 1968, when court-ordered desegregation was it its peak, nationwide nonpublic school enrollments climbed to 14 percent of the total school population.[23]

This growth resulted primarily from the formation of hundreds of "white

[23] U.S. Department of Health, Education, and Welfare, *A Century of U.S. School Statistics* (Washington, D.C., 1974).

academies" in southern states. Prince Edward County, Virginia, attempted to aid segregation by closing its public schools. Mississippi rescinded its compulsory school attendance law and attempted to arrange state tuition payments for students attending segregated private schools. These and similar efforts were eventually found to be illegal. Under the pressure of court decisions,[24] Internal Revenue Service investigations, and sheer economics, white academies began to close.

By 1975, the proportion of students enrolled in nonpublic schools had been halved. Undoubtedly, white fears of racially mixed schools had been at least partially assuaged, and this accounted for the closing of many segregated private schools. However, no sooner had nonpublic school enrollment proportions declined to 7 percent than they began once again to ascend. By 1980 it was estimated that nonpublic school enrollments had rebounded to between 10 and 11 percent of total kindergarten through twelfth grade enrollments. Legislative proponents in states such as New York, Minnesota, and Pennsylvania enacted state-aid provisions benefiting nonpublic schools. Such aid took various forms—direct aid to nonpublic schools for supplies and to cover costs of state-mandated operations such as testing, transportation of students, and state income tax credits and deductions to households paying school tuition. Whatever the political popularity or moral rectitude of such provisions, they generally were found to be constitutionally unacceptable.[25] However, in a 1983 decision, *Mueller* v. *Allen,* the U.S. Supreme Court ruled that tuition tax credits were constitutional if a state statute permitted deductions for both private and public school payments. Presumably this represents a more accommodating judicial position toward public subsidy of private schooling. The long-run consequences of this decision are not yet easily predictable.[26]

Nonpublic school advocates have enjoyed greater success in their efforts to obtain federal financial aid. In an extraordinarily adroit political compromise, Johnson administration education officials were able to fashion an agreement between the National Education Association and the National Catholic Welfare Conference that permitted enactment of the 1965 Elementary and Secondary Education Act.

Simultaneously frustrated by their inability to obtain judicial approval for a major plan for state aid to nonpublic schools and heartened by the ESEA federal assistance breakthrough, nonpublic school aid advocates subsequently attempted to implement an even more dramatic strategy—congressionally approved tuition tax credits. A concerted tuition tax credit coalition effort was mounted beginning in 1977. Proponents put forth bills that would grant households a federal income tax credit proportional to nonpublic school tuition payments. The plans, if enacted, would cost the federal treasury several billion dollars annually in lost tax revenues. However, throughout the 1970s and into the 1980s, federal revenue deficits were sufficient to dampen congressional enthusiasm for the idea.

[24] *Griffin* v. *County School Board,* 377 U.S. 218 (1964).

[25] Patrick S. Duffy, "A Review of Supreme Court Decisions on Aid to Nonpublic Elementary and Secondary Education," *The Hastings Law Journal,* 23, no. 3 (March, 1972), 966-89.

[26] *Mueller* v. *Allen,* 51 U.S.L.W. 5050.

There was yet another avenue by which private school proponents attempted to gain public financial support—voucher plans. Direct government aid to students (who then selected the school of their choice) was popularized for higher education with the advent of the so-called "GI Bill" following World War II. In 1955, Milton Friedman, a Nobel Prize-winning economist, advocated a similar strategy for returning efficiency and responsiveness to lower education. Friedman's idea began to receive greater attention during the onset of the efficiency movement in the 1960s. Finally, one small local school district, Alum Rock, in the area of San Jose, California, consented to undertake a diluted voucher trial. The Alum Rock demonstration concluded with mixed reviews.[27] Privatization critics continued to assert that vouchers were imperfect, and even proponents contended that the experiment was flawed in that private sector schools did not participate.[28]

Responsiveness

The 1960s and 1970s were a period of intense public school criticism. One dimension of these complaints was that American schools were insensitive to the preferences of clients, parents, and students. Public policy diagnosticians attributed the problem to excessive influence by educational professionals, administrators, and teacher organizations. The prime remedy was judged to be a restoration of local control—greater citizen participation. Toward this end, four reform surges took place between 1955 and 1980: (1) the so-called "community control" movement; (2) efforts to establish "alternative schools"; (3) administrative decentralization; and (4) school site management and parent advisory councils.

Community control. In the mid-1960s, the Ford Foundation sponsored a study of New York City schools.[29] The report it issued recommended that steps be taken to disaggregate the huge New York City school district into presumably more manageable subunits. Three experimental "community control" districts emerged and rapidly became the focus for substantial conflict. Eventually, the New York legislature enacted a bill that divided the city's schools into thirty-one elementary districts with elected boards subject to the overall authority of the city's central school board. Each of these subdistricts contained more pupils than the overwhelming majority of school districts throughout the United States. Community control proponents were dismayed that the new subbureaucracies would be touted as a way to return schools to the "people." Moreover, early political analyses asserted that newly elected local boards were heavily dominated by citizens supported by teacher

[27] Daniel Weiler, *The Public School Voucher Demonstrations: The First Year at Alum Rock* (Santa Monica: The Rand Corporation, June 19, 1974).

[28] David K. Cohen and Eleanor Farrar, "Power to the Parent? The Story of Education Vouchers," *The Public Interest,* 48 (Summer), 72–97, 1977.

[29] Mayor's Advisory Panel on Decentralization of New York City Schools, *Reconnection for Learning: A Community School System for New York City* (1967), sometimes referred to as the "Bundy Report."

unions and thus unrepresentative of "the community."[30] Much discussion was given to similar disaggregating proposals in other city districts, but little came of it practically.

Alternative schools. This concept, much like accountability, was and continues to be a semantic umbrella of sufficient breadth to encompass numerous schooling ideas, some of them antithetical to one another. In the 1960s, several notable authors wrote educational critiques and asserted that public schools were debilitatingly uniform, repressive, stifling student and staff creativity, and administered in a mindless fashion.[31] "Alternative education," using a British primary school model, was proposed as a reform. It was thought that the relatively unstructured learning experiences in such schools would more easily assist in the transition from home to scholarly activities. Many parents removed their children from public schools to place them in private "alternative" schools. Public school systems themselves, unwilling to forego their market share, established public "alternative" school experiments. By the end of the 1970s, the movement had run its course, and several of its major ideologues had revised their opinions, confessed a change of heart, and advocated more structured schools.[32]

Administrative decentralization. Large city school districts underwent a wave of decentralization during the 1960s and 1970s. The general justification was that disaggregation would permit schools to be more responsive to clients and employees. The typical pattern was to divide the district into several administrative subunits, each with an administrative office nominally in charge of all the schools in the subdistrict. Districts varied with regard to the degree of decision-making discretion permitted these subunits. In most instances, fiscal authority continued to be centralized. Personnel administration also typically remained a central office function. Curriculum planning and instructional emphasis were often permitted to vary in accord with the tastes of the subdistrict administrator. Only in New York City was disaggregation accompanied by political reform, namely, the election of subdistrict school boards. In other cities, such as Detroit, Los Angeles, and Washington, D.C., the central school board continued to be the policy-making body for the entire district. Consequently, critics contended that decentralization accomplished little more than added costs and insertion of yet another bureaucratic layer between local schools and "downtown" decision makers. It was difficult, outside of city school central offices and subdistrict administrators, to identify those favorable to the reform.[33]

[30] Marilyn Gittell, *Participants and Participation: A Study of School Policy in New York City* (New York: Center for Urban Education, 1967). Also see Henry M. Levin, ed., *Community Control of Schools* (Washington, D.C.: Brookings Institution, 1969).

[31] Jonathan Kozol, *Death at an Early Age* (Boston: Houghton Mifflin, 1967).

[32] Jonathan Kozol, *Children of the Revolution* (New York: Delacorte, 1978).

[33] George R. LaNoue and Bruce L. R. Smith, *The Politics of School Decentralization* (Lexington, Mass.: Lexington Books, 1973).

School site management. The relative failure of community control, alternative schools, and administrative decentralization encouraged yet a fourth effort to infuse schools with greater citizen participation. This additional reform was described in detail initially by a New York State reform commission that utilized the label "school site management."[34]

The plan intended both to gain a greater measure of lay control and to provide more "accountability" by using the school, rather than the district, as the basic decision-making unit for personnel and curriculum. School district central offices would continue to handle fiscal and business matters and serve as planning, coordinating, and record-keeping bodies. A parent advisory council (PAC) at each school would be responsible for selection and evaluation of the school principal and for advising him or her on curriculum, instructional, and personnel matters. Principals were to be on multiyear contracts, renewal of which was subject to parent advisory committee approval. Within specified boundaries, the principal and parent advisory council would have discretion over funds budgeted for the school by the central office. Each school's budget allocation was to be determined by a set of uniform decision rules, including criteria such as number, grade level, and achievement records of pupils assigned to the school. The parent advisory council would issue an annual evaluation report including plans for the subsequent year.

Several states adopted parent advisory council components for their state categorical aid programs. Portions of the idea were also favorably received by federal authorities, who began to include parent advisory council requirements for schools receiving categorical aid funds under programs such as ESEA, Title I, Emergency School Assistance Act (ESAA), and bilingual categorical funds. The idea became so pervasive that school administrators were soon to ask that the parent advisory councils undergo consolidation lest principals' nights consist of one council meeting after another and little else.

Aside from the widespread adoption of PACs, there is little positive evidence regarding their effectiveness. In many instances, little budget discretion was ceded to parents, collective bargaining agreements with teachers continued to render most decisions a central office matter, parents claimed they were too easily coopted by administrators, and few principals were attracted to the idea of their job security being tied to parental approval. These factors inspired the impression that the reform, though widely adopted, was only superficial.[35]

CONCLUSION

Almost every reform effort demonstrates that isolated pursuit of one value is virtually impossible. The coalition building necessary to define, fashion, and implement a widespread reform almost always necessitates concessions to proponents of yet

---

[34] James W. Guthrie, "Social Science, Accountability, and the Political Economy of School Productivity," in John E. McDermott, ed., *Indeterminacy in Education* (Berkeley: McCutchan Publishing Corp., 1976).

[35] *Improving Education in Florida: A Reassessment.* Prepared for the Select Joint Committee on Public Schools of the Florida Legislature (Tallahassee, 1976).

another value stream. Successful school reform coalitions, up to 1980, were most often formed by proponents of equality and efficiency. In state after state, redistribution of spending and taxing authority was accompanied by productivity reforms such as statewide achievement testing, spending limits, state prescribed teacher-training procedures, state mandated teacher-pupil ratios, and additional reporting requirements. The outcome in almost every instance was reduced decision-making discretion for local school authorities. Whether or not this consequence will, in time, foster counterpressures of reforms in the dimension of liberty (for example, tuition tax credits), remains to be seen.

SUMMARY

Americans have long held a favorable, if pragmatic, view of education. It is valued as a major means for fulfilling both individual and societal ambitions. Accordingly, for more than three centuries there has occurred a constant expansion of the nation's educational opportunities. Current systems provide formal instruction for almost 60 million students ranging from preschool enrollees to postgraduates. The annual expense involved in these undertakings is approximately $250 billion.

Despite their awesome size and comprehensive nature, America's systems of education undergo unceasing change. This is true in large measure because of the persistent tension between proponents of equality, efficiency, and liberty. The continued necessity of striking a new balance in the pursuit of these virtues renders schools uncommonly vital. This dynamism is crucial if education is to serve society well. However, desire for change must constantly be weighed against the need for appropriate institutional continuity. Finding and maintaining a reasoned balance between dynamism and stability will continue as a central challenge for educational administrators.

STATE GOVERNMENT AND AMERICAN EDUCATION

chapter 2

State governments comprise the major organizational base for America's system of schooling. As we describe in greater detail in Chapter Four on *Federal Government and Education,* the Constitution is silent with regard to national authority for the operation of educational systems. This fact, when combined with the Constitution's Tenth Amendment, preserving for states those powers not specifically assigned to the federal government or expressly prohibited to the states, renders education a state function. Constitutions of the fifty states contain clauses which assume state government responsibility for the provision of school services.

Numerous court cases have reinforced state legislatures' plenary authority in the field of education.[1] This is a particularly important concept for professional educators to comprehend because state government is the major determinant of United States' school policies. Also, it is a concept which is misunderstood by many members of the public and stands in contrast to the procedures with which individuals from most foreign nations are familiar.

To better explain the significance of state government for American education, this chapter portrays the historic evolution of school governance in the United States, provides an analytical model of the state policy-making process, and describes the contemporary structure and function of state agencies concerned with education.

[1] See for example, *Buck* v. *MacLean,* 115 So.(2d) 764 (Fla. 1959).

THE EVOLUTION OF STATE GOVERNANCE

Even in the early years of our nation's history, states held the legal authority for education. Nevertheless, the process whereby states exercise this authority has undergone a slow and uneven evolution. For the eighteenth and much of the nineteenth centuries, transportation and communication were slow and laborious. This condition, when coupled with early American resistance to centralized authority, explains the initial reliance of states upon local units of government to operate schools. State capitals were usually remote both geographically and governmentally. Residents paid for local schools by private fees or with community taxes. The students were their children who were then going to work in their home community. Thus, it seemed only natural that local officials should make the bulk of school decisions.

Over time, as social conditions changed, distances shrank, and technological advances occurred, state officials began to assume a larger role in the shaping of local school procedures and educational policy. The latter portion of the nineteenth century saw state influence increase dramatically. Similarly, the last quarter of the twentieth century also has been a time of accelerated involvement by state educational authorities. Several historic milestones in this evolutionary trend in state authority are particularly significant for understanding contemporary conditions.

HISTORIC EVOLUTION

The land that was to become the United States was colonized by western European settlers and commercial entrepreneurs in the seventeenth and eighteenth centuries. The dominant colonial culture became that of the English. They brought with them views about education which reflected the class structure of their homeland and the assumption that the household was the primary agent of education. English social policy throughout the sixteenth century, established by the House of Tudor, emphasized the role of the family as the systematic educator of the child. The Royal Injunctions of Henry VIII (1536), for example, required fathers, mothers, masters, and governors to "bestow their children and servants, even from their childhood, either to learning or to some other honest exercise, occupation or husbandry." Apprenticeships were compulsory for everyone who was not otherwise employed or whose parents had not made educational arrangements.

Colonial Roots[2]

New England states. The first American educational ordinances were enacted by the Massachusetts colonial legislature, then called the General Court, in 1642. These statutes reaffirmed the family's primary responsibility for instilling the abil-

[2] See Lawrence Cremin, *American Education: The Colonial Experience: 1607-1786* (New York: Harper & Row, Pub., 1970).

ity to read and for providing vocational training for children. They also established a public responsibility for education. If a household failed to provide for a child's education, the town's elected officials, known as *selectmen,* were required to remove the child from the home and place him or her in a suitable apprenticeship situation.

Similar compulsory education laws were subsequently enacted by all the New England and Middle Atlantic colonies, except Rhode Island. These early compulsory education statutes prescribed minimum standards, but did not prescribe schools. It became apparent, however, that formal instruction would be needed to provide the amount and kind of education deemed necessary by colonial leadership. Thus, beginning in 1635, a number of towns in Massachusetts and other New England colonies established schools. By 1647, eleven of the sixty towns in New England had voluntarily established, and were managing and supporting, town schools.[3]

In 1647, the Massachusetts General Court enacted the first legislation referring to schools. This act required all towns of fifty or more families to provide a teacher of reading and those of one hundred families to provide a Latin grammar school. This legislation became known as the "Old Deluder Satan" act, and its explicit purpose was to ensure that everyone in the Bible Commonwealth be able to read and understand the principles of religion and capital laws.

American colonists found it difficult to support their schools in the English manner, which was through royal grants, endowments, and church and guild sponsorship. Owing to lack of capital in the New World, they found it necessary to supplement endowments, investments, and tuition fees by various types of aid from the towns, including taxes levied on households. Though the colonists did not particularly intend it as such, these tax subsidies represented a new departure in the financing and control of schools.[4]

During the colonial period, laws were enacted that established the authority of the state legislature to determine whether towns should be required to maintain schools, kinds of schools they should be, length of term, means of support and control, and qualifications of teachers. In so doing, the Massachusetts General Court initiated a principle that education is a function of the state. Deliberately, however, the legislature emphasized the town as the unit of local school administration. Town meetings, comprised of those who had the right of local suffrage, were the source of local authority.

As towns grew in size and complexity, matters relating to education were increasingly delegated to town selectmen. In 1692, the Massachusetts General Court granted to selectmen the power to supervise schools and employ teachers. The selectmen, in turn, began to delegate educational responsibilities to special school committees comprised initially of their own members and later expanded to include

---

[3] Marcus Jernegan, *Laboring and Dependent Classes in Colonial America: 1607-1783* (Chicago: University of Chicago Press, 1931), p. 82.

[4] David B. Tyack, ed., *Turning Points in American Educational History* (Waltham, Mass.: Blaisdell, 1967).

others who were not selectmen. This was the beginning of education being a function of "special government" rather than included within the ambit of all government decisions, or "general government."

In 1789, the Massachusetts General Court established by law many of the actual practices that had developed in the state. With respect to control and supervision of the schools, the law stated:

> And it shall be the duty of the minister or ministers of the Gospel and the selectmen (or other such persons as shall be specially chosen by each town or district for that purpose) of the several towns or districts to use their influence and best endeavors, that the youth of their respective towns and districts, do regularly attend the schools appointed . . . and once in every six months at least . . . to visit and inspect the several schools in their respective towns and districts. . . .[5]

This law placed responsibility for certification of teachers with selectmen, rather than town ministers and preachers; it gave legal recognition to the school committee as an official group charged solely with control and maintenance of local schools; and it officially recognized the district as a level of community organization involved in the establishment and control of schools. Here can be seen the roots of lay control, special government, and local district administration.

Following the revolution of 1776 against the English crown, most New England states adopted the district form of organization, and powers of the local school district grew in the following three decades. For example, the Massachusetts legislation of 1789 that authorized district organization also delegated revenue raising authority to districts. This was accompanied by the power to form a district "prudential" committee certified to select teachers and raise money for the building and maintenance of schoolhouses. The Education Act of 1826 in Massachusetts made the maintenance of school committees compulsory for all towns. The legislation required the selection of a committee that would not be part of the regular town government, but would have a special function of school governance. It also reinforced the principle of lay control—nowhere did it mention particular ministerial, professional, or educational standards required for membership on the committee. "By the end of the second decade of the nineteenth century, Massachusetts had virtually accepted the principle of community control for public supported common schools," and throughout the colonial and early national period, laws in Maine, Vermont, New Hampshire, and Connecticut followed the example set by Massachusetts.[6]

The South. Southern colonies displayed greater regional variations than did New England in the control of public education. Towns were small, the population

---

[5] *The Acts and Resolves, Public and Private, of the Province of Massachusetts Bay,* Vol. I, *Acts of 1789,* Chapter XIX, cited in Lawrence Cremin, *The American Common School* (New York: Teachers College, Columbia University, 1951), p. 130.

[6] Cremin, *The American Common School,* pp. 136–37.

was widely dispersed, the economy was rooted in agriculture and relied heavily upon the exploitation of slave labor, and there was not one overarching religion.

During the eighteenth century, endowed, free, and tuition schools, as well as a number of private academies, were founded. Plantation owners, who had amassed huge holdings at the beginning of the eighteenth century, frequently employed tutors for their children. Wealthy families also sent their sons, and sometimes their daughters, to England to be educated. Others were sent to schools and universities in Scotland and in Europe. By and large, however, social, economic, and religious traditions of the South placed full responsibility for providing training and education directly upon the family. Therefore, a sharp differentiation in the provision of education arose between upper and lower economic strata. The rich had tutors or attended private schools, while children of rural poor had few formal educational opportunities. Formal education of slaves was neglected almost completely.

In 1779, Thomas Jefferson and his William and Mary law school mentor, George Wythe, issued a far-reaching plan for a comprehensive system of publicly supported elementary, secondary, and college schooling. However, the plan, "A Bill for the More General Diffusion of Knowledge," was ahead of its time and was not implemented in the South. Fifty years later, Horace Mann began to advocate many of the same concepts and oversaw their implementation in Massachusetts.

Mid-Atlantic development. In contrast to New England, the populations of the Middle Atlantic colonies, New Netherland (New York), New Jersey, Pennsylvania, and Delaware were characterized by a high degree of ethnic, cultural, and religious diversity. The close historical association between church and school, and proliferation of religious sects prevented any one group from establishing common schools, as the Puritans had done in Massachusetts.

The middle colonies shared with their southern counterparts a tradition of private provision of education, through family or church, and philanthropic schooling for the poor. Public support for instruction of paupers was accepted, at least in principle. By far the most common means of acquiring education was through private instruction, either at home by family or tutors, or in the many private schools that developed during the eighteenth century.

Western land. By 1820, the number of inhabitants living in this area had increased to the point where they represented one-fourth of the entire population of the United States.[7] The New England tradition of public education exerted a strong influence over federal policies for the new territory. The federal ordinances of 1785 and 1787 reserved the sixteenth section of land in each township for the "maintenance of public schools within townships," thereby establishing in each new state a tradition favoring public support of education.[8]

---

[7] Newton Edwards and Herman Richey, *The School in the American Social Order* (Boston: Houghton Mifflin, 1947), p. 214.

[8] Cremin, *The American Common School*, pp. 88–90.

Nineteenth Century Development of the Common School

During the period from the American Revolution to the 1830s, a number of changes were occurring in the political and social life of the new nation that would ultimately have a profound effect on education. The United States began to experience rapid population expansion, urbanization, extremes of wealth and poverty, and the unregulated use of child labor in factories. A widespread democratization of politics occurred and the process of defining an American culture provoked the rise of self-conscious nationalism.[9]

One outcome of these trends was a major reform movement, humanitarian in nature, led by those in the upper and middle classes and the intellectual community. It was during this era that education for the first time was offered as a panacea for society's ills. It was argued that a system of free, high quality *common* schools (meaning that the schools would be open to all children), could preserve America's democratic institutions, inculcate patriotism and spiritual and moral virtue, and increase economic productivity.

On balance, leadership for this movement came from influential community members who had careers outside education. For example, Horace Mann resigned as president of the Massachusetts State Senate in order to become secretary of the first Massachusetts board of education. At the urging of Mann, the legislature established a state board of education, created the office of State Superintendent of Schools, and established a state normal school for the preparation of teachers. The legislature also reduced the power of local districts by insisting that town school committees take responsibility for certification and supervision of teachers, required towns of specified size to maintain a high school, and finally, in 1852, passed the nation's first compulsory school attendance law. Mann's efforts in Massachusetts were the best publicized. In addition, other education leaders such as Henry Barnard of Connecticut, Caleb Mills of Indiana, John D. Pierce of Michigan, John Swett of California, and Calvin H. Wiley of North Carolina had similar roles in their respective states. Thus, by 1865 all states outside the South had enacted legislation similar to that of Massachusetts.

By the end of the nineteenth century, the ideological and legal framework for governance of America's present-day system of schools had been formulated. Education was well established as a public function, rooted in state statute, and administered primarily by local officials. Education was a function of special government, especially at the local level. However, even at the state level, special governmental arrangements, such as the state board of education and the state superintendency, had begun to emerge.

School districts served as the primary unit of local management. Each district had a governing board, members of which were laypersons. They were, ideally, to represent the general public in making educational policy. It is sometimes alleged

[9] *Ibid.*, p. 1.

Vista Library

that, in fact, these school officials occasionally reflected the views of an elite.[10] Regardless of their standing, they usually were in frequent face-to-face contact with their constituents. Schools were expected to perform educational miracles but the governmental mechanisms for their control were rooted in myriad down-to-earth practicalities—lay supremacy, substantial local autonomy, and public support.

Twentieth Century School Governance

By the beginning of the twentieth century, the United States was in a period of dramatically increasing population growth and industrialization. Public school systems—*common* schools—were now an integral part of every community in all states. By 1900, the national population had increased to 72 million, and there were nearly 110,000 local school districts. State government continued to bear the major burden of overseeing educational policy. The primary movement in this regard was the effort to consolidate small rural school districts into larger operating units. Proponents argued that larger school districts would be more efficient economically and could offer students a wider range of academic programs. Consequently, between 1900 and the beginning of World War II, the number of U.S. school districts was reduced almost fourfold to less than 30,000. Concomitant enrollment increases meant that the resulting districts were not only larger geographically but also contained many more schools and students.

The ever larger size of school districts rendered them increasingly resistant to management by elected lay school board members. Whereas once there had been an elected school board member for every 138 citizens, by World War II it was already the case that, on average, each school board represented literally thousands of constituents. Such conditions promoted the preparation and employment of professional school managers.

The twentieth century use of professional school administrators was encouraged by yet another movement. The so-called "progressive era" in American politics began near the turn of the twentieth century. In an effort to overcome the machine politics and corruption rampant in many large cities, state and local political charters were reformed so as to rid the system of what was described as "an excess of politics." One result was to insulate school governance from the mainstream of partisan political activity. Professional superintendents were ceded even greater authority, and school boards, if still elected, were admonished not to cross the "boundary" between policy and administration.

Professional school administrators were encouraged even further by the widespread adoption, prior to World War II, of so-called "scientific management principles." This was the era of efficiency in which time and motion studies were promoting substantial productivity gains in private business. The assertion on the part of scientific management proponents in education was that schools could be made equally productive by following private sector management patterns. The

---

[10] This view is expressed by Michael B. Katz, in *Class, Bureaucracy, and Schools* (New York: Praeger Publishing, 1975).

movement, in retrospect, does not appear either to have reduced school costs or enhanced pupil achievement. What it did do, without question, was to promote the authority of professional school managers. Thus, immediately before and for some time after World War II, the United States possessed a decentralized system of education with overall state authority, strong historic roots in delivering school services based on local districts, and a burgeoning number of professional school administrators.

CONTEMPORARY AMERICAN EDUCATIONAL POLICY PROCESS

Describing the political processes by which U.S. public policy is created is much like peeling an onion—there seemingly is always another layer. Education as a particular dimension of the overall public policy process is no exception. Participants include members of the general public, interest groups and their representatives, members of the education profession, and numerous public officials. Federal, state, and local governments are all involved. Within any level of government, all three branches—executive, legislative, and judicial—may participate. Why is schooling compulsory? Why are the age ranges of compulsory attendance not the same among all states? Why is schooling compulsory, but attendance need not be at public schools? How can schooling be compulsory, but under specified circumstances, parents in some states may be permitted to instruct their children at home? These questions illustrate the kaleidoscopic complexity of the American educational policy process. Because states have the prime responsibility for educational policy, we undertake an explanation of contemporary policy-making procedures here in the context of state educational governance.

Education and Politics

Americans are not always comfortable considering the linkage between education and politics. Indeed, much of the ethos of professional education is filled with the need to sustain a separation between political activity and public schooling. Historians and political analysts refer to this condition as education's "apolitical myth." For decades the myth suffused the literature of professional education and colored the public's view regarding educational policy.[11] Much of this myth can be traced to progressive era reforms which, at the turn of the nineteenth century, attempted to separate educational policy making from the mainstream of partisan politics. The graft and corruption which characterized politics in many American cities in the latter part of the nineteenth century spilled over to the management

---

[11] See David Tyack, *The One Best System* (Cambridge: Harvard University Press, 1965); Frederick M. Wirt and Michael W. Kirst, *Schools in Conflict* (Berkeley: McCutchan, 1982), Chapter One; and Diane Ravitch, *The Great School Wars: New York City 1805-1973* (New York: Basic Books, 1974).

of public school systems. The awarding of teaching positions by school board members to electoral campaign supporters and illegal rebates on supply and repair contracts were all too common. The diagnosis of these ills was that education suffered from an excess of partisan politics.

The proposed cure was to insulate school decision making from mainstream electoral undertakings. The practical outcome was to reinforce special government—local governing boards which had public schools as their exclusive purview. School boards were to have their own taxing authority so as to be fiscally independent of municipal political machines. School boards were to represent the entire city, so as to make members more publicly visible. School board member selection was to be accomplished by relatively nonpartisan procedures, such as appointment or by running for office in a politically unaffiliated manner. When school boards were to be elected, the voting was to occur on a different date than municipal elections. State boards of education and other education officials were also made nonpartisan, and chief state school officer positions were sometimes made appointive. By the second decade of the twentieth century, the apolitical myth and its practical consequences were firmly entrenched in statute and in the American cultural outlook toward education, and educational politics had a unique course at the state and local level.

Whatever the public perception, the reality was, and to a growing degree is, that education is part of the political system. An undertaking which commands in excess of 7 percent of gross national product, touches the lives of more than fifty million students, employs more than four million individuals, and is looked upon as a major institution responsible for inculcating societal values can hardly expect to go unnoticed by the political system.

Political Systems Theory

Systems theory provides a useful model for capturing much of the complexity of contemporary policy making. The systems model describes the linkage between the subsystem responsible for the authoritative allocation of values—the political system—and the broader society and its other subsystems, such as those concerned with the economy and religion. Figure 2.1 schematically models the political system and its relationship to the broader social environment.[12]

The environment. It is difficult to specify the boundaries of the political system. For example, where is the line between economics and politics to be drawn? A nation's fiscal policy can easily influence actions of elected officials and political parties and vice versa. Distinguishing boundaries for the educational policy system is even more complicated. It is the case that much of educational policy at

---

[12] This explanation of a political systems model is based upon David Easton, *A Framework for Political Analysis* (Englewood Cliffs, N.J.: Prentice-Hall, 1965). An extended application of this model to education is provided by Wirt and Kirst, pp. 23-38.

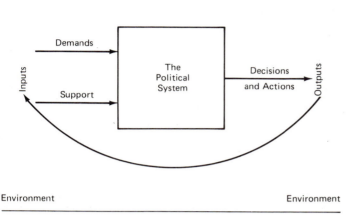

Environment   Environment

Environment   Environment

Figure 2.1 A Simplified Model of a Political System. Reprinted from
A Systems Analysis of Political Life, by David Easton, by
permission of the University of Chicago Press, © 1965,
1979 by David Easton. All rights reserved.

the federal and state levels is a product of the general political system responsible
for overall public policy. Thus it is easy for educational policy to become embodied
in political party campaign platforms or a presidential candidate's political promises. For example, in 1976, the National Education Association (NEA) openly supported the candidacy of Jimmy Carter. Subsequently, President Carter advocated
formation of a federal cabinet-level Department of Education. This was widely
viewed as a reward to the NEA for its electoral support. In 1980, the NEA again
endorsed Carter and opposed Ronald Reagan. Once becoming President, Reagan
initially advocated abolition of the Education Department. The idea was not a high
priority and it did not come about during the first Reagan term. Nevertheless, it
illustrates the extent to which education can become a partisan political issue.

In most local communities, education still takes the form of special government. A locally elected board of education responsible only for public school
policy renders the boundary-setting process somewhat neater than it is at the state
and federal levels. Even locally, however, the matter is not altogether simple. For
example, though not technically responsible for schools in the narrowest legal
sense, an elected mayor might advocate the position of local constituents and oppose closing a neighborhood school. A mayor, even if able to act only through persuasion, can exercise substantial informal influence in such a situation.

The boundary between the larger society and the portion of the political
system responsible for educational policy is a permeable membrane through which

significant exchanges occur. Across the boundary come *inputs,* upon which the policy system acts, transforming them into policy *outputs.* The latter are themselves fed back into the social system and subsequently serve to influence the environment of future demands and supports.

Schools, at the simplest level, can be viewed as processing inputs and converting them into outputs. The educational system receives expectations from society to socialize students into the ideology and mechanisms of the political system. Students are mandated to attend school. Schools are supported by public resources—taxes. The societal expectation for political socialization is a policy *demand.* Tax revenues are a *support.* School systems process such supports and demands and produce an output. In this instance, output takes the form of a politically socialized population which is itself then the source of successive demands and supports. Output influences the environment, hence the "feedback" loop included in Figure 2.1.

Inputs. Political *demands* made upon the educational policy system by the larger environment take several forms. Demands are classified as *extractive, regulatory, participatory,* or *symbolic.* Extractive demands are exemplified by a public expectation for vocational training, restoration of music or art courses in the curriculum, or for construction of a new neighborhood school. Regulatory demands are exemplified by the judicial ruling to dismantle racially segregated dual school systems or by the mandate that students not be dismissed from school without a "due process" hearing. Participatory demands are illustrated by the judicially supported requests of parents of handicapped students that their children be better served. The request that schools teach the pledge of allegiance and flag-salute or honor a dignitary such as Martin Luther King, Jr. by commemorating his birthday as a national holiday are demands for symbolic displays.

Supports. These comprise the other component of policy inputs. *Material* items—tax receipts, trained teachers, school buildings, and school supplies—constitute support. In addition, it is necessary to have nonmaterial supports such as *obedience* and *deference* in order to transform demands into outputs. For example, if there were no societal deference to the flag, or to the significance of Martin Luther King, Jr. for American history, then flag-salutes and holidays would be empty undertakings. Similarly, parental obedience to school policy mandates such as compulsory attendance is necessary for the system to sustain itself.

Outputs. As mentioned, the educational policy process converts inputs, demands, and supports into outputs. We have already illustrated a range of outputs such as new or added school services, regulations regarding attendance, provisions for added participation, and symbolic displays. These outputs are fed back into the larger political environment where they subsequently serve to influence successive sets of demands and supports upon the educational policy system.

Conversion processes. Transforming demands and supports into outputs requires both political and governmental actions. Political actions, in this context, are *interest articulation* and *interest aggregation*. The former comprises a means by which policy expectations are transported across the boundary between the larger society and the educational policy system. No matter how widespread or intense a public desire may be, until it is in some practical fashion expressed it cannot easily be acted upon and become an output. For example, if parents desire the school day to be longer, or if they want the state to relieve property taxes by funding a larger share of school support, then these expectations must be voiced. This is the process of interest articulation and it can occur in many ways. It may take a form as simple as a phone conversation with an elected official or a letter to the editor of a newspaper. It may take the form of an electoral campaign position by a candidate for a school board or state legislative position. A political party may incorporate an expectation in its campaign platform. However it happens, the result is to introduce into the conversion process an idea which is potentially eligible for transformation into a policy output.

It is sometimes the case that even when articulated, interests must be packaged, shaped, or bundled together so as to attract sufficient support to undergo enactment. For example, demands for greater equality in the delivery of school service are frequently packaged with demands for greater school efficiency. In this manner a coalition can be built to attract sufficient supporters to gain enactment. This process is known academically as interest aggregation. Politicians know it as political side payments.

Governmental functions. There are three avenues by which demands, once articulated, and supports are converted into and expressed by government as outputs. The three governmental avenues within a political system are *rule making, rule implementation,* and *rule adjudication.* Typically, these are thought of as being performed by separate branches of government—legislative, executive, and judicial. In fact, practical divisions are nowhere so neat. Legislative bodies influence rule implementation, for example, when they conduct oversight hearings. A local school board, presumably a rule-making body, in selecting a superintendent, has the potential to substantially influence rule implementation. Similarly, a court will periodically undertake a rule-implementation function when the judge directly oversees a school racial desegregation plan or orders a court master to devise a new school finance plan. Generally, however, in the United States, each of the three branches of government concentrates on the function constitutionally assigned to it.

Inputs from the society penetrate the boundary of the political system and are potential grist for the conversion process to transform them into policy outputs. Whether or not a particular input is in fact converted depends upon many factors, such as the strength of the demand and the availability of supports. To a substantial degree, the success of a demand may depend upon the degree to which it is aligned with one or more of the three value streams which underlie United States public policy.

GROWING SIGNIFICANCE OF STATE POLICY

Education is a policy area to which state officials have turned with increasing attention.[13] Given the nation's substantial history of strong local responsibility for education, what explains the expanded state role in the last quarter of the twentieth century? There appear to be several answers that are part of a trend unlikely to be altered in the short run. For the reasons described below, the clear trend is toward a strengthened and sustained state role.

School finance. States have access to the revenue base with the greatest elasticity of yield—personal and corporate income taxes and sales taxes. As schooling has become more expensive, taxpayers have frequently exhibited reluctance to contribute a larger proportion of property tax proceeds to its support. Hence the demand is that states bear a greater share of the burden. By 1980, this demand had resulted in states contributing a larger proportion of school support than local authorities. It continues to be the case that there is widespread variability. In Hawaii, excepting federal funds, all school support is from state sources. In California, more than eighty cents out of every school support dollar comes from the state. New Hampshire, at the opposite end of the continuum, relies upon the state for only 10 percent of school support. Nevertheless, despite exceptions such as New Hampshire, the trend is toward greater state financing.

This trend is strengthened by school finance reform efforts aimed at achieving greater equality in the distribution of school funding. The equal protection court cases to which we refer in detail in Chapter Five call upon state legislatures to distribute resources with substantially greater equality. Because property tax bases vary widely among local school districts, a central authority, the state, is called upon to undertake readjustments. General fund revenues place the state in a good position to smooth out local differences in revenue-raising capacity.

The power of the purse is substantial. Though there is no logical linkage between revenue raising and decision making, there is almost always a practical connection. An elected state official, be it a governor or legislator, is reluctant to be seen as responsible for raising taxes and then deferring to some other authority— local school districts—over control of the money's expenditure. Hence, there is a growing state presence in the management of local schools.

Political centralization. Education has become vitally important in the lives of Americans, and this political reality also accounts for a growing state role in education. With tens of millions of students enrolled and millions of employees, education touches the lives of many households. An educated workforce is seen as important for keeping the nation economically competitive. It is also viewed as important by public officials for maintaining a state or community's economic base. In most instances, schools account for approximately one half a state's total

---

[13] See James W. Guthrie and Paula H. Skene, "The Escalation of Pedagogical Politics," *Phi Delta Kappan,* 54, February 1973, pp. 386–89.

revenue allocations. The composite of these factors renders education a policy issue of such importance as to command state attention.

State involvement is self-reinforcing. Once state executive and legislative bodies begin to play a more extensive role in educational matters, interest groups focus greater attention at the state level, including participating in the electoral campaigns of candidates for state office. The support of interest groups in turn assures that successful office holders will subsequently pay attention to the concerns of their interest group campaign supporters. Thus, as education in the United States has become more involved in overt political activity, one almost inevitable outcome is the wider involvement of state officials in educational matters. This involvement, in turn, results in a dilution of autonomy for local school officials.

Efficiency. Public concern for enhancing student achievement and making schools more efficient triggered the "accountability and testing" movements to which we referred in Chapter One. These movements relied heavily upon statewide testing programs and state imposition of graduation standards. Similarly, the fiscal containment efforts of the 1970s—an effort to limit revenues available to the public sector—depended upon states as the policy instrument. Taxes, mandated minimum graduation requirements, and statewide testing all fall within the policy purview of the state, and the result has been a diminution in power for local educational authorities.

These trends toward centralized decisions show no sign of reversing. Hence, it appears that a strong state government role will characterize American education into the twenty-first century.[14]

STRUCTURE AND FUNCTION
OF STATE EDUCATIONAL SYSTEMS

States are assuming an increased policy significance for education, and a systems model is a useful paradigm for viewing relationships between the educational policy subsystem and society as a whole. However, an understanding of educational policy systems necessitates a look at significant agencies, actors, and their appropriate functions. We begin this explanation by describing state legislative activities connected with educational administration.

The Legislative Branch

With the exception of a unicameral arrangement in Nebraska, every state has a two-house legislative body. However, there is much variation in this arrangement. Some legislatures are relatively small in size. California has 80 members of the As-

[14] States differ in the extent of their control over education. See Frederick M. Wirt, "School Policy, Culture, and State Decentralization," Chapter VI, *Seventy-Sixth Yearbook of the National Society for the Study of Education,* Part III, pp. 164–87 (Chicago: University of Chicago Press, 1977).

sembly and 40 members of the Senate. New Hampshire has 399 members in its lower house and 24 in the Senate, rendering it the largest state legislature in the United States. Populous states such as New York and California, in which legislatures meet virtually year-round, often pay their elected officials full-time salaries and depend heavily upon paid staff to undertake the formulation and evaluation of policy proposals. Other states such as Nevada or Arkansas have part-time legislators and relatively small staff resources. Be that as it may, functional similarities among state legislatures are substantial.

State legislatures typically depend upon the committee system in order to carefully examine proposed policies. Both the upper and lower house will have an education committee chaired by an elected member of rank from the majority party. Presiding officers of such committees frequently acquire remarkable understanding of educational policies, and can become influential not only because of their position but also because of their expertise. Generally, education committees are standing committees. On occasion, a legislative body may also appoint one or more *ad hoc* committees to examine particular education-related matters, such as school finance. Legislatures sometimes also rely upon interim committees, which are active between regular sessions of the legislature, to examine a policy proposal more closely than time permits during the regular session. Occasionally, the two houses of a legislature will agree to appoint a joint or joint interim committee for a similar purpose.

Most state legislatures follow the congressional model and separate authorizing legislative functions from financial appropriations. Authorizing committees are charged with assessing the value of a policy proposal. Should they enact the proposal, a budget process subsequently appropriates funds. The appropriations process is usually complicated and involves an additional set of political actors.

Rule making is the function primarily assigned to state legislatures, and this certainly accounts for the major portion of their activity. Legislative bodies also become involved in rule implementation. Once responsible for enactment of a policy, it is not unusual for an influential legislator to be particularly concerned regarding the manner in which the policy is administered. Generally, this influence is exercised through informal means, such as conversations with executive branch officials. On occasion it can become more overt, such as legislatively specifying creation of a separate administering agency. Sometimes legislative committees also hold so-called "oversight hearings" to formally inquire about administrative procedures and to assess the success of a program.

Legislative bodies often establish agencies to assist them in compiling information and conducting research related to proposed policies and existing programs. Hiring a nonpartisan legislative analyst is a frequent pattern. There may also be research offices. Since education is such a substantial portion of the state's budget, it may attract careful scrutiny by such analysts and research agencies. Many of the staff may become particularly knowledgeable about state education matters and come to wield great influence.

The Executive Branch

A governor is a state's chief executive, presiding over the entire rule-implementation branch of state government. Often the governor is one of but a small handful of state-elected officers. The governor is usually the head, at least titulary, of his or her political party in the state. If the same political party controls both the executive and legislative branches, the governor is in a particularly powerful position. For all of these reasons, a governor is often the most visible public official within a state. Thus, when they choose to become involved in education, they are potentially among the most influential actors.

Education represents a more complicated, substantive area for a governor than any other of the policy dimensions which fall within the purview of states. Unlike transportation, criminal justice, health, or tax policy, governors typically do not have sovereignty over executive branch activities when it comes to education. They frequently share authority either with an elected chief state school officer (CSSO) or an elected state board of education. Only in a few states does the governor appoint the state board of education which then selects a CSSO or does the CSSO serve as an appointed member of the governor's cabinet. Progressive era reforms, in an attempt to insulate education from partisan politics, set education aside as a special policy area. Thus, governors must take additional executive branch actors and agencies into account when proposing or implementing educational policies.

Executive office of the Governor. Education is of such importance politically and financially within a state that increasingly governors appoint an education adviser. In five states, this adviser role has been formalized under the title Secretary of Education. When there is not such an adviser or Secretary, a governor may rely heavily upon the CSSO for counsel on educational matters. It is also often the case that a governor's budget officials, whether they are from an agency equivalent to the federal government's Office of Management and Budget (OMB), or from a state Department of Finance or Planning Office, almost always will attempt to fit the governor's position on educational policy into the overall fiscal plan for the state.

Governors can influence educational policy for a state by platform positions in electoral campaigns, submitting education messages and proposing bills to the legislature, issuing public statements, and by vetoing bills submitted by the legislature. Beyond advocacy for educational policy, or establishing boundaries for the state's role in financing education, governors may be influential through yet another channel, the appointment process. Where state boards of education are appointive, it is often the governor, with legislative approval, who nominates individuals to serve. This is also the case if a state has one or more separate boards to govern higher education. Some states have independent teacher licensing boards and these are generally comrpised of gubernatorial appointees as well.

Chief state school officers (CSSOs). As already mentioned, state governance for education is more complicated than for other policy areas. This complexity stems from the constitutional authority of CSSOs and state boards of education. Figure 2.2 illustrates this complexity. Eighteen states constitutionally specify the CSSO as an officer to be elected. Thirteen states allow partisan elections for the post. In the remaining five states it is listed as nonpartisan. In twenty-seven states the CSSO is an official appointed by a state board of education. In five states the CSSO is appointed by the governor. Thirty-two states utilize mechanisms to render the CSSO position nonpartisan, whether it is elective or appointive. However effective such arrangements have been in providing the public with the illusion that education and politics are separate, it has made for cumbersome governmental arrangements.

State boards of education. Forty-nine states have state boards of education.[15] In several states they are comprehensive bodies responsible for general and vocational education as well as higher and lower education. In thirty-two states the governor appoints members of the state board. In twelve states board members are elected (five partisan and seven nonpartisan). In four states board members are appointed by the legislature. This is the case for the powerful Board of Regents in New York State. In two states, the board of education is small and is comprised of individuals who are members as a consequence of holding other state offices. That is, they are state board of education members *ex officio.* This used to be the

Figure 2.2   Chief State School Officer (CSSO) and State Board of Education (SBE) Selection Patterns and Possibilities.

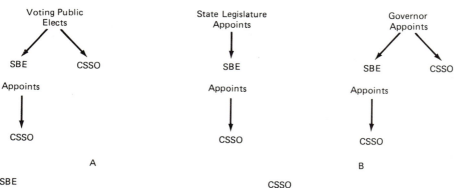

The only combination which presently does not exist is A3/B3

[15] Wisconsin is the exception. It has only a state vocational education board.

pattern throughout the United States. Now it is only the case in Florida and Mississippi. In Mississippi, the *ex officio* board is made up of only three members. In Ohio, the elected board consists of twenty-three members. The common range is between seven and thirteen members. The tendency is to have members serve from seven to nine years for the sake of continuity. State board members are generally lay persons who serve without pay. It is difficult to link methods of selection, size of board, or length of service to policy difference.

As legislatures have become increasingly involved in establishing educational policy, state boards of education have had their authority diminished. Additionally, where the CSSO is an elected official, possessed of an electoral base independent of the governor, legislature, and state board of education, the potential for policy conflict is substantial. At the least, a clear-cut demarcation between rule making and rule implementation implied by civics textbook descriptions is muddied by such mixed arrangements. Whether or not separation of authority actually makes a difference in terms of classroom activities, teacher behavior, curriculum content, or student performance is difficult to know.

State education departments.   The state education department (SED) is the main administrative agency for public schooling, and sometimes higher education, in each state. This agency is located in the state capital, and in large states may have one or more regional branches. Its chief executive is the CSSO. With the exception of relatively few near the top of the department's administrative hierarchy, the majority of employees will come under a civil service code and have the accompanying security of employment. The number of professionals employed typically ranges from 200 to 400.

State Board of Education and State Education Department Functions

Variability among states regarding the relative functions of the state board of education and the state education department is sufficient that anyone desiring precise information regarding a specific state is well advised to obtain detailed knowledge. For example, in New York State, there exists a Board of Regents, the members of which are appointed by the legislature on the basis of the state's congressional districts. This is an unusually powerful board. It has responsibility for both lower and higher education not only in administrative matters but, for selected areas, exercises judicial authority as well. New York's chief state school officer is legally empowered to replace local school board members if there is reason to do so. On the opposite side of the nation, the gubernatorially appointed State Board of Education in California is virtually powerless in a legal sense—it may only issue guidelines for legislatively enacted statutes, distribute admonitions to local school districts, and grant exemptions to teaching credential requirements.

Regardless of the authority of a particular state, the following general functions are characteristic of state education departments throughout the fifty states.

School finance.   State legislatures are responsible for statutorily determining finance distribution formulas, appropriation levels, and tax mechanisms for generating revenues. Administration of disbursements consistent with statute, however, is a state education department function. Administration of formulas and determination of local district apportionments is a large and complicated task. Funds are typically dispersed by the state treasurer; it is unusual for warrants or checks to be issued by state education departments.

Teacher certification.   A few states have a legally established agency, separate from the state board of education and state education department, responsible for determining teacher training and certification standards. However, in the majority of states this too is a function performed by the state education department and the state board of education.

Textbook selection.   A number of states perform a screening, selection, and purchasing function for local school districts in the area of textbooks and other instructional materials. Typically, this task is performed more often for elementary texts than those at the secondary level.[16] In that textbooks are a visible reflection of the values schools are expected to transmit, a state selection process can become highly controversial. Such has been the case in the 1970s and 1980s because of the intense pressure brought to bear in states by fundamentalist religious groups seeking a portrayal of values sympathetic to their own.[17]

Instructional standards.   Minimal graduation requirements, length of the school day and school year, and subject matter proficiency standards are illustrative of items legislatively established that are enforced by state education agencies.

Testing.   More than half the states utilize a statewide testing program. These examinations are increasingly patterned after the federally funded National Assessment of Educational Progress (NAEP) (see Chapter Four). Such examinations appraise students' knowledge in areas such as reading, mathematics, writing, and civic knowledge. In a few states, every student is tested at selected grade levels, but this is the exception. More typically, a representative group of students is chosen from a few grades of the elementary and secondary span. Several states test students for higher-order subject matter achievement in fields such as science, mathematics, English literature, history, and foreign language. New York State's Regents Examinations are famous in this regard. Passage of specialized examinations leads to the award of a prestigious "Regents Diploma." These state exams are separate from the Scholastic Aptitude Test described in Chapter One.

---

[16] A few states actually purchase plates from publishers and print textbooks themselves. This is done to save money. The degree of actual savings is arguable.

[17] See Dorothy Nelkin, *Science Textbook Controversies and the Politics of Equal Time* (Cambridge: MIT Press, 1977); and Franklin Parker, *Battle of the Books: Kanawha County* (Bloomington: Phi Delta Kappa, 1975).

Data collection and distribution. State education agencies collect information from local school districts and issue reports regarding matters such as finance, personnel, student attendance, and, if there is a state testing program, pupil performance. Such reports are generally done for state legislative bodies. They are useful to researchers and policy analysts. It is an unusual state in which such reports are written and distributed in a fashion that is also useful to the public.

State education departments are ideally suited to undertake analyses of educational programs and provide the public and policy makers with current evaluations of those which are effective and those which need to be altered or abandoned. Regrettably, it is unusual for a SED to have a well-developed analytic capacity.

Federal programs. In the time since enactment of the 1965 ESEA, one of the most significant functions of state education departments has been the administration of federally funded government programs. Title V of the ESEA specifically authorized use of federal funds for strengthening SEDs as they coped with these added administrative tasks. The general assessment is that SEDs have responded well to the challenge and have become the critical link between local districts and the federal Education Department.[18]

Facilities and transportation. State agencies are generally responsible for ensuring that architectural plans for local school buildings meet state standards for safety. In instances where the state funds construction completely, the SED may play an even larger role in the approval of building plans, including determination of whether a building is needed and granting permission to undertake construction. States may perform a similar function in approving school bus purchases, and state police are often responsible for undertaking periodic inspections of district bus fleets. In a similar vein, states may assist local districts in the purchasing of buses and other large pieces of equipment where quantity or bulk purchase may enable vendors to submit lower competitive bids than otherwise would be the case.

Regulation of nonpublic schools. Statutory and case law regarding the rights and responsibilities of SEDs in regulating nonpublic schools is mixed and no clear pattern has yet emerged. On one hand, state statutes sometimes require regulation when nonpublic schools receive some form of public aid. On the other hand, federal court decisions warn of excessive "entanglement" which might restrict First Amendment freedoms of nonpublic schools.

Interest Groups

One of the major means by which demands are transported through the boundary between the social environment and the political system is through the actions of interest groups and their representatives. As educational policy matters

---

[18] Jerome T. Murphy, *State Education Agencies and Discretionary Funds* (Lexington: Lexington Books, 1974).

have moved to the state level within the last two decades, interest groups have become more active in state capitals. Educational interest groups can be classified in three categories—those representing professional organizations, those constituted of clients of school services, and those initially established for other purposes but which have a periodic interest in education policy matters.

Professional education groups. These groups are generally comprised of school board and administrator organizations, teacher unions, and specialized education groups such as those concerned with vocational education, physical education, special education, bilingual education, and traditional subjects such as mathematics and English. On many issues, their views coincide, and they may even engage in collective lobbying to influence executive and legislative branch officials. School finance bills ensuring most or all districts added funds are illustrative of an issue about which such groups could probably reach agreement. Other issues, collective bargaining bills for example, are likely to divide these groups into those aligned with management, school boards and administrators, and those representing "labor"—teacher unions and classified employee groups.

Client groups. These groups include the Parent Teacher Association, League of Women Voters, Junior League, parents' unions, and an assortment of clients associated with more specialized school programs—those designed for handicapped students, child care or preschool, limited- or non-English speaking, gifted and talented, and benefactors of compensatory education programs. They have less cohesion than the professional education and school employee lobbies. Also, they have less money to spend in the support of particular political campaigns. Nevertheless. on specific issues they can be politically potent.

Generalized groups. Taxpayer associations, agriculture lobbies, summer camps, and business groups such as the Chamber of Commerce are primarily concerned with matters other than schooling. Nevertheless, where school issues cross their more immediate interests they can become intensely active politically.

The role of state-level special interests groups underwent substantial alteration in the 1960s and 1970s. The two changes of greatest note are their intensified political activities and their substantial fragmentation. The advent of collective bargaining offers at least a partial explanation of this phenomenon. Educational interest-group politics prior to and immediately following World War II were characterized by cohesion and consensus. Coalitions formed to lobby state officials were generally in agreement on state policy proposals. However, such groups were almost always heavily dominated by school administrators.[19] As collective bargaining movements grew among teacher unions in the 1960s, their leaders became increasingly frustrated by this fact and began to separate themselves from organizations weighted toward administration.

Another change is the increased participation of educational interest groups

---

[19] Stephen K. Bailey et al., *Schoolmen and Politics: A Study of State Aid to Education in the Northeast* (Syracuse: Syracuse University Press, 1962).

in political campaigns. Teacher unions have large campaign treasuries, raised from their dues-paying members, which are directed toward the election of state officials predicted both to win and likely to be favorably disposed toward teacher interest particularly and education generally. Teacher union political action committees (PACs) are among the best financed and most effective of such organizations.

The Judicial Branch

Chapter Six contains a more detailed description of the U.S. legal system and the role of courts in shaping educational policy. Suffice it to state here that rule interpretation in education plays an increasingly important role at the state level. Education has not escaped the trend toward litigiousness in American society. School finance cases have been particularly significant since the 1970s, but state court decisions in areas regarding access to school services, student discipline, teacher dismissal, racial desegregation, and school attendance have been important also.

SUMMARY

State government is primarily responsible for educational policy in the United States. This condition is complicated by the historic practice among states of delegating authority to local school districts for operational purposes. This convoluted situation evolved from colonial patterns of state authority, local operation, and lay control. Progressive era reforms seeking to insulate education from mainstream partisan politics promoted separate governmental procedures for education at both the state and local levels. Hence, while state legislatures and governors are mainly responsible for education, a mixed pattern of chief state school officers and state boards of education is also responsible for a limited policy-setting role as well as substantial administrative oversight of local school district activity. State courts also are involved in interpreting policy. An expanded judicial role is in large measure responsible for the increasing numbers of educational decisions made at the state level.

SELECTED READINGS

Campbell, Roald F., Luvern L. Cunningham, Raphael O. Nystrand, and Michael D. Usdan, *The Organization and Control of American Schools,* 4th ed. (Columbus, Ohio: Charles E. Merrill, 1980).

Fuller, Edgar, and Jim B. Pearson, eds., *Education in the United States: Nationwide Development Since 1900* (Washington, D.C.: National Education Association, 1969).

Thompson, John Thomas, *Policy Making in American Public Education: A Framework for Analysis* (Englewood Cliffs, N.J.: Prentice-Hall, 1976).

van Geel, Tyll, *Authority to Control the School Program* (Lexington: Lexington Books, 1976).

Wirt, Frederick M., and Michael W. Kirst, *Schools in Conflict* (Berkeley: McCutchan, 1982).

GOVERNING AMERICA'S SCHOOLS:
the role of local agencies

chapter 3

The approximately 15,000 local school districts in the United States and their nearly 90,000 individual schools comprise the fundamental operational units of American education. It is at the local level that the overwhelming majority of educational professionals are employed. This is the locus of curriculum planning and instruction. It is here that most school administrators receive their initial and probably more formative professional experiences. It is at this level that America's educational systems are the most visible, and it is here that the public frames its views regarding the success or failure of schools.

Since the 1950s, state legislative and executive branch agencies have intruded remarkably upon the conventional decision-making prerogatives of local school officials. Similarly, the federal government now occupies a substantial policy-making niche in American education. Despite such changes, local educational agencies continue to play a significant role. Regardless of the degree to which decisions of higher levels of government are just and inspired, success or failure of those policies depends crucially upon the understanding, ability, and insight of local educators. It is local officials who tailor broad state and federal policies to fit the educational preferences and conditions of individual students, parents, and citizens.

Because of these significant features, it is incumbent upon an educational leader, regardless of his or her eventual career objective, to be well informed about the structural and dynamic components of local educational systems. That is our purpose here. This chapter describes: structural features of school districts; governmental arrangements and political patterns surrounding local school boards; historic development, contemporary role, and personal characteristics of school board members and professional school administrators; organizational and political dynamics which characterize school board-administrator interactions; and the managerial role of school principals and so-called "intermediate agencies."

SCHOOL DISTRICT CHARACTERISTICS

School District Size

Both in terms of geography and enrollments, the variation among U.S. school districts matches the diversity which characterizes the nation as a whole. New York City and Los Angeles, with nearly one-and-a-half million students between them, occupy one end of the scale. At the opposite extreme there continue to be, though small in number, nonoperating school districts with no pupils in them whatsoever.[1] Some districts encompass but a few square miles. In contrast, Elko, Nevada, is a district covering 18,000 square miles.

The number of local districts reached its peak in the 1920s when nearly 130,000 were in existence. The overwhelming proportion of these were small rural districts, most operating only one school. An early twentieth century network of academic officials, college presidents, and professors of educational administration, operating in tandem with efficiency-oriented spokesmen for the business community, argued that small districts were wasteful of public resources and incapable of providing students with high-quality educational services.[2] They succeeded in triggering an astoundingly successful school district consolidation campaign. By 1950 the number of districts had been reduced to 80,000. By 1984, the number was only slightly in excess of 15,000, but this is something of a deceptive figure. Fully one-third of all U.S. school districts are contained within five states: California, Texas, Illinois, Nebraska, and New York. Other states have smaller numbers of districts. In particular, southern states have fewer districts because their local educational agencies are often coterminous with counties (see Table 3.1).

The consolidation effort has slowed, but it has not lost momentum altogether. It also remains controversial. Without question, legislative inducements and mandates for consolidation have been successful. However, it is arguable whether or not the advantages claimed for consolidation have been realized, and the costs of this effort may have been high. Research findings on the "optimum" size of school districts is mixed. It is difficult to identify a consistent relationship between school

---

[1] These anomalies are, effectively, tax shelters within which property owners are able to pay but a minimum in property taxes.

[2] See David B. Tyack, *The One Best System* (Cambridge: Harvard University Press, 1974); and Diane Ravitch, *The Great School Wars: New York City 1805-1973* (New York: Basic Books, 1974).

Table 3.1 DATA FILE: NUMBER AND ENROLLMENT OF OPERATING SCHOOL DISTRICTS*

STATE	DISTRICTS	SCHOOL YEAR 1971–72 ENROLLMENT			DISTRICTS	SCHOOL YEAR 1981–82 ENROLLMENT		
		Under 1,000	1,000–9,999	10,000 or more		Under 1,000	1,000–9,999	10,000 or more
Alabama	124	3.2%	87.9%	8.9%	127	3.1%	89.8%	7.1%
Alaska	29	69.0	24.1	6.9	52	76.9	19.2	3.8
Arizona	283	71.0	25.1	3.9	210	57.6	37.6	4.8
Arkansas	384	72.9	26.0	1.0	369	71.5	27.4	1.1
California	1,057	53.6	35.2	11.2	1,041	53.3	37.7	9.0
Colorado	181	64.6	28.2	7.2	181	61.3	30.4	8.3
Connecticut	169	26.0	63.9	10.1	165	30.3	66.1	3.6
Delaware	26	15.4	73.1	11.5	19	5.3	78.9	15.8
District of Columbia	1	.0	.0	100.0	1	.0	.0	100.0
Florida	67	4.5	58.2	37.3	67	4.5	56.7	38.8
Georgia	189	8.5	82.5	9.0	187	7.5	84.0	8.6
Hawaii	1	.0	.0	100.0	1	.0	.0	100.0
Idaho	115	62.6	34.8	2.6	115	59.1	38.3	2.6
Illinois	1,142	61.4	36.8	1.8	1,010	61.0	37.4	1.6
Indiana	315	17.5	75.6	7.0	304	14.8	79.3	5.9
Iowa	452	66.2	32.3	1.5	441	75.7	22.7	1.6
Kansas	311	70.7	28.0	1.3	306	72.9	25.8	1.3
Kentucky	190	17.4	79.5	3.2	180	18.9	77.8	3.3
Louisiana	66	.0	71.2	28.8	66	.0	68.2	31.8
Maine	242	63.6	36.0	.4	226	61.9	38.1	.0
Maryland	24	.0	37.5	62.5	24	.0	37.5	62.5
Massachusetts	373	39.9	54.7	5.4	346	38.4	58.7	2.9
Michigan	615	34.1	61.0	4.9	573	30.7	65.3	4.0
Minnesota	442	60.6	35.5	3.8	434	64.7	32.9	2.3
Mississippi	155	9.0	88.4	2.6	153	6.5	92.2	1.3

State								
Missouri	629	70.6	26.7	2.7	548	69.2	28.6	2.2
Montana	684	95.3	4.4	.3	561	94.8	5.2	.0
Nebraska	1,321	96.8	3.0	.2	994	96.3	3.4	.3
Nevada	17	35.3	52.9	11.8	17	23.5	64.7	11.8
New Hampshire	156	73.1	25.6	1.3	157	68.2	30.6	1.3
New Jersey	578	42.0	54.3	3.6	584	48.5	49.1	2.4
New Mexico	89	52.8	40.4	6.7	89	57.3	38.2	4.5
New York	736	27.9	66.3	5.8	715	29.8	67.3	2.9
North Carolina	152	.7	80.3	19.1	143	1.4	77.6	21.0
North Dakota	349	95.1	4.0	.9	290	95.2	4.8	.0
Ohio	625	15.2	80.0	4.8	615	16.6	80.2	3.3
Oklahoma	653	84.7	14.5	.8	619	82.2	16.6	1.1
Oregon	340	72.4	26.5	1.2	310	69.4	29.0	1.6
Pennsylvania	511	4.5	89.6	5.9	500	5.6	92.6	1.8
Rhode Island	40	22.5	65.0	12.5	40	22.5	70.0	7.5
South Carolina	93	4.3	78.5	17.2	92	6.5	73.9	19.6
South Dakota	222	86.0	13.1	.9	187	86.6	12.3	1.1
Tennessee	147	15.6	76.2	8.2	146	15.8	75.3	8.9
Texas	1,147	66.4	29.6	4.0	1,074	60.8	33.5	5.7
Utah	40	27.5	55.0	17.5	40	22.5	55.0	22.5
Vermont	250	89.6	10.4	.0	247	92.3	7.7	.0
Virginia	135	5.2	78.5	16.3	135	6.7	77.0	16.3
Washington	318	62.3	32.7	5.0	300	57.0	36.7	6.3
West Virginia	55	.0	80.0	20.0	55	.0	78.2	21.8
Wisconsin	449	50.8	46.1	3.1	433	53.3	44.8	1.8
Wyoming	79	70.9	26.6	2.5	49	46.9	49.0	4.1
Total	16,768	56.0%	39.6%	4.4%	15,538	54.1%	41.9%	4.0%

*Operating school districts are self-contained, public school systems run by local boards. Nonoperating systems do not run schools, but pay tuition to operating systems to educate children residing within their boundaries.

Source: U.S. Department of Education

45

or school district size and either economies of scale or student performance.[3] For example, whereas large schools and school districts appear to be more economical in areas such as utility costs, it may frequently be the case that transporting students to a central site increases fuel costs. Educationally, the answer is also far from clear. Whereas schools with larger enrollments can often afford to offer more specialized courses, for example, in advanced science, math, and foreign language, it is also the case that problems of student and employee alienation and indifference may increase with the size of the operational unit.[4] Bigger need not necessarily be better either educationally or financially.

Classifications of School Districts

Beyond big and little, rich and poor, school districts fit a number of different classifications. The most common variety are *unified school districts,* which sponsor kindergarten through twelfth grade instruction for all public school pupils within a specified geographic area. The district may contain one school or hundreds of schools, and the grade organization in school buildings may vary—it may be grades K-6, 7-9, 10-12; or grades K-8, 9-12; or grades K-6, 7-8, 9-12; or K-5, 6-7-8, 9-12. All schools and grades are under the administrative authority of a single district that has one governing board within that district.

There are also *elementary school districts,* which operate schools containing only grades K-6 or K-8. Where such districts exist, they usually feed into a geographically larger *secondary school district* that operates schools for grades 9-12. In addition, there are *union districts,* a label connoting the combining of two or more elementary or secondary districts into a single operating authority.

Beyond these typical labels there exist specialized districts and other categories of school districts tied to historical developments within individual states. In some areas, counties serve both as operating units—actually delivering school services—as well as providing specialized services—data processing and record keeping—to independent operating school districts within their boundaries. In some states there are vocational education districts, separate from local school districts, that are responsible for providing academic preparation.

There are *intermediate units* in almost every state. These may be organized along county lines, sometimes including more than a single county. In California, these are known as County Offices of Education. In New York, they are labeled Boards of Cooperative Educational Services (BOCES). In Texas, they are Educational Service Units. These agencies provide a variety of specialized services to local school districts. We provide additional explanations of their functions at the end of this chapter.

---

[3] See James Van, "School Size: A Regional Case Analysis" (unpublished Ed.D. dissertation, University of California, Berkeley, 1982).

[4] See Barker and Gump, *Big School: Small School* (Stanford: Stanford University Press, 1963). Also James W. Guthrie, "Organizational Scale and School Success," *Educational Evaluation and Policy Analysis,* Winter 1979, vol. 1, no. 1.

In keeping with both the historic development of education and its status as a special form of government, school districts generally do not follow the lines of municipal boundaries. There are exceptions to this. Large city district boundaries frequently are coterminous with those of their respective municipalities. Similarly, in the Midwest, school districts resulting from land survey ordinances of the late eighteenth century are frequently coterminous with township boundaries. However, 80 percent of U.S. districts have boundaries which are not coincidental with those of other governments. Public confusion frequently results.

Most school districts have taxing authority. Within legal boundaries established by legislatures, school boards can levy property taxes for the support of local educational services. Such districts are labeled *fiscally independent*. City school districts are the frequent exception. They must rely more often upon city councils or county boards of supervisors to approve their budgets and thereafter levy whatever taxes will be needed to raise revenues.[5] This is also the case for all school districts in Maryland, North Carolina, and Virginia. Hawaii, which has no local districts, is a special example in this regard. Such arrangements are labeled *fiscal dependence*.

Educators frequently assert that only by possessing taxing authority can local school districts remain unfettered by inappropriate political influence either from municipal governments or from state and federal authorities. Such an argument is intuitively attractive. However, social science researchers have not yet been able to identify what, if any, differences accrue to fiscal independence. Districts that have their own taxing authority appear not to differ significantly from fiscally dependent districts in terms of spending patterns.[6]

Legal Standing

State statutes vary regarding the legal standing granted local school districts. In some states, school districts are said to be municipal corporations. More typically, however, school districts are classified as *quasi corporations,* quasi in this instance meaning "acting as if." Edwards offers the following description of the distinction:

> Strictly speaking, a school district is not a municipal corporation: it is a quasi-corporation. A municipal corporation proper is a city or town incorporated primarily for purposes of local government. While such a corporation is in part an agency of the state established to assist in the affairs of civil government, it is created, in the main, to enable the locality to regulate and administer its own local concerns. Local interest and advantage rather than execution of state policy are its determining characteristics. In order to effectuate the purposes of their creation, it is obvious that municipal corporations must be granted considerable powers of a legislative and regulatory nature. A quasi-

[5] Since the 1978 enactment of Proposition 13, California's more than 1000 school districts, while nominally fiscally independent, in fact have not had the ability to generate local revenues. They depend entirely upon the state legislature to determine their revenues.

[6] See H. Thomas James, J. Alan Thomas, and Harold J. Dyck, *Wealth, Expenditures and Decision Making for Education* (Stanford: Stanford School of Education, 1963), p. 99.

corporation, on the other hand, is purely a political or civil division of the state; it is created as an instrumentality of the state in order to facilitate the administration of government.[7]

Several significant points follow from the fact that most school districts are quasi corporations. For example, in the majority of circumstances school board members are acting to facilitate state objectives. In so doing they typically are limited to the authority expressly granted to them by state statute.

The fact that school districts are not part of general government, not included within the authority of a city council, is often confusing to laypersons and is generally regarded as a flawed arrangement by political scientists.[8] The latter's concern is that government should benefit from integrated decision making, wherein representative officials have the authority at hand to comply with the general will of the public. Schools command substantial resources—local as well as state and federal. Citizens expect school services to be efficiently delivered and coordinated with other municipal endeavors such as transportation and zoning. Thus, it is argued that elected municipal officials should have authority to ensure such coordination. For their part, education administrators, supported by the majority of the public to this point, have argued that education is too important to risk being politicized in the manner that occurred at the end of the nineteenth century. Hence, special government status is utilized in an attempt to insulate education from narrow and inappropriate partisan political decision making.

Regardless of what is correct in this controversy, school districts are increasingly engaged in cooperative ventures with municipal government. Joint purchasing arrangements enable both municipal government and schools to derive the economic benefits from bulk buying. Transportation is also sometimes a cooperative undertaking. Joint use or leasing of surplus property offers an opportunity for local governmental bodies to cooperate. Such cooperation must be approached cautiously to ensure that the needs of neither governmental body is jeopardized. However, school administrators should be alert to the prospect of useful cooperation so as to both save resources badly needed for other services and to assure citizens that public revenues are being used in the most productive manner.

SCHOOL BOARDS

Mark Twain is alleged to have stated that "God first made school board members for practice and then created monkeys." However apocryphal, this statement represents the status of school board members in the hierarchy of America's elected officials. The nation has in excess of 90,000 school board members. This is by far

---

[7] Newton Edwards, *The Courts and the Public Schools* (Chicago: The University of Chicago Press, 1955), p. 54.

[8] See Roscoe C. Martin, *Government and the Suburban School* (Syracuse: Syracuse University Press, 1963), pp. 102–105.

the largest category of representative public officials. Yet school board members are frequently held in low regard by members of city councils, county boards, and state and federal elected officials. Also, until quite recently, it was an area of government which was substantially neglected by political science scholars. Low regard in the eyes of polemicists, politicians, and political analysts is matched by apparent low understanding by the public.

School boards are seldom viewed as important political bodies, and, thus, it is surprising to think that school board members may be politically ambitious. Nevertheless, many are. President Jimmy Carter and U.S. Supreme Court Justice Lewis Powell were local school board members. They are outstanding examples of the approximately 56 percent of school board members who responded to an inquiry regarding their motives by stating that they ran for office to achieve personal goals or represent an interest group. Although the survey was published in 1959, and its findings may no longer hold, its findings clash with the "apolitical myth" of the selfless, idealistic school board member.[9]

Who Serves?

It is clear from major surveys that contemporary school board members, like their predecessors from other eras, tend to be middle class individuals, generally drawn from business and professional occupations.[10] A 1982 survey revealed that U.S. school board members are predominantly male (72 percent), Anglo-American (91 percent), middle aged, professionally or managerially employed (67 percent), better educated than the general public in terms of completing four or more years of college (63 percent), and earning a good income (57 percent had annual earnings above the national median family income). The average length of service on a board is close to six years, and more than 94 percent are elected. They usually serve without pay and the average length of an election term is four years. They are generally elected at large from throughout a district. They almost always run without formal political party alignment. Board size ranges from three to more than twenty members. However, the present trend is toward five members.

School superintendents frequently lament that boards now lack the quality they once possessed. Such assertions are difficult to document empirically. It does appear accurate that large city boards of education have changed over time, with many more of their members being drawn from the minority groups that now dominate city demographics.[11] This is to be expected, and is altogether a measure

[9] Donald J. McCarty, "Motives for Seeking School Board Membership" (Ph.D. dissertation, University of Chicago, 1959).

[10] "Readout: All About Who You Are," *American School Board Journal,* January 1983, 170, no. 1, 23-24. George S. Counts, *The Social Composition of Boards of Education,* Supplementary Education Monograph no. 33 (Chicago: University of Chicago Press, 1927); and Alpheus L. White, *Local School Boards: Organization and Practice* (Washington, D.C.: U.S. Office of Education, Department of Health, Education, and Welfare, U.S. Government Printing Office, 1962).

[11] See Anne E. Just, "City School Politics" (unpublished Ph.D. dissertation, University of California, Berkeley, 1983).

of the vitality of the American representative system of government. If such individuals lack expertise in governing, and it is not altogether clear that such is the case, it may be because of prior lack of opportunity and experience.

Governmental Functions of School Boards

Despite school boards' long history, citizens appear remarkably uninformed regarding their governmental purposes and legal prerogatives. A 1983 survey in six midwestern states resulted in the following findings: Only 22 percent of public respondents were able correctly to state the number of members on their local school board. Ten percent thought the school board and administration were simply separate labels for the same agency. Eighteen percent thought the board merely rubber stamped administration decisions. Forty-three percent thought the board and administration were legally required to arrive at decisions acceptable to both. Eleven percent thought the board had total control. The remainder had no opinion. The substantial majority of respondents simply did not know or were badly misinformed regarding the role of school boards. When queried about the source of their information, most listed local newspapers. Fewer than 6 percent had ever attended a board meeting, and only 4 percent had ever read a board communique.[12]

Despite such apparent misunderstanding, local school boards are generally constitutionally and statutorily empowered to make a number of significant decisions. Seldom can a board make a decision and be totally unencumbered. There are almost always legal limits placed upon decisions. The decisions are, nevertheless, significant. Here is a composite listing of the major powers typically granted to local school boards.

> *Select Chief Executive Officer (CEO).* This is a decision which is generally considered the most significant of all school board actions. The CEO, Superintendent, is responsible for implementing board policies, recruitment and evaluation of employees, and a wide assortment of professional matters regarding curriculum and instruction. Regardless of the wisdom embodied in the board's policies, unless they are appropriately administered by able individuals, they may come to naught. Also, this is the person who more than any other is likely to establish the organizational climate for the district and shape the public's perceptions of local schools.

> *Approve Budgets.* In most states, generation and distribution of revenue for schooling purposes is a major school board responsibility. State law circumscribes discretion of boards in this regard. For example, fiscally independent school boards are not empowered to raise property taxes to any level of their choosing—there are state-imposed tax ceilings above which voter approval will be necessary. On the expenditure side, state mandates also curtail local discretion. For example, it is not uncommon for state law to specify the minimum proportion of a district's budget which must be spent upon certificated salaries or the maximum amount that can be spent for administration. Re-

---

[12] Gerald R. Boardman and Myrna Cassell, "How Well Does the Public Know Its School Boards?" *Kappan,* June 1983, 64, no. 10, 740.

gardless, within such boundaries, financial decisions of school boards are important in establishing educational directions for a school district.

Determine School Sites and Attendance Boundaries. In many ways it is through these actions that a school board is most visible to its local clients. Selecting the site for constructing a new school, deciding to close a building, remodeling an old building, or rearranging attendance boundaries are instances in which one group of constituents is likely to be advantaged and another disadvantaged. This can be the occasion for substantial community conflict. There are no "tricks" which will enable a school board to escape what may be intense conflict over such issues. School administrators may well be caught in the political heat. This is exactly the kind of resource allocation decision that the political system is established to render. The challenge is to make the decisions on grounds which are widely viewed as impartial and responsible. The only defensible approach is for a board and its administrative staff to undertake thorough and fair analyses so as to ensure a legitimate decision which benefits the largest number or minimizes disadvantages.

Enter into Contracts. School boards possess legal authority to contract for goods and services. State law generally prescribes contract procedures, e.g., bidding on purchases in excess of a minimum dollar level. Once made, however, a contract between a board and a vendor or individual is legally binding on both parties and cannot easily be broken by a subsequent board with a different view.

Bargain Collectively. Collective bargaining agreements or contracts with employees are negotiated with the school board being the agent of the district. A district administrator may represent the board at the bargaining table or the board may employ an experienced negotiator particularly for such purposes. Either alternative may be appropriate. What is seldom effective is to have one or more board members personally and directly engaged in negotiating. The board needs to have sufficient distance from the bargaining process to be objective and consider the district's best interests without risking intense emotional involvement. To paraphrase another homily: the board which represents itself at the bargaining table has a fool for a client. The bargaining process should be coordinated carefully with the budget process.

Establish Criteria for Employing School District Personnel. Other than the position of CEO, it is generally useful for school board members to delegate hiring authority to district administrators. However, the board should not absolve itself of responsibility for establishing qualifications for various positions.

Determine Curriculum. State statutes influence a local district's curriculum. However, there is almost always room for local discretion. For example, a state may require a specified number of units or mandate a minimum number of years of mathematics for a high school diploma. A local board has the option of exceeding such minima. Whether or not it does and, if so, in which direction, is a matter which should depend upon a careful assessment of community expectations and professional advice. However, the ultimate formal decision is the school board's to make.

There are numerous other domains in which school boards possess decision-making authority—procedures for evaluating students and employees, selection of instructional materials, architectural design, financing of capital purchases, personnel assignment policies, pursuit of categorical aid funds, and codes of student conduct. In these, as well as most other areas, school board decisions are narrowed by various environmental and organizational circumstances. For example:

> *State Statutes.* In that school boards are legal extensions of state authority, it is state statutes which impose the greatest restraint on discretion. For example, it is an unusual state that has no minimum qualifications for a school district's CEO. To be a superintendent typically takes a minimum level of experience, education, and licensure. Similarly, we have already mentioned that revenue generation and distribution is not an activity in which a board can engage unfettered.

> *Information.* It is virtually a maxim that decision makers never have sufficient information. One can almost always imagine an additional set of facts or analyses which would be helpful in arriving at a conclusion. However, information is often costly in terms of the time and resources it takes to collect and digest. The relative absence of information as well as the source of that information can limit the choices available to school boards. In that the superintendent and other administrators are major suppliers of information for school board members, they have substantial influence over the outcome of decisions.

> *Resources.* It is probably obvious that school districts have finite resources and thus are limited in the number of endeavors they can undertake. What is not so obvious is that a school board is also constrained by constituent opinions. Such constraints are seldom rigid. Leadership on the part of the board or administration can often shape public opinion. However, a board cannot consistently violate public expectations without paying politically in terms of electoral defeat or the threat of recall.

Political Functions of School Boards

The decision-making discretion of school boards has been altered sufficiently over time that one analyst has suggested that they no longer serve a full range of political functions. H. Thomas James, after having analyzed school board decision making for a number of years, speculates that whereas the nineteenth century boards were themselves responsible for rule making, rule implementation, and rule adjudication, the advent of professional school managers and the expansion of federal, state, and judicial authority, transformed school boards so that their current major function is only rule adjudication. He contends that boards spend most of their time interpreting rules made at other levels of government and tailoring their applications to a local setting. This transforms school boards, and to some degree superintendents into lightning rods which by attracting community conflict away from classrooms enables instruction to proceed relatively uninterrupted.

School Boards, Community Politics, and Administrators

Politics is the set of dynamic activities whereby a society decides upon the distribution of scarce items such as physical goods, power, participation, and prestige.[13] For education, these decisions involve complicated interactions between

---

[13] A more formal definition of politics is provided by David Easton in *A Framework for Political Analysis* (Englewood Cliffs, N.J.: Prentice-Hall, 1965). Also, the most famous definition of politics is that of Harold Lasswell, *Politics: Who Gets What, When, How?* (New York: McGraw-Hill, 1936).

constituencies and multiple layers and branches of government. We have pointed out many of the state-level actors and agencies in the preceding chapter, and we discuss the federal government in Chapter Four. Board members and professional educators in school districts are an important component of this interaction. In order to be effective, educational administrators must be cognizant of local political interactions and understand how they influence school policy and practice. In this section we describe appropriate findings and trends from the academic study of community politics.

"Community power." In every society and in almost every social setting, it is clear that particular individuals have greater influence or authority than others. The United States system of constitutional government attempts to ensure by legal means that each citizen is equally enfranchised. Still, it is the case that because of factors such as personal wealth, intellect, physical force, charisma, and family or friendship connections, some are more influential than others in political matters. Given this seemingly inescapable condition of inequality, it is often comfortable to conclude that a nation, state, or local community is controlled by a relatively narrow group of influential individuals.[14] Such reasoning continues by asserting that access to this "power elite" facilitates favorable decisions. For example, if a local superintendent wants a tax increase, funding for a new building, authority to hire additional staff, then he or she is advised to persuade the "power structure" and gain approval. However attractive, this scenario is, at best, vastly oversimplified and may prove altogether inaccurate.

Do "power elites" exist in school districts? What is the relationship between school board members, school administrators, and a community's power structure? Beginning in the late 1920s, social scientists undertook systematic studies of communities and their social systems. Among the best known were analyses of two midwestern towns, Muncie, Indiana (*Middletown,* by Robert S. and Helen M. Lynd), and Morristown, Illinois (*Elmtown's Youth,* by August B. Hollingshead).[15] Findings from these classic studies suggested that there was a relatively small group of business and government officials who exercised disproportionate influence over town matters, and schools were part of their sphere of influence. This type of research was interrupted by World War II, but was subsequently continued in Floyd Hunter's exhaustive study of a large southern city.

In *Community Power Structure,* Hunter portrayed Atlanta as having a central, controlling elite, the membership of which was substantially interconnected.[16] In 1960, Robert Dahl, a Yale political scientist who had served as Mayor of New Haven, Connecticut, studied his hometown using a research procedure different from Hunter's. His thesis in *Who Governs* is that "power" is widely distributed in

[14] This concept was applied to the United States by the sociologist C. Wright Mills in his book *The Power Elite* (New York: Oxford University Press, 1959).

[15] Robert S. and Helen M. Lynd, *Middletown* (New York: Harcourt Brace Jovanovich, 1929); and August B. Hollingshead, *Elmtown's Youth* (New York: John Wiley, 1949).

[16] Floyd Hunter, *Community Power Structure* (Chapel Hill: University of North Carolina Press, 1955).

a community and that the influential actors tend to vary by political issue.[17] If this view is correct, then the politics of education may be different than the politics of public works, economic development, or waste disposal. Among social scientists, substantial controversy occurred regarding the validity of the two theories.[18] Is "power" held by a ruling elite in all instances or is it dispersed contingent upon the issue? Additionally, debate took place regarding the research methodology most appropriate for discerning a community's power structure. Hunter used a "reputational" approach involving interviews inquiring about those who were perceived as influential. Dahl utilized "decision analysis," which depends upon interviews with parties on varying sides of a controversial proposal.

Hunter's and Dahl's research triggered literally dozens of additional community power studies in the 1960s. Many focused exclusively upon education politics and their relation to school administrators. From these efforts several components of "community power" emerged more clearly.[19] "Power" as a social science concept is imprecise. Whereas the term may have utility in colloquial conversation, it is not particularly useful for guiding research.[20] Second, the structure of influence is likely to vary from community to community. Small towns such as those studied by the Lynds and Hollingshead may well have a power structure different from larger cities such as New Haven or a major metropolitan center such as Atlanta. Suburban communities may vary yet again in terms of having either a centralized or pluralistic "power structure."[21] Whatever the current character of a community's political network, it may change over time. Regrettably, social science has only confirmed the variability of community political relationships. It is not yet able to discern a pattern to "community power" or explain why a community conforms to a particular model.

Practical politics.   Given such indeterminacy, what is the best course for educational administrators? We offer this advice:[22]

> Attempt to become informed regarding political relationships in your local district or school community. The absence of practical knowledge in this regard may impede your effectiveness.
>
> Employ an eclectic approach in determining the "power structure." The reputational techniques of Hunter, the issue-oriented research of Dahl, the case

[17] Robert A. Dahl, *Who Governs?* (New Haven: Yale University Press, 1960).

[18] See, for example, Nelson W. Polsby, *Community Power and Political Theory* (New Haven: Yale University Press, 1963).

[19] An excellent review of these studies is provided by Frederick M. Wirt and Michael W. Kirst, *Schools in Conflict* (Berkeley: McCutchan, 1982).

[20] See James G. March, "The Power of Power," in *Varieties of Political Theory,* David Easton, ed. (Englewood Cliffs, N.J.: Prentice-Hall, 1966), pp. 39–70.

[21] Warner Bloomberg et al., *Suburban Power Structures and Public Education* (Syracuse: Syracuse University Press, 1963).

[22] Useful practical advice in undertaking political analyses is provided by William D. Coplin and Michael K. O'Leary in *Every Man's Prince: A Guide to Understanding Your Political Problems,* revised edition (North Scituate, Mass.: Duxbury, 1982).

study approach of Vidich and Bensman,[23] and other procedures all have benefits. An administrator need not conduct time-consuming social science analyses. It generally will suffice to make reasoned inquiries and listen carefully to answers. Wide reading in local newspapers and attendance at appropriate community meetings are also in order.

Avoid a preconceived mind set regarding the pattern of local relationships. They may be central, pluralistic, or something else.

Realize that vertical patterns of influence may be of equal or greater importance than horizontal patterns. Whereas local actors and agencies certainly influence political decisions relevant to schools, it is also the case that forces such as federal and state governments, large national corporations, and international events also exercise substantial influence in local decisions.

LOCAL SCHOOL DISTRICT ADMINISTRATORS

Prior to 1900 there were few "professional" educational managers—those working at that time were to be found almost exclusively in large eastern and midwestern cities. As these cities grew in size, and ward-based schools grew in number and enrollment, school board members increasingly requested assistance in the management of school affairs. Their part-time, unpaid status did not permit giving attention to the financial and business problems that were occurring as a consequence of organizational growth. Initial school board requests were for assistance in clerical or narrow financial areas. It was in this way that professional school managers came to be. The Buffalo, New York city council appointed a superintendent of common schools on June 9, 1837. Thereafter, in big cities, the number of such positions grew—by 1860 twenty-seven urban school districts had superintendents.[24]

By the beginning of the twentieth century a number of social conditions coincided to expand professional school management. Previously described Progressive Era political reforms intended to separate educational policy from partisan politics paved the way for full-time educational managers. By attempting to apply the same scientific management techniques to schools as were in vogue in the private sector, the efficiency movement created a demand for professional administrators. This movement also promoted consolidation of many rural and small school districts into larger units, and the amalgamation of ward- and section-based school boards in central cities in an attempt to escape corrupt political practices. These changes created larger organizations and popular demand for professional school administrators. This need was seen as an opportunity by schools of education to train managers and thus enhance their own status.[25]

[23] Arthur J. Vidich and Joseph Bensman, *Small Town in Mass Society* (Garden City: Doubleday, 1958).

[24] See Roald F. Campbell, Luvern L. Cunningham, Raphael O. Nystrand, and Michael D. Usdan, *The Organization and Control of American Schools,* 4th ed. (Columbus, Ohio: Charles E. Merrill, 1980), p. 218.

[25] For more information see David Tyack and Elizabeth Hansot, *Managers of Virtue: Public School Leadership in America, 1820-1980* (New York: Basic Books, 1982).

Current population increases, continued school district consolidation, intensified public expectations for schools, growth of suburban school districts, and a general trend toward societal bureaucratization have contributed to the contemporary, widespread use of school administrators at many organizational levels—superintendent, central office, school site, county, state, and federal agencies. Indeed, by 1980 the number of school administrators in the United States approximated 160,000, one out of every 1500 citizens.[26] Who are these individuals, and what duties do they perform? These are the questions to which we now turn, beginning with the role of superintendent.

School Superintendents

Most U.S. school districts employ a *superintendent* as a chief executive officer (CEO). Exceptions tend to be small rural districts that may combine the district manager role with that of a school principal, or may join with one or more other districts in order to employ a common superintendent. Much is written regarding the significance of the superintendent's position. Boards of education are admonished, correctly, to expend substantial care in the selection of such an individual because of his or her crucial importance for the success or failure of the community's schools. Not only is the superintendent expected to be the school district's chief operating officer, but he or she (the number of females is increasing but superintendents are still overwhelmingly male) is also probably the most visible individual in the community on education matters. The position is important both practically and symbolically.

Who serves? Given the widely ascribed significance to the superintendency, it is surprising how little is known about the individuals who fill the role. From past studies, the following profile emerges: Superintendents are male, white, middle-aged, began as teachers, assumed their first administrative position at approximately age thirty, and became a superintendent some six years later. Virtually all superintendents hold a college degree and more than 80 percent hold advanced degrees—masters and doctorates. Contrary to conventional perceptions, the majority, about 55 percent, have majored as undergraduates in English, social science, science, business administration, or the humanities. About 25 percent have majored in education or physical education.

Generally, superintendents were raised in rural areas and small towns, and that is where the majority of them continue to serve. They work long hours, more than fifty-six in a typical week. They apparently enjoy their work, however, because more than 70 percent respond in polls that they would choose the occupation again.[27]

When it comes to salaries, superintendents appear generally well paid, at least

---

[26] By comparison, there were 600,000 attorneys and 450,000 physicians.

[27] American Association of School Administrators, *Profile of a School Superintendent,* as presented in Campbell, Cunningham, Nystrand, and Usdan, *Organization and Control,* p. 223.

when compared to teachers. Also, in general, the larger the district, the higher the salary. This is not, however, a linear relationship. A study of New York superintendents revealed the ten highest paid school district executives in that state, among which there was only a $5000 salary variation, managed districts in which enrollment varied from 2500 to more than 13,000. The superintendent of the latter district was only at the median in the salary range.[28]

The qualities sought by school boards in selecting superintendents are not clear. In a 1977 study spanning thirty-two years of superintendent selections in Wisconsin, March and March found little relationship between characteristics of those selected and characteristics of districts doing the hiring. Indeed, the researchers assert that the selection pattern appears as though boards of education were picking at random.[29]

Campbell and colleagues point out that the Wisconsin sample used in the March study represented a large number of small rural districts among which there may not have been wide variation. If the study had been conducted in states with larger and more heterogeneous districts, the selection process might well have proved less random.[30]

Richard O. Carlson undertook an insightful analysis of social mobility data originally collected by sociologist Melvin Seeman.[31] Carlson concluded that the superintendency is an "open elite," meaning that occupants of the position change frequently. Carlson categorized superintendents in two ways—"career bound" and "place bound." The former had a term of office averaging 4.6 years. The latter averaged 8.3 years.[32]

Superintendents' functions.   In the majority of school settings, the superintendent is the executive officer for the board of education. Exceptions occur in those few districts where there is a coequal executive, usually a business manager, with whom the superintendent shares authority. It is also sometimes the case that a district will have a clerk of the board with whom the superintendent divides duties. When the superintendent is the sole chief executive, all other district employees are subordinate.

Is the superintendent an employee of the board or an officer of the district? At one time there was substantial controversy surrounding this question. If the results of a 1975 national school board poll remain valid, it is still a confusing mat-

[28] New York State Office of Education Performance Review, *The Superintendent of Schools: His Role, Background, and Salary,* 1974.

[29] James C. March and James G. March, "Almost Random Careers: Wisconsin School Superintendency, 1940-1972," *Administrative Science Quarterly,* 22 (September 1977), pp. 377-409.

[30] Campbell, Cunningham, Nystrand, and Usdan, *Organization and Control,* p. 233.

[31] Melvin Seeman, "Social Mobility and Administrative Behavior," *American Sociological Review,* 23 (December 1958), p. 642.

[32] Richard O. Carlson, *School Superintendents: Career and Performance* (Columbus, Ohio: Charles E. Merrill, 1971), pp. 140-44.

ter for members of the public. Almost half the respondents sampled believed that the school board was subordinate to the superintendent rather than the reverse.[33]

Whatever the public's perception or past confusion, the legal picture is increasingly clear. Gee and Sperry conclude:

> The only generalization that we can reach after careful study of many states' laws is that the statutory protection of the job tends to be minimal, with employment conditions dictated primarily by contractual agreement negotiated between the Board and superintendent. Thus, the superintendent who by law may have the right to exercise a good deal of initiative may in fact not be able to survive if the Board is determined to restrict or scrutinize his or her every move. Conversely, the superintendent who has little or no statutory authority ascribed to his or her position directly may exercise great liberty and initiative if the Board is willing to place faith and trust in the superintendent's judgment and give sustained approval to the administrator's ideas, suggestions, and actions.[34]

The manner in which superintendents perform has been shaped over time by the professional conception of the role. In an article for the *Administrator's Notebook,* Roald Campbell traces four historic conceptions of the superintendency. This begins with the so-called scientific management movement at the beginning of the twentieth century, which shaped initial expectations for superintendents.[35] This was followed in the 1930s and 1940s by the so-called "human relations approach,"[36] in the 1950s and 1960s by the "structural movement,"[37] and in the 1960s by the "systems approach." These are discussed in greater detail in Chapter Seven.

Superintendents' activities. Studies of the manner in which school CEOs spend their time are reasonably consistent. The picture that emerges is one of a superintendent representing the school administration and the school board to the public, a negotiator of conflict, and a rational planner. Only one-fifth to one-fourth of the superintendent's time is spent in matters related to instruction or pupil personnel. The overwhelming proportion of time is devoted to budgetary and finance

---

[33] National School Boards Association Research Report, *The People Look at Their Schools,* Report No. 1975-1 (Washington, D.C.: National School Boards Association, 1975).

[34] E. Gorden Gee and David J. Sperry, *Education Law and the Public Schools: A Compendium* (Boston: Allyn & Bacon, 1978), pp. A-19 and A-20.

[35] Frederick W. Taylor, *Scientific Management* (New York: Harper & Row, 1947); and Franklin Bobbitt, "Some General Principles of Management Applied to the Problems of City School Systems," in *The Supervision of City Schools,* Twelfth Yearbook of the National Society for the Study of Education, Part I (Chicago: The University of Chicago Press, 1913), pp. 7–96, as quoted in Campbell, Cunningham, Nystrand, and Usdan, *Organization and Control,* p. 26.

[36] See F. J. Roethlisberger and William J. Dickson, *Management and the Worker* (Cambridge: Harvard University Press, 1941); and G. Robert Koopman, Alice Miel, and Paul J. Misner, *Democracy in School Administration* (New York: Appleton-Century-Crofts, 1943).

[37] As illustration, see James G. March and H. A. Simon, *Organizations* (New York: John Wiley, 1958).

matters, personnel, facilities, and public relations concerns.[38] In these endeavors the superintendent is frequently called upon to explain and persuade, either by written communique or by speaking at meetings. Much of what a superintendent does cannot be easily anticipated. The nature of the job often involves reacting to events initiated elsewhere, which precludes a neat compartmentalization of duties. Aspirants to the superintendency are encouraged to develop their ability to use the English language and to plan to be interrupted by crises, many of which they will be unable to predict. We have more to say about such matters in Chapter Nine on the administrator's role.[39]

Relationship with school board. Superintendent-school board relations are filled with potential tensions. Local school districts are legally controlled by lay authorities. By virtue of position, expertise, experience, and control of information, a superintendent—a professional—can dominate school district decision-making processes. The matter is made more complicated by the absence of a clear demarcation between a board's rule-making and the superintendent's rule-implementation role. Each side frequently views the other as unnecessarily usurping its authority. The matter is made yet more complicated by lack of agreement regarding the goals and objectives of most school districts and the substantial influence other governmental agencies and outside forces exert upon schools.

The researcher who has focused most extensively upon the political consequences of school board-superintendent relationships is Harman Ziegler. After studying school board-superintendent interaction, Ziegler concludes

> Board members, lacking a meaningful relationship to an external political constituency, fall easy prey to the superintendent's claim for "expertise." The recruitment process—looking to the civic business world for the pool of eligibles—virtually guarantees that the notions of lay control will be subverted. We do not have lay control because, among other reasons, school board members do not want to control educational policy. Their background and expertise compels them to look toward the superintendent's office for leadership. As the ideological descendant of the nineteenth century reformers, today's school board member is doing a good job, he is leaving the governance of schools to the experts.[40]

William L. Boyd offers a rebuttal by asserting that an administrator's control over a board is nowhere as dominant as Ziegler suggests. The issue at hand, the size and complexity of the community, the character and number of constituencies

---

[38] Campbell, Cunningham, Nystrand, and Usdan, *Organization and Control,* p. 235.

[39] For studies of how superintendents use their time, see "Observation of Administrator Behavior" (Chicago: Midwest Administration Center, University of Chicago, 1959); Nancy Jane Pitner, "Descriptive Study of the Everyday Activities of the Suburban School Superintendents" (Ph.D. dissertation, Ohio State University, 1978); John Feilders, "Profile: The Role of the Chief Superintendent of Schools" (Belmont, CA: Pitman Learning Inc., 1982); and Larry Cuban, *Urban School Chiefs Under Fire* (Chicago: The University of Chicago Press, 1976).

[40] Harmon Ziegler, "Creating Responsive Schools," *Urban Review,* 6, no. 4 (1973), 40.

involved, and the influence of external agencies all mitigate superintendent-board interaction. Moreover, educators are more likely to be more responsive to the public than professionals in other policy areas, such as transportation, welfare, or pollution control. Indeed, an early 1970 study of six public agencies in nine major cities reveals education to be highly ranked in responsiveness and innovation.[41]

Wirt suggests a theoretical explanation involving variables, such as the issue at hand, public concern, and technical expertise, which interact to form a zone of tolerance within which a board of education may well permit the superintendent to exercise initiative and discretion without much constraint. Outside of this zone, the board may itself exercise substantial control. Research remains to be done on Wirt's theory, but the practical resolution of tensions between school boards and superintendents will continue to depend on specific agreements reached in each individual community.[42]

The Hierarchy of Local School Administration

In addition to the approximately 14,000 superintendents in the United States, there are another 145,000 administrators. About 60,000 of these are employed in central offices of local school districts, county offices of education and other intermediate agencies, state education departments, and federal government agencies. The functions and titles of these individuals are numerous. Typical divisions include instruction, business and financial affairs, personnel, facilities and transportation, and federal programs. The number employed in a local school district is related to the district's enrollment. In a small district, the superintendent may be responsible for all of these functions. In New York City or Los Angeles, each of these departments will itself be subdivided and contain hundreds of administrative personnel.

Administrative organization. We know of no single organizational arrangement which is appropriate for every school district. It is not simply the case that the number of pupils and geographic size of a district are the only important variables in designing a district's administrative structure. Matters such as a district's educational goals, composition and heterogeneity of its pupil and citizen clients, its financial resources, history, and the preferences of its policy makers and chief executive officer are also important determinants of administrative structure. Not only is there no one structure that suits every district—there is no one structure that is of eternal value for a particular district. Though of little utility for its own sake, organizational change is nevertheless occasionally to be expected. A district

---

[41] William L. Boyd, "The Public, The Professionals, and Educational Policy Making: 'Who Governs?'" (*Teachers College Record,* 77, May 1976), pp. 539–77; and Roland L. Warren, S. M. Rose, and A. F. Bergunder, *The Structure of Urban Reform* (Lexington: Heath, 1974.

[42] Frederick M. Wirt, "The Dependent City: External Influences Upon Local Autonomy," paper delivered at the September 1983 Annual Meeting of the American Political Science Association in Chicago.

may not need to alter its administrative structure regularly, but it should engage in periodic appraisals to ensure that the division of tasks and authority is appropriate and consistent with whatever changes have occurred over time.

Line and staff. "Line" authority is descriptive of an administrator who has direct operational responsibility. "Staff" are thought to perform supporting functions, provide advice, analyses, evaluations, and planning. Unless an organization is unusually large, for example the United States Army, the two roles can become confused. In a local school district, it is unusual to be able to afford administrators who are exclusively line or staff. There are those, often operating in the form of management consultants, much taken with the continued design of organizational charts who spend substantial energy delineating "line" and "staff" functions. On occasion, such an expenditure of energy may be appropriate—more often it is misdirected. It is more important to keep in mind that organizational arrangements need to be consistent with the functions to be performed, should provide for clear-cut lines of authority so as to avoid useless duplication of effort and blurred accountability, and should take into account characteristics of those available to perform administrative tasks. In that the crucial instructional functions for which school districts are formed generally take place at school sites, a good rule is to have as few administrative layers as possible between the superintendent and principals.

Principals

School districts are most often divided into attendance areas. These are school board-determined geographic boundaries. Children are directed to attend the school containing the appropriate grade level within their zone. There are conditions under which parents can petition to transfer to another zone. Each school within an attendance zone usually has an executive officer—a principal. When schools were generally small, there might well have been only one teacher, or, in the instance of schools with more than one teacher, a teacher in charge or head teacher.

Population growth, school district consolidation, and the agenda of conditions promoting formation of superintendencies also initiated the role of school executive—principal—a full-time administrator generally without teaching responsibilities. There continue to be relatively small schools with a head teacher, or two or more schools which share a single principal. Indeed, there are approximately 90,000 principals in the United States, with elementary principals outnumbering their secondary counterparts four to one. This principal pattern also characterizes nonpublic schools, though the title often is "head master."

Functions of principals. School districts vary substantially regarding the range of authority ceded to principals. There are clear instances in which a principal is a CEO empowered to perform for his or her building almost the entire range of functions a superintendent does for a district. At the opposite end of the continuum are uncommonly centralized districts in which principals are expected simply to enforce detailed district regulations and procedures. At one juncture in the 1970s, the New York City schools became sufficiently bureaucratized that school principals themselves unionized. They rejected the argument that they were "management" because they asserted they had too little discretion. They likened themselves to airline pilots, responsible for ferrying a plane and its cargo from one place to another in keeping with prescribed technical procedures, but not being part of airline management.

New York City's structure may have been on the rigid end of the administrative continuum, at least as perceived by principals.[43] Nevertheless, in the 1970s substantial criticism was leveled against schools in other city districts for being overly bureaucratic, inflexible, and unable to respond to the preferences of clients.[44] These criticisms coincided with revised opinions regarding the crucial nature of the principal in determining the success of a school. Numerous proposed reforms were aimed at restoring greater decision-making discretion to the school site. Among the ideas were "community control" of schools, alternative schools, and administration decentralization of large school systems.

One of the most comprehensive plans for restoring discretion to school sites was put forward in the 1970s by the New York State Education Commission.[45] This blue-ribbon panel proposed that local school districts be kept for many overall administrative and planning activities, but that the school site become the basic unit of educational management. This would occur by allocating lump-sum revenues to schools and permitting school officials, assisted by a parent advisory council, to determine their own expenditures. Parent advisory councils were to act as miniature school boards except that their authority was advisory, not final. Principals were to be on multiyear contracts, the renewal of which was subject to the approval of the advisory council. Each school was to publish and widely distribute to clients an annual report containing descriptions of the school's program and an assessment of the school year just completed. This assessment was to contain, among other data, a summary of pupil scores from the state-administered achievement testing program.

New York implemented the plan only in part, but the Florida legislature was favorably impressed with the ideas and enacted many of them into statute.[46] These ideas have been accepted partially in other states.

The 1970s reform era came and went, but it left a significant legacy for local school management. Parent advisory councils are now a frequent part of program administration at many school sites.[47] Principals have often been given substantially

---

[43] See Ravitch, p. 170.

[44] Charles E. Silberman, *Crisis in the Classroom* (New York: Random House, 1970).

[45] Commission on the Quality, Cost, and Financing of Elementary and Secondary Education in New York State, *The Fleischman Report* (New York: Viking Press, 1973).

[46] *Improving Education in Florida, A Report by the Governor's Citizens' Committee on Education* (Tallahassee, 1973).

[47] The school-site parent advisory council idea was assisted substantially by federal government categorical aid program requirements enacted in the 1970s. See Chapter Four for more discussion.

greater budgetary discretion than was previously the case. (For this reason we explain school-site budgeting in detail in Chapter Eleven.) The outcome has been to render principals more important than was the case for many decades.

Despite the just-mentioned legacy, the impetus of the movement toward school-site decision discretion was mitigated until recently by other conditions such as collective bargaining, shrinking finances, and declining enrollment.[48] Regardless of where the pendulum now stands on decentralized decision making, it is useful to remember that principals and their staff at a local school are educational professionals and any administrative arrangement which deprives them of reasonable autonomy to conduct the instructional program is at best wasteful of their talents and, if too restrictive, may in fact be counterproductive.

INTERMEDIATE EDUCATION AGENCIES

Approximately thirty-five states have an intermediate unit. These administrative and service organizations take a variety of forms and perform varying functions from state to state. They originated in instances where state administrative agencies were remote and there was a need to mediate between state and local authorities. In such circumstances, intermediate units played a substantial regulatory role. The county office of education was and continues to be the major intermediate unit, and the county superintendent of schools was often an "inspector" ensuring local compliance with state standards. In this way, intermediate units assisted in upgrading the quality of service offered by local districts.

In addition to performing a regulatory function, intermediate units did, and to a growing degree continue to, supply direct services to school districts within their geographic boundaries. Record keeping, data processing, fiscal accounting, personnel records, payroll, library and film distribution, special programs for handicapped and gifted students, transportation management, and consulting regarding business and instructional matters are illustrative of the services that intermediate units provide for local school districts. In general, the more rural the area, and the smaller the constituent districts in terms of enrollment, the greater the reliance upon an intermediate unit.

Since the 1970s, the intermediate units have begun to more fully assume operating functions. This is particularly true in specialized areas such as services for handicapped students and in vocational education. These are the kinds of services for which there can be substantial economies of scale. It may be far more costly for a single district to purchase the equipment and employ the specialized personnel required for programs for which there is but limited demand in a single district. By offering the services more centrally and spreading costs, particularly capital outlay, over a larger number of pupils, intermediate units can often assist students more economically. Such specialized service delivery sometimes arises as

---

[48] For a discussion of its more recent context see James W. Guthrie, *Kappan* (forthcoming).

a consequence of state mandates. It also happens when local districts agree to contract with the intermediate unit for a service. Using the latter mode permits local boards to retain a larger degree of control and ensures that the intermediate unit is responsive to client preferences.

On past occasions, the utility of intermediate units has been debated. However, the ability to offer otherwise costly services at more reasonable rates, growth of shared service contracts, and the continued need to provide assistance to small rural districts points strongly to their likely continuation.[49]

SUMMARY

Though diminished in importance because of the growing role of mid-twentieth century state and federal policy initiatives, the basic operating unit of American education continues to be the local school district. It is at this level that services are delivered to clients and the success or failure of an instructional system is most strongly determined. Lay boards of education exist to make policy for local districts, but such governing bodies depend heavily upon advice and assistance from school administrators. The chief executive officer of a school district is the superintendent. He or she, more than any other single individual, is likely to establish the tone for a local school district. Principals are in a similar position for individual schools.

SELECTED READINGS

Campbell, Roald F., Luvern L. Cunningham, Raphael O. Nystrand, and Michael D. Usdan, *The Organization and Control of American Schools* (Columbus, Ohio: Charles E. Merrill, 1980).

Wirt, Frederick M., and Michael W. Kirst, *Schools in Conflict* (Berkeley: McCutchan, 1982).

---

[49] An excellent summary of the historic development and contemporary role of intermediate units in education is provided by Campbell, Cunningham, Nystrand, and Usdan, *Organization and Control,* pp. 115–34.

THE FEDERAL
GOVERNMENT
AND PUBLIC EDUCATION

chapter 4

The United States is nearly unique among the world's nations in not having a national system of schooling. Nevertheless, since 1785 the federal government has played an important role in influencing the direction of America's state and local public educational systems. Federal school aid dollars generally constitute between 6 and 8 percent of elementary and secondary expenditures. This is not much money when viewed against the awesome backdrop of the nation's total school spending (see Chapter Five). However, the purposes for which such funds are distributed, the high public visibility surrounding federal actions, and the legal mechanisms available for enforcement enable federal programs to exert influence far in excess of the actual dollar amounts involved. It is for this reason that educational administrators, whether or not they are involved directly in the operation of such programs, need to understand federal education policies, their constitutional foundations, historic development, social purposes, operational principles, and political dynamics. These are the topics covered in this chapter.

CONSTITUTIONAL FOUNDATIONS

The absence of any provision explicitly concerned with education or schooling appears to have been a conscious choice among eighteenth century framers of the United States Constitution. Notes compiled by James Madison during the Philadelphia Convention suggest that thought was given to establishing a national university, but no formal proposal was made to provide the federal government with a role in lower education.

Others in attendance, for example, Thomas Jefferson[1] and Benjamin Franklin,[2] considered learning to be important and had given expression to their views on education in other settings. Thus, omission of the words "schooling" and "education" from the constitution was not simply a casual act. Whereas Alexander Hamilton advocated stronger central authority than did Jefferson, it is unlikely that even he espoused a large role in education for government. Rather, the probability is high that the Jeffersonian view that less government was better government pervaded the convention's thinking about education as well as other matters.[3]

In the eighteenth century, education was not yet firmly established as even a local government function, let alone an undertaking for a national authority. In many of the colonial settlements, schooling was an undertaking significant primarily for individual interpretation of biblical scriptures. Even when technical knowledge began to assume greater importance in the economic life of individuals, educational arrangements continued to be more private than public. It was only in the mid-nineteenth century that state-enacted compulsory attendance laws triggered the present model of public schooling.[4] Thus, those in attendance at the 1787 Constitutional Convention had little experience with government provision of education, and their negative reaction to the then strong British monarchy prejudiced them against granting a national authority the right to control such a potentially influential undertaking as schooling.

The U.S. Constitution's Tenth Amendment specifies that "The powers not delegated to the United States by the Constitution, nor prohibited by it to the States, are reserved to the States respectively or to the people." This provision strongly reflects the social contract theories of government which were vitally important to those framing the Constitution.[5] Individual self-determination was held to be an inalienable right of each human being and was to be ceded to representative governing bodies only in restricted dimensions. Hence, the Tenth Amendment explicitly asserts that the national government was to be imbued only with

---

[1] See for example Thomas Jefferson's "A Bill for the General Diffusion of Knowledge" proposed to the Virginia Assembly in 1779, reprinted in John S. Pancake, ed., *Thomas Jefferson: Revolutionary Philosopher, A Selection of Writings* (Woodbury, New York: Barron's Educational Service, Inc., 1976), pp. 212–221.

[2] "Proposals Relating to the Education of Youth in Pennsylvania" by Benjamin Franklin, reprinted in Background Reading for the July 20–21, 1965, White House Conference on Education, U.S. Department of Health, Education, and Welfare, Washington, D.C., pp. 5–8.

[3] See Jefferson's December 20, 1887, letter to James Madison on the subject of the new federal constitution, Pancake, *Ibid.*, pp. 84–88.

[4] James W. Guthrie, Diana K. Thomason, and Patricia A. Craig, "The Erosion of Lay Control" in National Committee for Citizens in Education, *Public Testimony on Public Schools* (Berkeley: McCutchan, 1975), pp. 76–121.

[5] See *Social Contract: Essays by Locke, Hume, and Rousseau* edited by Sir Ernest Barker (Oxford: Oxford University Press, 1947).

those powers expressly granted to it. All other authority was to be held by individual states, unless specifically denied by the Constitution. The Tenth Amendment's ending ". . . or the people." makes it clear that the citizenry is the source from which governing authority ultimately stems.

The absence from the Constitution of express national government responsibility for education and schooling, when coupled with the language of the Tenth Amendment, cedes plenary, meaning *ultimate,* legal authority for education to state government. Each state constitution contains an education clause explicitly acknowledging authority of the state in matters of education and schooling.

As a consequence of the above-described federal and state constitutional arrangements, the federal government has no widespread direct responsibility for the operation of education programs. (Direct federal governing administration of institutions such as the armed service academies, Galladet College for the Deaf, located in Washington, D.C., and the Overseas Dependent Schools are limited exceptions to this statement.)

Despite this condition of limited authority, the federal government has had a substantial history of involvement in educational matters. Beginning in the middle of the twentieth century, federal authorities inaugurated numerous educational programs which presently provide services throughout all fifty states, the trust territories, thousands of local school districts, and schools. It is unlikely that even a single American public school is untouched by federal educational policy. Given the absence of explicit constitutional authority, what comprises the legal basis for such undertakings? There are several answers to this question.

The federal government's constitutional authority to finance and regulate educational programs is derived from implied powers contained in several sections of the U.S. Constitution. Over the approximate two centuries since ratification, numerous judicial interpretations of constitutional provisions have substantially expanded the scope of the federal government's educational authority. These implied powers have stemmed from court decisions regarding the "general welfare clause," the First Amendment, and both the "due process" and "equal protection" clauses of the Fourteenth Amendment.

General Welfare Clause

Article 1, Section 8, clause 1 of the Constitution is commonly referred to as the "general welfare clause." It states "The Congress shall have the power to lay and collect taxes, duties, imposts, and excises, to pay the debts and provide for the common defense and *general welfare* of the United States." For a century or more following adoption of the Constitution, this was a controversial provision. Proponents of a limited national government, such as James Madison, desired a narrow interpretation whereas advocates of a strong central government, such as Alexander Hamilton, argued for a broad view of the statement. In the 1930s, decisions of the U.S. Supreme Court substantially altered the nature of the debate. In a case involving "New Deal" legislation sponsored by the Roosevelt Administration, the nation's highest court ruled that Congress had the authority to interpret the "general welfare clause" as long as it did not act arbitrarily.[6]

The Court also held that the clause could be interpreted differently from time to time as conditions necessitated redefinition of the nation's general welfare.[7] Since these judicial opinions, debate has shifted to whether or not a particular policy proposal is useful, not whether Congress possesses authority to undertake the endeavor. Consequently, federal educational programs are viewed as within the implied constitutional authority of Congress. This is not to assert that there is always agreement upon the wisdom of a particular legislative proposal or a new federal educational program. Contemporary educational initiatives can still provoke heated debate at the federal level.

Contractual Obligations

Article 1, Section 10 of the U.S. Constitution has been judicially interpreted to restrict the ability of states and local boards of education to impair the obligations of contracts. The Supreme Court has held that ". . . a legislative enactment may contain provisions which, when accepted as the basis of action by individuals, become contracts between them and the state or its subdivision."[8] This constitutional provision and the legal principles derived from it have also been applied to controversies between teacher unions and school boards over tenure rights and retirement agreements.

Separation of Church and State

The First and Fourteenth Amendments combine to provide a constitutional base for federal government control over the relationship between religion and public school funding. The First Amendment specifies that "Congress shall make no law respecting the establishment of religion or prohibiting the free exercise thereof." The Supreme Court has held that the First Amendment was intended to create a "wall of separation between church and state."[9] Consistent with this view, courts, both state and federal, have struck down repeated state efforts to provide direct financial subsidies to nonpublic schools.

The U.S. Supreme Court has evolved a three-pronged test to determine whether a private school aid plan violates the wall of separation: (1) the statute must have a secular legislative purpose; (2) the statute's "primary effect" must neither advance nor inhibit religion; and (3) the statute and its administration must avoid excessive government entanglement with religion.[10] The application of these

---

[6] *United States* v. *Butler,* 297 U.S. 1, 56 Sup. Ct. 312.

[7] *Helvering* v. *Davis,* 301 Dr. S.619, 57 Sup. Ct. 904.

[8] *State ex/rel Anderson* v. *Brand,* 313 U.S. 95.

[9] *Illinois ex/rel. McCollum* v. *Board of Education,* 333 U.S. 203 and *Everson* v. *Board of Education,* 330 U.S.1.

[10] *Lemon* v. *Kurtzman,* 403 U.S. 602; 91 Sup. Ct. 2105, 1971 and *Leeman* v. *Sloan,* 340 f. Suppl. 1356, 1972.

criteria has generally served to discourage state aid to private elementary and secondary schools. The 1983 U.S. Supreme Court decision in *Mueller* v. *Allen* approved a Minnesota statute providing state income tax deductions for school fees, both public and private.[11] The long-term consequences of this decision are not yet easily predictable. Regardless of *Mueller,* the issue has long been and undoubtedly will continue to be heated (see Chapter One on this topic). Negative decisions have not been extended to private higher education when courts have ruled a wider variety of government aid plans to be constitutional. The relatively greater maturity of college students is a crucial distinction for the courts.[12]

The Fourteenth Amendment

The Fourteenth Amendment, adopted in 1868, was one of three constitutional enactments during the Civil War intended to free slaves. It stretches the mantle of the first ten amendments so as to protect the civil liberties of citizens from encroachment by the states.[13] The Fourteenth Amendment contains two clauses of particular importance to federal government authority and influence over education—the so-called *due process clause* and the *equal protection clause.* The latter provision served as the basis for one of the most significant reforms ever undertaken in American public education—the overturning of the dual school systems, one for whites, another for blacks, which evolved historically and were supported statutorily in seventeen southern states and the District of Columbia.

Equal protection. In 1954 the U.S. Supreme Court issued a school desegregation decision[14] which overturned the "separate but equal" doctrine which had dominated U.S. race relations since the 1896 decision in *Plessy* v. *Ferguson.*[15] In *Plessy* the Court had let stand an 1890 Louisiana statute segregating races on railway cars as long as the facilities were deemed to be equal. In *Brown* v. *Board of Education,* by far the most noted of the desegregation cases, the opinion of the Court stated:

> We conclude that in the field of public education the doctrine of "separate but equal" has no place. Separate educational facilities are inherently unequal. Therefore, we hold that the plaintiffs and others similarly situated for whom the actions are brought are, by reason of the segregation complained of, deprived of the equal protection of the laws guaranteed by the Fourteenth Amendment.

[11] *Mueller* v. *Allen,* 54 U.S. L.W. 5050.

[12] For more on this topic see Richard E. Morgan, *The Politics of Religious Conflict: Church and State in America* (New York: Pegasus, 1968); and Chester E. Finn, Jr., "The Politics of Public Aid to Private Schools" in *The Changing Politics of School Finance* edited by Nelda H. Cambron McCabe and Allan Odden, Third Annual Yearbook of the American Education Finance Association (Boston: Ballinger, 1982), pp. 183–210.

[13] Michael W. LaMorte, "The Fourteenth Amendment: Its Significance for Public Educators," *Educational Administration Quarterly,* 10, no. 3 (Autumn 1974), 1–19.

[14] *Brown* v. *Board of Education,* 347 U.S. 483, 74 Sup. Ct. 686.

[15] 163 U.S. 537, 16 Sup. Ct. 1138.

The *Brown* decision, in conjunction with implementation decrees and numerous lower court decisions, was resisted, sometimes violently. The eventual result, however, was a dismantling of the *de jure* racially segregated school systems which had long characterized public schooling in the South. More subtle discriminatory mechanisms which contribute to *de facto* racial segregation have not so easily lent themselves to legal remedy.[16] Thus, the irony is that racial segregation currently pervades public school systems of northern and some western states to a greater degree than in the South.[17] *De facto* racial segregation persists despite federal government educational programs primarily designed to combat the condition—for example, the Emergency School Aid Act (ESAA).

The *equal protection clause* has also been used as the basis for a constitutional challenge to the school finance arrangements in many of the fifty states. In Chapter Five we explain the legal logic underlying this judicial reform strategy. Suffice it to state here that the practical outcome, though not wholly unsatisfactory, has been nowhere near the legal success of the school desegregation suits. Indeed, racial desegregation and school finance reform efforts simultaneously display the power and limits of the federal government's ability to influence public education. Because of the complexity of the United States' multitiered and many-faceted system of government, reform results in both racial desegregation and school finance have not been nearly as successful as advocates had hoped nor as devastating as opponents had feared.

Due process. The U.S. Constitution's "due process clause" also provides a major legal vehicle through which the federal government can influence public education. Generally the *due process clause* protects individuals. Judicial interpretations of this provision have come to guide much of the legal interaction between pupils, parents, and employees in their dealings with school districts and other educational agencies. We review these legal arrangements extensively in Chapter Six. Here it is important to understand that courts have also decided that there are occasions on which individuals' rights under the *due process clause* must be weighed against society's need to protect itself.

Though continually being redefined by courts, so-called "police powers" are inherent within the authority of government at all levels. For example, teachers and other school employees are not free simply to do or teach whatever they would like if such actions jeopardize society's need to protect itself. Courts have generally enforced the Smith Act, which makes it a crime punishable by fine and imprisonment to advocate the forceful overthrow of government. This establishes a limitation re-

---

[16] On this point see J. Harvey Wilkinson, *From Brown to Baake* (Oxford: Oxford University Press, 1976); Gary Orfield, *Must We Bus?* (Washington, D.C.: The Brookings Institution, 1978); and David L. Kirp, *Just Schools* (Berkeley: University of California Press, 1982).

[17] See *Progress,* a report of desegregation trends in the United States, Summer, 1980, a publication of the National Project Task Force on Desegregation Strategies jointly sponsored by the Education Commission of the States, the National Association of State Boards of Education, and the Council of Chief State School Officers. Education Commission of the States, 1980.

garding what can be taught in public as well as private schools. As Reller, Johns, and Morphet state: "Those who insist that the federal government should have no control whatsoever over the curriculum of public schools seem to be unaware of the inherent police powers of the federal government relating to matters of national concern."[18]

To this point, we have attempted to explain the legal basis for federal government participation in educational matters. The federal government's ability to influence America's system of schooling, however, is not limited to legal authority. Influence is also possible through means such as financial inducement, demonstration projects, dissemination of research findings, and evaluation efforts. We will discuss these additional mechanisms in a subsequent section of this chapter. We now move to a description and analysis of federal government educational programs.

THE EVOLUTION OF FEDERAL EDUCATIONAL PROGRAMS

In 1785, even before ratification of the Constitution by all the original colonies, central government policy was being made regarding education. The Land Survey Ordinance of that year, as well as the better known Northwest Ordinance enacted two years later in 1887, provided for several sections of land in each Township within newly formed territories to be reserved for the support of public schools.[19] The significance of these provisions is difficult to deduce retrospectively. At the least, they served as precedent for subsequent federal government policies regarding education. Their influence may even have been greater in that the preservation for public purposes of land which otherwise would have been ceded to private use perhaps reinforced whatever frontier desire existed for schooling.

Regardless, over the two centuries subsequent to these early enactments, various branches and agencies of the federal government have initiated and implemented a wide variety of educational programs. The general justification for such activities is that they meet national needs likely to be neglected by states acting independently or that, in economic terms, they are better managed by a central authority. Imagine, for example, that the nation's supply of highly skilled scientists or individuals possessed of a keen ability to speak languages other than English was so short as to jeopardize national defense or the balance of U.S. international trade. It is unlikely that individual states would enact programs to meet such shortages. These are national needs, and on several past occasions Congress has enacted and funded programs to solve problems such as these.

Similarly, some functions risk financial loss if performed by smaller units and would be best undertaken by a central authority. Data collection and research and

[18] Edgar L. Morphet, Roe L. Johns, and Theodore L. Reller, *Educational Organization and Administration* (Englewood Cliffs, N.J.: Prentice-Hall, 1982), p. 204.

[19] See Roald F. Campbell, Luvern L. Cunningham, Raphael O. Nystrand, and Michael D. Usdan, *The Organization and Control of American Schools* (Columbus, Ohio: Charles E. Merrill, 1980), pp. 26–27.

development activities are good examples. The initial congressional provision establishing the Department of Education in 1867 made prominent mention of the agency's role in collecting statistical information to be used in sustaining and improving the nation's schools. Though performed unevenly over time by the federal education authority, this is a task which nevertheless falls naturally to a central government. States, or even smaller units of government, are not well positioned to gather and analyze information from across the nation. Hence, the present day cabinet level Department of Education contains the National Center for Educational Statistics (NECS), which systematically collects, analyzes, and publishes information regarding the conditions of education in the United States.

In 1966 Congress authorized establishment of the National Assessment of Educational Progress (NAEP) to undertake systematic appraisals of the educational performance of students in the United States.[20] NAEP was initially operated by the Education Commission of the States (ECS), an interstate consortium with headquarters in Denver, Colorado. In 1983, the Educational Testing Service (ETS) in Princeton, New Jersey became responsible for NAEP's operation. This massive achievement assessment program, costing $5 million annually and involving the testing of thousands of students throughout the nation, is not an endeavor that individual states could easily organize or afford to operate for the entire nation. It more naturally falls to the federal government to conduct such an undertaking.

In attempting to meet otherwise unaddressed national needs and to perform functions which logically fall to a central authority, the federal government's educational efforts have generally been oriented toward fulfillment of two major value objectives: (1) equalization of educational opportunity; and (2) enhancement of educational productivity. Here again can be seen the significance of the value commitment to equality and efficiency described in Chapter One. We explain a number of federal educational endeavors within these categories, but there are now far too many federal educational programs to provide a detailed description of each. Hence, we have selected programs, be they historic or contemporary, important either for their dollar magnitude, a precedent they established, or an idea they embodied.

Enhancing Productivity

We begin with the value category of "efficiency" because the first major federally sponsored education activities were intended to expand the supply of activities in schools crucial to national economic development.

Land grants to aid higher education.   In the century following its formation, one of the federal government's largest economic assets was vast undeveloped lands

[20] For a history of the formative years of NAEP see Ralph W. Tyler, "National Assessment: A History and Sociology," in James W. Guthrie and Edward Wynne, *New Models for American Education* (Englewood Cliffs, N.J.: Prentice-Hall, 1971).

under its control. In 1862, Congress enacted the first Morrill Act, named after Senator Justin S. Morrill of Vermont, the bill's major proponent.[21] This statute allocated 30,000 acres of federal land to each state for each of its two senators and however many representatives to which it was then entitled. Income from sale or rental of these lands was to be used for establishing agricultural and mechanical arts colleges. These "A & M" colleges were to contribute to the new nation's supply of craftsmen and technicians. Such institutions were also to provide instruction in military science and tactics.

Each state benefited from this program. It has not always been a public institution, however, which has received financial proceeds from sale or lease of land. Cornell University in Ithaca, New York, and the Massachusetts Institute of Technology in Cambridge, Massachusetts, are both examples of prestigious private institutions which have received aid from Morrill Act lands. So-called land grant colleges received additional aid with the second Morrill Act of 1892 and Hatch Act of 1897.

Though these aid programs were directed at higher educational institutions, they are, nevertheless, important for elementary and secondary education in that they substantially abetted the precedent of federal assistance for education. Subsequent legislation was directed at assisting lower education.

Vocational education to assist industry and defense.   As the United States moved toward World War I, Congress was concerned regarding the availability of sufficient numbers of skilled workers to supply both American industry and the war effort. Consequently, the Smith-Hughes Act of 1917 was enacted. This statute appropriated federal funds to states to establish secondary school programs in agricultural and industrial trades, and homemaking. States were required to match the federal funds. This established precedent for matching grants, which subsequently have become a major lever by which federal officials induce program cooperation on the part of state and local agencies.[22]

The federal government's initial concern for vocational education has subsequently been strongly sustained. In 1929, Congress enacted the George-Reed Act; in 1935, the George-Ellzey Act; in 1937, the George-Dean Act; and, in 1946, the George-Barden Act. The 1963 Vocational Education Act, promoted by President John F. Kennedy, established a different direction for vocational education that has been subsequently pursued with systematic reauthorizations. By the mid-1980s, Congress was annually appropriating approximately $1 billion for the support of secondary school level vocational preparation. States and other agencies provide even more funds, but federal programs have acted as substantial incentives for establishment of a complex vocational training system (see Table 4.1).

[21] Morrill's first effort was enacted by Congress in 1858 only to be vetoed by President Buchanan. Morrill's "Reply to President's Veto of Land Grant Bill," is an articulate justification of federal government encouragement of educational activity. This speech is reprinted in *Background Readings for the 1965 White House Conference on Education*, p. 21.

[22] See "Debate on Smith-Hughes Vocational Educational Act" (1970), reprinted in *Background Readings, White House Conference on Education*, p. 47.

Table 4.1   DATA FILE: INSTITUTIONS OFFERING VOCATIONAL EDUCATION PROGRAMS, School Year 1978-79

State	Total	Public Comprehensive or Vocational Secondary Schools	Public Area Vocational Centers (Secondary)	Private Secondary Schools	Public Noncollegiate Postsecondary Institutions	Private Noncollegiate Postsecondary Institutions	2-Year Institutions of Higher Education	4-Year Institutions of Higher Education
Alabama	615	369	113	9	24	65	23	12
Alaska	190	150	2	2	3	22	10	1
Arizona	338	150	3	8	6	154	14	3
Arkansas	464	333	9	5	28	67	10	12
California	2,331	1,117	63	56	23	939	111	22
Colorado	414	252	17	7	9	102	16	11
Connecticut	344	167	16	6	17	109	18	11
Delaware	65	28	4	2	0	22	6	3
District of Columbia	57	16	1	4	2	27	0	7
Florida	665	316	28	18	30	231	30	12
Georgia	595	333	26	10	39	148	23	16
Hawaii	71	38	0	2	1	21	6	3
Idaho	174	124	2	0	11	30	3	4
Illinois	1,270	776	32	24	18	349	55	16
Indiana	605	358	31	19	10	144	17	26
Iowa	701	565	0	10	2	94	23	7
Kansas	383	246	14	5	14	65	24	15
Kentucky	479	252	72	9	24	96	10	16
Louisiana	611	389	18	11	36	135	5	17
Maine	155	62	22	11	7	37	6	10
Maryland	434	252	19	7	3	126	21	6
Massachusetts	541	247	22	24	30	164	41	13
Michigan	886	436	44	23	13	304	38	28

State								
Minnesota	673	422	61	7	41	110	23	9
Mississippi	378	228	61	8	3	52	21	5
Missouri	687	359	55	12	36	178	17	30
Montana	170	120	0	1	5	37	3	4
Nebraska	356	255	0	12	5	61	10	13
Nevada	91	50	1	1	0	34	3	2
New Hampshire	153	80	20	3	1	27	10	12
New Jersey	622	311	35	17	22	203	20	14
New Mexico	169	95	3	3	8	46	7	7
New York	998	420	72	52	22	317	79	36
North Carolina	608	386	8	8	5	109	74	18
North Dakota	209	148	9	5	0	34	7	6
Ohio	1,292	735	76	19	50	336	46	30
Oklahoma	683	475	35	5	30	110	19	9
Oregon	343	199	4	3	1	117	13	6
Pennsylvania	1,265	663	67	62	35	351	46	41
Rhode Island	106	51	0	6	1	38	2	8
South Carolina	397	242	33	4	25	56	26	11
South Dakota	222	160	6	7	8	27	2	12
Tennessee	572	287	62	7	44	125	23	24
Texas	2,436	1,769	117	17	55	397	61	20
Utah	159	85	2	1	9	50	7	5
Vermont	101	49	15	9	2	16	3	7
Virginia	492	252	39	9	7	152	25	8
Washington	528	302	4	13	5	173	27	4
West Virginia	300	150	50	3	25	50	8	14
Wisconsin	535	380	0	16	15	98	19	7
Wyoming	81	57	1	4	1	11	7	0
Total	27,014	15,706	1,394	586	811	6,766	1,118	633

Source: "The Condition of Education," 1983 Edition, National Center for Education Statistics

During the Great Depression of the 1930s, Congress established several anti-poverty programs which had significant educational components. Frequently, vocational training was a prominent feature of these undertakings. For example, the Civilian Conservation Corps (CCC) and the National Youth Authority (NYA), both provided vocational training opportunities for unemployed Depression youth. In 1965, as part of the Johnson administration "War on Poverty," the Federal Job Corps was established to enable out-of-school and out-of-work youth to gain job skills. The Depression era programs were operated directly by federal government agencies such as what was then called the War Department (now Defense Department), and Federal Security Agency (now the Department of Education). The Job Corps was operated by a variety of private organizations on direct contract with the now defunct Office of Economic Opportunity (OEO). Relative to programs in surrounding local school districts, these federally funded and operated vocational training endeavors were unusually expensive, costing up to twenty times as much per enrollee. Local and state public school officials insisted that they could perform the same function more efficiently. Such complaints, along with changing economic conditions, eventually terminated these antipoverty, direct federal government vocational training efforts, and virtually nothing of them remains today.[23]

In 1957, the Soviet Union launched the first successful earth-orbiting space satellite, Sputnik. This event soundly shook America's sense of technological superiority, and U.S. public education served as a convenient scapegoat for popular frustration and disappointment. The nation subsequently regained its poise and launched a massive federal program that resulted in the moon landing and other space successes of the 1960s and 1970s. Education also benefited, with enactment of the 1958 National Defense Education Act (NDEA). This statute utilized federal matching funds as an incentive for local school districts to upgrade their instruction in science, mathematics, and foreign languages. Higher educational institutions also gained through expanded financial support for college students entering science and math teaching. The NDEA was successful in assisting schools meet the heightened public expectation for scientific and technological supremacy.

Also, in the 1960s, the National Science Foundation (NSF) funded fellowships and training programs at many colleges and universities whereby science and math teachers could gain advanced training. The NSF also funded a number of science and math curriculum revision projects that substantially influenced secondary school instructional efforts.

In the early 1980s, the mass media and professional periodicals began reporting increasing shortages of qualified secondary school math and science teachers.[24] The fear of losing a competitive economic position in international sales of high technology products and procedures motivated President Reagan to propose, and Congress to consider, a federal program with many of the same purposes as the original 1958 NDEA. This was the 1983 American Defense Education Act.

[23] Henry J. Aaron, *Politics and the Professors* (Washington, D.C.: The Brookings Institution, 1978).

[24] James W. Guthrie and Ami Zusman, "Teacher Supply and Demand in Mathematics and Science," *Kappan,* September 1982, 64, no. 1, 28–33.

Research and development. As previously mentioned, there is diminished financial incentive to engage in a research activity when potential results may give an advantage to a host of others besides the initiating agency. Under such conditions, a tempting strategy is to wait and hope to "piggyback" on the research funded by another. Educational research and development can be viewed through this lense. Why should one state expend its scarce resources in undertaking basic research on, for example, human learning, when there is no reasonable way to require other states to share the expense? Under such circumstances, there is likely to be an underinvestment in an activity which might otherwise enhance educational efficiency and the productivity of the entire economy. In order to avoid such a condition, the federal government has long supported educational research and development.

In 1954, Congress passed the Cooperative Research Act which authorized federal funds for support of educational research in institutions of higher education. This statute was originally administered by the U.S. Office of Education, then one of several agencies comprising the newly formed (1953) Department of Health, Education, and Welfare (HEW). In 1965, the main features of the Cooperative Research Act were incorporated into Title IV of the Elementary and Secondary Education Act (ESEA). This provision substantially expanded the amount of federal money available for supporting educational research. Additionally, it established twenty regional educational laboratories and twelve university-based research and development (R & D) centers. These newly formed organizations were intended as a clearing house for the development of new ideas. R & D centers would transform them into practical applications which would then be distributed to school districts by the regional educational laboratories. This research, development, and dissemination strategy was patterned after the highly effective model utilized in U.S. agriculture.

In 1975, federal educational research functions were transferred to the newly established National Institute of Education (NIE), then within HEW, and now an agency within the Department of Education. By the late 1970s, however, federal expenses incurred by the war in Vietnam, large outlays for supporting domestic social programs, and diminished public affection for education had reduced NIE appropriations to the point where several of the R & D centers and laboratories were closed. The funding available to the remainder was insufficient to support large-scale research projects. Though NIE continued to be the major funding source for educational research throughout the 1970s and early 1980s, its impact was minimal in many respects, and there were even serious suggestions for its dissolution.[25] The long-run prospects for its success may improve with the mid-1980s' resurgence in public concern for education.

As with the surviving vocational education programs, all recent federally sponsored education efforts rely heavily upon existing structures—state agencies, local school districts, and colleges and universities—for the operation of services. The direct delivery approaches seen in the CCC, NYA, and Job Corps are no more

---

[25] Chester Finn, "What NIE Cannot Be," *Kappan,* February, 1983, 64, no. 6, 407–410.

popular politically in the 1980s than they were half a century ago. Whether this political attitude can be altered over time is presently unpredictable. However, the probability is high that, regardless of the delivery mechanisms involved, the federal government is likely to have an interest in using education to enhance national economic efficiency and productivity far into the future.

Promoting Equality of Educational Opportunity

Expanding the services available to groups of previously underserved students is a relatively recent function of the federal government's educational efforts. Except for the late nineteenth and early twentieth century attempts to provide for the education of various native American groups, it was not until the second half of the twentieth century that major federal programs began benefiting groups of students for whom full educational access previously had not been available. However, in the time since the U.S. Supreme Court's decision in *Brown* v. *Board of Education,* both the executive and the legislative branch have been substantially more attentive to claims for equal educational opportunity by racial minorities, children from low-income households, handicapped students, and non-English- and limited-English-speaking students. All of these groups, though not to the same degree, have been the focus of relatively recent federal education programs.

Educational Consolidation and Improvement Act (ECIA). In 1981 Congress accepted a Reagan Administration recommendation regarding education and consolidated many previously existing educational programs into two major statutory provisions of the ECIA. Chapter One of this act continues the major feature of the 1965 ESEA—federal funds for compensatory educational programs for students from low-income families. Appropriations under this authority comprise the largest federally-sponsored educational program. Funds are distributed to states based on a formula which takes into account numbers of school-age children from low-income households. States, in turn, distribute Chapter One funds to counties and local school districts. Districts are responsible for spending compensatory education funds in a manner consistent with federal regulations and guidelines. Chapter One funds generally are used for elementary programs to enhance pupils' reading and arithmetic achievement. However, it is possible to utilize the funds for other purposes, such as secondary remedial instruction, counseling, field trips, instructional materials, and, under limited circumstances, personal and health items such as eye glasses.

The compensatory educational program is classified as *categorical aid* because the funds can only be used by local school districts for the purpose of providing added educational services to a specified category of students—those who qualify as being from low-income circumstances. Local and state officials are sometimes unhappy with the relatively rigid spending requirements of the Act, and federal audit requirements are increasingly stringent. Evaluations of Chapter One programs are mixed, with a slight weighting of results toward the favorable end of the continuum.[26] Regardless, the program appears to have built itself a sufficiently broad political constituency so that only unusually fierce federal budgetary pressure would eliminate it. The great likelihood is that it will remain for many years to come, and the challenge to professional educators is to make it more effective.

Chapter Two of the ECIA consists of a *block grant* pieced together from twenty-eight previously enacted educational programs. Funds are allocated to each state based on a student population formula. Thereafter, each state establishes a plan based either upon school district enrollment or measures of student need. Local districts are free to spend the funds in whatever fashion they decide best meets their needs for added services.

Chapter Two's enactment involved substantial political controversy. Many local and state education officials had long desired that federal categorical aid programs be consolidated into a limited number of so-called "block grants," wherein states and districts would be permitted greater discretion over spending. The interest groups comprised of educators and citizens who benefited most directly from the categorical aid resisted such consolidation for fear their particular programs would not be part of local spending priorities under a block grant. In 1981, when the Reagan administration initially proposed consolidation, several major programs were to be included, the massive above-described compensatory education program being one of them. However, the eventual compromise was to preserve the categorical integrity of major programs and to combine many smaller authorities. ECIA Chapter Two is the result, and it remains too early to fully know the outcome of state and local decision making about these discretionary funds.[27]

Education for All Handicapped Children Act. Throughout the 1960s and early 1970s increasing political pressure was brought to bear upon state legislatures to correct substantial injustices regarding handicapped students. Many states did not then provide school services for severely handicapped students. Other states underfunded such programs. Following several important state court cases in which it was held that handicapped children also deserved "equal protection" of the law,[28] state legislatures as well as Congress enacted programs to ensure better schooling for the handicapped.

Public Law 94-142, the Education for All Handicapped Children Act (EHCA) enacted in 1976, was one result. This federal statute, funded by annual appropriations approximating $1 billion, distributes funds to states and ultimately local districts to assist in the provision of educational services to various categories of handicapped school children. In accepting funds, states and districts must agree to

---

[26] Stephen P. Mullin and Anita A. Summers, "Is More Better? The Effectiveness of Spending on Compensatory Education," *Kappan,* January 1983, 64, no. 5, 339-347.

[27] A preliminary appraisal of ECIA Chapter Two is reported in Paul D. Hood, Caroline S. Cates, William M. Herring, and Sue McKibbin in *School Improvements in the Far West* (San Francisco: Far West Laboratory for Educational Research and Development, 1982).

[28] *PARC* v. *Commonwealth,* 834 F. Sup. Ct. 1257 (ED Pa. 1971) 343 F. Sup. 279 (ED Pa. 1972) and *Mills* v. *Board of Education,* 348 F. Sup. 866 (DCC 1972).

a rigorous set of federal regulations to be followed in educating eligible students. In that the procedures are unusually legalistic, many local school officials are annoyed at the high level of implied distrust. Advocates for the handicapped reply that past abuses speak poorly for the integrity of local education officials on this score and contend that firm federal regulations are altogether necessary to ensure that handicapped students are fairly treated. Over time, one would hope the level of trust would build more favorably on both sides of the issue so that less energy is devoted to conflict and more attention is given to the instruction of students. Meanwhile a large population of students is now benefiting from services previously unavailable in many states and localities (see Table 4.2).

Emergency School Aid Act. From 1955 through the 1960s, judicial pressure was exerted upon southern districts to dismantle their dual school systems. Throughout much of this period the Justice Department and the HEW Office of Civil Rights, both within the executive branch, attempted also to bring pressure to bear upon school districts to undertake racial desegregation. Beginning in 1968, the Nixon Administration attempted to dilute judicial and executive branch mandatory desegregation pressures and proposed to substitute more federal government inducements for voluntary local school district desegregation. Proponents of racially

Table 4.2   **CHILDREN RECEIVING SPECIAL EDUCATION BY DISABILITY**
Education for All Handicapped Children Act, PL 94-142
and
Chapter 1 State Programs for Handicapped Children, PL 89-313

	1976–77[a]	PERCENTAGE OF ENROLLMENT[b]	1982–83	PERCENTAGE OF ENROLLMENT[c]
Mentally Retarded	969,546	2.19%	775,816	1.93%
Deaf	22,033	0.05	35,493	0.09
Hard of Hearing	89,395	0.20	38,452	0.09
Speech Impaired	1,302,666	2.94	1,135,105	2.83
Visually Impaired	38,274	0.09	28,646	0.07
Emotionally Disturbed	283,072	0.64	353,215	0.88
Orthopedically Impaired	87,008	0.20	57,676	0.14
Other Health Impaired	141,416	0.32	51,848	0.13
Learning Disabled	797,213	1.80	1,741,054	4.33
Deaf-Blind	—	—	2,514	0.00
Multihandicapped	—	—	65,743	0.16
Total	3,708,588	8.37%	4,285,606	10.67%

[a]First year of PL 94-142 child count.
[b]Based on 1976–77 public school enrollment of 44,317,000.
[c]Based on 1981–82 public school enrollment of 40,168,000 because 1982–83 figures were not yet available.

Source: Education Department

integrated schools were skeptical of such a strategy, but in 1972 Congress neverthe-less enacted the Emergency School Aid Act.

The intent of this legislation was to assist local school districts in integrating their schools by providing federal funds for the in-service training of teachers, em-ployment of teacher aides and instructional specialists for desegregated classrooms, or whatever else local school officials reasonably contended would assist their dis-trict in voluntarily desegregating schools. Appropriations for this statute reached their peak in the late 1970s with about $300 million. Thereafter, funding de-creased, and the Emergency School Aid Act was one of the twenty-eight combined in 1981 to form Chapter Two of the Education Consolidation and Improvement Act. The extent to which local districts utilize Chapter Two funds for the same purposes as ESAA was intended is not yet known, but there has almost assuredly been a diminution of effort in this regard.[29]

Bilingual education. As the United States moved into the second half of the twentieth century, large numbers of immigrants, particularly from Spanish-speaking and Asian nations, created a problem for selected local school districts. The chil-dren of many of these new Americans had only limited, if any, ability to speak and read English. Ironically, these youngsters were compelled by state statute to attend school, but thereafter many of them sat in classrooms where the medium of instruc-tion, English, was unintelligible to them. In San Francisco, site of a heavy influx of non-English-speaking Asians, students and their parents filed suit against the school district in order to receive language assistance in school. The case, *Lau* v. *Nichols,*[30] eventually was decided in favor of the plantiffs. Based on Section 601 of the 1964 Civil Rights Act, the court found that the students were discriminated against un-fairly and mandated that the school district provide multilingual instructors and other educational assistance to these children.

The legal precedent became established that school districts were responsible for assisting limited- and non-English-speaking students. In order to cope with the added costs of such services, several state legislatures enacted categorical school aid programs, and Congress added Title VII to the 1965 Elementary and Secondary Education Act. This provision allocates funds, through states, to local school dis-tricts to assist with bilingual instruction. Federal appropriations were never large, reaching $100 million in 1979.

Enhancing Liberty or Choice

The federal government's concern for education has historically focused on the objective of efficiency. The various manpower training acts have been consis-tent with this direction. Concern for equality is more recent, but this objective has

---

[29] *School Finance News,* "How States Are Spending Their Block Grants," April 7, 1983, 2, no. 7, 3.

[30] *Lau* v. *Nichols,* 483 F2d (9COR., 1973), 94 S. Ct. 786 (1974).

received more support in terms of dollar appropriations. The value area which has received relatively less attention by the federal government is enhancement of choice, or liberty. Following World War II, Congress enacted the Service-man's Readjustment Act, PL 78-346, which provided financial assistance to veterans for postsecondary schooling. Literally millions of veterans took advantage of this aid to attend college, and the nation was probably much the better for having provided such assistance. The "GI Bill" was the forerunner of "voucher plans" in that the federal funds went to the individual, and he or she decided upon the institution to attend. However, in that the aid was for postsecondary schooling, no controversial questions of aid to nonpublic schools were provoked.

In the 1980s, the Reagan Administration proposed a tuition tax credit plan which would benefit elementary and secondary as well as postsecondary institutions. Controversy over such an arrangement is substantially more heated than was the case with the GI Bill. Tuition tax credits expand choice by permitting households to deduct all or a portion of *non*public school tuition payments from their federal income taxes. The allowable dollar amount is taken as a "credit" against federal income taxes owed, not simply as a before-tax deduction. Such a plan is viewed with favor by many nonpublic school officials and the parents of nonpublic school children. Conversely, public school advocates often view the plan with alarm. Opponents fear that such federal subsidies will undermine public schools, and they allege that the plan will violate First Amendment prohibitions regarding aid to religious schools.[31]

Prior to 1983, tuition tax proposals had passed in the U.S. Senate on six separate occasions. In 1979, the House of Representatives, by a narrow margin, enacted a tuition tax credit plan. President Jimmy Carter threatened a veto and, given that control of the Senate belonged to Democrats at the time, his threat was sufficient to stifle the bill. President Reagan's administration again proposed such a plan, but the prospect of awesome federal government budget deficits in the 1980s is by itself probably sufficient to dissuade congressional approval. Aside from economics and politics, however, the constitutionality of such a plan may have perhaps been enhanced by the U.S. Supreme Court's decision in the previously mentioned case, *Mueller* v. *Allen*.

Another mechanism for expanding choice in education is the use of vouchers. We describe voucher plans in greater length in Chapter Five. Suffice it here to mention that there were federal government voucher advocates and even one quite small federally-funded voucher experiment in the 1970s. On balance, however, the previously described tuition tax credit idea has proven to be a more attractive mechanism for the federal government to enhance educational choice. Tuition tax credits could encourage educational choice and not necessitate the federal administrative

---

[31] See James S. Catterall, *Tuition Tax Credits: Fact and Fiction* (Bloomington: Phi Delta Kappan Educational Foundation, 1983).

overhead of a voucher plan. In that tuition tax credit plans have not yet succeeded, it is unlikely that vouchers will either. Indeed, as long as federal government revenues are substantially below projected expenditures for existing programs, the probability is small that any new educational initiatives will result. The possible exception is in those areas where education can more easily be connected with either improvement of the economy or national defense.[32]

It is an unusual categorization scheme which neatly encompasses every item, and ours is no exception. Many of the federal government's educational programs can be described as having been undertaken in pursuit of efficiency or equality, but there are other programs which fall outside of this framework. One of the most significant is the so-called *impact aid program.*

At the outset of World War II and again in the early 1950s with the Korean War, local officials frequently found their school district faced with virtually unmanageable growth problems. Nearby military bases and other federal installations would expand quickly and public schools would often have to absorb hundreds of additional pupils in a short period of time. The matter was made worse by the fact that federal installations were not subject to local taxation. In order to compensate for this condition, in 1940 Congress enacted and subsequently renewed the Lanham Act, PL 81-874. This *in lieu* of tax statute compensates local districts for loss of property tax revenue resulting from the "impact" of federal activity. Hence the funds have come to be known as *impact aid.* Local school districts annually conduct a census among pupils to determine eligibility. Thereafter, they can use the funds as though they were general revenues. There is also a modest amount of impact aid for school construction purposes—PL 81-815.

To this point we have described federal government educational programs administered directly by educational agencies. In addition there are numerous federal education-related endeavors which are administered by departments other than Education. For example, the federal Department of Agriculture administers an enormous lunch and breakfast program which provides school districts with funds, advice, and surplus agricultural commodities. The Department of Defense operates Overseas Dependent Schools for the children of Americans stationed in foreign nations. The now defunct Office of Economic Opportunity (OEO), which was not within a department, but reported directly to the president, operated numerous important educational programs. (The remains of these efforts have been shifted to the Department of Education.) However, even if we do not allocate substantial space to these other efforts, their significance should not go unnoticed. Table 4.3 displays the full range of federal programs, both in higher and lower education, operated by the U.S. Department of Education in 1983.

---

[32] For an extended description of future federal educational policy options, see James W. Guthrie, "The Future of Federal Education Policy," in *Education and Urban Society,* 14, no. 4, August, 1982 (Beverly Hills: Sage Publications, Inc.), 511–530.

Table 4.3   DEPARTMENT OF EDUCATION BUDGETS

	1983 Appropriations	1984 Appropriations	1985 President's Request	1985 Appropriations	1986 President's Request
			(dollars in thousands)		
DEPARTMENT OF EDUCATION					
ELEMENTARY AND SECONDARY EDUCATION					
Programs for Disadvantaged Students					
(ECIA Chapter 1)					
Basic grants	$2,727,588	$3,003,680	$3,034,519	$3,200,000	$3,200,000
State agency programs					
Migrants	255,744	258,024	229,626	264,524	222,976
Handicapped	146,520	146,520	146,520	150,170	150,170
Neglected and delinquent	32,616	32,616	32,616	32,616	32,616
State administration	33,180	34,414	30,973	35,607	35,607
Evaluation and studies	4,746	4,746	5,746	5,246	5,246
Subtotal, Chapter 1	3,200,394	3,480,000	3,480,000	3,688,163	3,646,615
Migrant education					
High school equivalency program (HEA IV-A)	6,300	6,300	....	6,300	....
College assistance migrant program (HEA IV-A)	1,200	1,950	....	1,200	....
Subtotal, Migrant Education	7,500	8,250	....	7,500	....
Education Block Grant					
(ECIA Chapter 2)	450,655	450,655	685,655	500,000	500,000
Secretary's discretionary fund					
Book distribution	5,850	6,500	6,500	7,000	7,000
Arts education	2,025	2,125	2,125	3,157	3,157
Alcohol and drug	2,850	2,850	3,000	3,000	3,000
Other	18,040	17,290	31,599	18,752	18,752
Subtotal, Secretary's discretionary fund	28,765	28,765	43,224	31,909	31,909
Subtotal, Chapter 2	479,420	479,420	728,879	531,909	531,909
Other Programs					
Math and science education	....	....	50,000	100,000	100,000
Magnet schools	....	....	....	75,000	....
Follow Through	19,440	14,767	....	10,000	....
Territorial teacher training assistance	960	1,000	....	2,000	....
General assistance for the Virgin Islands	1,920	1,920	....	2,700	....
Ellender fellowships	3,000	1,500	....	1,500	....
Women's educational equity	5,760	5,760	....	6,000	....
Training and advisory services (CRA IV-A)	24,000	24,000	....	24,000	16,000
Excellence in education	....	....	....	5,000	....
Subtotal, Other Programs	55,080	48,947	50,000	226,200	116,000
School Assistance in Federally Affected Areas					
(Impact Aid)					
Maintenance and operations (P.L. 81-874)					
Payments for "A" children	390,161	457,500	476,630	513,000	513,000
Payments for "B" children	45,039	77,500	....	130,000	....
Special provisions	15,000	20,000	20,000	22,000	20,000
Disaster assistance	10,000	25,000	10,000	10,000	10,000
Subtotal, Maintenance and Operations	460,200	580,000	506,630	675,000	543,000
Construction (P.L. 81-815)	80,000	20,000	....	20,000	....
Subtotal, Impact Aid	540,200	600,000	506,630	695,000	543,000

KEY TO EDUCATION LAWS

ECIA — Education Consolidation and Improvement Act
HEA — Higher Education Act
CRA — Civil Rights Act
IEA — Indian Education Act

EHA — Education of the Handicapped Act
RA — Rehabilitation Act
VEA — Vocational Education Act
AEA — Adult Education Act

GEPA — General Education Provisions Act

Table 4.3   (cont.)

	1983 Appropriations	1984 Appropriations	1985 President's Request	1985 Appropriations	1986 President's Request
			(dollars in thousands)		
Indian Education					
Payments to local educational agencies and non-LEAs (IEA Part A)	48,465	50,900	51,350	51,350	50,323
Special programs for Indian students (IEA Part B)	12,600	12,000	12,000	12,000	11,760
Special programs for Indian adults (IEA Part C)	5,531	3,000	3,000	3,000	2,940
Program administration					
Salaries and expenses (GEPA)	2,409	2,700	2,200	2,200	2,051
National advisory council (GEPA)	180	180	230	230	218
Subtotal, Indian Education	**69,185**	**68,780**	**68,780**	**68,780**	**67,292**
Total, Elementary and Secondary Education	**4,351,779**	**4,685,397**	**4,834,289**	**5,217,552**	**4,904,816**
VOCATIONAL AND ADULT EDUCATION					
Vocational and Adult Education					
Vocational education (VEA)					
State grants and innovative programs					
Basic grants (Part A)	558,155	566,969	731,314	566,969	716,136[1]
Program improvement and supportive services (Part A)	99,590	99,590	------	99,590	------
Programs of national significance (Part B)	7,678	8,178	------	8,178	8,178
Special programs for the disadvantaged (Part A)	14,356	14,356	------	14,356	------
Consumer and homemaking education (Part A)	31,633	31,633	------	31,633	------
State advisory councils	6,500	7,000	------	7,000	7,000
State planning	3,588	3,588	------	3,588	------
Permanent appropriation (Smith-Hughes Act)	7,161	7,161	7,161	7,148	7,148
Subtotal, Vocational Education	**728,661**	**738,475**	**738,475**	**738,462**	**738,462**
Adult education grants to states (AEA)	95,000	100,000	100,000	100,000	100,000
Total, Vocational and Adult Education	**823,661**	**838,475**	**838,475**	**838,462**	**838,462**
BILINGUAL EDUCATION AND MINORITY LANGUAGES AFFAIRS					
Grants to school districts	84,126	89,567	100,459	99,230	104,165
Bilingual desegregation grants	2,400	------	------	------	------
Training grants	31,288	32,610	25,000	28,500	24,000
Support services	16,340	13,502	10,100	11,535	11,100
Bilingual vocational training	3,686	3,686	3,686	3,686	3,686
Emergency immigrant aid	------	30,000	------	30,000	------
Total, Bilingual Education	**137,840**	**169,365**	**139,245**	**172,951**	**142,951**
SPECIAL EDUCATION AND REHABILITATIVE SERVICES					
Education for the Handicapped					
State assistance (EHA)					
State grant program (Part B)	1,017,900	1,068,875	1,068,875	1,135,145	1,135,145
Preschool incentive grants (Part B)	25,000	26,330	26,330	29,000	29,000
Subtotal, State Grants	**1,042,900**	**1,095,205**	**1,095,205**	**1,164,145**	**1,164,145**
Special Purpose Funds					
Deaf-blind centers (Part C)	15,360	15,000	12,000	15,000	12,000
Severely handicapped projects (Part C)	2,880	4,000	4,000	4,300	4,300
Early childhood education (Part C)	16,800	21,100	21,100	22,500	22,500
Postsecondary programs (Part C)	2,832	5,000	5,000	5,300	5,300
Innovation and development (Part E)	12,000	15,000	12,000	16,000	16,000
Media services and captioned films (Part F)	12,000	14,000	14,000	16,500	16,500
Regional resource centers (Part C)	4,130	5,700	4,500	6,000	6,000
Recruitment and information (Part D)	720	1,000	1,000	1,025	1,025
Special education personnel development (Part D)	49,300	55,540	37,640	61,000	50,000
Special studies (Part B)	435	3,100	2,000	3,170	2,000
Architectural barrier removal	40,000	------	------	------	------
Transitional services	------	6,000	6,000	6,330	6,330
Subtotal, Special Purpose Funds	**156,457**	**145,440**	**119,240**	**157,125**	**141,955**
Subtotal, Education for the Handicapped	**1,199,357**	**1,240,645**	**1,214,445**	**1,321,270**	**1,306,100**

[1] Basic grants are expanded to accommodate the *Carl D. Perkins Vocational Education Act* and now include funding for disadvantaged populations, program improvement, expansion and innovation, and state planning.

Table 4.3   (cont.)

	1983 Appropriations	1984 Appropriations	1985 President's Request	1985 Appropriations	1986 President's Request
			(dollars in thousands)		
Rehabilitative Services and Handicapped Research					
Rehabilitative services					
Basic state grants (RA I)	943,900	1,037,800	1,003,900	1,100,000	1,100,000
Client assistance	------	6,000	------	6,300	6,300
Service projects (RA III and VI)	31,094	27,900	27,500	32,800	29,300
Keller national	------	4,000	3,700	4,200	4,200
Independent living (RA VII)	19,400	19,400	21,000	27,000	22,000
Training (RA III)	19,200	22,000	5,000	22,000	15,000
Subtotal, Rehabilitative Services	**1,013,594**	**1,117,100**	**1,061,100**	**1,192,300**	**1,176,800**
National Institute of Handicapped Research (RA II)	31,560	36,000	30,060	39,000	39,000
Evaluation	------	2,000	500	2,000	600
Subtotal, Research and Evaluation	**31,560**	**38,000**	**30,560**	**41,000**	**39,600**
Total, Special Education and Rehabilitative Services	**2,244,511**	**2,395,745**	**2,306,105**	**2,554,570**	**2,522,500**
POSTSECONDARY EDUCATION					
Student Financial Assistance					
Pell (Self-Help) Grants (HEA IV-A)	2,419,040	2,800,000	2,800,000	3,575,000	2,691,000
Supplemental Educational Opportunity Grants (HEA IV-A)	355,400	375,000	------	412,500	------
College Work-Study (HEA IV-C)	590,000	555,000	850,000[1]	592,500	------
Work Study/Grants	------	------	------	------	850,000[1]
State Student Incentive Grants (HEA IV-A)	60,000	76,000	------	76,000	------
National Direct Student Loans (HEA IV-E)	193,360	180,860	4,000	215,000	28,000
Guaranteed Student Loans (HEA IV-B)	3,090,000	2,256,500	2,840,677	3,079,477	2,714,482
Subtotal, Student Aid	**6,707,800**	**6,243,360**	**6,494,677**	**7,950,477**	**6,283,482**
Higher and Continuing Education					
Special programs for the disadvantaged (HEA IV-A)	154,740	164,740	82,370	174,940	82,370
Veterans cost-of-instruction (HEA IV-A)	3,000	3,000	------	3,000	------
Institutional aid programs (HEA III)	134,416	134,416	134,416	141,208	141,208
Cooperative education (HEA VIII)	14,400	14,400	------	14,400	------
International education/foreign language studies					
Domestic programs (HEA VI)	21,000	25,800	------	26,550	------
Overseas programs (Fulbright-Hays Act)	5,000	5,000	------	5,500	------
Minority institutions science improvement	4,800	4,800	4,800	5,000	5,000
Graduate/professional fellowships (HEA IX-A and -B)	10,000	11,000	------	11,750	------
Public service grants and fellowships (HEA IX-A and -B)	1,920	2,500	------	2,500	------
Javits fellowship	------	------	------	2,500	------
Construction interest subsidy grants (HEA VII)	25,000	24,500	18,775	18,775	23,500
Academic facilities grants	22,500	------	------	28,000	------
Construction projects	------	------	------	22,000	------
Fund for the Improvement of Post-secondary Education	11,710	11,710	11,710	12,710	------
Legal training for the disadvantaged (HEA IX-D)	1,000	1,000	------	1,500	------
Law school clinical experience (HEA IX-E)	605	1,000	------	1,500	------
General Daniel James Memorial at Tuskegee	9,000	------	------	------	------
Carl Albert Congressional Research and Studies Center	2,000	------	------	------	------
Taft Institute of Government	750	------	------	750	------
Wayne Morse Chair of Law and Politics	335	------	------	------	------
Maureen and Mike Mansfield Foundation	------	5,000	------	------	------
Land grants for Samoa and Micronesia	------	------	------	6,000	------
Guam assistance	------	------	------	500	------
Subtotal, Higher and Continuing Education	**422,176**	**408,866**	**252,071**	**479,083**	**252,078**

Proposed consolidation of Supplemental Education Opportunity Grants and College Work-Study; institutions could use up to 50 percent of proposed Work/Study grants for supplemental opportunity grants.

Table 4.3   (cont.)

	1983 Appropriations	1984 Appropriations	1985 President's Request	1985 Appropriations	1986 President's Request
	(dollars in thousands)				
Educational Research and Training Activities Overseas (Special Foreign Currency Program)					
Grants to American institutions (Fulbright-Hays Act)	516	1,133	------	------	------
Subtotal, Foreign Currency	516	1,133	------	------	------
Higher Education Facilities Loan and Insurance					
Higher education facilities loan and insurance fund					
Annual appropriation (HEA VII-C)	20,143	19,846	14,194	14,194	17,996
Permanent indefinite appropriation (HEA VII-C)	134	------	------	------	------
Subtotal, Facilities	20,277	19,846	14,194	14,194	17,996
College Housing Loans					
Permanent indefinite appropriation (Housing Act IV)	40	------	------	------	------
Subtotal, Housing Loans	40	------	------	------	------
Total, Postsecondary Education	7,150,809	6,673,205	6,760,942	8,443,754	6,553,556
RESEARCH AND IMPROVEMENT					
Educational Research and Statistics					
National Institute of Education	55,614	48,231	54,231	51,231	51,231
National Center for Education Statistics	8,589	8,747	8,747	8,747	8,747
Subtotal, NIE and NCES	64,203	56,978	62,978	59,978	59,978
Library and Learning Technologies					
Public libraries	60,000	65,000	------	75,000	------
Public library construction	50,000	------	------	25,000	------
Interlibrary cooperation	11,520	15,000	------	18,000	------
College library resources (HEA II-B)	1,920	------	------	------	------
Training and demonstrations (HEA II-B)				1,000	
Library career training	640	640	------	------	------
Research and administration	240	240	------	------	------
Research libraries (HEA II-C)	6,000	6,000	------	6,000	------
Subtotal, Libraries	130,320	86,880	------	125,000	------
Total, Research and Improvement	194,523	143,858	62,978	184,978	59,978
SPECIAL INSTITUTIONS AND ED ADMINISTRATION					
Special Institutions					
American Printing House for the Blind	5,000	5,010	5,010	5,510	5,510
National Technical Institute for the Deaf	26,300	28,000	31,400	31,400	30,080
Gallaudet College	52,000	56,000	46,835	58,700	58,889
Howard University	145,200	156,200	158,230	158,230	151,230
Subtotal, Special Institutions	228,500	245,210	241,475	253,840	245,709
Salaries and Expenses					
Office for Civil Rights (CRA)	44,868	44,396	42,633	45,000	42,938
Office of the Inspector General	12,840	14,961	15,312	15,312	14,837
Departmental management	232,955	230,000	243,505	241,075	219,567
Subtotal, Salaries and Expenses	290,663	289,357	301,450	301,387	277,342
Total, Institutions and Administration	519,163	534,567	542,925	555,227	523,051
TOTAL, DEPARTMENT OF EDUCATION	$15,422,286	$15,440,612	$15,484,959	$17,967,494	$15,545,314

Source: U.S. Department of Education

MAKING AND IMPLEMENTING
FEDERAL EDUCATIONAL POLICY

The procedures responsible for federal policy are not fundamentally different from the political mechanisms which result in educational policy at the state and local levels (see Chapters Two and Three). However, we undertake an abbreviated discussion here of the basic political processes and governmental structures involved in the formation of federal educational policy.

The iron triangle. Conventional wisdom holds that federal policy for almost any endeavor, not just education, is a consequence of political interactions between components of the so-called "iron triangle." Its three components are educational units of the executive branch, congressional committees, and interest groups. The idea for a new piece of legislation may arise within any one of these groups or from a large number of other sources—a new book, a study supported by a philanthropic foundation, a journalist's article, or an academic research project. Once an executive branch agency or a member of Congress becomes interested in sponsoring the idea, arranging for the concept to be drafted in bill form is relatively easy, either by using counsel in an executive branch agency or the Legislative Drafting Service in the House or Senate.

Identifying potential supporters of an idea and subsequently negotiating the compromises that may be necessary before important factions agree to support a bill may be difficult. Obviously, the more important the bill, the more groups likely to be affected, and the larger the federal appropriation involved, the greater the likelihood of controversy. Many more bills are defeated than enacted. In order to be successful, an idea frequently must be repeatedly submitted over a number of years before gaining enough acceptance and popularity to be adopted. Also, whereas an idea may stem from many sources and be initiated by any one component of the iron triangle, conventional wisdom holds that eventually the other two components must also agree before passage will occur. Brokering the multifaceted agreements necessary to ensure enactment of a bill is an art which is seldom fully appreciated by the public.[33]

Implementation. In the conventional civics textbook explanation, policy is made by the legislative branch and thereafter implemented in a politically sanitized executive branch agency. This is but another form of the frequently promulgated myth that a clear distinction can be made between policy making and administration. In fact, political conflicts left unresolved in the enactment process are almost inevitably reflected in efforts to implement the legislation. Consequently, adminis-

[33] Alternatives to the iron triangle concept of policy formation are presented by Michael Kirst and Gail Meister in "The Role of Issue Networks in State Agenda Setting," Project Report 83-80A1, Institute for Research in Educational Finance and Governance, School of Education, Stanford University, February, 1983.

tering federal educational policy is far from a mechanically simple, politically sterile technocratic undertaking.

Once an education bill has been approved by both houses of Congress, it is often necessary to convene a joint "conference committee," composed of members from both the House and Senate to resolve differences between the two versions of the bill. Assuming presidential approval, the bill then becomes public law, and is numbered such that the initial set of digits refers to the Congress in which the bill was enacted, and the second set refers to the bill's place in the sequence of statutes becoming law. For example, Public Law 94-142 denotes the 142nd bill to become a statute in the 94th session of Congress. Thereafter, the specified administering agency within the executive branch is responsible for drafting the regulations which will inform implementation of the new statute.

Regulations are necessary because in the enactment phase it is not generally possible to place sufficient language in the statute itself to cover every contingency connected with implementation and administration. Also, the political dynamics of enactment frequently necessitate a degree of ambiguity and vagueness. The greater the abstraction, the greater the probability that political agreement can be reached. "Do good and avoid evil" is an admonition so vague as to be vapid—however, few oppose the principle. As soon as legislation becomes specific, providing details regarding which groups will get how much money for what purposes, the prospect of political conflict increases. Thus, in order to dampen controversy and attract a greater number of supporting votes, legislation is sometimes deliberately vague, and it is left to the drafting of regulations to tidy up the rules of administration. In the instance of statutory ambiguity, interest groups may lobby as assiduously to influence the regulations as they did to influence the initial legislation itself.

An education bill is likely to fall to the administrative province of the Department of Education. This cabinet level department was created in 1978 upon the recommendation of President Jimmy Carter. Prior to that time, the U.S. Office of Education (USOE) as well as the National Institute of Education (NIE) were agencies within the Department of Health, Education, and Welfare (HEW). The latter is now Health and Human Services (HHS), reflecting the relegation of education to its own niche.

Department of Education lawyers are responsible for drafting regulations. In this process they pay particular attention to the "legislative history" of the bill. This is derived from committee hearing records and committee reports in both the House and Senate. Additionally, whatever debate accompanied passage of the bill on the floor of each house and the Conference Committee report, if any, also becomes part of the bill's legislative history. From such records the intent of the bill is more fully deduced, and prescriptions for administration are drafted which are intended to guide the actions of state and local officials as they implement the legislation. Regulations specify purposes for which federal funds can be used, state and local plans which may be required by the Department of Education, and rules by which local projects will be audited.

Regulations, once drafted, are submitted to the appropriate congressional committees for approval. They are also published and distributed in the *Federal Register* so that educators and others in the field can let their opinions be known. When the approval process is complete, the regulations are inserted in the *Federal Administrative Code* and carry the weight of law. Often, "guidelines" are provided state and local officials to assist in interpreting the regulations and the statute itself. Federal guidelines are typically written in much more straightforward language and provide examples of procedures and programs to assist local administrators.

Appropriations.   To this point, we have focused upon the procedures concerned with enacting and implementing "authorizing" legislation—the substantive bill which specifies the purposes of the federal government educational program and authorizes funds to be spent. The actual dollar amount Congress will allocate to the purposes for which spending is authorized is established by the "appropriations" process. This endeavor is virtually a separate legislative track involving interaction with executive branch budget officials. It relies heavily upon the Congressional Office of the Budget (COB) and appropriations committees and subcommittees in both the House and Senate. It is not sufficient for professional educators to be sophisticated regarding the dynamics of authorization politics. It is also the case that knowledge of appropriation politics, which is characterized by a separate political culture, is necessary. We recommend a thorough reading of *The Politics of the Budgetary Process* by Aaron Wildavsky in order to gain a comprehensive view of this important issue.[34]

GAINING ADMINISTRATIVE COMPLIANCE

Federal officials are anxious that education funds be spent in compliance with statutes and regulations. Inducing compliance is a topic about which substantial thought has been given by experts in public administration.[35] Here we wish simply to mention a few of the strategies utilized by the federal government. Keep in mind that the United States governmental system is multitiered, with each layer concerned with guarding its historically evolved prerogatives.

The major strategy pursued with educational programs is to require state and local agencies to submit a plan for the use of forthcoming federal funds.[36] The plan must comply with the guidelines for the legislation involved. Thereafter, it is as-

[34] Aaron Wildavsky, *Politics of the Budgetary Process* (Boston: Little, Brown, 1980).

[35] Paul Berman and Milbrey McLaughlin, *Federal Programs Supporting Educational Change,* vol. 8; Implementing and Sustaining Innovations (Santa Monica: Rand Corporation, 1978); and Michael S. Knapp et al., *Cumulative Effects of Federal Education Policies on Schools and Districts* (Menlo Park: SRI International, 1983).

[36] Such plans generate a great many reports. See, for example, Mary Bankston, "Organizational Reporting in a School District: State and Federal Programs." *IFG Policy Perspectives,* report of the Stanford University School of Education Institute for Research on Educational Finance and Governance, 1982.

sumed that local administrators will operate in a manner consistent with the submitted plan. Periodically, a local or state agency may be audited, either by state officials, the Auditor General of the Department of Education, or by the General Accounting Office of Congress. The purpose of an audit is to ensure that program spending is consistent with the locally submitted plan and with federal regulations.

Another strategem pursued in gaining compliance is to require local or state matching of federal funds. The hope is that by requiring a mix of monies, local officials will be committed to the success of the federally subsidized endeavor as if it were wholly their own. Yet another strategy is to empower local clients or program recipients to exert pressure on local districts to ensure compliance. There are at least two expressions of this strategy. One is to be found in PL 94-142 wherein parents of handicapped youngsters can request a "fair hearing" with local officials and even be represented by an attorney in the process. Such an adversary process is intended to protect the statutory rights of clients and provide them with a lever to gain local district compliance. Somewhat more subtle is the creation of school-site advisory councils and parent advisory councils such as are required by a number of federal program regulations (see Chapter Three). The hope here is that parents, presumed benefactors of the program, will advise and appropriately oversee actions of local education officials.

There are a few examples of education agencies violating federal legislative intent. On balance, the overwhelming experience has been that local and state officials attempt to operate federal programs in an honest and effective manner.

NATIONALIZING INFLUENCES
UPON AMERICAN EDUCATION

Despite the United States' relatively decentralized system, there are a substantial number of dimensions in which schools in one part of our nation are similar to those in another. This homogeneity extends beyond what would be necessary to simply instruct students of a similar age and grade. Moreover, this similarity is a function of influences far beyond those exerted by federal officials. Rather, there exists a host of additional nationalizing influences that are extragovernmental in nature.

For example, the use of test results by an overwhelming proportion of colleges and universities to determine admission eligibility renders the Scholastic Aptitude Test (SAT), along with college admissions standards, one of the major determinants of U.S. secondary school curricula. Regional accreditation agencies operating throughout the United States exert influence upon secondary school curricula offerings, instructional procedures, and book procurement by school libraries. Textbook publishers have greater profit potential if they serve a large market—hence their desire to publish texts which are widely attractive, regardless of the values in a particular section of the nation or tastes of local decision makers. Nationwide organizations such as the American Association of School Administrators (AASA), National School Board Association (NSBA), National Education Association (NEA), and American Federation of Teachers (AFT) are in a position to influence state and local practices through their nationwide communication channels, which cut across local and state boundaries.

The probability is high that the majority of nationalizing forces have been beneficial for American elementary and secondary education. They frequently have as their purpose the elevation of standards. We mention the process simply to alert educational administrators to the almost omnipresent prospect of outside influence.[37] A professional educator is obligated to consider the consequences of such nationalizing forces for the students and organization for which he or she is primarily responsible. This is true whether or not the expression of these forces is a textbook which is only marginally acceptable, and thus should be rejected, a state college or university admission requirement which has the prospect of distorting the cohesion of local secondary school curricula, or a proposed federal educational program which might disrupt local procedures. Under conditions such as these, the appropriate professional stance is that of reasoned effort to alter the offending conditions.

SUMMARY

Unlike most other nations, the central government of the United States does not have a primary role in education. State governments are the primary policy makers while the federal government funds programs—governed by state educational agencies and operated by local school districts—intended to promote equality of educational opportunity and greater school productivity. Federal support for education began in the eighteenth century, but significant financing did not occur until the mid-twentieth century with enactment of major bills such as the National Defense Education Act (1958), the Elementary and Secondary Education Act (1965), the Education for All Handicapped Children Act (1976), and the Education Consolidation and Improvement Act (1981). Federal funds for education approximated $18 billion in 1985, and were divided almost equally between K-12 programs and higher education. The latter is generally devoted to student aid. Federal judicial decisions such as those in *Brown* v. *Board of Education* (1954) have also exerted substantial influence over U.S. education.

[37] A more extensive treatment of this topic is provided by Stephen N. Barro in "Federal Education Goals and Policy Instruments: An Assessment of the 'Strings' Attached to Categorical Grants in Education," in Michael Timpane, ed., *Federal Interest in Financing Schooling* (Santa Monica: The Rand Corporation, 1978), pp. 229–86; and Henry M. Levin and Man C. Tsang, "Federal Grants and National Educational Policy," Project Report no. 82-18, Institute for Research on Educational Finance and Governance, Stanford University, School of Education, 1982.

SELECTED READINGS

Advisory Commission on Intergovernmental Relations, *The Future of Federalism in the 1980s* (Washington, D.C.: AIR, 1980).

Bailey, Stephen K., and Edith K. Mosher, *The ESEA: The Office of Education Administers a Law* (Syracuse: Syracuse University Press, 1967).

Kaufman, Herbert, *Administrative Feedback: Monitoring Subordinates' Behavior* (Washington, D.C.: Brookings Institution, 1973).

Miller, Robert A., ed., *The Federal Role in Education: New Directions for the Eighties* (Washington, D.C.: Institute for Educational Leadership, 1981).

Timpane, Michael, ed., *The Federal Interest in Financing Schooling* (Cambridge: Ballinger, 1978).

FINANCING AMERICA'S SCHOOLS

chapter 5

The high degree of decentralized decision making which characterizes American school governance is directly reflected in the means by which revenues for the support of public education are generated and distributed. In this chapter we describe and analyze the general principles underlying United States school finance. Before turning to this topic in detail, however, there are certain general conditions which bear explanation.

SCHOOL FINANCE AND PUBLIC VALUES

The constitutional provisions, statutes, court decisions, regulations, and administrative guidelines shaping the financing of America's schools are remarkably complicated. Moreover, as we have already suggested, they vary substantially from state to state. This complexity is a consequence of the major social and economic conditions which shape school financing. First, a state's school financing provisions represent an effort to insert into public policy society's expectations for the function of schools and the performance of students. When seen through the eyes of a public policy analyst, school financing is complicated because it reflects the unusual value diversity of the United States in general and the states in particular. Our political system must accommodate proponents of equality, liberty, and efficiency. At their philosophic roots, these values conflict with each other.

However valid their positions, there are individuals and groups who believe schools should spend more money and others who believe current spending levels are already excessive. There are advocates for and opponents of aid to nonpublic schools. Some believe that public school spending should be absolutely equalized; still others propose that school spending, however unequal, should be completely a matter of local choice. Some groups propose far-reaching property tax revisions; yet others want education funded only from state sources or from state lotteries and gambling revenues. Somehow, this vast spectrum of beliefs must be consolidated, mediated, and codified. That is the function of the political system, and the resulting crazy-quilt pattern among states is but a reflection of constantly shifting public opinion throughout our nation.

Each state is in effect a microcosm of much of the United States. Thus in this chapter we are not able to encompass the details of each state's school finance system. To understand the specific arrangements of a particular state, readers are encouraged to acquire documents regularly published by most state education departments and organizations such as the Education Commission of the States and the National Education Association. However, the general concepts and principles we describe in this chapter should render understanding of any state's specific plans substantially easier than otherwise would be the case.

MAGNITUDE OF THE U.S. SYSTEM OF SCHOOL FINANCE

Not only is the United States system of decentralized school financing complex, it is also far larger than that of other countries. Approximately one out of every six members of our population is enrolled in a public school, and the absolute number of enrollees is growing. To deliver public education services to such a vast student population—an estimated 42 million in 1984—requires the employment of over four million individuals, three million of whom are licensed education professionals, teachers, counselors, and administrators. In addition, America's approximately 15,000 local school districts must annually purchase literally millions of tons of various supplies—fuel, food, paper, paint, equipment, and vehicles. Public education, kindergarten through twelfth grade, is one of the nation's largest governmental undertakings, of the same order of magnitude as other publicly subsidized human services such as health delivery, welfare arrangements, and transportation. Thus, it is not surprising that its operation and maintenance require awesome levels of financial resources. Here are a few statistics to underscore this point.

Total spending among United States public schools, kindergarten through twelfth grade stood at $105 billion in 1981. By 1990 this amount is projected to grow to between $170 and $190 billion. This translates to $2613 per pupil in 1981 and more than $4000 per pupil in 1990 (Table 5.1 displays past spending patterns).

The foregoing are nationwide average figures, and variation among the fifty states is substantial. For example, in 1980 the highest average annual expenditure per pupil among the forty-eight contiguous states was $3452 in New York State.

Table 5.1   EXPENDITURES FOR PUBLIC EDUCATION, 1940–1980

YEAR	Expenditures per Pupil CURRENT $	CONSTANT (1967) $	PER CAPITA EXPENDITURES	PERSONAL INCOME	%
1940	92	195	17.7	596	3.0
1945	115	213	19.3	1,224	1.6
1950	232	321	39.3	1,810	2.2
1955	335	418	61.4	2,027	3.0
1960	433	488	87.1	2,226	3.9
1965	475	503	123.0	2,782	4.4
1970	767	660	200.2	3,955	5.1
1975	1,294	803	304.0	5,857	5.2
1980	2,168	878	427.0	9,490	4.5

Source: National Center for Educational Statistics, *Revenues and Expenditures for Public Elementary and Secondary Education,* FY 1980 and 1972-73. U.S. Bureau of the Census, *Historical Abstracts of the United States, Colonial Times to 1970.*

On the low end of the spending continuum was Arkansas at $1564 per pupil. Moreover, states differ in their projected rates of population growth, adaptation to high technology industries, access to inexpensive energy sources, and preferences for quality of education. Thus, these per pupil spending differences are predicted by the NIE National School Finance Project to increase over time unless there is a major federal aid program enacted that reduces interstate disparities.

Whether or not school spending, approximately $150 billion in 1985, is sufficient for the nation's needs is subject to debate. However, historical and cross-cultural comparisons are informative. For example, in 1940, at the end of the Great Depression and before the formal declaration of U.S. involvement in World War II, the nationwide average annual expenditure per pupil was $100. Even discounting inflation, expenditures per pupil have increased almost 500 percent since that time. This is faster growth than in any other major public sector service, with the exception of subsidized health care. The previously mentioned Table 5.1 depicts school spending trends and adjusts them for changes in the consumer price index (CPI). The next two tables, 5.2 and 5.3, display public school spending as a percent of gross national product (GNP) from 1940 through 1980, and compare U.S. school spending in this regard to selected other nations.[1]

What can be seen in these tables is that the United States allocates a large proportion of GNP to education when compared to many nations. Also, one can see the long-term trend of education spending. The school expansion necessary from 1950 to 1970 in order to serve the World War II baby boom necessitated larger shares of the nation's total resources. In the time from 1970 to the 1980s, a declining school age population, a "surplus" of teachers, increased competition from other public sector services, and uncertainty in the nation's economy triggered decreased allocation of GNP to education.

[1] Spending and GNP figures for the U.S. differ in these tables because of varying bases of comparison used by government sources.

Table 5.2 PUBLIC SCHOOL EXPENDITURES
AS A PERCENT OF GROSS NATIONAL
PRODUCT, 1940–80

YEAR	EXPENDITURES	Billions $ GNP	%
1940	2.7	100.0	2.7
1945	3.2	212.4	1.5
1950	7.1	286.5	2.5
1955	10.1	400.0	2.5
1960	19.4	506.5	3.8
1965	35.3	691.1	5.1
1970	56.8	992.7	5.7
1975	64.8	1,549.2	4.2
1980	95.9	2,633.1	3.6

Source: U.S. Bureau of the Census, *Statistical Abstract of the United States,* various years.

Table 5.3 PUBLIC SCHOOL EXPENDITURES INTERNATIONAL COMPARISONS

COUNTRY	YEAR	Expend. (MIL.)	% OF GNP	% OF TOTAL PUBLIC EXPEND.
United States	1977	120,700	6.3	17.7
Australia	1977	6,402	6.5	16.2
Austria	1978	3,280	5.7	8.0
Brazil	1979	1,043	5.6	(NA)
Canada	1978	16,153	8.1	18.5
Colombia	1978	513	2.3	19.9
France	1978	25,301	5.3	(NA)
Germany (Fed. Rep.)	1979	34,699	4.6	(NA)
India	1977	2,923	2.9	9.9
Japan	1978	55,563	5.7	16.1
Mexico	1979	6,103	5.2	(NA)
Saudi Arabia	1979	4,841	7.8	10.2
Soviet Union	1978	47,431	7.4	12.0
Sweden	1978	7,850	9.1	13.1
United Kingdom	1976	14,177	6.3	14.3
Zaire	1979	363	5.0	25.8

Source: U.S. Bureau of Census, *Statistical Abstract of the United States, 1983.*

GENERAL SCHOOL FINANCE PRINCIPLES

In the absence of a national educational system in the United States, it is state-level government which has ultimate responsibility for financing public schools. The federal government contributes only approximately 6 percent of the total cost for kindergarten through twelfth grades. Consequently, this chapter concentrates upon the principles involved in state-level revenue generation and distribution. We divide our discussion of this topic into (1) the means by which states raise revenues for schools and (2) a description of the means used to distribute those revenues.

Revenue Generation—Taxation

The longer one goes to school, the greater the probability of earning higher income. Figure 5.1 displays this relationship for data collected in 1980. Notice that a college graduate could then expect to earn almost twice as much as a high school graduate over an entire lifetime. Notice also the restricted earning opportunities for women. While these earning figures are correlates of schooling, they cannot be interpreted solely as the results of schooling.

If schooling benefited only the individual, we would speak of it as a consumer good or a personal investment item, and the justification for public support of education would be substantially weaker. However, analyses have continually demonstrated substantial economic returns to a society, as well as to individuals, from investing in education (the results of these analyses are displayed in Table 5.4). This is less true at the postsecondary level where returns on educational investment become more blurred between the advantage to the individual and the advantage to the entire society. Because the *spillover benefits* are less clear, the economic argu-

Figure 5.1   Education Pays. National Education Association based on 1980 census data.

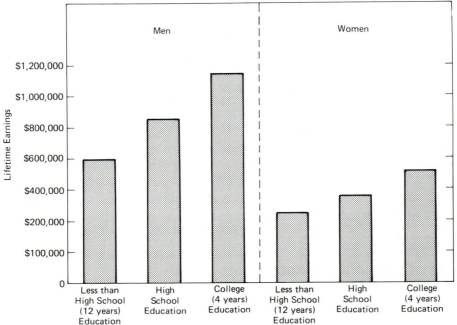

Table 5.4   **INTERNAL RATES OF RETURN TO SECONDARY EDUCATION**
             IN THE UNITED STATES

AUTHOR(S)	SAMPLE YEAR	IROR (percent)	
		PRIVATE	SOCIAL
Hansen (1963)	1950	14.5	11.4
Becker (1964)	1939	16.0	
	1949	20.0	
	1956	25.0	
	1958	28.0	
Hanoch (1967)	1960	16.1	
Hines, Tweeten, and Redfern (1970)	1960	19.5	14.0
Mincer (1974)	1960	13.0	
Carnoy and Marenbach (1975)	1940	49.1	18.2
	1950	22.7	14.2
	1960	14.6	10.1
	1970	18.9	10.7

Source: Elchanan Cohn, *The Economics of Education,* 1979.

ment for full public subsidy of higher education is less strong. For elementary and secondary education, however, the returns to the entire society from investment in schooling have been found to be high. Thus, public funds are justified for the support of schooling. Economists view this as an investment in *human capital.*

Keep in mind that public support need not imply public provision. It is possible to generate public funding for a service, but to have the service provided privately. This is what characterizes much of government-subsidized medical care, and there are ardent proponents of such a model in public education. The use of public funds to subsidize private providers is a highly controversial public policy issue, and we explain the topic more fully later in this chapter. It is even possible for government to require both private payment and private provision for schooling. Such proposals have been made but never adopted in the United States. Here, however, we concentrate on the means by which public funds are raised to support public schools. First we explore the characteristics of taxes and then explain the operation of specific broad-based taxes used to support public education—income, sales, and property taxes.

Characteristics of Taxes[2]

Basis.   There are four general bases upon which taxes can be levied—*wealth, income, consumption,* and *privilege.* All of these involve money, though such is the case much more directly for the first three than the last. We will illustrate each.

[2] The ensuing discussion is based substantially on the description of taxes and school finance distribution formulas contained in Walter I. Garms, James W. Guthrie, and Lawrence C. Pierce, *School Finance: The Economics and Politics of Public Education* (Englewood Cliffs, N.J.: Prentice-Hall, 1978).

A tax on *wealth* is based on the ownership of property, either real or personal. The property tax and the federal estate tax are examples. Note that the size of the tax need not bear a relationship to the income earned by the property but only on the assigned value of the property.

A tax on *income* is applied to the taxable income of individuals (or corporations). Taxable income is the income that remains after allowable expenses and deductions. One of the virtues of the income tax is that the amount of the tax is related to the income used to pay it.

A tax on *consumption* is usually known as a sales tax, particularly if it applies to all or most sales in a political jurisdiction. If it applies only to the purchase of a particular class of items (such as the tax on theater admission or telephone use), it is known as an *excise* tax. Import duties on particular classes of goods are also known as *excise* taxes. The *value added tax* (VAT), widely used in Europe, in which a tax is calculated on the value of an item at each stage of production is a consumption tax variant. A federal tax on individual consumption has been proposed periodically as an inducement for persons to save and invest—not spend.

A tax on *privilege* generally takes the form of a license fee imposed on an individual or company engaged in the performance of a task subject to government regulation. For example, most states impose a fee to license teachers, physicians, and others who charge for providing services to the public. Other privilege taxes are simply for permitting the holder to engage in an activity or hold a possession and have no direct relationship to earning income—dog licenses, gun licenses, and drivers' licenses.

Privilege taxes were initially collected to cover the cost of government regulation involved with the activity in question. However, over time, the total amount of revenue collected in such fees has become quite large, and it is now often the case that the size of the fee far outstrips whatever bureaucratic costs of regulation are involved. Though far from the general rule, school districts can benefit from such fees—for example, taxes on safety deposit boxes or for parking permits are used in some localities to contribute to school support.

Equity.   Taxes are a financial burden imposed on all by the will of the majority or its representatives. Hence, there is a desire for taxes to be equitable. Defining and measuring what is equitable can be a difficult task. Three standards have emerged for evaluating this intangible: (1) equal treatment of equals, (2) being taxed in relationship to benefits received (or burdens imposed), and (3) ability to pay.

1. Equal Treatment of Equals. Treating equals equally is a relatively easy equitability test. For example, two individuals earning the same level of taxable income should pay the same in income taxes, and two individuals owning property of equal value should pay the same amount in property taxes. This is known as *horizontal equity*. There are a few exceptions in practice, particularly with regard to the property tax which we will discuss in a later section. On balance, however, most United States taxes fare well when judged against this standard.

2. Being Taxed in Relation to Benefits Received. Because not all individuals in society are equal, it is necessary to have additional criteria against which to judge the equity of taxes. One such additional standard is the extent to which a tax imposed is consistent with benefits received. Examples are federal and state taxes imposed on gasoline, proceeds from which are specified for highway maintenance. The further one drives, within limits, the higher one's consumption of fuel. The added taxes, presumably, pay for upkeep of the roadway. Similarly, assessments imposed by the front foot on property owners to pay for various civic improvements are intended to be in proportion to benefits received. This standard, as with its predecessor, has difficulties attached to its application. For example, who benefits most from a strong military defense and, thus, who should pay for it? Similarly, who benefits most from an effective local police force? Should crime victims have a portion of their municipal taxes refunded? Because of such difficulties, another standard is also used to judge taxes – ability to pay.

3. Ability to Pay. Progressive and Regressive Taxes. Regardless of the basis upon which a tax is imposed – wealth, income, privilege, or expenditure – if we are to appraise the tax in terms of ability to pay, we must make the judgment relative to the individual's income. It is from income, not wealth or expenditure, that taxes are paid. Thus, in order to impose this standard of equity we measure the amount of tax to be paid against income. If the amount paid is evenly related to income, the tax is said to be *proportional*. If the tax falls more heavily upon high income individuals, the tax is said to be *progressive*. Conversely, if the tax falls more heavily upon individuals with low income, it is said to be *regressive*. Table 5.5 illustrates these three conditions relative to individual income levels.

The federal personal income tax is a good illustration of a *progressive* tax. The higher one's taxable income level, the larger the proportion of one's income has to be paid in taxes. Being in a "higher bracket" translates to paying a higher proportion of income in taxes. Periodically, proposals are discussed to convert the federal personal income tax to a straight percentage of income. In the unlikely event such a system of taxation came about, then the federal income tax would more closely approximate a proportional tax. Because individuals do not strictly consume housing in proportion to their income, the property tax has the potential to be a regressive

Table 5.5 COMPARISON OF PROPORTIONAL, PROGRESSIVE, AND REGRESSIVE TAXES

INCOME	Proportional			Progressive			Regressive		
	TAX	RATE		TAX	RATE		TAX	RATE	
$10,000	$ 3,000	.30		$ 500	.05		$ 5,500	.55	
20,000	6,000	.30		3,000	.15		9,000	.45	
30,000	9,000	.30		7,500	.25		10,500	.35	
40,000	12,000	.30		14,000	.35		10,000	.25	
50,000	15,000	.30		22,500	.45		7,500	.15	
Total tax	$45,000			$47,500			$42,500		

tax. We explain this more fully in a later description of the specific operation of property taxes.

Impact and incidence. To this point in our discussion we have acted as though taxes were paid by the person actually billed. This is not always the case. The terms *impact* and *incidence* denote an important distinction in the division of the tax burden. The individual or company that physically pays the tax bears the impact. This may be the department store consumer paying a sales tax or a property owner sending a check to the tax collector. Determining the impact of a tax is a relatively trivial matter. However, the ultimate burden of the tax may not be borne by the person initially paying.

The term *incidence* denotes the point at which the burden of the tax ultimately comes to rest. Incidence can be difficult to discern because taxes can be shifted. A few examples help to illustrate the point. The tax bill for an apartment house is sent to the property owner of record, who will send a check to the tax collector. However, if there is a shortage of rental units in the geographic area, then the tax incidence is likely to be borne by the building's tenants. Property taxes will be embedded in the rents charged—this is a forward *tax shift*.

Imagine that property taxes are raised in a city, and a bakery owner now must pay a higher annual tax amount on his property. He would like to raise the retail price of bread, but to do so would render his products less competitive with a bakery located in a nearby community. Thus, he cannot easily shift his taxes forward to the consumer. Instead, he shifts them laterally to his employees in the form of lower wages or lower wage increases than he was otherwise planning to pay.

In yet other examples, the owner of a property might shift a tax backward in the form of lower profit to himself. Obviously, tax shifts can occur in all manner of combinations depending upon the competitive nature of the economy in the location involved. However, what is important is to realize that taxes are not always what they appear to be and that their ultimate burden may fall in a different area than that of their initial impact.

Individuals often inquire whether or not the United States tax system is an equitable one from the standpoint of ability to pay. A nationally known economist, Joseph Pechman, offers the following analysis (see Table 5.6).[3] He calculates that the sum of all federal, state, and local taxes has an incidence roughly proportional throughout a wide range, with most households paying approximately 27 percent of their total income in taxes. At the lowest income levels, the sum of all taxes tends to be regressive. At the other end of the income scale, the sum of all taxes tends to be progressive. Thus, at extremes of income, both rich and poor households are paying more than 27 percent in taxes.

Pechman makes an adjustment for so-called *transfer payments*. This is the technical term for government payments for purposes such as welfare, unemployment, and social security. They are *transfers* in the sense income is taken from one

---

[3] Joseph Pechman, "The Rich, The Poor, and the Taxes They Pay," *The Public Interest*, no. 17 (Fall, 1969), 21–43.

Table 5.6   TAXES AND TRANSFERS AS PERCENT OF INCOME, 1965

INCOME CLASS	FEDERAL TAXES	STATE AND LOCAL TAXES	TOTAL TAXES	TRANSFER PAYMENTS	TAXES LESS TRANSFERS
Under $2,000	19	25	44	126	−83*
$2,000-$4,000	16	11	27	11	16
4,000- 6,000	17	10	27	5	21
6,000- 8,000	17	9	26	3	23
8,000-10,000	18	9	27	2	25
10,000-15,000	19	9	27	2	25
Over 15,000	32	7	38	1	37
All classes	22	9	31	14	24

*The minus sign indicates that the families and individuals in this class received more from federal, state, and local governments than they, as a group, paid to these governments in taxes. They paid 44 percent of their income exclusive of transfer payments in taxes, but received 126 percent as much in transfer payments as in other income, leaving them with a net of 83 percent more after taxes and transfer payments than before either. (Totals vary slightly because of rounding.)

Source: Reprinted with permission of Joseph Pechman, *The Public Interest,* no. 17 (Fall 1969). Copyright © 1969 by National Affairs, Inc.

person and granted to another without the exchange of a good or service. Not surprisingly, lower income households benefit from such payments more than high income households. This feature tends to relieve the regressivity of the overall tax system. If the assumptions contained in Pechman's calculations are generally valid, then the United States tax system is, on balance, equitable. This is not to claim, however, that the system is uniformly equitable in every state, community, or for every individual.

Yield. The yield of a tax is its ability to generate revenue. Generally speaking, the broader the base to which a tax is applicable, the higher will be its yield. The federal personal income tax is unusually broad, and its annual yield typically covers half of federal operating outlays. On the other hand, taxes applied to the "privilege" of owning a dog—dog license fees—are narrow and raise relatively small revenues.

When discussing taxes, economists are interested in the degree to which yield is related to changes in personal income. *Elasticity* is the measure of the relationship between tax yield and income. The "income elasticity of yield" is calculated by dividing percentage change of tax yield by percentage change in national (or regional) income. Take a hypothetical example in which tax revenues from alcohol sales (an excise tax) increased 20 percent, but personal income increased only 15 percent. Twenty divided by 15 equals 1.33, an income elasticity of yield of 1.33. An elasticity of yield less than 1.0 is referred to as an *inelastic* tax. A yield higher than 1.0 is known as an *elastic* tax.

The federal personal income tax is a remarkably elastic tax with a yield approximating 1.5. When individuals' incomes increase, they are pushed into higher "tax brackets," and pay a greater proportion of their incomes in taxes. Sales taxes tend to be only mildly elastic. Property taxes are also only mildly elastic. Property reassessments tend to lag behind gains in personal income. However, in favor of the property tax, it should be said that when personal income drops, the property tax is resilient—its yield typically does not drop proportionately.

Cost of administration and compliance. The cost of tax administration is the cost to the government of levying and collecting a tax. *Compliance costs* refer to the costs to the taxpayer of complying with the requirements of the tax. *Tax efficiency* refers to the relationship between administration and compliance costs and the yield of a tax. Administering excise taxes on alcohol or cigarettes is relatively inexpensive. The government collects the taxes at the factory, and there are relatively few manufacturers. In that there are many parcels of property subject to reassessment, administrative costs associated with property taxation are higher.

Variations in compliance cost. Property taxes have a low compliance cost because the property owner need only write a check one or two times a year to the tax collector. Conversely, federal personal and corporate income taxes have high compliance costs. Each of these taxes necessitates the taxpayer keeping elaborate records and undertaking numerous calculations.

Economic, social, and political effects. If a tax has as its prime purpose the generation of revenue, then it should be as *neutral* as possible. That is, it should not affect economic decisions made by suppliers and consumers, nor should it influence social well being. In fact, it is difficult to create an absolutely neutral tax. For example, an excise tax on cars will either increase the vehicle's price to the consumer, decrease wages to employees, decrease profits to owners, or a combination of the three. Income and sales taxes can drive economic exchanges "underground" in an effort to exclude them from taxation. It is sometimes alleged that property taxes deplete the stock of housing which would otherwise be available to low income tenants. These are unintended consequences of taxes. It should be remembered, however, that some taxes are deliberately designed to effect changes in consumer or supplier behavior. Import taxes intended to protect domestic manufacturing are an illustration.

General Taxes

The general taxes in widest use in the United States are the personal income tax, sales tax, and property tax. The first two of these are employed to support general government and serve as the revenue base for state-level subsidies for public education. We provide only a brief description of each of these. The property tax, however, is historically the local revenue source most associated with the support of education and, thus, we provide greater detail regarding its operation.

Personal income tax. The *federal personal income tax* generates more revenue than any other U.S. tax. It serves as the major foundation for federal revenues. It even provides funds, though minimal, for the operation of state and local programs in the form of *federal revenue sharing grants.* This tax is also the major source of funds for federal categorical aid for states and local school districts (see Chapter Four). In addition, forty states rely upon a personal income tax to generate state revenues. A few states authorize a local income tax, but this is the exception rather than the rule.

Taxes are legally withheld from paychecks by employers for the overwhelming majority of wage earners. Self-employed individuals are legally required to make quarterly estimated tax payments. At the end of the calendar year, individual earners and households are responsible for filing income tax statements with the federal Internal Revenue Service and its state equivalents. Taxes owed must be paid at this time, or tax refunds requested.

As mentioned previously, the personal income tax is generally progressive. Being highly elastic in yield, it has the added benefit to government of generating revenue even faster than general economic growth. The disadvantage is that in an economic downturn, income tax receipts shrink even faster than the decline in personal income. Lastly, the compliance burden is high with the income tax. In 1981, personal income tax revenues totaled $332.9 billion. The federal government collected $291 billion and the remainder was collected by the states.

General sales taxes. This is the preferred tax for state governments. Forty states levy a statewide sales tax, and for many it is their principal source of general revenue. The tax is relatively efficient in terms both of administration and compliance. It is also moderately elastic, generating added revenues when the economy is expanding. It is easy for a state to authorize local governments to levy sales taxes. They can be collected by the state and redistributed to the appropriate local government agency with substantial ease. Unless food and pharmaceutical drugs are excluded from taxation, however, the sales tax can be regressive—otherwise it tends to be proportional. In 1981, sales tax collection for states and their localities totaled $90.42 billion.

Property taxes. Public opinion polls suggest that the property tax is among the least liked taxes. However, it is the mainstay of local government support, schools included. In 1981, $76 billion was collected in state and local property tax revenues. Local governments collected $68 billion, and approximately one-half of this amount went to support schools. This much money would be difficult to replace by other means. Consequently, while there will undoubtedly be continued efforts to reform the manner in which the property tax is administered, the prospect of its complete elimination seems remote.

The property tax is a tax on wealth. For taxing purposes, property has two classifications—*real* and *personal*. Real property consists of *land* and *improvements* that are firmly attached to land—items such as buildings, power lines, and railroad tracks. Personal property consists of *tangible* items of intrinsic value—for example, automobiles, airplanes, and business inventories. Intangible personal property consists of items of wealth generally devoid of intrinsic value—for example, stocks, bonds, and mortgages. Real property is subject to taxation almost everywhere. Much tangible personal property is also taxed. Little intangible personal property is taxed because of the difficulty of gaining access to it for accurate tax purposes.

Property tax procedures. In order to be taxed, property must be assigned a value. In this process two functions take place. Accurate records must be kept regarding location of the property, the official owner, and whatever financial transactions have transpired regarding the property, such as sales and liens. Generally, a locally appointed official known as a *recorder* is charged with these duties.

Another official, an *assessor,* is responsible for assigning a value to the property. Under some circumstances this is a difficult task. One of the guides available to assessors in arriving at the value of property is the market place. If a parcel of property, or a parcel quite similar to it, has recently changed hands, then an assessor can rather easily fix its *market value.* However, if the type of property involved seldom sells, for example a race track or copper mine, then other procedures may have to be employed. One such alternative is to take into account the income-earning capacity of property and then assign it an assessed value. This is frequently done for farmlands, factories, utilities, and extractive industries and is known as *capitalizing* the value of the earning.

Once *market value* is established by acceptable means, the assessor must then assign an *assessed value* to the property. Assessed value is almost always less than market value. This will be the case even when state law calls for property to be assessed at full value. The primary reason for the differential is that assessors are reluctant to expose themselves to the controversy associated with assigning a specific value which can be easily questioned. By establishing assessed values lower than market value, a degree of protection is afforded in the event of an appeal. There are also less praiseworthy reasons for underassessment. It has not been unknown for elected assessors, recognizing where votes are located, to systematically underassess residences, leaving commercial properties within their jurisdiction to bear an unfair tax burden.

The total assessed value (AV) of a school district is the property wealth available to be taxed. In order to compare the property wealth of school districts, total assessed value is divided by the number of pupils in the district. This provides a unit measure of property wealth—assessed value per pupil (AV/PP). It is important to keep in mind that this represents property wealth and not necessarily the income of school district residents. The value of property is also by no means equally distributed among school districts. One need only remember that industrial properties are frequently concentrated in areas where there are few homes. In such instances, assessed valuation per pupil may be unusually high, but the income of residents need not reflect this. For example, cities and urban districts may appear "wealthy" by property measures, but many of their residents may be subsisting on low incomes.

Conversely, suburbs may consist of concentrated housing with little commerical or industrial property. The outcome here, regardless of residents' incomes, is a school district of low property wealth (assessed valuation per pupil). It is important to distinguish between these various measures of wealth.

Once value is assigned and systematic reassessments are made to ensure that property values remain current, the job of the assessor is completed. Thereafter, locally elected government officials, municipal councils, special enterprise districts (flood control, mosquito abatement, sanitation, fire protection, etc.), and school boards determine the amount of their budget that must be raised from property taxation. This is a complicated process which involves judgments about what spending levels should be and what level of taxation is politically feasible. The budget requirements of a governmental unit less its anticipated income leaves the amount to be raised through property taxes. The following simplified illustration depicts the logic of the process.

School District Budget	$ 10,000,000
Other Income (state funds)	5,000,000
To be raised by Property Taxes	5,000,000
District Assessed Valuation	250,000,000
Tax Rate	0.020

Property tax rates customarily are expressed in one of three ways depending upon the state. Using the above example, the tax rate could be expressed as 20 mills per $1.00 of assessed value, $20 per $1,000 of assessed valuation, or $2 per $100 of assessed valuation. Tax rate is determined by dividing the specified local revenue amount by the assessed valuation. In the above example, a 20 mill rate will generate the $5 million sought in local revenues:

$$\frac{\$5,000,000}{\$250,000,000} = 0.020$$

Approximately 70 percent of the 15,000 or so school boards in the United States have taxing authority. These are labeled *fiscally independent* districts. They do not rely, except perhaps in the most technical sense, upon another local body of government to establish their tax rates. The remaining districts, those which are *fiscally dependent*, must submit their budgets to another unit of government for approval. The approving body then levies the appropriate tax. Typically, in eastern and midwestern cities this will be a city council; in the south it may be county government. In California, it is state government. Hawaii, on the other hand, having been a monarchy before entering statehood, does not use local property taxes for general public school support.

One of the reasons why the property tax sometimes fares so poorly in terms of public opinion is that it is an exceedingly "visible" tax. Income tax withholding schemes, and the incremental manner in which consumers pay sales taxes renders these two broad taxes relatively invisible to the taxpayer. Conversely, the property tax is typically paid in one or two large annual installments. As a result a property owner, though probably not a tenant, is conscious of suddenly having a smaller bank account.

Another frequent criticism leveled at the property tax is that it is regressive. In fact, economists have mixed views about this.[4] To the extent the property tax is regressive, there are means by which the condition can be alleviated. A hypothetical example follows.

	HOMEOWNER A	HOMEOWNER B
Annual Income	$ 50,000	$20,000
Assessed Value of Home	100,000	60,000
Property Tax rate	30 mills (.03)	30 mills (.03)
Property Taxes	3,000	1,800
As percent of annual income	6 percent	9 percent

In this illustration Homeowner A pays substantially higher taxes than Homeowner B. However, as a percent of annual income, the criterion against which regressivity is measured, B pays more. In this simplified instance, the property tax is regressive. As we stated previously, to the extent that individuals do not consume housing proportionate to their income, the property tax has the potential to be regressive. In this example, Homeowner individual A would have had to own a home valued at $150,000 to have consumed housing proportionate to income.

Several means are available to state legislatures for relieving property tax regressivity. One mechanism is to shield a portion of assessed value so that it is not exposed to taxation. This is done in states by the statutory provision of *exemptions* such as the so-called homeowner's exemption, or property tax exemptions for the elderly, disabled, or veterans. By exempting, for example, the initial $10,000 in property value on a home, the owner pays taxes only on the remainder.

Another frequently used mechanism for tax relief is known as a *circuit breaker.* The analogy is to the electrical device by the same name which offers protection by interrupting the flow of power should there be a surge in electrical voltage beyond some preestablished level. Similarly, with a property tax circuit breaker, taxes in excess of a predetermined annual income level are taken as a credit against state income taxes.

For instance, using the previously provided hypothetical example, if the state in which the two homeowners reside had established 7 percent of annual income as the circuit breaker cutoff point, then Homeowner B would have had a state income tax credit of $400, the property tax payment in excess of the cutoff rate. By having Homeowner A pay an additional $500, the property tax would have been altered to be proportional. However, no state currently enforces such symmetry.

For more than a century the property tax has served as the revenue mainstay for local government, and for schools in particular. Since 1980, states have assumed

[4] For differing views regarding property tax regressivity, see Dick Netzer, "Property Taxes," *Municipal Finance,* 44, no. 2 (November 1971), 36; and Henry J. Aaron, *A New View of Property Tax Incidence* (Washington, D.C.: The Brookings Institution, 1974).

a slightly larger role in financing schools, and general state funds now pay more than fifty-one cents out of every school revenue dollar. However, the property tax continues to be an important feature of school finance, raising approximately forty-three cents out of every school dollar nationwide. The tax generates a sufficient amount of revenue so that state policy makers are not likely to eliminate it. What appears more important is to reform the tax so that the potential difficulties associated with it are ameliorated. When this is done, the tax can serve as a basis for an equitable system of school finance. We turn now to an explanation of how school revenues are distributed.

DISTRIBUTING SCHOOL DOLLARS

No two states have an identical school finance distribution system. Each is the product of its unique mixture of historical development, taxation schemes, preferences for particular kinds of schooling, and governmental arrangements. At one end of this funding continuum is Hawaii, which depends almost exclusively upon state school financing and federal categorical aid, using no local property taxes for current support. At the other extreme is New Hampshire, which depends almost exclusively upon locally generated property tax revenues for school support. In the middle are the majority of states, which depend heavily upon both state and local funding. Even given this modal arrangement, it is impossible to generalize about the entire system of school financing. What can be done is to explain several model school finance distribution formulae, which most states utilize.

Classification of funds. Before undertaking these descriptions of formulae, it is useful to distinguish between classifications of school spending. The largest classes are *operating* funds and *capital* funds. Capital spending is money utilized for financing physical projects such as buildings, vehicles, and durable equipment. Schools in the United States expend approximately $12 billion annually in this area and, though less than 10 percent of operating expenditures, it is still a large amount of money. Space does not permit a detailed description of state capital spending provisions. Suffice it here to specify that the arrangements for building schools and buying large equipment are different than the mechanisms for distributing other funds, and a more specialized textbook reference is in order for those interested in the topic.[5]

The other major classification of school money, funds for *current operation,* is sometimes labeled *operation* and *maintenance.* These are monies which officials use to pay salaries, purchase supplies, and maintain buildings and vehicles. Operating funds are themselves subdivided into two classifications, so-called *general* funds and *categorical* funds. The former are revenues which, within defined legal boundaries, can be spent at the discretion of local school officials. These are the funds

[5] See Chapter 14 of Garms, W., Guthrie, J., and Pierce, L., *School Finance: The Economics and Politics of Public Education* (Englewood Cliffs, N.J.: Prentice-Hall, 1978).

which support the core instructional program of a school district. Categorical funds are monies granted by another level of government, either state or federal, to local school districts to enable the latter to undertake a specific endeavor. In the case of federal categorical aid, state or local officials are legally obligated to utilize categorical funds in the manner specified by the higher authority. Sometimes categorical funds are authorized for a specific instructional purpose, such as upgrading reading. Sometimes they must be spent on a specified target population, for example, students from low income households or handicapped students. Occasionally, categorical aid must be spent on specified materials, such as science and mathematics instructional equipment. Whatever the purpose, categorical funds cannot be spent at the total discretion of local decision makers, but must be used in accord with state or federal specifications.

Nationwide, categorical aid constitutes approximately 10 to 15 percent of total school operating expenditures. Federal categorical programs are described in Chapter Four. Later in this chapter we describe several common components of state categorical aid programs. First, however, we concentrate on general funds.

The Importance of the State

At selected points throughout this text we refer to the plenary authority of state government regarding public schools. Here again it is important to remember this constitutional condition because it is the fifty state legislatures which are legally responsible for the manner in which public schools are financed. State legislatures are responsible for whatever state general fund revenues flow to schools. Additionally—and this is often not understood—state legislatures are legally responsible for local property taxes raised for school support. Even when a local school board is fiscally independent and levies a property tax, that is technically a state tax. Schools are state agencies, even if administered by local officials with authority delegated to them by the state. Consequently, in describing finance distribution schemes, we do so from the perspective of the state.

The Desirable and the Practical

Focusing upon the social purposes of public schooling, and omitting for the moment concern for individual benefits, it would be desirable for the state to specify with substantial precision the level of achievement expected of each student at each grade level or state of instruction. These agreed upon criteria would be the goals for that student at his or her grade level. We will represent this set of goals by "Y." Again, ideally, a diagnosis would be undertaken for each pupil, and his or her level of achievement relative to the set of goals would be specified by "X." Presumably the student would be short of full understanding, and some gap would exist between X and Y. Filling this gap would constitute the instructional objective for that grade or unit.

If education were a science, it might be possible to prescribe the school resources necessary to elevate the student to wherever he or she should be—from X to

Y. This resource level could be converted to a dollar amount, Z, for each pupil, and the budget of a classroom, school, school district, and state could be computed by totaling all the Zs for the organizational unit involved.

Even if such precision were desirable, and it gives the appearance to some of being frighteningly technocratic, it currently is far from being practically possible. One reason for the impracticality of such procedures is the controversy surrounding the purposes of schooling. Are reading and writing more important than youngsters learning to get along with one another? This, and dozens of other value questions, is difficult to answer in absolute terms. One of the majestic features of the American political system has been its overall ability to mediate such conflicts so that society maintains reasonable stability. However, the modest price of such stability is an imprecision regarding the full range of school purposes.

Faced with uncertainty of this nature, state officials nevertheless must construct mechanisms for funding schools. However imprecise and blunt, state distribution mechanisms are intended to direct resources from the state to local schools so that students can be expected to make reasonable progress in learning. One of the important components in a state distribution scheme is the basis upon which funds will be allocated to local school districts.

Allocation Units

Every state relies upon a tally of the number of students to be schooled as a means for allocating general funds to local school districts. Approximately half the states utilize a measure of actual attendance, usually *average daily attendance* (ADA), as the allocation unit. The remainder utilize a measure of *enrollment* or *membership* (ADE or ADM). Attendance (ADA) is an attractive measure from a state policy point of view because it induces local officials to encourage pupils to come to school. Conversely, local school administrators contend they incur expenses whether or not a student actually attends. Once a student is enrolled, teachers must be paid, fuel bills still arrive, and so on. A few states attempt to resolve this controversy by combining ADA and ADE into an average figure.

States frequently use pupil weightings in their allocation processes. The term WADA or WADM denotes *weighted average daily attendance* or *membership.* Assigning an added weight to a category of pupils is a means for more closely approximating what state officials believe ought to be spent. The most commonly utilized weighting schemes are for categorical aid programs. For example, states frequently weight handicapped pupils proportionate to the severity of the disability, for example, 1.1 for a speech impairment and 2.5 for an orthopedically or neurologically handicapped student. Similarly, a state may assign an added weight to youngsters from low income households or those who are low achievers. Weightings are derived from past practice, professional judgment, available finances, and political compromise. They are seldom an outcome of science. They represent a politically practical estimate of the additional costs of educating classes of students upon whom, arguably, more should be spent.

Most states provide added funding for secondary students because the smaller and more specialized high school classes typically involve higher labor and supply costs. Elementary educators frequently contend, however, that if more money were spent in the early years of schooling, the need for remedial spending would be reduced later. Florida recognizes this argument by providing added weighting in grades one through four, as well as nine through twelve.

Distribution Schemes

States have taken responsibility for the financial support of local school districts since the early part of the nineteenth century. Initially, state aid took the form of flat grants—that is, a specified dollar amount allocated to a local jurisdiction intended to pay total school operating costs. Subsequently, the flat grant was altered, becoming a flat grant per pupil. Flat grant arrangements frequently continue as an anachronistic, insignificant feature of many state school finance plans. Currently, the flat grant provision by itself nowhere suffices to cover full operating costs. Fortunately for schools, other financing features have been added.

In the 1920s two school finance experts, George Strayer and Robert Haig, advocated a system which came to be widely adopted throughout the nation. Their distribution scheme involved establishment of a spending foundation and thereafter specified a means by which a state could equalize the ability of local school districts to generate property tax revenues to meet the state foundation-spending level. In simplified form, *foundation plans* contain a state established minimum-per-pupil spending level. This dollar amount is intended to serve as a floor, the least amount spent on each student. Also, the foundation amount is interpreted to represent a school resource level sufficient for students to succeed personally and occupationally. It is also an amount intended to protect the state against ignorance—that is, it presumably satisfies the state's need for an educated citizenry. The foundation amount, or minimum spending level, is established by legislative action. As with pupil weighting schemes, there is little science involved in arriving at a foundation-spending figure. Past practice, political feasibility, and the fiscal condition of the state are determining factors.

Foundation plan.   Figure 5.2 graphically illustrates the operation of a foundation distribution scheme. The highest level horizontal line depicts the $2400 amount of the foundation guarantee, supposedly representing the cost of a minimal program. The section labeled "Required Local Effort" is the amount raised by the local property tax at a state specified required rate of 15 mills. The amount in the section labeled "State Aid" is contributed by the state, with a foundation level of $2400. For District A, the required local effort (RLE) raises little money ($1200) and the state contribution ($1200) is high; for District B, the district raises more of the guarantee ($1800) than the state contributes via subsidy ($600); and for District C, the district raises the guaranteed amount ($2400) and receives nothing from the state. The solid sloping line at the top is the dollar increment that would be

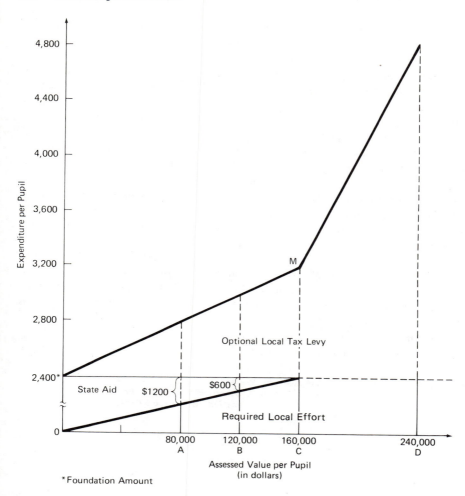

Figure 5.2   Distributing State Education Dollars.

raised if all districts chose to levy an optional local tax at the rate of 5 mills above the required 15 mill tax. District B can raise more than District A, and District C can raise more than District B. The slope becomes steeper at point M because beyond that, districts already raise more than the guarantee by using only the required rate, thus making the total property revenue they collect that much higher.

It may be argued that this required rate is unfair for some districts because they happen to be rich in property and have more money to spend from levying the required tax rate than do property-poor districts. If the required tax is indeed a state tax, then the amount raised above the guarantee could be returned to the state to be used elsewhere. This concept is called *recapture* or *recycling,* and its potential effect is shown by the dashed lines on Figure 5.2. With recapture on the 15 mills of RLE, the amount raised by any district is shown by the dashed diagonal line.

Percentage equalizing and power equalizing. The difficulty with the foundation approach has been that states have typically been reluctant to equalize spending capacity beyond the minimum foundation level. Districts with higher levels of property wealth have been able to spend more per pupil, have lower property tax rates, or a combination of the two. These unequal conditions, though widely justified on grounds that such a system protects "local control" of school decisions, triggered substantial reform efforts in the 1970s. We subsequently describe the legal logic of the lawsuits involved and explain the reforms which have resulted. However, even before the reform era of equal protection suits began, a distribution mechanism existed and had been implemented in several states to reduce the potential for unequal spending and taxing. This distribution scheme is called *percentage equalizing,* a variant of which is *power equalizing.*

Percentage and power equalization guarantee to each of a state's local school districts the same amount of assessed valuation per pupil. (This sometimes leads to these plans being labeled *guaranteed yield plans.*) Equalization is accomplished mathematically, not by redrawing district boundaries to geographically encompass the same amounts of property wealth.

Figure 5.3 illustrates the manner in which a percentage or power equalizing plan operates. Notice that school district officials select the per-pupil spending level.

Figure 5.3 Percentage Equalizing. From Walter I. Garms, James W. Guthrie, and Lawrence C. Pierce, School Finance: *The Economics and Politics of Public Education* (Englewood Cliffs, N.J.: Prentice-Hall, 1978).

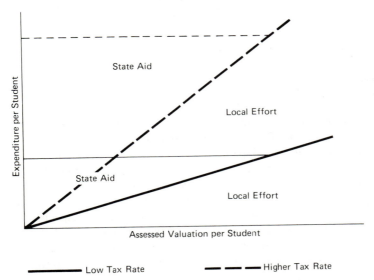

Generally there is a state-specified spending minimum and maximum. Within that range, districts are free to select the spending level they believe is appropriate for students. Spending levels can be legislatively arranged to be different for varying grade levels, or even can accommodate pupil weighting.

Once a local spending level is selected, the district's property tax rate is then scheduled accordingly. If the local application of the attendant tax rate does not raise the per-pupil amount specified, then state general funds subsidize the district for the difference. If an excess amount is raised, the surplus should then be "recaptured" by the state and recycled to other districts. However, such recycling is highly visible and politically unpopular. States generally have not engaged in recapture, and where it has happened, it has been at less than full rate. In the 1970s the Florida legislature was artful in designing such a plan around the state's wealthiest district, Dade County. In this fashion, all counties were free to select their pupil spending level, but there was no recapture since application of a scheduled tax rate never generated a per-pupil funding level in excess of the amount specified.

Full state funding. Yet another means for financing schools is simply to have the state specify the per-pupil funding level for every classification of student and thereafter impose a uniform property tax throughout the state to fund the plan. In those districts where the statewide standard property tax rate generates insufficient revenue for the specified per-pupil spending level, the state makes up the difference. If more than enough revenue is raised, then the state recaptures the excess for distribution elsewhere.

Categorical aid programs. State appropriated general funds are intended to cover whatever are judged to be the educational needs of "average" students. However, not all districts are alike in terms of their concentrations of students in need of higher than average cost services. It is also frequently the case that districts have unusual geographic features which render delivery of educational services more expensive. To compensate for such conditions, state legislatures authorize payment of *categorical funds* intended to cover the costs of specified programs. Handicapped students, students from low income households, low achieving students, gifted and talented students, and vocational students are among the categories most frequently included in state categorical funding programs. Additionally, school districts, generally in rural areas, judged to be necessarily small in terms of their enrollment are frequently provided with added funds per pupil to compensate for these diseconomies of scale. Similarly, city school districts are sometimes compensated for the high density of the populations from which their enrollments are drawn. School construction, school lunches, and preschool programs are also usually categorically funded undertakings.

Cost differentials. Within the boundaries of a state it is frequently the case that the cost of delivering an equivalent education program will differ from district to district. *Cost of living differences* may increase labor prices in urban school districts. Similarly, long distance and isolation may drive up delivery and fuel costs for rural areas. Increasingly, state school finance distribution formulae are sensitive to these cost differentials. One approach, limited to states which undertake periodic regional cost of living analyses, is to index spending levels for both general and categorical aid, to whatever price differences exist throughout the state. Florida pioneered this approach in the 1970s. A more sophisticated approach now undergoing examination is to carefully analyze regional cost variations in delivering a standardized set of educational services. Funding per pupil in each district is then adjusted in accord with these regional *educational cost differentials.*

REFORMS

Foundation programs widely used by states since the 1920s were judged to be a substantial improvement over their flat-grant predecessors. However, in that their equalization provisions did not prevent widespread spending and taxing differentials, there grew an ever more critical constituency claiming that school finance systems were inequitable. In the late 1960s two independent scholarly efforts laid the constitutional groundwork for seeking judicial reform of these inequalities.

The essential ingredient in this legal argument was that state school finance plans violated the equal protection clause contained in the U.S. Constitution's Fourteenth Amendment as well as comparable provisions of state constitutions. Further, it was argued, school finance provisions discriminated in two crucial ways. First, they delivered services unevenly to individuals in three so-called "suspect classifications"—race, income class, and geographic location. Second, the contention was made that state provisions violated the rights of citizens in the delivery of education, a service crucial to the fulfillment of so-called "fundamental interests." Freedom of speech, the right to vote, and freedom of assembly are among civil liberties classified as fundamental constitutional interests because of their significance for the fulfillment of democratic processes. Violations against those in suspect classifications or in regard to a citizen's fundamental interests may be sufficient to trigger a particularly strict court test, a *compelling interest* test. Taken together, such alleged violations would necessitate proof on the part of state governments that they possessed more than just a *rational basis* for their school finance plans. If the rational basis test is all that is necessary, the court asks only that the justification be reasonable, not arbitrary or capricious. If the justification is rational, the court does not substitute its own values.

In 1973, in a landmark case, the United States Supreme Court decided by a narrow five to four margin that the system of school financing in Texas, then one of the most extreme in terms of the spending and taxing differentials it permitted, did *not* violate the U.S. Constitution's Fourteenth Amendment.[6] The nation's highest court decided that plaintiffs, pupils, and parents in a low wealth school district

---

[6] *San Antonio* v. *Rodriguez,* 411 U.S. 1, 35 (1973).

had not adequately demonstrated existence of a suspect classification, nor had they been persuasive in making the argument that education was a fundamental interest. After all, the court majority argued, the federal constitution makes no mention of education or schooling. The Court also questioned whether students upon whom only the minimum was spent were being "damaged" as a consequence.

School finance reform advocates were disheartened by the decision. However, only three weeks later the New Jersey Supreme Court, in a case based on that state's constitution, with no federal question involved, ruled that New Jersey's school finance plan violated the state's education clause that charged the legislature with the statewide provision of a ". . . thorough and efficient system of education." [7] What precisely comprises a thorough and efficient system of education was not clear to the Court, or to anyone else. The Court, however, reasoned that the system then in place, whatever its virtue, was not thorough and efficient, and ordered substantial legislative revisions.

Subsequent to the New Jersey decision, literally dozens of other cases were filed in other states. Many of these were successful—California, Washington, Minnesota, West Virginia, and Connecticut among them. Many were unsuccessful, for example, New York, Colorado, and Oregon. Regardless of the precise nature of a court's actions, legislatures often reacted to the pressure to reform, and during the 1970s did so at a pace more rapid than at any other time in the history of school finance. By no means were intrastate spending disparities eliminated. However, the extent of such differentials were substantially reduced from what had previously been the case. [8]

School Finance Reform Alternatives

From the equal protection suits and other recent efforts to reform school finance through the judicial system, there emerged the so-called *principle of fiscal neutrality*. Negatively stated, this standard provides a measure against which the equity of a school finance system can more easily be appraised. The principle specifies that "The quality of a child's schooling should not be a function of wealth, other than the wealth of the state as a whole." [9] Note that this standard does not specify what the quality of schooling should be. That is a philosophically difficult question, to which the answer, should it be forthcoming, might lift the lid off a state's treasury. However, by stating the principle in the negative, it is possible to judge what a school finance system should not do. It should not tie school service quality, translated as dollar resource levels per pupil, to measures of local property wealth.

[7] *Robinson v. Cahill*, 2 N.J. 472, 303 A2d 273 (1973).

[8] As mentioned in Chapter One, the effects of this reform movement are assessed in the Spring 1983 issue of the *Journal of Education Finance*, 8, no. 4.

[9] This standard is the intellectual contribution of Arthur Wise, *Rich School Poor Schools* (Chicago: University of Chicago Press, 1970), and John E. Coons, William H. Clune, and Stephen D. Sugarman, *Private Wealth and Public Education* (Cambridge: Harvard University Press, 1970).

Three major plans have emerged to render a state school finance system compatible with the principle of fiscal neutrality. Two of these plans, full state funding and district power equalizing, have proved politically more practicable than the third, a system of state subsidized vouchers.

Full state funding.   This is the mechanism which states such as California, Washington, New Mexico, and West Virginia have adopted in the wake of equal protection suits. It is a system which Hawaii adopted in 1959, the time of its entry into the union. The complexities are legion, but the essence of the plan is that the state specifies spending levels per pupil. Thereafter, the state subsidizes districts wherein a state-mandated property tax rate is insufficient, ensuring that each district receives the appropriate revenue level regardless of whether local tax sources are adequate to generate the revenues involved. This solution to the problem stresses expenditure and taxing equality. In order to achieve this, the district relinquishes a large degree of local discretion. School district officials have no taxing authority and have no choice regarding the level of spending in their district.

District power equalizing.   We explained this system previously as a variant of percentage equalizing plans. In effect, the state guarantees each district that an equal amount of property wealth is available to be taxed to support education. Districts may choose various spending levels, and at any specified taxing level any two districts will receive identical per-pupil revenues. Hence, the principle of fiscal neutrality is met because local wealth is not the determinant of school quality. A system such as this exists nowhere in a pure form. However, states such as Michigan, California, and Florida have utilized it in part. This system trades a measure of equality on school spending and taxing in order to preserve a degree of local decision-making authority.

Vouchers.   This plan, should any state adopt it, not only would alter school financing, but would also dramatically change the pattern of school governance. A voucher plan was enacted by Congress following World War II to assist returning military veterans in paying for their higher education.[10] A voucher plan has never been enacted by any state. Efforts were made by the now defunct federal Office of Economic Opportunity in the 1970s to induce school districts to experiment with the idea. Only one, Alum Rock, near San Jose, California, accepted the offer. Alum Rock dropped the plan within three years. The idea, usually espoused by fiscal conservatives and political libertarians, and sometimes by those who view it as a means of empowering school choice among the poor, has not yet proven attractive to a political majority either nationally or in a particular state. However, in the mid-

---

[10] Serviceman's Readjustment Act, P.L. 78, 346.

1980s there were renewed efforts at the state and federal levels to enact voucher plans.[11]

Fundamentally, a voucher plan would involve a state legislature providing households with a financial warrant for each school-age child, redeemable only for the cost of schooling. What the characteristics of eligible schools would be is a crucial component of the voucher controversy. Most voucher proponents contend that both public and nonpublic schools should be eligible to accept vouchers. Others suggest that the idea is a good one in that it would inject a substantial measure of market competition into schooling and might thus induce higher quality and more productive schools. However, they are also fearful that social cohesion might suffer if individual household preferences for styles of schooling paralleled racial, religious, or income stratification in society. These latter voucher advocates would restrict redemption to public schools.

Vouchers can be made more complex by weighting students such that, for example, the handicapped receive a voucher of higher dollar value than others. Similarly, there are other features which can be imposed upon voucher plans in an effort to render them more socially sensitive. For example, requiring any school which redeems vouchers to accept any pupil who applies might be a mechanism for reducing racial or social discrimination.

Despite the fact that no state has seen fit to adopt such a plan, the proposal continues to be made. In 1983, a presidentially appointed national school finance panel recommended that federal categorical aid programs for low income students be transformed into a voucher plan. Similarly, President Reagan espoused tuition tax credit plans, the U.S. Senate has passed tuition credit bills six times, and the House of Representatives once enacted such a plan. This last case was in 1979, and the threat of President Carter's veto was then sufficient to discourage Senate approval. Regardless, the idea is likely to be the topic for debate for years to come.

SUMMARY

The United States annually spends in excess of $150 billion for the support of its K-12 public schools. School financing is primarily a state responsibility. State revenues, generally from sales and income taxes, comprise slightly more than 50 percent of school spending. The overwhelming proportion of the remainder is derived from local property tax proceeds.

Revenue distribution formulae of states vary substantially. Nevertheless, the majority rely upon a "foundation plan" variant which mixes state and local funds to ensure that each pupil has an expenditure floor below which no local district can fall. Heavy reliance upon local property wealth for revenues facilitates expenditure

---

[11] See for example the proposal by Governor Perpich of Minnesota described in the March 6, 1985 *Education Week*, p. 6.

and tax rate differentials among school districts within a state. During the 1970s, progress was made in dampening the range of interstate spending and taxing disparity. The reform was achieved in large measure by pursuit of "equal protection" suits through state judicial systems.

SELECTED READINGS

Benson, Charles S., *The Economics of Education* (3rd ed.). Boston: Houghton Mifflin Company, 1979.

Coons, John E., and Stephen D. Sugarman, *Education by Choice: The Case for Family Control.* Berkeley: University of California Press, 1978.

Garms, Walter I., James W. Guthrie, and Lawrence C. Pierce, *School Finance: The Economics and Politics of Public Education.* Englewood Cliffs, N.J.: Prentice-Hall, Inc., 1978.

Guthrie, James W., ed., *School Finance Policies and Practices: The 1980's, A Decade of Conflict.* Cambridge: Dallinger, 1980.

Lehn, Richard, *Quest for Justice: The Politics of School Reform.* New York: Longman, 1978.

LEGAL ENVIRONMENT FOR EDUCATION IN THE UNITED STATES

chapter 6

The laws to which educational institutions are subject are derived from legislative and executive branch rule-making efforts and judicial system rule-interpretation processes. Rule making results in public legal documents such as constitutions, charters, statutes, codes, and regulations. Rule interpretation results in court decisions, so-called case law. Previous chapters examined the rule-making role of local, state, and federal governments in shaping educational policy and practice. In this chapter we focus upon rule-interpretation contributions of courts. We first describe the U.S. judicial system and then explain important features of the law regarding teachers and students. In Chapter Twelve we discuss the law as it relates to collective bargaining.

THE U.S. JUDICIAL SYSTEM

The United States judiciary is comprised of a dual system of federal and state courts. Each system has specific spheres of jurisdiction and contains several levels. In the federal court system there are district courts (lowest), circuit courts of appeal, and the supreme court (highest). Parallel judicial structures exist in each of the fifty states. Although names may differ, each state system typically has lower and trial courts, intermediate appeals courts, and a final appeals or supreme court.

The highest court is the U.S. Supreme Court. It is the final arbiter in cases regarding questions of constitutional and federal law and in matters regarding disputes between states or, in certain cases, citizens of different states. It was created by the U.S. Constitution, Article III, Section I, which specifies

> The judicial power of the United States, shall be vested in one supreme Court, and in such inferior Courts as the Congress may from time to time ordain and establish.

State courts derive their authority from state constitutions and legislative enactments. Cases decided by state courts may involve questions of federal or state law. In contrast, federal courts are more restricted and generally exercise jurisdiction only over cases involving diversity of state citizenship and questions pertaining to constitutional or federal law. In deciding cases, state and federal courts adhere to the U.S. Constitution and federal statutes. Where these bodies of law are silent, state law prevails. Hypothetical opinions on the legitimacy of laws cannot be rendered by courts. They must result from legal questions raised in actual disputes between parties. In restricted civil matters, a state attorney general may provide advice, but this is not binding on a court.

Cases are initiated in the appropriate federal or state trial courts. At this level evidence is presented, usually by lawyers before a jury and a judge. Typically, a verdict is rendered by the jury and a judicial opinion issued by the judge in accord with state or federal law. Such decisions may be appealed to a higher court within the judicial system in which the case originates if either party to the dispute believes the decision to be inconsistent with state or federal law. The appeal process culminates at the state supreme court in matters concerning state law, and the decision of this court in these instances is final. For matters pertaining to the U.S. Constitution, federal statutes, or diversity of citizenship cases, U.S. Supreme Court reviews may be sought. Cases heard by the U.S. Supreme Court may come to it directly or from a Federal District Court, U.S. Circuit Court of Appeals, or state supreme court.

Whether a case will be heard by the U.S. Supreme Court is a matter of the Court's choice. Generally, the Supreme Court will only accept cases in which a substantial federal or constitutional question is involved. If the Court decides not to hear a case on appeal, the ruling of the lower court will stand. If a case is not heard, it should not be inferred that the Supreme Court concurs with the lower court's decision. It may simply mean that the case failed to gain the necessary votes for a hearing from the nine justices. No reasons are given.

Decisions of the U.S. Supreme Court are binding throughout the nation. Decisions of U.S. Circuit Courts of Appeals and Federal District Courts apply to geographical regions over which they have jurisdiction. Rulings of state appellate courts pertain only to the geographical district in which the court decisions are rendered. Thus, precedental value of decisions emanating from various courts on education-related and other issues may vary. Decisions issuing from any court must be consistent with the U.S. Constitution, federal law, and opinions of the U.S. Supreme Court.

RIGHTS OF TEACHERS

In many instances, legal rights are logical and self-evident. A school administrator acting sensibly and courteously is not likely to violate them. Nevertheless, one is well advised to be knowledgeable about matters in which litigation is possible. The overview of school-related legal matters presented, however, is not intended to replace the advice of an attorney in a specific instance.

Legal rights of teachers are fundamentally associated with conditions of employment, retention, and federal and state constitutional and statutory guarantees of civil liberties. School board policy or action can be challenged when teachers believe an undertaking infringes upon their constitutional or statutory rights, or their contractual rights in instances when a teacher contract is involved. These legal challenges are adjudicated in federal and state courts. Several facets of teacher rights and responsibilities are discussed in this section: (1) who is qualified to teach; (2) hiring-contractual obligations; (3) security of employment—tenure; (4) professional rights—selection of teaching materials and methods, dissent and protest, and sexual conduct; (5) discrimination in employment—race, sex, age, handicap; (6) liability for student injury; and (7) dismissal of tenured and nontenured teachers.

Who Is Qualified to Teach

Individuals must first possess a valid credential or license before they are considered qualified to teach. Credentials are generally issued by a state through its designated agency to applicants meeting specific requirements. In most states the minimum requirement for a teaching credential is the baccalaureate degree, including certain course requirements.[1] Additional requirements may include an age minimum[2] or maximum,[3] U.S. citizenship, good health,[4] good moral character,[5] and acceptable performance on a teacher proficiency examination or test of basic information both in areas of general knowledge and subject specialization.[6] Mere possession of a credential does not bestow a right to teaching employment. It simply

[1] *Klot* v. *Wilson,* 156 N.Y.S. 2d 425 (1956).

[2] For example in California, the minimum age for obtaining a teaching credential is eighteen.

[3] New York had a maximum age of forty-six for obtaining a credential. This was upheld by the court when an applicant older than forty-six passed an examination for a regular license as a high school laboratory assistant. See *Sobel* v. *Bogen,* 190 N.Y.S. 2d 562 (1959).

[4] *Conlon* v. *Marshall,* 59 N.Y.S. 2d 52 (1945).

[5] *Bay* v. *State Board of Education,* 223 Ore. 601, 378 P. 2d 588, 96 A.L.R. 2d (1963).

[6] *Cheasty* v. *Board of Examiners of Board of Education of City of New York,* 230 N.Y.S. 2d 234 (1961).

indicates that the individual earning a credential meets minimum legal requirements for teacher employment in a particular state. Credentials for other school positions such as counselor, psychologist, administrator, or supervisor must also be obtained by meeting state minimum legal requirements.

The state or its delegated representative may not refuse to issue a credential to an individual who meets specified requirements. On the other hand, credentials may be refused when there is good cause. For example, in overturning a trial court decision, the state court of appeals upheld the Oregon Board of Education's refusal to grant a five-year elementary teaching credential to an applicant because he lacked good moral character. This determination was made because the applicant had been convicted of breaking and entering stores and grand larceny, including safe burglaries, while he held a position of trust as a night policeman.[7] In another instance, a Georgia court held that presenting false claims against the United States indicated a lack of good character.[8]

In refusing to grant a credential to an applicant, the responsible granting state board or agency must make a reasonable and honest judgment on the basis of the relevant evidence available to it.[9] When an applicant is denied a credential, however, he or she is entitled to a hearing or administrative review[10] and ultimately a judicial review if the action of the board is believed to be arbitrary or unreasonable.

Individuals may be issued temporary, emergency, or conditional credentials. These do not automatically become permanent, however. Typically, such credentials are issued for a specified period of time, such as one year, and must be renewed or the holder must provide evidence sufficient to warrant a permanent credential.

Credentials also may be revoked for sufficient cause and on the basis of clearly articulated state law. Sufficient cause may include immoral or unprofessional conduct, incompetence, or willful neglect of duty.[11] Revocation may not be based on race, religion, or on grounds that abridge the credential holder's constitutional rights.[12]

Hiring: Contractual Obligations

Upon obtaining the requisite school credential, a teacher may be employed by a local school board. Terms and conditions of employment should be agreed to by both the school board and teacher and placed into a contract which, if properly executed, is legal and binding. A teacher could, however, be hired without a formal contract. Where a contract does exist, it must satisfy the following conditions: (1) a

---

[7] *Bay* v. *State Board of Education,* 233 Ore. 601, 378 P. 2d 558, 96 A.L.R. 2d 529 (1963).

[8] *Huff* v. *Anderson,* 90 S.E. 2d 329 (Ga. 1955).

[9] *Devlin* v. *Bennet,* 213 A. 2d 725 (Conn. 1965).

[10] *Cochran* v. *Levy,* 25 N.Y.S. 2d 960 (1940).

[11] For example, California Education Code, Article 3, Sec. 44932, 44933, 87732 (1979).

[12] *Council* v. *Donovan,* 244 N.Y.S. 2d 199 (1963).

meeting of the minds of both parties with respect to the terms of the contract; (2) valid consideration regarding what is to be performed and compensation for that performance; (3) legal subject matter, which recognizes that there is no requirement to perform or engage in activities that are considered criminal or contrary to public policy; (4) be entered into by competent parties—those who have the mental capacity to understand contract terms and who are of legal age as defined by the state in which the contract is tendered; and (5) have terms sufficiently clear so that each party understands what is required.[13] Depending upon state law, teacher contracts may be oral. They are usually written, however, and become valid when approved by the local school board acting within the authority it derives from state statute. Written contracts also are easier to prove if legally challenged.[14]

Contracts may be terminated because of a breach of terms by either party or upon the teacher's submission of a resignation and its acceptance by the school board. A breach of contract may, for example, result from dissatisfaction with expected and stipulated performance or organizational changes that necessitate teacher dismissals. Contracts also may be terminated because it is impossible for a teacher to perform required duties—for instance, when a teacher is physically or mentally unable to instruct. The local school board may be required to compensate a dismissed teacher if it breaches the contract. Conversely, a teacher who resigns before the expiration date or without fulfilling terms of a contract may be required to compensate the local school district.[15]

Security of Employment: Tenure

Tenure provides for continuing employment of teachers who are subject to dismissal only for a cause prescribed by state law. In most states, teachers acquire tenure after successfully completing a period of probationary instruction, typically three years in duration. While conditions that must be satisfied in order to acquire tenure are delineated by state statute, and thus must be observed throughout a state, job security under the statutory provisions of tenure holds only in the school district in which tenure is granted. It is not transferable between school districts, within or between states. Tenure may be acquired when employment is continuous after the probationary teaching period, when a board neglects to notify the teacher by a certain date before completion of the final year of probationary teaching that his or her services will no longer be needed,[16] when the board fails to comply with state law,[17] or when pay is uninterrupted beyond the probationary period.[18]

It is usually the case that teaching is full-time during the period of probation.

---

[13] Louis Fischer, David Schimmel, and Cynthia Kelly, *Teachers and the Law* (New York: Longman, 1981), pp. 4–5.

[14] For example, see *Kapustic v. School District,* 111 A. 2d 169 (Pa. 1955).

[15] *Bowbells Public School District No. 14 v. Walker,* 231 N.W. 2d 173 (N.D. 1975).

[16] *Vittal v. Long Beach Unified School District,* 87 Cal. Rptr. 319 (Cal. App. 1970).

[17] *Morse v. Wozniak,* 398 F. Supp. 597 (E. D. Mich. 1975).

[18] *Wooten v. Byers School District No. 32J,* 396 P. 2d 964 (Colo. 1964).

The granting of tenure, therefore, is generally predicated on full-time teaching. In some instances, however, tenure may be granted to part-time[19] and substitute teachers.[20] Of course, teachers need not be rehired after completion of probationary teaching and thus can be denied tenure.[21] Reasons for not rehiring a probationary teacher may be "no reason or any reason."[22] Nevertheless, there are several conditions that may thwart a school district intending not to rehire a probationary teacher. Among them are abridgments of constitutional rights, state statutory provisions, and expectations of continued employment.

Tenure is frequently criticized because it provides not only for the continuing employment of competent teachers but also for the retention of incompetent ones. Unquestionably, there is some merit in this position. What is overlooked in such criticism is that incompetent teachers can be dismissed. It must be realized that the intent of tenure is not simply to guarantee lifetime employment but also to protect teachers from unjust dismissal and to provide a clear set of procedures to be followed when dismissal is recommended. These procedures are discussed in a later section.

Professional Rights of Teachers

Teachers' professional rights are generally discussed and litigated under the label of academic freedom. Although the precise meaning is elusive, the term typically encompasses the right of teachers to select teaching techniques and instructional materials that are relevant, engage in research of their choice, speak and write freely about social, political, and economic issues, associate with whom they desire, and be accorded legal due process. These rights are protected by the First, Fifth, and Fourteenth Amendments of the United States Constitution. In other words, teachers have the same constitutional rights as do all citizens. As stated in a celebrated case concerning the rights of students to engage in symbolic speech, ". . . neither students nor teachers shed their constitutional rights to freedom of speech or expression at the schoolhouse gate."[23] The right of teachers to engage in private speech as opposed to symbolic speech, for example, criticizing a school principal in private, is likewise protected under the law.[24]

This does not mean that teachers may say or do anything they desire. In making a determination of the latitude teachers may exercise with respect to academic freedom, the Supreme Court has sought "a balance between the interests of the teacher, as a citizen, in commenting upon matters of public concern and the in-

[19] *State ex. rel. Saxtzoph* v. *District Court, Fergus County,* 275 P. 2d 209 (Minn. 1954).

[20] *McSherry* v. *City of St. Paul,* 277 N.W. 541 (Minn. 1938).

[21] *Carl* v. *South San Antonio Independent School District,* 261 S.W. 24 560 (Tex. App. 1978).

[22] *Schultz* v. *Board of Education of Dorchester,* 222 N.W. 2d 578 (Neb. 1974).

[23] *Tinker* v. *Des Moines Independent Community School District,* 393 U.S. 503, 89 S.Ct. 733, 21 L.Ed. 2d 731 (1969), [Id. at 506].

[24] *Givhan* v. *Western Line Consolidated School District,* 99 S.Ct. 693 (1979); also, *Johnson* v. *Butler,* 433 F. Supp. 531 (W.D. Va. 1977).

terest of the State, as an employer, in promoting the efficiency of the public services it performs through its employees."[25] The Supreme Court has further stated
that "the right to academic freedom . . . like all other constitutional rights, is not
absolute and must be balanced against the competing interests of society."[26] Several cases represent dimensions of academic freedom.

Selection of teaching materials and methods. A teacher's right to select
materials containing words that may be considered offensive has been upheld in
Keefe v. *Geanakos.*[27] In this instance the school committee of the Ipswich Massachusetts Public School System sought to discipline and discharge one of its tenured
high school teachers who also was head of the English department. The school committee's action was precipitated by the plaintiff, who gave his senior English class
a copy of the *Atlantic Monthly* magazine (September 1969) and assigned an article
for reading that contained a vulgar and offensive term. In discussing the article, the
plaintiff explained the contextual use of the term and also provided an opportunity
for any student who felt that assignment to be distasteful to have an alternate one.
The question addressed by the court in this case was "whether a teacher may, for
demonstrated educational purposes, quote a 'dirty' word currently used in order to
give special offense or whether the shock was too great for high school seniors to
stand" [Id. at 361]. After reading the article in question the court found that "the
single offending word, although repeated a number of times, is not artificially introduced, but, on the contrary, is important to the development of the thesis and conclusions of the author." While the court noted that classroom speech is subject to
"some measure of public regulation," it found that the educational value of the
assigned article and its discussion in class was appropriate. The school committee
was thus prevented from discharging the plaintiff, and the right of teachers to use
relevant classroom methods and materials was upheld.

In another case[28] the court ruled that the plaintiff could not be dismissed
from his teaching position because of his class discussion of a taboo word. This case
involved a teacher in the Lawrence (Massachusetts) High School who, in using the
students' discussion of an outside reading assignment to make the point that certain
classroom seating assignments in Kentucky were ridiculous, drew attention to other
things that were also ridiculous. To explain his point the teacher wrote on the
blackboard the taboo word "fuck" and asked for volunteers to define it. One student defined it as sexual intercourse. The teacher indicated in the discussion that
followed that one term was acceptable and one not, and illustrated other taboo
words.

On the complaint of a parent, the principal of the school asked the head of
the English department to determine what had happened in the class. In the inves-

[25]*Pickering* v. *Board of Education,* 391 U.S. 563, 88 S.Ct. 1731, 20 L.Ed. 2d 811
(1968), [Id. at 568].

[26]*Parducci* v. *Rutland,* 316 F. Supp. 352 (M.D. Ala. 1970), [Id. at 355].

[27]*Keefe* v. *Geanakos,* 418 F. 2d 359 (1st. Circ. 1969).

[28]*Mailloux* v. *Kiley,* 323 F. Supp. 1387 (D. Mass. 1971).

tigation of the incident the teacher admitted he had written the taboo word on the blackboard but that he had not called on any particular individual student to define it. Acting on this evidence the superintendent suspended the teacher for seven days with pay. Subsequently, following a hearing, the school committee dismissed the teacher on the charge of conduct unbecoming a teacher. The teacher initiated legal action because in discharging him for his classroom conduct the school system deprived him of his rights as set forth in the First and Fourteenth Amendments to the United States Constitution.

While there were conflicting views from experts on the appropriateness of the plaintiff's use of the taboo word and his teaching methods, the court held that there was no evidence that the plaintiff's teaching method was contrary to school system rules, professional opinion, or ethical canons. Thus, the court ruled that "inasmuch as at the time he acted plaintiff did not know and there was no reason that he should have known, that his conduct was proscribed, it was a violation of due process for the defendants to suspend or discharge him on that account" [Id. at 1393].

The right of teachers to select teaching materials that are appropriate is further demonstrated in *Parducci* v. *Rutland*.[29] Parducci assigned Kurt Vonnegut's *Welcome to the Monkey House* as outside reading for her English class. The following morning the school's principal, Rutland, along with the school system's associate superintendent conferred with Parducci, informed her of their displeasure with the story, conveyed the distress of several parents, and advised her not to teach the story. Parducci argued that she considered the story to be a fine literary work and believed she "had a professional obligation to teach the story." Parducci was subsequently dismissed from the school district. She appealed in a court action on the basis that the dismissal violated the First Amendment, her right to academic freedom. Finding that the defendants failed to show that the assignment of *Welcome to the Monkey House* was inappropriate or that it created a significant school disruption, the court ruled in her favor. In its decision the court stated:

> This court is well aware of the fact that 'school officials should be given wide discretion in administering their schools' and that 'courts should be reluctant to interfere with or place limits on that discretion.' Such legal platitudes should not, however, be allowed to become euphemisms for 'infringement upon' and 'deprivations of' constitutional rights. However wide the discretion of school officials, such discretion cannot be exercised so as to arbitrarily deprive teachers of their First Amendment rights [Id. at 357].

The foregoing cases notwithstanding, not every action of a teacher regarding the conduct of his or her class can be approved on grounds of academic freedom. *Ahern* v. *Board of Education of School District of Grand Island*[30] serves to illustrate this view. Ahern was a high school economics teacher employed by the Grand

---

[29] *Parducci* v. *Rutland*, 316 F. Supp. 352 (M. D. Alabama, 1970).
[30] 456 F. 2d 399 (8th Cir., 1972).

Island, Nebraska, Board of Education. She embraced a teaching philosophy which encouraged students to make decisions regarding subjects for daily discussion, course materials, and classroom behavior. During an approved absence to attend a conference, a substitute teacher slapped one of the students in her class. Upon learning of this incident, Ahern, in speaking to her pupils, called the substitute a "bitch" and suggested that if such an incident again occurred in her absence that students walk out. She also encouraged and assisted the students in formulating a school regulation concerning corporal punishment. As this activity became the focus of her economics class, the principal called Ahern into conference and admonished her for labeling the substitute a "bitch" in the presence of her class. He further directed her to teach economics rather than politics and to use more conventional teaching methods. During this conference, which also was attended by the assistant principal of the school and the head of Ahern's department, she was warned that failure to follow the principal's directions could result in her suspension from teaching. She purposely failed to comply with the principal's directions and was dismissed. Subsequently, the school board voted unanimously to discharge Ahern for insubordination.

Ahern brought suit against the school board on the basis that she had been denied freedom of speech, her right to teach, and due process. The federal district court upheld the board's right to discharge Ahern for insubordination. On appeal the circuit court of appeals affirmed the decision of the lower court. In its decision the court stated:

> . . . our conclusion is that Miss Ahern was invested by the Constitution with no right either (1) to persist in a course of teaching behavior which contravened the valid dictates of her employers, the public school board, regarding classroom method, or (2), as phrased by the district court, 'to teach politics in a course in economics' [Id. at 403–404].

Dissent and protest.   Teachers generally enjoy the right to dissent and protest national governmental or local school policies on or away from school sites as long as these activities do not disrupt school operations. In the previously cited *Pickering,* the U.S. Supreme Court held that "a teacher's exercise of his right to speak on issues of public importance may not serve as a basis for his dismissal from public employment."[31] Clearly, teachers' First Amendment rights cannot be violated.

In another case a university instructor in English, Keyishian, was dismissed because he refused to sign a certificate (the so-called "Feinberg Certificate") stating that he was not a communist or, if he was, that the fact had been communicated to the President of the State University of New York. In this instance the Supreme Court ruled that a teacher cannot be dismissed for merely belonging to the Communist Party.[32]

---

[31] *Pickering* v. *Board of Education,* 391 U.S. 563 (1968), [Id. at 574].

[32] *Keyishian* v. *Board of Regents of University of State of New York,* 385 U.S. 589, 17 L.Ed. 629, 87 S. Ct. 675 (1967).

The right of a teacher not to participate in school flag salute ceremonies also has been upheld.[33] Russo, a high school art teacher, refused to recite the flag salute (the Pledge of Allegiance). Instead, she stood and silently faced the flag with her arms at her side while students and the senior teacher in the homeroom saluted the flag and recited the Pledge of Allegiance. Although there was no classroom disruption stemming from her action, or evidence that she tried to influence students, the school board dismissed her. Russo brought legal action against the board, but the trial court upheld the Board's decision. On appeal the circuit court of appeals ruled in favor of Russo. In so doing it stated:

> Public employment is not a sinecure to be retained regardless of merit simply by shouting loudly that any threat of dismissal is motivated by an anti-First Amendment animus. But where in fact, as in this case, a dismissal is directed because a teacher has engaged in constitutionally protected activity, that dismissal may not stand [Id. at 633].

Teachers also may not be denied the right to protest by wearing a symbol, such as an armband, as long as such a symbolic gesture does not seek to persuade students, interfere with the teacher's classroom performance, or disrupt the school. Illustrative of this fact is the case in which an English teacher in New York was dismissed by the school board because he refused to discontinue wearing an armband in school to protest the Vietnam War. The court ruled that such protest was permissible under the U.S. Constitution's First Amendment.[34]

While courts have upheld the right of teachers to protest and dissent, this right is not sacrosanct. For example, the action of a high school principal in displaying the Confederate battle flag in his office was judged to be "a symbol of resistance to school integration and, to some, a symbol of white racism in general."[35]

Sexual conduct.   Several issues pertaining to school-related sexual activities of teachers have come before the courts. These issues include homosexuality and sexual relations, sexual advances, discussion of sexual matters, and sexual activity with students. In general, no clear pattern in court decisions emerges except for those cases involving sexual relations and sexual advances of teachers toward minor students. In these instances courts have upheld the right of school boards to dismiss teachers. The following cases are illustrative.

A deputy sheriff discovered a community college teacher, Joseph Stubblefield, having sex with one of his students in a parked car one night. The teacher was dismissed on grounds of immoral conduct. The board action was upheld by the court although Stubblefield argued that the behavior for which he was dis-

[33] *Russo* v. *Central School Dist. No. 1,* 469 F. 2d 623 (2d Cir. 1972), cert. denied, 411 U.S. 932 (1973).

[34] *Charles James* v. *Board of Education of Central District No. 1,* 461 F. 2d 566 (2d Cir. 1972).

[35] *Smith* v. *St. Tammany Parish School Bd.,* 316 F. Supp. 1174 (E.D.La. 1970), aff'd, 448 F. 2d 414 (5th Cir. 1971), [Id. at 1176].

missed occurred outside of school.[36] In another case a teacher was dismissed because the high school student he had dated became pregnant, and he admitted to being the future father. Even though the student was not enrolled in the school in which the teacher worked and there was thus no adverse effect on his teaching, the dismissal was sustained.[37]

In another case an excellent tenured teacher was dismissed for touching and tickling girls all over their bodies in an auto van during a field trip. They in turn displayed similar behavior toward him. Moreover, the conversation between the students and the teacher, as reported by another adult chaperone, was suggestive and sometimes vulgar. As a result of these activities the teacher was found guilty of immorality and dismissed by the school board, an action upheld by the court.[38]

School districts have also dismissed teachers for homosexual activities on grounds that such behavior was immoral or unprofessional. Such dismissals have not always been upheld by the courts, however. For example, in the case of Morrison,[39] the California Supreme Court stated:

> Terms such as 'immoral or unprofessional conduct' or 'moral turpitude' stretch over so wide a range that they embrace an unlimited area of conduct. In using them the Legislature surely did not mean to endow the employing agency with the power to dismiss any employee whose personal, private conduct incurred its disapproval. Hence the courts have consistently related the terms to the issue of whether, when applied to the performance of the employee on the job, the employee has disqualified himself [Id. at 224–225].

The court further stated that the Board of Education's characterization of conduct in the Morrison case as "immoral," "unprofessional," or "involving moral turpitude" was inappropriate unless such conduct indicates unfitness to teach.

In a somewhat similar case a school board, using a state statute on immorality, dismissed a female teacher who confessed to being homosexual.[40] In negating the board's action, the court held that the statute was too vague since it failed to define immorality—thus homosexuality could not be considered immoral. In denying the board's action the court stated "[t]he statute is vague because it fails to give fair warning of what conduct is prohibited and because it permits erratic and prejudiced exercise of authority" [Id. at 255].

In two other cases the courts reached an opposite conclusion and upheld the dismissal of teachers for homosexuality. In the first of these cases, Sarac, a California teacher, was arrested because he made a "homosexual advance" to a

---

[36] *Board of Trustees of Compton Junior College District* v. *Stubblefield,* 94 Cal. Rptr. 318 (1971).

[37] *Denton* v. *South Kitsap School District No. 402,* 516 P. 2d 1080 (Wash. 1973).

[38] *Weismann* v. *Board of Education of Jefferson County School District,* 547 P. 2d 1267 (Colo. 1976).

[39] *Morrison* v. *State Board of Education,* 1 Cal. 3d. 214, 461 P. 2d 375, 82 Cal. Rptr. 175 (1969).

[40] *Burton* v. *Cascade School District Union High School No. 5,* 353 F. Supp. 254 (D. Ore. 1973).

plainclothes policeman at a public beach. Because Sarac had a history of homosexuality, and admitted his guilt on the criminal charge of making a public homosexual advance, the California Supreme Court upheld revocation of his teaching credentials.[41] In the second case, a Washington state high school teacher admitted to his vice-principal that he was homosexual and was subsequently dismissed by the school board. The board's action was upheld by the Washington Supreme Court on the basis that knowledge of the teacher's homosexuality would cause disruption in the school and adversely affect his teaching.[42]

Courts also have upheld dismissal of teachers for openly engaging in sexual activity, which called into question their fitness to be a teacher. In the case of *Pettit*,[43] it was revealed that the plaintiff had openly engaged in sexual acts with men other than her husband at a swinger's club affair in Los Angeles. In upholding the board's dismissal of Pettit, the court indicated that her actions rendered her unfit to be a public school teacher. Similarly, a tenured elementary school teacher in Florida was dismissed for engaging in a sexual act with his nine-year-old step-daughter. The court upheld his dismissal on the basis of immoral conduct. The court stated that the teacher's "conduct is an incident of a perverse personality which makes him a danger to school children and unfit to teach them."[44]

Discrimination and Employment

In keeping with mandates of the equal protection clause of the Fourteenth Amendment of the U.S. Constitution and numerous federal statutes and regulations,[45] discrimination in employment because of race, sex, age, religion, or handicap is prohibited. Such prohibitions may also be covered by state law. Federal statutes are more encompassing, however, and supercede state laws.

Title VII of the Civil Rights Act of 1964 is the most comprehensive of anti-discriminatory employment laws. The intent of Title VII, the elimination of artificial barriers to employment because of race, sex, religion, or national origin, is forcefully specified in *Griggs* v. *Duke Power Co.*[46] Here the Supreme Court stated:

> Congress did not intend by Title VII . . . to guarantee a job to every person regardless of qualifications. What is required by Congress is the removal of artificial, arbitrary, and unnecessary barriers to employment when the barriers operate invidiously to discriminate on the basis of racial or other impermissible classification [Id. at 430–431].

[41] *Sarac* v. *State Board of Education*, 57 Cal. Rptr. 69 (1967).

[42] *Gaylord* v. *Tacoma School District No. 10*, 559 P. 2d 1340 (Wash. 1977).

[43] *Pettit* v. *State Board of Education*, 513 P. 2d 889 (Cal. 1973).

[44] *Tomerlin* v. *Dade County School Board*, 318 So. 2d 159 (Fla. Ct. App. 1975), [Id. at 160].

[45] Civil Rights Act of 1866, 1870; Title VI and Title VII of the Civil Rights Act of 1964; Equal Employment Opportunity Act of 1972; Executive Order 11246, as amended by Executive Order 11375; Title IX of the Education Amendments of 1972; Age Discrimination in Employment Act Amendments of 1978; Equal Pay Act of 1963; and Rehabilitation Act of 1973 as amended.

[46] *Griggs et al.* v. *Duke Power Co.*, 401 U.S. 424 (1971).

Racial discrimination. Following the 1954 *Brown* decision[47] many cases regarding displacement and hiring of minority teachers who had worked in segregated school systems were litigated.[48] In general, courts have held that teachers and professional and administrative staff who work directly with children "must be hired, assigned, promoted, paid, demoted, dismissed, and otherwise treated without regard to race, color, or national origin."[49] Further, reduction in staff resulting in dismissals or demotions are not to be made unless "objective and reasonable nondiscriminatory standards are used to select individuals to be dismissed or demoted."[50]

Race may be taken into account in school staffing under court-ordered desegregation to ensure racial balance.[51] If, however, no desegregation order exists and there is no desegregation-related incidence of staff reductions, dismissals, or hirings, then the most qualified applicants, regardless of race, must be sought out.[52]

Discriminatory practices pertaining to prerequisites for teaching have also precipitated litigation and have been found to be impermissible. For example, a Mississippi school district required either a specified minimum score on the Graduate Record Examination (GRE), a Master's degree in any field, enrollment in a program leading to a Master's in Education within a two-year period of time, an AA Teaching Certificate, or a minimum score on the National Teacher's Examination in order to be employed as a teacher. This district had operated a dual system of segregated schools prior to a court order in February 1970 requiring desegregation. The above requirements served to disqualify many Black teachers when school desegregation began. In reversing the Fifth Circuit Court of Appeals' ruling that GRE use was inappropriate, but the Master's degree and AA Teaching Certificate were not, the Supreme Court held that the GRE, the Master's degree, and the AA Teaching Certificate could not be used as a basis for teacher employment. The court reasoned that there was no relationship between teacher employment requirements imposed by the school district and the knowledge and skills necessary for teaching. Use of the requirements was "unreasonable and discriminating."[53]

Sexual discrimination. Discrimination in employment on the basis of sex is clearly proscribed in Title VII of the Civil Rights Act of 1964. Teachers' mandatory maternity leaves are another form of discrimination associated with sex that has received considerable attention. The requirement that pregnant teachers leave their

[47] *Brown* v. *Board of Education of Topeka*, 347 U.S. 483, 74 S.Ct. 686, 98 L.Ed. 873 (1954).

[48] For example, *Lee* v. *Roanoke City Board of Education*, 466 F. 2d 1378 (5th Cir. 1972); *Chambers* v. *Hendersonville City Board of Education*, 364 F. 2d 189 (4th Cir. 1966); *Wall* v. *Stanly County Board of Education*, 378 F. 2d (4th Cir. 1967).

[49] *Singleton* v. *Jackson Municipal Separate School District*, 419 F. 2d 1211, 1219 (5th Cir. 1970) (en banc), [Id. at 1218].

[50] *Ibid.*

[51] *Morgan* v. *Kerrigan*, 509 F. 2d 580 (2d Cir. 1974).

[52] *Lee* v. *Conecuh County Board of Education*, 464 F. Supp. 333 (S.D. Ala. 1979).

[53] *Armstead et al.* v. *Starkville Municipal Separate School District et al.*, 461 F. 2d 276 (5th Cir. 1972).

positions several months in advance of child delivery and not return for several months after giving birth has been found unconstitutional. For example, in simultaneously considering two similar cases that had gone before federal district courts and circuit courts of appeals, the Supreme Court held that "mandatory termination provisions . . . violate the Due Process Clause of the Fourteenth Amendment, because of their use of unwarranted conclusive presumptions that seriously burden the exercise of protected constitutional liberty."[54]

The related question of whether teachers could be excluded in employee disability programs for normal pregnancy was answered affirmatively by the court.[55] In legislative rebuttal, Congress later enacted the Pregnancy Disability Act, which is contained in Section 701 of Title VII of the Civil Rights Act of 1964, 42 USC 2000. It states:

> The terms 'because of sex' or 'on the basis of sex' include but are not limited to because of or on the basis of pregnancy, childbirth or related medical conditions and women affected by pregnancy, childbirth or related medical conditions shall be treated the same for all employment related purposes including receipt of benefits under fringe benefit programs as other persons not so affected but similar in their ability or inability to work, and nothing in sec. 703h of this Title shall be interpreted to permit otherwise.

With respect to equal pay, differences are impermissible on the basis of sex unless such differences are a function of merit, seniority, productivity, or other sex-neutral factors. The Equal Pay Act of 1963 mandates that equal pay must be provided for men and women if they perform similar work. The question of equal pay for male and female coaches, regardless of the sport, however, has not been resolved by the courts.[56]

Age discrimination. The law specifies that individuals who are at least forty but less than seventy should not be discriminated against in any area of employment by employers of twenty-five or more persons.[57] In education, several challenges regarding age discrimination have occurred in the area of mandatory retirement. In general, courts have held that forced retirement at age seventy is permissible[58] but may not be required at age 65.[59]

Discrimination based on handicap. Generally, handicapped individuals are not to be discriminated against in employment where their particular handicap poses no barrier to job performance.[60] The Rehabilitation Act of 1973, which be-

---

[54] *Cleveland Board of Education* v. *La Fleur,* 414 U.S. 632, 94 S.Ct. 791, 39 L.Ed. 2d 52 (1974), [Id. at 651].

[55] *Geduldig* v. *Aiello,* 417 W.S. 484 (1974).

[56] See *Keyes* v. *Lendir-Rhyme College,* 552 F. 2d 579 (4th Cir.) cert. denied 434 U.S. 904 (1977).

[57] The Age Discrimination in Employment Act Amendments of 1978, 29 U.S.C.A. sec. 621.

[58] *Palmer* v. *Ticcione,* 576 F. 2d 459 (2d Cir. 1978).

[59] *Kuhar* v. *Greersburg-Salem School District,* 466 F. Supp. 806 (W.D. Pa. 1979).

[60] *Carmi* v. *Metropolitan St. Louis Sewer District,* 471 F. Supp. 119 (E.D. Mo. 1979).

came effective in 1977, prohibits school districts receiving federal funds from discriminating against "otherwise qualified handicapped individuals."

The question of what constituted "otherwise qualified" was raised in the case of Frances Davis,[61] a licensed practical nurse, who was denied admission into Southeastern Community College's nursing program because of a hearing disability. Finding the college's action discriminatory, the circuit court ruled that the college had to reconsider the Davis application without regard to her hearing disability. The opinion of the circuit court was reversed by the Supreme Court.[62] The Court held that "Southeastern's unwillingness to make major adjustments in its nursing program does not constitute . . . discrimination" [Id. at 413]. The Supreme Court further stated:

> It is undisputed that respondent could not participate in Southeastern's nursing program unless the standards were substantially lowered. Section 504 [The Rehabilitation Act of 1973] imposes no requirement upon an educational institution to lower or to effect substantial modification of standards to accommodate a handicapped person [Id. at 413].

Liability for Student Injury

Under the principle of *in loco parentis,* teachers, administrators, and other school staff assume the role of parent for students in their care. Thus, they are liable for injuries sustained by students which result from negligent behavior. Negligence refers to a failure to exercise reasonable care in protecting students from physical injury or injury to one's reputation. Compensation may be sought by an injured student through civil action brought against school staff under provisions of torts and tort liability.

Tort law is a specialized branch of law beyond the scope of this text.[63] Simply stated, a tort is a civil wrong not covered by contract. Applied to teachers and school staff, torts are generally unintentional and include negligent behavior that results in injury to a student. As stated by the Indiana Supreme Court, "[t]ort of 'negligence' is composed of three elements: (1) a duty on the part of the defendant in relation to the plaintiff; (2) failure on the part of the defendant to conform its conduct to the requisite standard of care required by the relationship; and (3) an injury to the plaintiff resulting from that failure."[64] These three elements must be established before a legal claim may be satisfied. Two cases are cited to illustrate court findings on teachers' liability for negligence.

In the first case, an Indiana fifth grade student who had sustained injuries from an explosion of a detonator cap in a classroom during recess brought action against the teacher, school principal, and school corporation.[65] The plaintiff alleged

[61] *Davis* v. *Southeastern Community College,* 574 F. 2d 1158 (4th Cir. 1978).

[62] *Southeastern Community College* v. *Davis,* 442 U.S. 397 (1979).

[63] For an excellent coverage of Tort law see William L. Prosser, *Handbook on the Law of Torts,* 4th ed. (St. Paul, Minn.: West Publishing Co., 1971).

[64] *Miller* v. *Griesel et al.,* 308 N.E. 2d 701 (Ind. 1974), [Id. at 702].

[65] *Miller* v. *Griesel et al.,* 308 N.E. 2d 701 (Ind. 1974), [Id. at 703].

that there was "failure to use reasonable and due care to provide adequate supervision." The court ruled in favor of the defendants as the plaintiff "failed to present a prima facie case" in which the duty of school authorities "to exercise ordinary and reasonable care and supervision for the safety of children under their control" was breached.

In the second case, a student who lost the sight of an eye after she was struck with a pebble thrown by another student on a playing field was awarded compensation for injury. In this case a teacher escorted twenty eighth-grade girls to the athletic field and had them sit on a log located along the third base line of a baseball field. The teacher left the girls there and returned to the school. On her departure, eighth-grade boys who had been playing on the baseball field began throwing pebbles at the girls. One of the pebbles struck a student, Margaret Sheehan, in the eye, causing loss of sight. The court held that with adequate supervision the injury was one which could reasonably have been foreseen.[66]

In the Sheehan case, the defendants unsuccessfully attempted to introduce the matter of contributory negligence—a failure on the part of the injured party to exercise due care and thus to contribute to the injury sustained. Contributory negligence, however, may not be assigned to a student who is too young to understand the danger that may be inherent in the activity in which he or she is engaged.[67] In disallowing the defendants' use of contributory negligence, the court noted in the Sheehan case that this issue was not raised until two years after the accident. Introduction of a new issue at the moment of trial is impermissible.[68]

Dismissal of Tenured Teachers

Teachers who have acquired tenure can be dismissed only for specified cause or for any just or good cause indicated by state statute. A local school board wishing to dismiss a teacher for cause has an obligation to prove the teacher's unfitness to discharge his or her duties and responsibilities.

In proposing to dismiss a tenured teacher the board must follow state-prescribed procedures which generally include written notification of the specific charges upon which the proposed dismissal is based, sufficient time for the teacher to prepare a defense against such charges, and the right to a hearing at which the teacher may be represented by legal counsel and witnesses may be cross-examined. Prescribed procedures also provide, generally, for the number of days following notification of dismissal charges within which the teacher may request a hearing, the number of days following the request in which the hearing must begin, and a time limitation regarding the occurrence of past incidents that may be introduced as hearing evidence. The right to court appeal of the hearing officer's verdict also may be indicated. Where dismissal procedures are prescribed, they must be followed precisely.

---

[66] *Sheehan* v. *St. Peter's Catholic School,* 188 N.W. 2d 868 (Minn. 1971).

[67] *Weems* v. *Robbins,* 9 So. 2d 882 (Ala. 1942).

[68] *Sheehan* v. *St. Peter's Catholic School,* 188 N.W. 2d 868 (Minn. 1971).

Causes for which a tenured teacher may be dismissed vary by state. Some of these were cited in the earlier discussion. The most prevalent causes, however, include incompetency,[69] immorality or unprofessional conduct,[70] insubordination,[71] physical or mental illness,[72] designated criminal convictions,[73] or necessary and justifiable reduction in staffing requirements or reduction in force ("riffing").[74] Whether a specific cause for dismissal is specified by state statute or the stipulation for dismissal is any "just or good cause," charges may not be arbitrary or capricious.

Dismissal of Nontenured Teachers

In many states, upon written notification by a specified date, a nontenured or probationary teacher may not be rehired. In some states, reasons for dismissal or nonrenewal of contract must be provided (Illinois, California), or the probationary teacher must request such reasons in writing (Connecticut).

The right of a nontenured teacher to a hearing, if notified of dismissal or the intent not to renew the teaching contract, has been reviewed by the U.S. Supreme Court in two major cases. In ruling on these cases the Supreme Court made clear the scope of liberty and property interests embraced by the Fourteenth Amendment to the U.S. Constitution, which requires procedural due process. The particular language of the Fourteenth Amendment interpreted in these cases is "no state shall . . . deprive any person of life, liberty or property, without due process of law . . ."

In the first case,[75] an assistant professor, David Roth, was hired for one academic year and was informed by his employer, Wisconsin State University-Oshkosh, that he would not be rehired the following year. Roth brought action in federal court arguing that the decision not to rehire him without a stated reason and an opportunity to a hearing denied his Fourteenth Amendment due process rights.

[69] For example, see *Horosko* v. *School District of Mt. Pleasant Township School District,* 335 Pa. 369, 6 A. 2d 866 (1939); *Mims* v. *West Baton Rouge Parish School Board,* 315 So. 2d 349 (La. App. 1975); *Manchester* v. *Lewis,* 507 F. 2d 289 (5th Cir. 1974); *Blunt* v. *Marion County School Board,* 515 F. 2d 951 (5th Cir. 1975).

[70] For example, see *Petitt* v. *State Board of Education,* 10 Cal. App. 3d 29, 109 Cal. Rptr. 665 (1973); *Sarac* v. *State Board of Education,* 57 Cal. Rptr. 69 (1967); *Weissman* v. *Board of Education of Jefferson County School District,* 547 P. 2d 1267 (Colo. 1976); *Watson* v. *State Board of Education,* 99 Cal. Rptr. 468 (Cal. App. 1971).

[71] For example, see *Johnson* v. *United School District,* 191 A. 2d 897 (Pa. 1963); *Tichener* v. *Orleans Parish School Board,* 144 So. 2d 603 (La. 1962); *Gilbertson* v. *McAlister,* 403 F. Supp. 1 (D. Conn. 1975).

[72] For example, see *Alford* v. *Department of Education,* 91 Cal. Rptr. 843 (1971); *Riggins* v. *Board of Education,* 300 P. 2d 848 (Cal. 1956); *Wishart* v. *McDonald,* 500 F. 2d 1110 (1st Cir. 1974).

[73] For example, see *Skripchuk* v. *Austin,* 379 A. 2d 1142 (Del. 1977); *Caravello* v. *Board of Education of Norwich City School District,* 369 N.Y.S. 2d 829 (1975); *Kiner* v. *State Board of Education,* 344 So. 2d 657 (Fla. 1977).

[74] *Tressler* v. *Upper Dublin School District,* 373 A. 2d 755 (Pa. 1977); *Beers* v. *Nyquist,* 338 N.Y.S. 2d 745 (1972); *Smith* v. *Board of Directors of Harmony School District,* 328 A. 2d 883 (Pa. 1974).

[75] *Board of Regents* v. *Roth,* 408 U.S. 564, 92 S. Ct. 2701, 33 L. Ed. 548 (1972).

Roth also argued that the real reason for his dismissal was based on critical statements he had made about the administration of the university. The latter issue was not before the court, however. At issue was whether the university had a right not to rehire a nontenured teacher. In upholding this right of the university not to rehire Roth, the court held that there had been no violation either of Roth's liberty or property interests under the Fourteenth Amendment that would require a due process hearing. The court indicated that

> The state, in declining to rehire the respondent, did not make any charge against him that might seriously damage his standing and associations in his community. It did not base the nonrenewal of his contract on a charge, for example, that he had been guilty of dishonesty, or immorality . . . there is no suggestion whatever that the respondent's interest for his 'good name, reputation, honor or integrity' is at stake.
>
> Similarly, there is no suggestion that the State . . . imposed on him a stigma or other disability that foreclosed his freedom to take advantage of other employment opportunities [Id. at 558–559].

Thus the court held that Roth had not been deprived of a liberty interest when the university did not rehire him.

In addressing the scope of property interests under the Fourteenth Amendment the court stated:

> To have a property interest in a benefit, a person clearly must have more than a unilateral expectation of it. He must, instead, have a legitimate claim of entitlement to it. It is a purpose of the ancient institution of property to protect those claims upon which people rely in their daily lives, reliance that must not be arbitrarily undermined. It is a purpose of the constitutional right to a hearing to provide an opportunity for a person to vindicate those claims [Id. at 561].

Hence, the court likewise found that there was no infringement on Roth's "property" interest. It held that "the respondent surely had an abstract concern in being rehired, but he did not have a property interest sufficient to require the university authorities to give him a hearing when they declined to renew his contract of employment" [Id. at 561].

In the second case, a professor at Odessa Junior College (Texas) who had been employed for four successive years at that college was notified that the yearly contract under which he worked was not to be renewed.[76] He was provided no formal statement of charges upon which his dismissal was based nor an opportunity for a hearing. Charges were filed by the professor in federal court on the basis that his constitutional guarantee of due process under the Fourteenth Amendment had been violated and that his First Amendment rights had been abridged. The professor believed the real reason he was being dismissed was his public criticism of the policies of the administration of the college. While the court reaffirmed its view

---

[76] *Perry* v. *Sindermann*, 408 U.S. 593, 92 S.Ct. 2694, 33 L.Ed. 2d 570 (1972).

that "the nonrenewal of a nontenured public school teacher's one year contract may not be predicated on his exercise of First and Fourteenth Amendment rights," the respondent did not show that the mere nonrenewal of his contract resulted from his exercise of free speech (First Amendment) or a deprivation of liberty or property interests (Fourteenth Amendment). The court did find that the college had a *de facto* tenure system in which the plaintiff had a legitimate claim and a property interest in continued employment. As such, he was entitled to "continued employment absent 'sufficient cause'." The court stated further that "the respondent must be given an opportunity to prove the legitimacy of his claim of such entitlement in light of the 'policies and practices of the institution'" [Id. at 580]. Thus the court held that the professor was entitled to be informed of the specific charges upon which the nonrenewal of his contract was based and a hearing at his request where such charges could be challenged.

RIGHTS OF STUDENTS

The federal and state constitutional rights of students in or out of school are as inviolate as those of any other citizen of the United States. An abundance of court decisions exemplifies the extent to which school policies and procedures must ensure students' constitutional rights. In this section we provide brief discussions in the following areas: freedom of speech; school sanctions—corporal punishment, suspensions, expulsions, grade reductions; searches and seizures; marriage, pregnancy, and motherhood; student records; and equal educational opportunity—school desegregation, student classification and placement, bilingual education, sex discrimination, and handicapped students.

Freedom of Speech

In *Tinker,*[77] the U.S. Supreme Court provides a clear statement regarding the constitutional guarantee of freedom of speech for students. In this case, five students were suspended for wearing black arm bands to protest the war in Vietnam. Upon learning that some of the students planned to wear armbands, principals in the Des Moines, Iowa, schools developed a suspension policy which specified that students wearing armbands were to be sent home and suspended until they returned without them. Three students who were sent home did not return to school until after the period planned for the Vietnam War protest by a concerned group of citizens, which included their parents.

The students' suspensions were legally challenged, and their rights were ultimately upheld by the Supreme Court. In ruling in favor of the plaintiffs, the Supreme Court observed that the students' passive protest involved "direct, primary First Amendment rights akin to 'pure speech'" [Id. at 738]. It noted that only a few of the 18,000 students wore arm bands, that there was no disruption of school

[77] *Tinker* v. *Des Moines Independent Community School District,* 393 U.S. 503 (1969).

classes, and that the rights of other students were not threatened. Thus, the court held that wearing of black arm bands was a fundamental First Amendment right. Students could not, therefore, be denied their right of expression. The court stated:

> In our system, students may not be regarded as closed-circuit recipients of only that which the State chooses to communicate. They may not be confined to the expression of those sentiments that are officially approved. In the absence of a specific showing of constitutionally valid reasons to regulate their speech, students are entitled to freedom of expression of their views [Id. at 740].

In rendering its opinion, the court recognized, however, that there are limits of tolerance regarding free speech. In the words of the court, ". . . conduct by the student in class or out of it, which for any reason—whether it stems from time, place, or type of behavior—materially disrupts classwork or involves substantial disorder or invasion of the rights of others is, of course, not immunized by the constitutional guarantee of freedom of speech" [Id. at 741].

Students also enjoy the right to express themselves freely in student newspapers and publications even though the school may finance the publication and it may be produced off the school's campus. In exercising these rights, school operation must not be disrupted or the rights of others violated.

In *Scoville* v. *Board of Education,*[78] two students were expelled after writing material in a publication critical of school authorities and policies. Although published off campus the publication was sold in school to faculty and students. In reaching its decision, the federal district court found that distribution of the publication "constituted a direct and substantial threat to the effective operation of the high school." Thus, the school board's action in expelling the students was upheld. On appeal the circuit court reversed the opinion of the district court and indicated that "at no time . . . was expulsion of plaintiffs justified on grounds other than objectionable content of the publication" [Id. at 12]. Nor did the appeals court find that the board could have "reasonably forecast that the publication and distribution of this paper to students would substantially disrupt or materially interfere with school procedures." The court held that the grounds upon which the students were expelled was "an unjustified invasion of plaintiff's First and Fourteenth Amendment rights" [Id. at 10].

School Sanctions

Schools have used a variety of negative sanctions against students when their conduct has not conformed to school policy. Among the punishments imposed have been corporal punishment, suspension, expulsion, and grade reduction.

Corporal punishment. Unless specifically prohibited by state statute or state or local school board policy, corporal punishment, if reasonably administered, is

[78] *Scoville* v. *Board of Education of Joliet Township High School District 204,* 425 F. 2d 10 (7th Cir. 1970), cert. denied, 400 U.S. 826 (1970).

a permissible remedy for student misbehavior.[79] Many school districts have adopted a policy wherein corporal punishment must be administered by a school site administrator, for example, the principal, in the presence of an adult witness and with prior parental approval. In the absence of such policy, teachers may administer corporal punishment. Its use, however, has been challenged when considered to be cruel and unusual, an infringement on the proscriptive right of the parent, or a denial of due process. Several cases illuminate the extent to which schools are immune from such challenges.

In *Glaser* v. *Marietta*,[80] the right of the school to use corporal punishment was challenged "on grounds that it constitutes cruel and unusual punishment and . . . it usurps parental rights." In deciding this case the court found that there was no violation of the constitutional rights of the minor plaintiff and that use of corporal punishment is acceptable except when the parent expressly notifies school authorities that it is not to be used. The court stated, however, that

> [i]f a parent is unwilling to grant discretion to the school officials, if he is unwilling to delegate authority to paddle or spank whenever that is indicated, then he must be prepared to take the steps needed to effectively discipline his errant child [Id. at 561].

The court further indicated that the action of the parent must be active and prompt so that the errant behavior of the child does not disrupt the school or infringe upon educational pursuits of other children.

In another case, plaintiffs sought to restrain use of corporal punishment without prior parental permission on grounds that it violated their Eighth and Fourteenth Amendment rights.[81] In this case the plaintiffs charged that use of corporal punishment, without parental approval, denied due process rights of the Fourteenth Amendment and that it "constitutes cruel and unusual punishment in violation of the Eighth Amendment as applied to states through the Fourteenth Amendment" [Id. at 658]. While the court did not judge the wisdom of the school district's corporal punishment policy which gave rise to this case, it held that the policy was not "arbitrary, capricious, unreasonable or wholly unrelated to the competency of the state in determining its educational policy" [Id. at 659]. The court also held that use of corporal punishment in this instance was not cruel or unusual punishment and that the judgment of the school "outweighs any claims based on parental rights" [Id. at 660].

In *Ingraham* v. *Wright*,[82] pupils in Dade County, Florida, charged school officials with violating their Eighth and Fourteenth Amendment rights for two

---

[79] States in which corporal punishment is prohibited by state statute include Massachusetts and New Jersey. It is banned by the state school board in Maryland and by local board policy in New York City.

[80] *Glaser* v. *Marietta*, 351 F. Supp. 555 (W.D. Pa. 1972).

[81] *Ware* v. *Estes*, 328 F. Supp. 657 (N.D. Tex.), aff'd 458 F. 2d 1360 (5th Cir. 1972), cert. denied 409 U.S. 1027.

[82] *Ingraham et al.* v. *Wright et al.*, 430 U.S. 651 (1977).

reasons: (1) an exceptionally harsh paddling they had received; and (2) they were not granted a hearing. In ruling against the plaintiffs the Supreme Court held that the cruel and unusual punishment clause of the Eighth Amendment was intended to protect individuals convicted of crimes, and thus did not extend to use of corporal punishment for disciplinary purposes in public schools. It further held that the Due Process Clause of the Fourteenth Amendment did not require a notice and hearing before corporal punishment could be administered. On this point the Supreme Court cited and upheld the opinion of the lower court that stated ". . . we refuse to set forth, as constitutionally mandated, procedural standards for an activity which is not substantial enough, on a constitutional level, to justify the time and effort which would have to be expended by the school in adhering to these procedures or to justify further interference by federal courts into the internal affairs of public schools."[83]

Corporal punishment also was challenged by a sixth grade student and his mother in North Carolina.[84] Here it was claimed that the student's constitutional rights were violated when he was paddled by his teacher although his mother had explicitly indicated to school officials that she did not wish her son subjected to corporal punishment. It was further claimed that the student's procedural due process rights were violated. On the first point the court held that indeed the rights of parents to control disciplinary practices to be used with their children is encompassed within the liberty interest of the Fourteenth Amendment. Nonetheless, because the state must assume a responsibility for behavior of students in school, the court disallowed "the wishes of a parent to restrict school officials' discretion in deciding the methods to be used in accomplishing the not just legitimate, but essential, purpose of maintaining discipline."[85]

On the second point the court held that minimal procedural due process rights under the Fourteenth Amendment should be accorded students. These rights are: (1) unless "acts of misconduct are so antisocial or disruptive in nature as to shock the conscience," the student must be informed of what behavior will result in corporal punishment; (2) other remedies should be attempted before using corporal punishment; (3) when corporal punishment is administered it must be witnessed by a second school official who is to be informed of the reason the student is being corporally punished in the student's presence and prior to its use; and (4) the parent of the child must be provided, upon request, with a written report containing reasons for corporal punishment and the name of the witness.[86] Thus, procedural due process must now be provided students with respect to the use of corporal punishment.

In *Hall* v. *Tawney*,[87] the court addressed the question of substantive due

[83] *Ingraham et al.* v. *Wright et al.,* 525 F. 2d 909 (1976), [Id. at 919].

[84] *Baker* v. *Owen,* 395 F. Supp. 294 (M.D.N.C. 1975), aff'd 423 U.S. 907, 96 S. Ct. 210, 46 L. Ed. 2d 137 (1975).

[85] *Baker* v. *Owen,* 395 F. Supp. 294 (M.D.N.C. 1975), [Id. at 301].

[86] *Baker* v. *Owen,* 395 F. Supp. 294 (M.D.N.C. 1975), [Id. at 302].

[87] *Hall* v. *Tawney,* 621 F. 2d 607 (4th Cir. 1980).

process rights in cases of cruel and brutal corporal punishment. In rendering its decision the court stated:

> As in the cognate police brutality cases, the substantive due process inquiry in school corporal punishment cases must be whether the force applied caused injury so severe, was so disproportionate to the need presented, and was so inspired by malice or sadism rather than a merely careless or unwise excess of zeal that it amounted to a brutal and inhumane abuse of official power literally shocking to the conscience [Id. at 613].

On the basis of this case, the cruel and unusual punishment clause of the Eighth Amendment, held to be inapplicable to school corporal punishment cases in general,[88] may in certain school cases be grounds for violation of a constitutional right.

Suspension and expulsion. Suspensions and expulsions ostensibly provide a means for punishing students for severe misbehavior or refusal to obey a reasonable school rule. Generally, suspensions are used to exclude students from school for periods of one to ten days while expulsions are used for longer periods. Although suspensions and expulsions may sometimes be necessary disciplinary action, in many schools use of both has been criticized as being ineffective and discriminatory.[89] Nevertheless, such actions are legal. When used, however, due process rights of students must be respected. These rights are clearly specified in *Goss* and in *Wood.*

Goss v. *Lopez*[90] resulted from the suspension of Dwight Lopez and Betty Crome from the Columbus, Ohio, Public School System without a hearing. A sharply divided court held that under the Due Process Clause of the Fourteenth Amendment students had a legitimate property and liberty interest which entitled them to an education. Thus, the court held that "[n]either the property interest in educational benefits temporarily denied nor the liberty interest in reputation, which is also implicated, is so insubstantial that suspensions may constitutionally be imposed by any procedure the school chooses, no matter how arbitrary" [Id. at 736]. The court therefore held that the due process procedures to which schools must adhere for a suspension of ten days or less are as follows: The student must be (1) informed orally or in writing of charges being levied against him or her; (2) given an explanation of the basis upon which these charges are made if they are denied by the student; and (3) be provided an opportunity to present his or her interpretation of the occurrence. In general, notice and hearing must precede actual suspension of the student, and these may immediately follow behavior for which suspension is sought. In those situations in which the student's presence "poses a

---

[88] See *Ingraham* v. *Wright,* 430 U.S. 651 (1977).

[89] A penetrating and comprehensive study reveals that minority youth, in particular Black and Hispanic youth, are suspended and expelled from school at alarmingly high rates and that many such suspensions are unnecessary. See *School Suspensions. Are They Helping Children?* A Report by the Children's Defense Fund of the Washington Research Project, Inc. (Cambridge, Mass.: Children's Defense Fund, 1975).

[90] *Goss* v. *Lopez,* 419 U.S. 565, 95 S.Ct. 729, 42 L.Ed. 2d 725 (1975).

continuing danger to persons or property or an ongoing threat of disrupting the academic process," the student may be removed from school immediately, without notice or hearing [Id. at 739]. In these instances, notice and hearing should follow as quickly as possible.

The matter of school expulsion, due process requirements, and a related issue pertaining to liability of school board members in depriving students of constitutional rights is addressed in *Wood* v. *Strickland*.[91] In this Arkansas case, three sixteen-year-old tenth grade students were expelled for approximately three months for "spiking" punch served at a school meeting attended by parents and students. The court held that students' due process rights had been violated and that school board members were not immune from liability for compensating damages under the Civil Rights Act of 1871, 42 U.S.C. sec. 1983.

Reduction in grades. As a further sanction against students, some schools have lowered grades when a pupil has been suspended from school. This practice is essentially an additional punishment and has been judged illegal.[92]

Searches and seizures. If school officials have reason to believe that students have in their possession, either in a school locker or concealed in their clothing, illegal objects or materials, then searches are permissible. Searches of students have been frequently challenged on grounds that they infringe upon Fourth Amendment rights to be secure against unreasonable searches and seizures. In general, courts have sought to balance Fourth Amendment rights of students against the school's need to maintain discipline and order. Courts also have held that since school officials stand *in loco parentis,* they have the right to exercise supervision and control over students as well as an obligation to protect them while they are entrusted to the school.

In *People* v. *Overton*,[93] the court ruled that a locker search authorized by a school official and conducted without a search warrant was legal. In this case, the vice-principal, accompanied by a detective, school custodian, and the student, opened the student's locker after it had been determined that the locker contained marijuana. The court held that the school not only had the right to inspect a student's locker but also "that right becomes a duty when suspicion arises that something of an illegal nature may be secreted there" [Id. at 480].

In another case,[94] a student reported to school officials that someone identified only as wearing a corduroy coat with a fur collar had taken his wristwatch. The uniformed service officer to whom this complaint was eventually transmitted saw a student wearing the type of coat indicated in the report and asked the student into the dean's office. There the student was requested to show his wrist watch. It was not the one stolen. Noticing a bulge with a brown envelope protrud-

[91] *Wood et al.* v. *Strickland et al.,* 420 U.S. 308 (1975).
[92] *Dorsey* v. *Bale,* 521 S.W. 2d 75 (Ky. Ct. of App. 1975).
[93] *People* v. *Overton,* 24 N.Y. 2d 522, 301 N.Y.S. 2d 479, 249 N.E. 2d 366 (1969).
[94] *People* v. *Bowers,* 72 Misc. 2d 800, 339 N.Y.S. 2d 783 (1973).

ing from the top pocket of the student's dungarees, the dean asked the student to empty his pockets. A survey of the contents of his pockets revealed that the student possessed marijuana. He was then arrested. In a court action, the student charged that the seizure was illegal and sought to have the evidence suppressed. The court noted that there was nothing to indicate that the student possessed marijuana when he was stopped and invited into the dean's office. Thus, the court held that the seizure was unlawful and granted the motion to suppress the evidence. The court stated that "[t]his case involved neither probable cause for a lawful arrest nor consent nor abandonment nor exigent circumstances" [Id. at 787].

In a far-reaching decision, the United States Supreme Court overturned a decision of the New Jersey Supreme Court and held that school officials have the right to conduct student searches depending on the reasonableness of the search. The Court noted that a search of a student is justified "where there are reasonable grounds for suspecting that the search will turn up evidence that the student has violated or is violating either the law or the rules of the school." Continuing, the Court indicated ". . . such a search will be permissible in its scope when the measures adopted are reasonably related to the objectives of the search and not excessively intrusive in light of the student's age and sex and the nature of the infraction." While the Court noted that the Fourth Amendment prohibits unreasonable searches and seizures, it ruled that "striking the balance between school children's legitimate expectations of privacy and the school's equally legitimate need to maintain an environment in which learning can take place requires some easing of the restrictions to which searches by public authorities are ordinarily subject." Thus, "school officials need not obtain a warrant before searching a student who is under their authority. Moreover, school officials need not be held subject to the requirement that searches be based on probable cause to believe that the subject of the search has violated or is violating the law. Rather, the legality of a search of a student should depend simply on the reasonableness, under all circumstances, of the search."[95]

The action that precipitated this ruling involved a juvenile girl who was caught smoking with another student in the girls' lavatory of a New Jersey high school. A teacher who witnessed this event escorted the girls to the vice-principal's office and accused them of breaking the school's no-smoking rule. The vice-principal asked one girl, T.L.O., if she had been smoking. She denied doing so. The vice-principal then demanded to see her purse and upon opening it found a package of cigarettes and other paraphernalia thought to be associated with drugs. Upon further examination, the assistant vice-principal found marijuana, a pipe, plastic bags, $40.98 in money, a list of names of students who owed T.L.O. money, and two letters implicating her in selling marijuana. She was suspended from school three days for smoking and seven days for possession of marijuana. T.L.O. appealed for reinstatement in school and sought to have the evidence suppressed. At the initial hearing in 1980, the judge found that the search conducted by the vice-principal

---

[95] *New Jersey* v. *T.L.O.*, No. 83-712, 53 USLW 4083 (January 15, 1985).

violated Fourth Amendment guarantees. The case then moved to the New Jersey Juvenile and Domestic Relations Court, Middlesex County, New Jersey (N.J., 428 A. 2d 1327). Here the court ruled that the search was justified and did not violate the Fourth Amendment's prohibitions against illegal searches and seizures. It further adjudged T.L.O. to be a delinquent and placed her on a one-year probation. The Appellate Division of the New Jersey Superior Court in 1982 upheld the trial court's decision regarding the Fourth Amendment but vacated the adjudication of delinquency (N.J. Super. A.D., 448 A. 2d 493). The New Jersey Supreme Court, 463 A. 2d 934 (N.J. 1983) reversed the Superior Court decision and held that the search was unreasonable. As indicated earlier, the U.S. Supreme Court in *New Jersey* v. *T.L.O.* overturned that ruling and held the search to be reasonable and not in violation of the Fourth Amendment.

Body searches of students have not been viewed favorably by courts. For example, a strip search of a student suspected of carrying drugs was found by the court to be unreasonable. In this case,[96] the court held that

> . . . although the necessities for a public school search may be greater than for one outside the school, the psychological damage that would be risked on sensitive children by random search insufficiently justified by necessities is not tolerable. And it must also be emphasized that the scope of permissible search and, for that matter, the scope of undue risk of psychological harm will vary significantly with the age and mental development of the child [Id. at 490].

Marriage, Pregnancy, and Motherhood

Students who are married enjoy the same right to an education as do other students.[97] They may, however, be temporarily excluded from school following marriage. The period of exclusion varies in length but is generally less than one year. A court of appeals in Kentucky invalidated a school regulation that required any student who married to withdraw from school one full year and then to be readmitted only as a special student with permission from the principal.[98] The school board adopted this rule, contending that the period immediately preceding and proceeding the marriage caused much discussion among students and was disruptive of the school's environment. The regulation was enacted to avoid disruption. In practice, the regulation had not been applied with exactitude—students were permitted to remain in school for six weeks following marriage. The court held that the regulation was inconsistent with its intent and was thus arbitrary and unreasonable.

In contrast, a Tennessee school district implemented a school regulation that required students who married to be expelled for the remainder of the school term. Those who married during the summer could return to school the term immediately

---

[96] *People* v. *Scott D.*, 34 N.Y. 2d 483 (1974). See also, *M.M.* v. *Anker*, 607 F. 2d 588 (2d Cir. 1979).

[97] *McLeod Trustees Moss Point Public School* v. *State*, 122 So. 737 (Miss. 1929); *Bell* v. *Lone Oak Independent School District*, 507 S.W. 2d 636 (Tex. 1974).

[98] *Board of Education of Harrodsburg* v. *Bentley*, 383 S.W. 2d 677 (1964).

following. The school held that the period of time immediately after a marriage was disruptive because of the excitement and discussion it caused among students. The court found the school regulation to be reasonable and it was thus upheld when legally challenged.[99]

In several school districts, policies have been implemented prohibiting married students from participating in extracurricular school activities. Prior to 1972, courts upheld this sort of regulation and supported school officials' argument that such policy served as a deterrent to teenage marriage and school dropouts.[100] Since 1972, school regulations barring participation of married students in extracurricular activities have been found to be invalid.[101] In *Holt v. Shelton,* the court held such a prohibition to be an infringement upon the right to an education and upon the due process and equal protection of the law.[102]

The right of pregnant students or those who have already given birth to receive an education is undisputed. Whether a pregnant high school student or one with a child may be excluded from attending school, however, has been at issue as well as the subject of litigation.

In *State v. Chamberlain,*[103] the court upheld a school policy that required pregnant students to withdraw from school. In such instances the students continued academic work by receiving assignments and examinations from teachers at home. They were given full academic credit toward graduation requirements. In reaching its decision the court found that school regulations were intended to protect the health of the pregnant student and were not punitive. Consequently, the regulation was "neither unreasonable, arbitrary, nor contrary to law."

An opposite conclusion was reached in the case of an eighteen-year-old pregnant, unmarried student when the school policy to exclude such students was challenged.[104] The court held this policy to be invalid. Here the court noted that the challenged policy was directed at unwed pregnant students since married pregnant students were permitted to attend school. It is instructive to note the following summary statement of the court:

> . . . no danger to petitioner's physical or mental health resultant from her attending classes during regular school hours has been shown; no likelihood that her presence will cause any disruption of or interference with school activities or pose a threat or harm to others has been shown; and no valid educational

[99] *State v. Marion County Board of Education,* 302 S.W. 2d 57 (Tenn. 1957).

[100] For example, see *Kissick v. Garland Independent School District,* 330 S.W. 2d 708 (1959); *State Ex Rel. Baker v. Stevenson,* 189 N.E. 2d 181 (1962); *Starkey v. Board of Education of Davis County School District,* 381 P. 2d 718 (Utah 1963); *School District of Waterloo v. Green,* 259 Iowa 1260, 147 N.W. 2d 854 (1967).

[101] See *Moran v. School District #7, Yellowstone County,* 350 F. Supp. 1180 (Montana 1972); *Bell v. Lone Oak Independent School District,* 507 S.W. 2d 636 (Tex. 1974); *Hollon v. Mathis Independent School District,* 491 F. 2d 92 (5th Cir. 1974); *Indiana High School Athletic Association v. Raike,* 329 N.E. 2d 66 (Ind. 1975).

[102] *Holt v. Shelton,* 341 F. Supp. 821 (Tenn. 1972).

[103] *State v. Chamberlain,* 12 Ohio Misc. 44, 175 N.E. 2d 539 (1961).

[104] *Ordway v. Hargraves,* 323 F. Supp. 1155 (1971).

or other reason to justify her segregation and to require her to receive a type of education treatment which is not the equal of that given to all others in her class has been shown [Id. at 1158].

Efforts to exclude unmarried mothers from regular school attendance also have been invalidated upon legal challenge. This is evidenced in *Perry* v. *Grenada.*[105] While the court held that unwed mothers may not be excluded from school attendance, it indicated that such students could be denied the right of school attendance if after a fair hearing for readmission they were "found to be lacking in moral character or that their presence in schools will taint the education of other students" [Id. at 748].

Student Records

Information about students contained in school records is subject to statutory regulations prescribed by the Family Educational Rights and Privacy Act of 1974 (also known as the Buckley Amendment, after former Senator James Buckley of New York, its leading sponsor).[106] The Buckley Amendment provides procedural regulations which, if not followed by educational institutions, constitute a basis for discontinuing federal funding. The Amendment's fundamental purposes are to curtail dissemination of information about students to third parties without consent; to provide parental, and under certain conditions, student access to school records; to specify procedures for challenging school-maintained information about students; and to require schools to institute and publicize a policy whereby parents can see their children's school records.

Students' records may be released without consent (1) to other school officials and teachers who have legitimate educational interests; (2) to schools which the student seeks to transfer, provided the parent is notified and a copy of the record is made available upon request, and provided the parent is given an opportunity for a hearing to question the accuracy of the record; (3) to authorized federal and state officials who may need the records for audit or evaluation purposes, provided the identity of students and their parents will be kept confidential and the records will be destroyed when no longer needed; (4) to institutions in conjunction with an application for financial aid; (5) to organizations conducting studies pertaining to predictive tests, improving instruction, and administering student aid programs, provided the data will be treated in a confidential manner and destroyed when the studies have been completed; (6) to accrediting organizations for purposes of accreditation; (7) to parents of dependent students; (8) to individuals who may need the information for the health or safety of the student or others; and

---

[105] *Perry* v. *Grenada Municipal Separate School District,* 300 F. Supp. 748 (1969).

[106] The Family Educational Rights and Privacy Act of 1974, 20 U.S.C. Sec. 1232 g. The federal regulations pertaining to this act also should be carefully reviewed. See Regulations for the Family Educational Rights and Privacy Act of 1974, Subtitle A–Department of Health, Education, and Welfare, Parts 99–99.67.

(9) to comply with a judicial order or subpoena, provided the parent and the student are notified prior to releasing the records.

Parents or eligible students may waive any rights they have to information access by signing a written waiver. Waivers can be made known to parents and eligible students but this is not required. When rights are not waived, access to educational records as permitted must be granted upon request within a reasonable period of time but within forty-five days.

Educational agencies or institutions must inform parents and eligible students of their rights under this Act and must maintain a record of individuals, agencies, or organizations requesting and obtaining access to the student's record as well as a record of the legitimate interests of such agencies and organizations in this regard.

Equal Educational Opportunity

In the words of the U.S. Supreme Court, "[i]n these days, it is doubtful that any child may reasonably be expected to succeed in life if he is denied the opportunity of an education. Such an opportunity, where the state has undertaken to provide it, is a right which must be made available to all on equal terms."[107] It follows, then, that wherever barriers exist to the full accord of equal educational opportunity they should be removed. The removal of such barriers has precipitated a wide spectrum of litigation. Considerable progress has been made, but the goal of full equality of educational opportunity has not been met completely. In this section we discuss equality of educational opportunity in these areas: school desegregation, student classification, bilingual education, sex discrimination, and handicapped students.

School desegregation. It has been clearly established that school segregation on the basis of race is unconstitutional. In the landmark case of *Brown* v. *Board of Education*,[108] the Supreme Court held that segregated school systems denied minority students equal protection under the law guaranteed by the Fourteenth Amendment. In another case, heard on the same day as *Brown*, in which the validity of segregated schools in Washington, D.C. was challenged, the Court held that school racial segregation in that city constituted a denial of due process law under the Fifth Amendment.[109] Racial discrimination perpetuated by dual segregated school systems was thus rendered unconstitutional on the basis of the Equal Protection Clause of the Fourteenth Amendment and the Due Process Provision of the Fifth Amendment.

Because of the unconstitutionality of segregated school systems, the Supreme

[107] *Brown* v. *Board of Education of Topeka (Brown I)*, 347 U.S. 483, 74 S. Ct. 686, 98 L. Ed. 873 (1954), [Id. at 880].

[108] *Brown* v. *Board of Education of Topeka (Brown I)*, 347 U.S. 483, 74 S. Ct. 686, 98 L. Ed. 873 (1954), [Id. at 880].

[109] *Bolling* v. *Sharpe*, 347 U.S. 497, 74 S. Ct. 693, 98 L. Ed. 884 (1954).

Court mandated that they be dismantled "with all deliberate speed."[110] The reluctance of some districts to desegregate their schools in compliance with this mandate, expressed in *Brown II (1955)*, led the Supreme Court in 1969, fourteen years later, to hold that "the obligation of every school district is to terminate dual school systems at once and to operate now and hereafter only unitary schools."[111]

A variety of tactics have been used to delay school desegregation. These have included abolition of the public school system,[112] selling school buildings which would then be used as private, all-white academies,[113] educating white children in the city's school system and contracting with an outside district to educate black students,[114] freedom-of-choice plans,[115] and manipulation of school attendance zones.[116] Each of these actions, and others similar in nature, have been declared illegal or inadequate by the courts.

A number of permissible remedies to segregated schools can be noted: transportation of students or busing to achieve desegregation, remedial altering of school attendance zones, and optional majority-to-minority school transfer arrangements,[117] desegregation of faculty and other school staff,[118] school pairing and magnet schools,[119] compensatory or remedial programs for students who have been previously subjected to *de jure* segregation, and in-service training for school staff.[120]

Many large urban areas have substantial enrollments of minority students. However, segregated residential housing patterns restrict the ability of school districts in these areas to desegregate effectively. To address this problem, Detroit proposed an interdistrict or metropolitan solution in which the school district

[110] *Brown* v. *Board of Education (Brown II)*, 349 U.S. 294, 75 S. Ct. 753, L. Ed. 1083 (1955), [Id. at 1106].

[111] *Alexander* v. *Holmes County Board of Education*, 396 U.S. 19 [Id. at 20], 90 S. Ct. 29, 24 L. Ed. 2d 19, reh. den. 396 U.S. 976, 90 S. Ct. 437, 24 L. Ed. 2d 447 (1969).

[112] *Griffin* v. *County School Board of Prince Edward County*, 377 U.S. 218, 84 S. Ct. 1226, 12 L. Ed. 2d 256 (Va. 1964).

[113] *Wright* v. *City of Brighton*, 441 F. 2d 447 (5th Cir. 1971).

[114] *Goins* v. *County School Board*, 186 F. Supp. 753 (Va. 1960).

[115] *Green* v. *County School Board of New Kent County*, 391 U.S. 430, 88 S. Ct. 1689, 20 L. Ed. 2d 716 (1968).

[116] *Keyes* v. *School District No. 1, Denver, Colorado*, 413 U.S. 189, 93 S. Ct. 2686, 37 L. Ed. 2d 548 (1973).

[117] *Swann* v. *Charlotte-Mecklenburg Board of Education*, 402 U.S. 1, 91 S. Ct. 1267, 28 L. Ed. 2d 554 (1971).

[118] *Singleton* v. *Jackson Municipal Separate School District*, 419 F. 2d 1211 (5th Cir.), cert. den. 402 U.S. 944, 91 S. Ct. 1611, 29 L. Ed. 2d 112 (1970).

[119] *Northcross* v. *Board of Education*, 466 F. 2d 890 (6th Cir. 1972). Although the Supreme Court ruled that the Court of Appeals for the Sixth Circuit exceeded its power in prescribing a systemwide remedy broader in scope than that authorized by the District Court, remedies referred to in this instance had been implemented with no apparent problem. See *Dayton Board of Education* v. *Brinkman*, 433 U.S. 406, 97 S. Ct. 2766, 53 L. Ed. 851 (1977).

[120] *Milliken* v. *Bradley (Milliken II)*, 433 U.S. 267, 97 S. Ct. 2749, 53 L. Ed. 2d 745 (1977). In this case, the Supreme Court held that the state of Michigan should pay one-half the cost of the remedial and in-service training programs the local school district (Detroit) wished to implement.

would transport its minority students to suburban school districts. In ruling on the validity of the plan, the majority opinion of a sharply divided Supreme Court (5-4) held that the approval of this remedy would "impose on the outlying districts, not shown to have committed any constitutional violation, a wholly impermissible remedy based on a standard not hinted at in *Brown I and II* or any holding of the Court. . . ."[121] This opinion notwithstanding, it is evident that in many urban centers effective desegregation based on pupil assignment cannot be achieved without some form of interdistrict solution. In 1983, the St. Louis school district and several surrounding suburban districts implemented such a metropolitan desegregation remedy.[122]

Student classification and assignment. Classification of students on the basis of test scores, ostensibly for the purpose of providing learning or educational activities at an appropriate level, is a questionable practice.[123] One negative effect of this practice is to restrict students' life-chances.[124] Thus, classification procedures demand careful application and continuing educational, parental, and judicial scrutiny.[125] This is not to deny that some students have special needs that can best be met in separate classes. For example, students with severe brain damage or who are autistic should receive special assistance. Many students, however, because of I.Q. scores, are incorrectly labeled EMR (Educable Mentally Retarded) and assigned to special education classes or are assigned to nonacademic ability groups or tracks. Deleterious effects of such practices are increasingly apparent, and several court decisions have questioned placement procedures.[126]

[121] *Milliken* v. *Bradley (Milliken I)*, 418 U.S. 717, 94 S. Ct. 3112, 41 L. Ed. 2d 1069 (1974), [Id. at 1091–1092].

[122] *Lidell, et al.* v. *Board of Education of the City of St. Louis, State of Missouri, et al.*, 567 F. Supp. 1037 (1983).

[123] For example, see Jerome Kagan, "The IQ Puzzle: What Are We Measuring?" in *Inequality in Education*, no. 14 (July 1973), 5–13; also, Kirby A. Heller, Wayne H. Holtzman, and Samuel Messick, eds., *Placing Children in Special Education: A Strategy for Equity* (Washington, D.C.: National Academy Press, 1982), pp. 53–58; 230–61.

[124] Kirby A. Heller, Wayne H. Holtzman, and Samuel Messick, eds., *Placing Children in Special Education: A Strategy for Equity* (Washington, D.C.: National Academy Press, 1982), pp. 53–58; 230–61.

[125] Kirp suggests that, among other constitutional remedies to present classification practices, students and their parents be afforded due process rights to protect against misclassification. See David L. Kirp, "Student Classification, a Public Policy, and the Courts," 44, 1 *Harvard Educational Review* (February 1974), 7–50.

[126] The Federal District Court invalidated California's system of classification of black children for EMR classes in 1975. The classification system used relied on various intelligence tests. In reaching its decision the court noted the disproportionate placement of black children in EMR classes (black children represented 25 percent of the population in these classes) and considered the testimony of experts regarding use of I.Q. tests. See *Larry P.* v. *Wilson Riles*, No. C-71-2270 RFP (Oct. 1979). In another similar case, an Illinois District Court, after analyzing each test item for cultural test bias against black students, found all but a few of the items on the Stanford-Binet and WISC-R intelligence tests to be valid for use in educational placement by the Chicago Public Schools. See *Parents in Action on Special Education* v. *Hannon*, No. 74-C-3586 (N.D. Ill. 1980).

Perhaps the most far-reaching judicial opinion regarding student classification is that rendered in *Hobson* v. *Hansen.*[127] Plaintiffs charged that the Washington, D.C., public school tracking system had become "a system of discrimination founded on socioeconomic and racial status rather than ability, resulting in the undereducation of many district students" [Id. at 512]. Through use of achievement and scholastic aptitude tests, students were assigned to one of four tracks: (1) honors—gifted; (2) regular—college preparatory; (3) general—average and students planning to work after high school; or (4) basic or special academic—slow learners, retarded.

Implicit in the use of this or any other tracking scheme is the view that an accurate assessment or measurement of student ability can be made. Such an assessment, reasoned the court, relied on tests which were incapable of predicting educational potential accurately. For a number of reasons—environmental, psychological, socioeconomic, racial—a majority of poor and minority students did not perform well on tests and were placed in lower tracks. The court concluded that the tracking system, rather than classifying students by their ability to learn, classified them according to socioeconomic or racial status or, more precisely, according to environmental and psychological factors that had nothing to do with innate ability. The court stated: "Considering the tests used to determine which children should receive the blue-collar special, and which the white, the danger of children completing their education wearing the wrong collar is far too great for this democracy to tolerate" [Id. at 515]. Thus, the court held that the system used in Washington, D.C., violated the equal protection (Fourteenth Amendment) and due process rights (Fifth Amendment) of the poor and a majority of the districts' black students and deprived them of equal educational opportunities.

Bilingual education. Students whose primary language is not English may be at a disadvantage in schools in which instruction is in English. Hence, courts have held that such students have a right to receive appropriate assistance. In *Lau* v. *Nichols,*[128] the Supreme Court reversed district and appeals court decisions and held that "students who do not understand English are effectively foreclosed from any meaningful education" [Id. at 4]. As a consequence, based on section 601 of the Civil Rights Act of 1964, the Court held that the San Francisco public schools had to provide a solution for the non-English-speaking Chinese students who brought suit against the district.

In a related case, Hispanic students legally challenged their school district for failing to provide opportunities to satisfy their educational and social needs, thus denying them equal educational opportunity.[129] The court held that in this district the constitutional right to equal protection was denied Hispanic students. Consequently, the district was instructed to provide specialized programs and Spanish-speaking teachers to address plaintiff students' needs.

---

[127]*Hobson* v. *Hansen,* 269 F. Supp. 401 (D.D. Cir. 1967), aff'd in part and appeal dismissed in part, sub nom *Smuck* v. *Hobson,* 408 F. 2d 175 (D.C. Cir. 1969).

[128]*Lau* v. *Nichols,* 414 U.S. 563, 94 S. Ct. 786, 39 L. Ed. 2d 1 (1974).

[129]*Serna* v. *Portales Municipal Schools,* 351 F. Supp. 1279 (D.N.M. 1972).

Sexual discrimination. Historically, female students have been prevented from participating on boys' athletic teams and provided unequal opportunity to engage in other organized, competitive sports. With the advent of Title IX of the Education Amendments of 1972, schools receiving federal funds must now make provisions for inclusion of females in all educational programs or activities. In the language of Title IX, "no person in the United States shall, on the basis of sex, be excluded from participation in, be denied the benefits of, or be subjected to discrimination under any education program or activity receiving Federal financial assistance. . . ."[130] While the intent of Title IX is clear, several court cases challenging sexual discrimination have instead been argued on the basis of the Fourteenth Amendment.

In Minnesota two students challenged a policy which barred females from participating with males in high school interscholastic athletics, specifically, the noncontact sports of tennis, cross-country skiing, and cross-country running. Teams for these events were provided for male students but not for females. In deciding this case, the court ruled that denial of the right to participate was discriminatory and an infringement of the Equal Protection Clause of the Fourteenth Amendment.[131] Participation of females with males in noncontact sports where there are no teams available for females is generally permissible.[132] In some cases, however, prohibition of females participating with males in contact sports—for example, soccer—also has been found in violation of the Equal Protection Clause of the Fourteenth Amendment.[133]

The intent of the law is to prohibit arbitrary or unreasonable discrimination on the basis of sex in all school-related activities, including allocation of funds for various athletic activities. Courts have been particularly sensitive to situations in which athletic teams exist for boys but not for girls. Where separate school athletic teams in the same activity exist for boys and girls, courts have not found such arrangements to be impermissible.[134]

At another level, sexual discrimination regarding use of separate examination scores for boys and girls in determining school admission was the impetus for the legal challenge in *Bray* v. *Lee*.[135] In this case, which originated in Boston schools, higher examination scores were required of girls for entry into the Girls Latin School than for boys for entry into the Boys Latin School. Ruling in favor of the plaintiffs, the court held that "the use of separate and different standards to evaluate the examination results to determine the admissibility of boys and girls to the Boston Latin School constitutes a violation of the Equal Protection Clause of the

---

[130] 20 U.S.C. sec. 1681—Educational Amendments of 1972, Title IX, Sec. 901.

[131] *Brenden* v. *Independent School District 742,* 477 F. 2d 1292 (8th Cir. 1973).

[132] In addition to *Brenden*, see *Lee* v. *Florida H.S. Activities Association,* 291 So. 2d 636 (Fla. 1974); *Gilpin* v. *Kansas State High School Activities Association, Inc.,* 377 F. Supp. 1233 (Kan. 1974).

[133] *Hoover* v. *Meiklejohn,* 430 F. Supp. 164 (D. Colo. 1977).

[134] *Bucha* v. *Illinois High School Association,* 351 F. Supp. 69 (N.D. Ill. 1972).

[135] *Bray* v. *Lee,* 337 F. Supp. 934 (D. Mass. 1972).

Fourteenth Amendment, the plain effect of which is to prohibit prejudicial disparities before the law."[136]

At yet another level, schools which discriminate on the basis of sex have been held to be in violation of the law if the purpose was for segregation.[137] On the other hand, separate, single-sex high schools where attendance at either of the two was voluntary and which were equal in size, academic quality, and prestige have been upheld as being a reasonable arrangement for academically talented boys and girls.[138] In principle, therefore, the court has held that "a legitimate educational policy may be served by utilizing single-sex high schools."[139]

Handicapped students. Recognizing educational inequities experienced by handicapped students or, more appropriately, children with special needs, federal legislation now prohibits discrimination against the handicapped student. Using the principle of equal educational opportunity as expressed in *Brown,*[140] Congress enacted two pieces of legislation guaranteeing and reinforcing rights of the handicapped.

The first is the Education for All Handicapped Children Act, Public Law 94-142.[141] This act includes the following provisions for handicapped students:

1. free appropriate education
2. protection of their rights and those of their parents or guardian
3. assistance to states and localities in providing for their education
4. assessment and assurance that the educational efforts used are effective

Public Law 94-142 also mandates that an individualized educational program (IEP) be prepared for each handicapped student. In preparing this program a representative of the local or intermediate education agency, teacher or teachers of the handicapped student, parents or guardian of the student, and the child, if appropriate, are to be involved. Should parents or the guardian disagree with the educational placement of the handicapped child, they may require a hearing in accord with their due process rights.[142]

Public Law 94-142 further specifies that handicapped children be educated with nonhandicapped children "to the maximum extent appropriate," thus adhering to the principle of the least restrictive educational environment. Additionally, tests, materials, or methods used to evaluate special needs of the student must be nondiscriminatory.

A second legislative act designed to ensure handicapped rights is the Rehabili-

---

[136] *Bray* v. *Lee,* 337 F. Supp. 934 (D. Mass. 1972), [Id. at 937].

[137] *U.S.* v. *Hines County,* 560 F. 2d 619 (5th Cir. 1977).

[138] *Vorchheimer* v. *School District of Philadelphia,* 532 F. 2d 880 (3rd Cir. 1976), aff'd 430 U.S. 703 (1977).

[139] *Vorchheimer* v. *School District of Philadelphia,* 532 F. 2d 880 (3rd Cir. 1976), aff'd 430 U.S. 703 (1977), [Id. at 896].

[140] *Brown* v. *Board of Education of Topeka,* 347 U.S. 483 (1954).

[141] 20 U.S.C. Sec. 1401 *et seq.*

[142] See HEW Regulations, 41 *Federal Register* 56965 (December 30, 1976).

tation Act of 1973 (**PL 93-112**), section 504.[143] The Act stipulates that "[n]o otherwise qualified handicapped individual in the United States . . . shall, solely by reason of his handicap, be excluded from the participation in, be denied the benefits of, or be subjected to discrimination under any program or activity receiving Federal financial assistance." In addition to reinforcing educational provisions of PL 94-142, this act provides for nondiscrimination in employment and removal of physical or architectural barriers impeding access to buildings and facilities used by the handicapped.

SUMMARY

The Constitution of the United States, while not specifically mentioning education, guarantees the personal rights of all citizens. The Supreme Court has emphasized that neither teachers nor students leave their constitutional rights at the schoolhouse gate. School leaders must be aware of the legality of policies and procedures, enacted or contemplated, that affect teachers or students. This chapter has provided an overview of the legal implications of selected school issues. Court cases and federal legislation have been cited and summarized to illustrate legal protection for school staff and students.

The judicial system in which issues of law are interpreted consists of both federal and state courts. Both systems contain trial and appellate courts. At the state level, trial, appeals, and superior courts form a tripartite system. District and appeals courts, designated by geographic territory, and the Supreme Court form the basic structure of the federal system. The highest court in the nation is the U.S. Supreme Court. Its decisions are binding on all other courts and become the law of the land.

SELECTED READINGS

Fellman, David., ed., *The Supreme Court and Education* (3rd ed.). New York: Teachers' College Press, 1976.

Fischer, Lewis, David Schimmel, Cynthia Kelly, *Teachers and the Law.* New York: Longman, 1981.

LaMorte, Michael, *School Law: Cases and Concepts.* Englewood Cliffs, N.J.: Prentice-Hall, 1982.

Levine, Alan H., *The Rights of Students.* New York: Avon, 1977.

Morris, Arval A., *The Constitution and American Education.* American Casebook Series. St. Paul, Minn.: West Publishing Co., 1974.

Peterson, Leroy J., Richard A. Rossmiller, and Marlin M. Volz, *The Law and Public School Operation* (2nd ed.). New York: Harper & Row, Publishers, Inc., 1978.

Sorgen, Michael S., Patrick S. Duffy, William A. Kaplin, and Ephraim Margolin, *State, School and Family: Cases and Materials on Law and Education* (2nd ed.). New York: Matthew Bender, 1979.

---

[143] 29 U.S.C. 794 *et seq.* See also Federal Regulations, 42 *Federal Register* 22676 (May 4, 1977).

THE ORGANIZATIONAL NATURE OF SCHOOLS

chapter 7

American elementary and secondary school systems evolved from rather simple beginnings more than two hundred years ago. Today they encompass a complex range of small to large school districts throughout the nation. In some ways schools resemble other complex organizations—corporations, for instance. However, because of their governance structure, relationships to their environment, and staff and student internal interaction patterns, they are organizationally unique. This chapter, therefore, attempts to provide insight into the complicated organizational nature of schools and suggests implications for school management and policy implementation.

We first explain the organizational structure of schools, and follow with a discussion of major themes of organizational theory that are relevant for schools. Next, the formal organizational structure of schools is described. Schools as a loosely coupled or selective linkage system are next discussed. Following a brief description of the informal structure of schools, the chapter concludes with an analysis of educators as professionals and bureaucrats within the organizational structure of schools.

THE ORGANIZATIONAL STRUCTURE OF SCHOOLS

State Public School Systems

As discussed earlier (see Chapter Two), the establishment and operation of schools are legitimized by state statute. Except for Hawaii, which has a state operated educational system, all U.S. public educational systems are state regulated and supported, but locally operated. Administration and operation of school systems occur through a multilayered organizational system consisting of state, intermediate, and local boards, and state departments of education. A basic framework for initially viewing the public school system is displayed in Figure 2.1 of Chapter Two.

What Figure 2.1 depicts is the state's ultimate authority over school operation. Local school boards, however, have the responsibility of operating local public school districts as an arm of state government consistent with state and federal law.

Local Public School Organization[1]

In many respects, the basic organizational structure of local school systems (see Figure 7.1) reflects a hierarchical arrangement in which: (1) there is a relatively clear separation of authority relationships; (2) there is a fixed division of labor;

Figure 7.1   Basic Organizational Structure of Local School Systems.

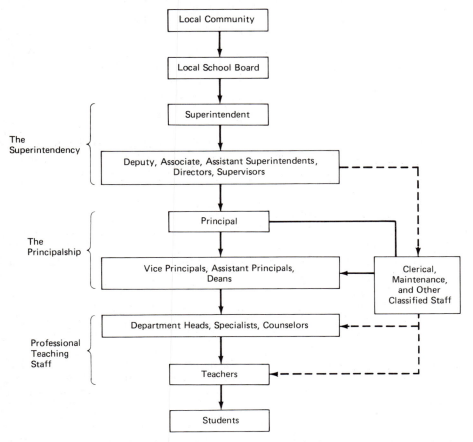

[1] We provide a more extensive discussion of local school educational systems in Chapter Two.

(3) professional personnel are selected on the basis of technical knowledge; (4) there are implicit rules governing performance; and (5) personnel are separated from official property or the ownership of the means of production. Taken together, these characteristics define schools as a bureaucratic structure. In reality, however, the authority relationships suggested by this hierarchical depiction are not so precise.[2]

The organization of schools, not unlike that of other organizations, reflects an implicit desire to facilitate control, coordination, and organizational effectiveness. Historically, the pyramidal structure characteristic of most school systems has been influenced by at least three fundamental schools of thought: (1) classical; (2) human relations; and (3) open systems.[3] These viewpoints are discussed below since they contribute to our understanding of influences on the school's organizational structure and on effective school management.

Classical Theory of Organization

The conceptual base for the classical or rational school of organizations and administrative thought is provided in substantial measure by Max Weber. His theory of "bureaucracy" as a rational administrative system for the effective management of complex organizations has had a profound effect on organizational theory. A second major force on the rational approach to organizational effectiveness is Frederick Taylor, who postulated that organizational productivity could be increased through use of "time and motion" studies and by providing economic incentives for workers. We briefly discuss their contributions below.

Bureaucracy. As defined by Weber, bureaucracy refers to an ideal design for organizational effectiveness.[4] The "bureaucracy" is a rational system of organizing human means to accomplish specific ends. Its underlying structural principles include

Explicit rules and regulations.

Spheres of competence allowing for a clear division of labor and selection of office holders by ability.

Technical training, competence, and expertise—the basis for the authority of each position in the hierarchy.

Hierarchical structure in which each higher office has control and supervision of a lower office.

Administrative staff separate from ownership of the means of production.

Acts, decisions, and rules recorded and utilized as bases for policy.

[2] Charles E. Bidwell, "The School As a Formal Organization," *Handbook of Organizations,* ed. James G. March (Chicago: Rand McNally & Company, 1965), pp. 973-76.

[3] Scott views organizations as rational, natural, or open systems which selectively encompass either classical, human relations, or open systems theories or concepts. For a full discussion of this very interesting approach, see W. Richard Scott, *Organizations. Rational, Natural, and Open Systems* (Englewood Cliffs, N.J.: Prentice-Hall, Inc., 1981), pp. 55–132.

[4] For a comprehensive view of Weber's concepts regarding the bureaucracy, see Max Weber, *From Max Weber: Essays in Sociology,* ed. Hans H. Grath and C. Wright Mills (New York: Oxford University Press, 1946).

According to Weber, these principles maximize rational decision making; in approximating them, organizations become more efficient.

At the root of Weber's bureaucratic model is the concept of authority, which is distinct from other forms of personal and social influence such as power and persuasion. Weber views power within a social relationship as the probability that a given individual will exert his or her will regardless of the resistance of others. In contrast, authority is seen as a function of the probability that the commands of a given individual will be followed by others. Inherent in Weber's notions about authority is the concept of *legitimacy,* or the willingness of others to accept the exercise of power because it coincides with their values.[5] Since power in its coercive form is alienating, Weber posits that authority, defined as legitimate power, is more appropriate for enforcement of organizational rules and regulations.

Weber distinguished between three types of legitimate rule or authority as follows:

> *Traditional authority* – authority legitimated by the sanctity of tradition. Traditional authority tends to perpetuate the existing social order and is ill suited for adaptation to social change. Patriarchal authority represents its pure form.
>
> *Charismatic authority* – rests on the affectual and personal devotion to the leader and a conviction that his actions embody the newly adopted ideals. It is unstable because it is authority that is linked to one person.
>
> *Legal authority* – legitimated by a belief in supremacy of the law. It assumes existence of a formally established body of social norms designated to organize conduct for rational pursuit of specified goals. The basic premise is the idea that laws can be enacted and changed at will by formally correct procedure.[6]

The purest type of legal authority is represented in Weber's notions of bureaucracy.

Several criticisms can be levied against "bureaucracy" as an organizational model. First, some bureaucratic principles are dysfunctional—that is, they have negative consequences (though not necessarily equal in force).[7] For example, the functional utility of hierarchical authority structures is that they are said to encourage willing compliance and coordination. Dysfunctionally, this principle perpetuates rigidity and adherence to rules as end results rather than as means to an end. Second, the principle of impersonality was described by Weber to be functionally rational yet it contributes to low morale and alienation. Third, efficient use of technical knowledge was seen by Weber as a dimension of the division of labor; in fact, it sometimes stifles initiative.

Weber's bureaucratic model can also be criticized because it focuses upon the

---

[5] Amitai Etzioni, *Modern Organizations* (Englewood Cliffs, N.J.: Prentice-Hall, Inc., 1964), p. 51.

[6] Peter M. Blau and W. Richard Scott, *Formal Organizations* (San Francisco: Chandler Publishing Co., 1962), pp. 30–32.

[7] For more comprehensive analyses of these dysfunctions, see Robert K. Merton, "Bureaucratic Structure and Personality," *Social Forces,* 18 (1940), 560–568; P. Selznick, *TVA and the Grass Roots* (Berkeley: University of California Press, 1949); Alvin Gouldner, *Patterns of Industrial Bureaucracy* (Glencoe, Ill.: The Free Press of Glencoe, 1954); and Blau, P. and Scott, W., *Formal Organizations,* pp. 34–36.

formal, impersonal components of an organization while ignoring informal relations. While important, the formal structure of bureaucracy fails to recognize that organization members interact not only in occupational roles but also as individuals seeking to fulfill social and psychological needs. Several empirical studies support the view that friendship patterns, informal exchange systems, and unofficial natural leaders arise to modify formal organizational arrangements.[8]

A final criticism of Weber's theory of the bureaucracy is specified by Gouldner who calls attention to an implicit contradiction in Weber's conception.[9] Gouldner contends that emphasis on expert judgment based on technical knowledge is inconsistent with the Weberian concern for disciplined compliance or response to directives of superiors. Weber implies that these principles are not conflicting and the superior's authority will partially be legitimated on the basis of technical expertise. While top executives in complex organizations are experts in some areas, they generally do not have the same level of competence in all areas of specialization. Because of this, individuals under their jurisdiction will likely be experts in other areas. The exercise of authority as a function of technical knowledge, therefore, creates tension between superiors who have expertise in limited areas and subordinates whose expertise lies in other areas. Indeed, as we later suggest, the structural looseness in school systems is influenced by the technical competence and expertise of non-executive individuals (teachers) and others below the level of the superintendent.

Scientific management. At the same time Weber championed the bureaucratic model as being essential for organizational effectiveness, Frederick W. Taylor (1856–1915) postulated that management and nonmanagement employee interests could be brought together through principles of self-interest. By making a company maximally efficient, increased benefits could be distributed to everyone. Taylor's ideas were particularly influential in shaping early twentieth century school management.

Taylor proposed that there was one best way to do a job. Through scientific analysis and time and motion studies, a determination could be made of maximum human productivity. Reduction of fatigue also was a fundamental concern of these studies. Taylor's view was that productivity could be increased if muscular and physiological motions of workers within a given time span were less fatiguing. By analyzing the work process in the handling of pig iron at Bethlehem Steel, Taylor was able to specify worker pace and movement, work sequence, and equipment size necessary for greater productivity. He also believed that pay could be tied to output, thereby inducing maximum worker effort. Although Taylor's views had a

---

[8] See, for example, C. H. Page, "Bureaucracy's Other Face," *Social Forces,* 25 (1946), 88–94; L. Iannaccone, "An Approach to the Informal Organization of the School," *Behavioral Science and Educational Administration,* ed. Daniel E. Griffiths (Chicago: University of Chicago Press, 1964), ch. 10; R. H. Turner, "The Navy Disbursing Officer as a Bureaucrat," *American Sociological Review,* 12 (1947), 342–48.

[9] A. W. Gouldner, *Patterns of Industrial Bureaucracy,* p. 227.

great effect on management thought and work organizations, the analysis of every facet of work to increase efficiency and the notion that optimum work performance could be motivated through pay incentives were not completely supported by management or workers.

Human Relations Approach

While principles of bureaucracy and scientific management dominated organizational thought from 1910 to about 1935, the period from approximately 1935 to 1950 saw a shift in emphasis to a concern for human relations. The major assumption undergirding this approach was that fulfillment of employee social and psychological needs would serve as motivation for greater productivity. Essentially, the human relations strategem stresses the informal dimensions of organization.

Experimental and analytical procedures used by proponents of the human relations school to understand workers' organizational behavior is reminiscent of Taylor's scientific analysis. However, whereas Taylor held a mechanistic view of workers as extensions of machines, the human relations approach emphasized the importance of human variables such as feelings, attitudes, and the social climate of organizations. These variables became manifest in the Hawthorne studies described by Mayo, Roethlisberger, and Dickson.

Conducted at the Hawthorne plant of Western Electric, the Hawthorne studies were initially designed to examine scientific management assumptions regarding productivity. One assumption examined was whether or not worker productivity could be enhanced through increased illumination in the work place. The experiment designed to test this assumption revealed that no matter what degree of change occurred in illumination, except when it became too low for accurate vision, productivity improved. Related experiments regarding variations in work conditions, such as length of rest breaks and room temperature, produced a similar result—increases in worker output were not a function of the variables manipulated but of human factors.[10] It became evident that experimental subjects respond not only to the attention they receive but also to the novelty of the experiment. As a result of these findings, observable effects in other social science research in which subjects are given special attention and in which there is some novel component have come to be known as "the Hawthorne effect." That is, increases in efficiency can be associated with attention given to the social and psychological needs of individuals.

The bank-wiring room experiment constituted another phase of the Hawthorne studies. In this experiment a group of fourteen men were placed in a separate room to be observed for six months while they wired telephone switchboards (known as banks). The work to be performed required both individual and team effort. Experimental conditions were designed to be as similar as possible to regular

---

[10] Elton Mayo, *The Human Problems of an Industrial Civilization* (New York: Macmillan, Inc., 1933); Fritz L. Roethlisberger and William L. Dickson, *Management and the Worker* (Cambridge: Harvard University Press, 1939).

working conditions. The purpose of the experiment was to determine whether group productivity would increase as a function of financial incentives, an assumption postulated by the scientific management movement. It did not. Observational and interview data indicated that the group established an informal standard for what constituted a satisfactory day's work. Production greater than that which the group considered acceptable placed one's job in jeopardy. To produce less was judged unfair to management.

Generalizations from the Hawthorne studies stand in sharp contrast to several of the earlier notions of scientific management. What the Hawthorne studies were able to demonstrate was that (1) group norms were at least as, and maybe more important, in determining levels of productivity than managerial or administrative norms; (2) non-economic rewards were significant in inducing productivity; and (3) reaction to management standards and rewards occurs not only for individual workers, but also occurs for a group. Other organizational considerations emanating from the Hawthorne studies include (1) participatory decision making—group satisfaction and commitment are enhanced through participation in the decision-making process when appropriate (we discuss this more fully in Chapter Nine); (2) leadership style has an effect on group performance—a "democratic" style is more effective for group performance than either a "laissez-faire" or "authoritarian" style;[11] leaders who give relatively equal attention to initiating structure (task performance) and consideration (friendship, trust, respect, warmth, and concern) tend to be more effective as measured by worker satisfaction and performance[12] (see Chapter Nine); and (3) the existence and importance of formal and informal leaders in groups—formal, appointed leaders are concerned with task performance while informal leaders emerge from the group and attend to the group's social and psychological needs.[13]

The human relations approach to organizational effectiveness emphasized informal dimensions of the organization. Concepts of bureaucracy and scientific management had earlier brought into focus the importance of formal facets. What became clear was that organizational effectiveness and efficiency were not exclusively a function of either orientation. A third school of thought evolved which viewed organizations as open systems.

Open Systems Approach

Beginning about 1960, theorists became concerned with the interdependency of the organization's internal and external elements. The closed system view that characterized the thinking associated with organizational rationality espoused by

[11] Ralph White and Ronald Lippitt, "Leader Behavior and Member Reaction in Three 'Social Climates'," *Group Dynamics. Research and Theory,* 3rd ed., ed. Dorwin Cartwright and Alvin Zander (New York: Harper & Row, Publishers, Inc., 1968), pp. 318–35.

[12] Andrew W. Halpin and B. J. Winer, "A Factorial Study of the Leader Behavior Descriptions," *Leader Behavior: Its Description and Measurement,* ed. Ralph M. Stodgill and Alvin E. Coons (Columbus, Ohio: Bureau of Business Research, Ohio State University, 1957).

[13] Robert F. Bales and P. E. Slater, "Role Differentiation in Small Decision-Making Groups," *Family Socialization and Interaction Process,* ed. Talcott Parsons and Robert F. Bales (Glencoe, Ill.: Free Press, 1955).

the proponents of classical and human relations concepts was replaced with the notion that organizations are open systems which interact with their environment. Here, organizations are viewed as subsystems operating within suprasystems whose components interact with each other. They are seen as maintaining themselves by processing inputs from their environment and converting them into outputs. This input-throughput-output model is informed by feedback to which the organization must be responsive. Much of the open systems rationale derives from general systems theory, which we briefly discuss next.

General systems theory. The totality of interacting and interrelated components within a framework that separates an entity from the environment for the purpose of achieving goals is emphasized in the systems approach. This is not to say that boundary maintenance precludes interaction with the environment. Clearly, such interaction is essential for organizations since it is from the environment that they derive the energy, materials, and information necessary for their existence.[14]

In a broad context, systems may be viewed as being biological (living organisms), mechanical (automobiles), or social (organizations). We utilized a version of social systems theory in Chapter Two to describe the educational policymaking process. Systems are composed of *subsystems* which operate interrelatedly to achieve intended purposes. They also are part of a *suprasystem.* That is, they operate within a larger environmental context. For example, within an individual school, the curriculum, administrative services, and food services may be considered as interrelated subsystems that exist and function to achieve the purpose(s) of the school. The individual school itself operates within the larger context of a school district or suprasystem. Similarly, the school district in which the individual school is located can be viewed as a subsystem operating within the broader societal and environmental suprasystem.

In achieving their purpose(s), or *outputs,* systems depend on environmental *inputs* which are filtered into an interacting set of components maintained by a *boundary* which serves to differentiate internal and external interactions and interrelationships. As defined by Berrien, "the boundary [is] that region through which inputs and outputs must pass, during which exchanges with the system's environment undergo some modification or transformation."[15] Outputs may be assessed continuously for their adequacy. Such assessment data are fed back into the system for system adjustment. An illustration of a basic systems model is shown in Figure 7.2.

Several concepts are fundamental to systems. *System boundaries* separate systems from their environments and from other systems. Boundaries may be impenetrable or permeable. Impenetrable boundaries characterize *closed systems,* which derive few inputs from the environment. Closed systems are thought to be self-sufficient. But they move toward *entropy*—a movement to disorder, lack of

---

[14] Scott, W., *Organizations. Rational, Natural, and Open Systems,* pp. 109–110.

[15] F. Kenneth Berrien, *General and Social Systems* (New Brunswick, N.J.: Rutgers University Press, 1968), p. 23.

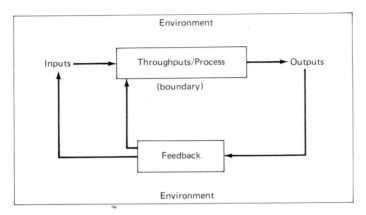

Figure 7.2 Basic Systems Model.

resource transformation, and eventually death.[16] Permeable boundaries characterize *open systems,* which exchange resources with their environments. Open systems exist in a relative state. That is, the extent of openness will vary among systems.[17] Thus, system openness can be viewed as a continuum.

System purpose is accomplished through interaction of subsystems and a system's interaction with the suprasystem in which it exists. Purpose determines the processes required, which in turn specify the kinds of components or subsystems that will constitute the system. The effectiveness or performance adequacy of a system can be assessed on the basis of how closely and how economically or efficiently the output of the system satisfies the purpose for which it exists.[18]

Homeostasis is a state in which the system is in harmony with its environment. It is a state of balance and stability, or *equilibrium,* between environmental resources and the system. A state of *disequilibrium* will exist when the system is unable to use resources as they are received from the environment or when its subsystems are out of balance.

From the vantage point of the systems approach, the effective design of an organization must consider interaction and relationships between subsystems within the organization and interrelationships between the set of subsystems and the environment or larger system. These subunits, their internal interrelationships, and interrelationships with the environment will differ by organization. Hence, there is no one best organizational structure within the open systems formulation. Organizational designs are contingent on the environmental constraints within which the organization exists.[19]

[16] Terence R. Mitchell, *People in Organizations: Understanding Their Behavior* (New York: McGraw-Hill Book Company, 1978), pp. 25–26.

[17] Berrien, F., *General and Social Systems,* p. 16.

[18] Bela H. Banathy, *Instructional Systems* (Palo Alto, Calif.: Fearon Publishers, 1968), pp. 12–13.

[19] See Paul R. Lawrence and Jay W. Lorsch, *Organization and Environment. Managing Differentiation and Integration* (Homewood, Ill.: Richard D. Irwin, Inc., 1969), pp. 185–210.

The importance of the environment in determining organizational structure and behavior can be viewed from two other perspectives: (1) resource dependence; and (2) natural selection.[20] In the latter instance, advocates posit that the environment naturally selects certain organizations to survive and to reproduce themselves because of their congruence with environmental characteristics.[21] The former designation is one in which organizations adapt to the environment; administrators manage the environment either to control their power over needed inputs or to decrease dependency on them.[22]

Systems theory has been criticized because it fails to account adequately for change which results from interactions of actors[23] and because of the probability that misconceptions may result from the use of analogies from one type of system to another, for instance, comparing "the thermostat-heater system to the control system of an organization."[24] Nevertheless, the open systems approach provides a logical and comprehensive design for the analysis of organizational behavior and effectiveness.

In summary, the three broad approaches to organizational conceptualizations—classical, human relations, and open systems—provide a rich and diverse perspective on what structure and arrangements have been viewed as being desirable, and perhaps necessary, for organizational effectiveness and efficiency. The traditional structure of organizations deriving from the bureaucracy concept is that of a pyramid with control residing at the top. Because of its division of labor and authority based on technical competence assumptions, more emphasis is placed on the office and position than on the social and psychological needs of individuals. These latter dimensions were the concern of the human relations approach, though advocates of this perspective failed to alter the basic bureaucratic organizational structure. Systems advocates attempt to bridge approaches advanced by the bureaucracy and human relations schools. Here interdependency and interrelations of organizational subunits with the environment are emphasized. Systems theorists also stress sociological functionalism—the function of anything is dependent upon (1) the smaller units of which it is composed; and (2) larger systems of which it is a subcomponent.[25] As we describe in the next section, components of these conceptualizations of organizations have influenced organizational structure and processes in individual schools and school systems.

---

[20] Howard E. Aldrich and Jefferey Pfeffer, "Environments of Organizations," *Annual Review of Sociology,* ed. Alex Inkeles, James Coleman, and Neil Smelser (Palo Alto, Calif.: Annual Reviews, Inc., 1976), 2, 79–105.

[21] Aldrich, H. and Pfeffer, J., "Environments of Organizations," 79–105.

[22] Jefferey Pfeffer and Gerald R. Salanick, *The External Control of Organizations* (New York: Harper & Row, Publishers, Inc., 1978).

[23] David Silverman, *The Theory of Organizations* (New York: Basic Books, Inc., 1971), p. 5.

[24] Scott, W., *Organizations. Rational, Natural, and Open Systems,* p. 120.

[25] Harold L. Hodgkinson, *Education, Interaction, and Social Change* (Englewood Cliffs, N.J.: Prentice-Hall, Inc., 1967), p. 49.

THE ORGANIZATIONAL STRUCTURE OF SCHOOLS:
FORMAL DIMENSIONS

In several respects, the organizational structure of schools and school systems resembles a rational, closed system quite similar to Weber's bureaucratic model. These systems are structured in a hierarchical manner, have a division of labor based on technical competence and specialization, have written rules and regulations, and have an authority structure between higher and lower offices.

Diagrammatically, as earlier displayed in Figure 7.2, it is apparent that schools can be viewed as embracing the scalar concept or a hierarchical structure of offices in which the highest authority resides at the top level. This hierarchical arrangement is sometimes perpetuated by the school system in school policies which sometimes result from teacher negotiations. For example, in grievance procedures, which frequently are negotiated, the aggrieved party must appeal unsatisfactory resolutions sequentially up the hierarchical ladder until the school board or its representative ultimately acts on the original grievance (see Chapter Twelve). Whether for convenience or control, or because of tradition, schools and school systems tend to structure themselves in a hierarchical arrangement.

School organization is also influenced by a division of labor based on technical competence and specialization. While administrators at the organization's higher levels generally must be certificated as teachers, they usually must also have administrative credentials and additional formal training. Teachers are required only to have a teaching credential, but principals and most other administrators must also possess an administrative credential. Whereas teachers may be appointed with little or no formal teaching experience, principals and other administrators generally are obligated to have spent several years as a classroom teacher. Moreover, principals and other high level officials may face a mandate to augment their administrative credentials with added formal training or advanced academic degrees. Certainly, these individuals are expected to possess technical competence and specialized knowledge compatible with the higher level positions they hold.

Schools are also characterized by written rules and regulations, which are frequently called policies. Such rules and regulations, which exist both for students and school staff, are used to control members' behavior and assure reasonable uniformity in task performance.[26] Rules and regulations also legitimize authority, routinize punishment, and provide a mechanism for bargaining.

In legitimizing authority, rules diminish the need for superiors to give orders. Importantly, they protect against the arbitrary use of power and routinize the consequences of infractions. Additionally, rules can serve as a mechanism for bargain-

---

[26] Max G. Abbott, "Hierarchical Impediments to Innovation in Educational Organizations," *Perspectives in Educational Administration,* ed. Max G. Abbott and J. T. Lovell (Auburn, Ala.: Auburn University, School of Education, 1965).

ing. That is, by withholding enforcement of some rules, superiors may bargain with subordinates for information and cooperation.[27]

On the negative side of the ledger, rules may serve to justify mediocrity. They may result in standardization and uniformity of lesson plans, curriculum guides, and excessive use of tests and textbooks. Students and their needs are diverse, and such standardization and uniformity may not serve their best interests. Enforcement of rules and regulations further encourages school staff to behave in impersonal ways toward outsiders. If there are clear rules regarding specific situations, there is little need for discussions with outsiders when problems arise.[28] Finally, rules and regulations serve to protect employees from outside requests they may consider inconvenient or inappropriate.[29]

SCHOOLS AS A SELECTIVE LINKAGE SYSTEM

Organizationally higher level positions in the school system have authority over those that are lower. In this manner schools reflect the hierarchical authority structure of Weber's bureaucratic model. The superintendent of schools is the chief executive officer of the school system and is in a position to exercise authority over other school staff consistent with board policy and contractual arrangements. Similarly, associate and assistant superintendents have authority over principals who in turn have authority over teachers. Technically, positions of authority such as these are considered to be *line positions,* those that have direct supervisory and evaluation responsibility, in contradistinction to *staff positions* (for example, director of personnel) that are advisory. In reality, however, in the school setting actual authority and control from higher levels over lower levels are rather imprecise. For instance, top administrator positions at the level of the superintendency have little day-to-day contact with teachers and little direct control over their teaching. Teachers generally have autonomy within their classrooms, particularly with respect to teaching techniques that are relatively impervious to administrative control from the central school office or superintendency or from their school principal.

Just as teachers have discretion over how instruction occurs in their classrooms, principals have considerable discretion in responding to central office directives. Although principals must be responsive to such mandates, they also must

---

[27] Alvin Gouldner, *Patterns of Industrial Bureaucracy* (New York: Free Press, 1964), pp. 162–80; see also, Charles M. Achilles and John L. Keedy, "Principal Norm Setting as a Component of Effective Schools," William A. Kritsonis' *National Forum of Educational Administration and Supervision,* 1, no. 1 (1983/84), 58–68.

[28] Ronald G. Corwin and Roy A. Edelfelt, *Perspectives on Organizations: Viewpoints for Teachers* (Washington, D.C.: American Association of Colleges for Teacher Education, 1976), p. 30.

[29] R. Bar-Yosef and E. O. Schild, "Pressures and Defenses in Bureaucratic Roles," *American Journal of Sociology,* 71, no. 6 (May 1966), 665–73.

arrange their schools in ways that minimize impersonality and disruption and maximize staff morale and program effectiveness. Hence, their response, say, to a central office directive that calls for surveying students' family occupations may not be immediately addressed if to do so would interfere with other school activities. In other instances, principals may find it necessary to disobey completely (but creatively) a central office directive. For example, the central office may desire to have principals spend one-third of their time in classrooms observing or supervising teachers. This might be avoided by building a schedule of other leadership or management activities that effectively eliminates the availability of time necessary to execute such directives. In other words, principals may occasionally either avoid or manipulate central office mandates if it is in the best interest of the school.[30]

From the foregoing discussion we can see that within the school's authority structure, those in higher authority levels do not exercise complete control over those at lower levels. What is portrayed, rather, is a school system in which authority and control is somewhat discontinuous and loosely coupled.[31]

In contrast to the foregoing discussion in which loose control between authority levels has been depicted, schools do exercise considerable control over other school-related matters. Who is eligible to teach or to serve as a school administrator in public schools is tightly controlled through state academic and credential requirements. Without appropriate credentials, individuals may not be employed as teachers or administrators unless the state temporarily waives regular credential requirements and authorizes the employment of uncredentialled individuals or the issuance of emergency credentials to meet shortages of professional personnel.

Schools also exercise tight control over the initial admission of students through minimum age requirements, over grade promotion, over graduation via curriculum unit and subject requirements, and, in many states, proficiency examinations.[32] Student placement in gifted programs or college preparatory curricula,

---

[30] For an excellent account of ways in which principals avoid or manipulate central office directives, see Van Cleve Morris, Robert L. Crowson, Cynthia Porter-Gehrie, and Emanuel Hurwitz, Jr., *Principals in Action, The Reality of Managing Schools* (Columbus, Ohio: Charles E. Merrill Publishing Company, 1984), pp. 149–77.

[31] There is a growing literature on schools as loosely coupled systems. For example, see Karl E. Weick, "Educational Organizations as Loosely Coupled Systems," *Administrative Science Quarterly*, 21, no. 1 (March, 1976), 1–19; John W. Meyer and Brian Rowan, "The Structure of Educational Organizations," *Environments and Organizations*, ed. Marshall W. Meyer and associates (San Francisco: Jossey-Bass Publishers, 1978), pp. 78–109; Terrence E. Deal and Lynn D. Celotti, *"Loose Coupling" and the School Administrator: Some Recent Research Findings* (Stanford University: School of Education, 1977), ERIC Reports, ED140436; Karl E. Weick, "Administering Education in Loosely Coupled Schools," *Phi Delta Kappan*, 63, no. 10 (June, 1982), 673–75.

[32] Currently, 14 states require passage of proficiency examinations as a condition of high school graduation. They are Alabama, Arizona, California, Delaware, Florida, Georgia, Hawaii, New Jersey, North Carolina, Oregon, Tennessee, Utah, Vermont, and Virginia. Louisiana will require high school graduation tests by 1992. In four states—Colorado, New Hampshire, Texas, Wisconsin—local districts have the option to require high school graduation tests. See Chris Pipho and Connie Hadley, "State Activity, Minimal Competency Testing," *Clearinghouse Notes* (Denver, Col.: Education Commission of the States, April, 1984).

generally determined by standardized testing, is another area in which the school's control is unequivocal. Schools also monitor student attendance closely since the allocation of state funds for school operation is determined by students' average daily attendance. Thus, it is apparent that schools maintain close control and authority over several important aspects of their operation. Yet they are loosely coupled when considering authority and control between higher and lower levels in areas in which technical competence, specialization, and managerial direction must be executed.

Schools give the appearance of being hierarchical and conforming to Weber's bureaucratic model. However, as we have pointed out, in important ways they do not adhere strictly to the tenets of that model. Schools are thus more appropriately viewed organizationally as being both tightly and loosely controlled systems. Functionally, therefore, schools can be thought of as a selective linkage system. In this regard, schools maintain complete control or tight linkage over such aspects as student entry, advancement, graduation, professional eligibility, and student record keeping. Conversely, the linkage between higher and lower authority levels for matters pertaining to classroom teaching and school management can be characterized as being loosely linked.

Schools may further be seen as a selective linkage system when viewing their relationship to the environment, as manifested in community relations. Local school systems must interact socially and politically with the community in which they are located. This interaction takes place through linkages with individual parents, parent-teacher associations, school advisory councils, and special interest groups.[33] School-community interaction is important in determining school goals, generating approval and support for the school's program, problem solving, and conflict resolution.[34]

Whereas school leaders understand the importance of forming selective linkages with the community to accomplish school purposes, this view is not always shared by teachers. Waller, for example, calls attention to the fact that solidarity results from their professional status and is strengthened by their detachment from the community.[35] Achilles and Keedy remind us that principals may employ an exchange system in their relations with teachers: In exchange for protecting them from community intrusions, they agree to comply with the principal's program.[36] Whether or not teachers themselves interact closely with the community, school of-

[33] For a discussion of mechanisms for linking the school and its community, see Eugene Litwak and Henry J. Meyer, *School, Family and Neighborhood: The Theory and Practice of School-Community Relations* (New York: Columbia University Press, 1974).

[34] Organizational and environmental interaction with particular attention given to how organizations in the business sector negotiate environmental change is discussed in Paul R. Lawrence and Jay W. Lorsch, *Organization and Environment. Managing Differentiation and Integration* (Homewood, Ill.: Richard D. Irvin, Inc., 1969).

[35] Willard F. Waller, *The Sociology of Teaching* (New York: John Wiley, 1932).

[36] Charles M. Achilles and John L. Keedy, "Principal Norm Setting as a Component of Effective Schools," William A. Kritsonis' *National Forum of Educational Administration and Supervision,* 1, no. 1 (1983/84), 58-68.

ficials must do so to garner programmatic support, resources, and legitimization. Community or environmental selective linkages are thus important in these regards.

Because schools are selective linkage systems, their response to crises and environmental change can be immediate and direct. Responses can be handled at the level of the superintendency, the principalship, or the classroom teacher. Hence, there is considerable merit to the school's selective linkage system. However, this advantage is mitigated by greater amounts of time needed for effective communication flow throughout the school system. Consequently, crises may expand because of ineffective school system communication.

THE ORGANIZATIONAL STRUCTURE OF SCHOOLS: INFORMAL DIMENSIONS

Most school system employees are members of myriad groups that comprise the informal system network. Such groups form because of similar work assignments, proximity of work location, vocational and recreational interests, age, sex, marital status, and shared values. Informal groups exhibit greater collective power than any single group member. They also are relatively enduring. Lortie, for example, found in studies conducted on primary group formation among teachers that informal groups not only exist from September to June while school is in session, but also that such groups are reconstituted with no significant change when school reconvenes the next year.[37]

From another informal organizational perspective, group norms are important determinants of group behavior. Evidence of this view in the school setting is provided by Willower's fourteen month study of a junior high school. In this study it was determined that the informal school organization was dominated by older and more experienced teachers. The most important norm of acceptable teaching, according to these experienced teachers, was maintenance of pupil control and discipline. Anyone using permissive methods was apt to be labeled a poor teacher.[38]

The informal organization of the schools must be recognized as a powerful force in enhancing organizational efficiency. Administrators who can identify informal group leaders and establish close working relationships with them are substantially advantaged in accomplishing organizational goals.

EDUCATORS AS PROFESSIONALS AND BUREAUCRATS IN THE SCHOOL'S ORGANIZATIONAL STRUCTURE

In most large organizations in which professionals are employed, it is inevitable that tension will exist between bureaucratic administrators and professionals who are more interested in pursuing activities associated with the profession to which they

[37] D. C. Lortie, "The Balance of Control and Autonomy in Elementary School Teaching," *Educational Organization and Administration,* ed. D. A. Erickson (Berkeley: McCutchan Publishing Co., 1977), pp. 335–71.

[38] Donald Willower, "The Teacher Subculture and Curricular Charge" (paper presented at a Faculty Seminar, Temple University, 1968), ERIC, Ed-202-588.

belong. The fundamental cause of this bureaucratic-professional conflict is the organizational authority system under which each operates. The full professional is guided by authority and control derived from a colleague reference group and technical or specialized knowledge. The bureaucrat derives authority from the hierarchical organizational structure which views superordinates as having authority over those at lower levels. Because of these orientations, decisions of the classic bureaucrat will be made in the interest of the organization, while decisions of the idealized professional will reflect the best interests of the client or norms of the profession.

In varying degrees this phenomenon exists in nonprofessional, professional, and semiprofessional organizations.[39] In *nonprofessional organizations,* those in which the primary goal is to make a profit, administrative activities are coordinated so that profits can be maximized. Here, final authority resides in line officers constituting the administrative chain of command. Professionals in these organizations are more likely to occupy specialized or staff advisory positions outside the line of authority. Thus, the bases for decisions will differ with each group correctly assuming their decisions are justifiable. In the final analysis, however, the organization's authority will prevail.

In contrast to the nonprofessional organization, *professional organizations* are those in which knowledge is produced, applied, preserved, or communicated, in which 50 percent or more of the staff are professionals, and in which professionals have control over the organization's major goal activities. In these organizations administrators provide support for the primary goal activity which is essentially controlled by professionals. Final authority resides with the professional. Included in this category are universities, research organizations, and hospitals.

Semiprofessional organizations are similar to those that are professional, but differ on the bases of the status of professional employees and their functions. Full professionals undergo an extended period of specialized preparation. Semiprofessionals spend less time in training. Functionally, there are differences in goals, matters with which professionals deal, and privileges. A professional organization is fundamentally concerned with the generation and application of knowledge. Professionals in these organizations may deal with matters pertaining to life or death, and they often have access to privileged communication. Semiprofessional organizations focus more on the communication of knowledge. Semiprofessionals employed in them, therefore, are usually not concerned with matters of life and death, nor do they have full access to privileged communications. Schools and social work agencies can be included in the category of semiprofessional organizations.

In coping with professional-bureaucratic tension at the organizational level, professional and semiprofessional organizations may seek as chief line officers individuals who have had specialized training in administration. Alternatively, they may seek individuals within the profession who possess an affinity for, and an interest in, management but who have not received specialized administrative training. Use of the former solution can be observed in primary and secondary schools; the latter in universities. Ideally, with a professional serving as the chief line administrator of

---

[39] This discussion of nonprofessional, professional, and semiprofessional organizations is based on Etzioni's concepts. See Etzioni, *Modern Organizations,* pp. 75–93.

an organization, the interests of both the professionals and the organization will be understood and accommodated.

At an individual level, professionals may address the professional-bureaucratic dilemma by manifesting a commitment to the organization or by seeking support, identity, and reinforcement from professional colleagues inside and outside of the organization. This tendency is dramatically demonstrated in Gouldner's study of organizational loyalty, commitment to professional skills, and outside reference group orientation.[40] Gouldner's findings revealed that for some individuals in a professional organization, a high commitment to professional skills as well as an orientation to an outside reference group was more highly valued than organizational loyalty. Individuals characterized by these traits were labeled "cosmopolitans." On the other hand, when loyalty to the organization was more dominant than commitment to professional skills and an orientation to outside reference groups, the individual was considered to be "local." Although Gouldner's study involved faculty at a small liberal arts college, existence of both cosmopolitans and locals in professional and semiprofessional organizations is generally assumed to reflect reality. Merton, who first used the terms "cosmopolitan" and local," also reports that workers can be characterized by job orientations that are cosmopolitan or local. Cosmopolitans are concerned with professional objectives and occupational status or recognition. Locals, on the other hand, seek recognition within the organization in which they work.[41]

There is some evidence to indicate that school superintendents also exhibit orientations that are "cosmopolitan" or "local." For example, the study by Carlson found that superintendents can be classified as being place-bound or career-bound.[42] Place-bound superintendents have a local orientation and are fully committed to the school district in which most of their professional career has been spent. In a manner analogous to the locals in Gouldner's study, they are loyal to the organization. In contrast, career-bound superintendents tend to be committed to a professional career rather than to a local community. We can infer from this finding that career-bound superintendents will have a tendency to be committed to an external professional reference group or association and not exhibit the same degree of loyalty to the local organization that characterizes place-bound superintendents. It also can be noted that there is some support for the view that professionals in professional and semiprofessional organizations may simultaneously display commitment to the organization and to the profession.[43]

[40] Alvin W. Gouldner, "Cosmopolitans and Locals: Toward an Analysis of Latent Social Roles—I," *Administrative Science Quarterly*, 2, no. 3 (1957), 281–306.

[41] Robert K. Merton, *Social Theory and Social Structure,* rev. ed. (New York: Free Press, 1957), pp. 393–95.

[42] Richard O. Carlson, *Executive Succession and Organizational Change* (Chicago: University of Chicago, Midwest Administration Center, 1962), pp. 7–15.

[43] For example, see William Kornhauser, *Scientists in Industry* (Berkeley: University of California Press, 1962).

Educators as Professionals

Features of professional-bureaucratic tension are associated with most formal organizations, including schools. Teachers and administrators employed in schools are subjected to the same tension noted in the last section. At an individual level the ability of educators to reduce such tension is conditioned by the autonomy and control they are able to exercise as professionals.

Blau and Scott view a professional as one who

1. Has universalistic standards; specialized knowledge; specialized training.

2. Has a specialization; professional expertness; qualifications to deal with problems in a strictly limited area; authority in sphere of expertise.

3. Has relations with clients characterized by affective neutrality.

4. Attains status through performance; professional success dependent upon outstanding performance in accordance with principles laid down by colleague group.

5. Makes decisions independent of practitioner's self-interest.

6. Is a member of a voluntary association for the purpose of self-control, which comes from
   a)   a body of expert knowledge and a code of ethics which governs professional conduct;
   b)   external surveillance of professional conduct by peers who are in a position to see the individual's work, who have skills to judge his or her performance, and because of a personal stake in the reputation of their profession, are motivated to exercise sanctions;
   c)   a view of colleagues as equal;
   d)   the right to license practitioners.[44]

By this set of criteria, it is evident that school teachers and administrators cannot currently be regarded as full professionals. First, neither group exercises complete control over entry into the field or over standards of performance. Second, acquisition of a specialized body of knowledge is accomplished in a relatively short period of time. Third, while they are organized into voluntary associations that have codes of ethics, enforcement of such codes is problematic. To their credit, teachers and administrators perform a personal service that is important to society. Thus, in considering preparation, service, and the voluntary associations to which they belong, the label "semi" or "quasi" professional appears more appropriate at present than that of full professional.

Toward Professional Status

The drive toward full professional status for educators is stimulated by the large numbers of teachers and administrators holding membership in professional associations. For example, the American Federation of Teachers (AFT) re-

---

[44] Blau, P. and Scott, W., *Formal Organizations,* pp. 60–63.

ported that they had 249,000 members in 1972 and 580,000 members in 1982. The National Education Association (NEA) had 1.1 million members in 1972 and 1.6 members by 1982. Membership in the American Association of School Administrators (AASA) was 19,335 in 1972 and 17,077 in 1982.

In keeping with efforts to be a full professional, each of these organizations has a code of ethics concerning the "professional" behavior of its members. Each has developed considerable political influence at both national and state levels in lobbying for educational initiatives and legislation. Each has been active in supporting candidates for federal and state legislative offices. As a result of these activities, there is the recognition of a growing sense of power. Nevertheless, there remain major impediments to professionalism, the removal of which constitutes a significant challenge. We discuss this challenge in Chapter Sixteen.

SUMMARY

Large-scale organizations dominate the worklife of most individuals in industrial societies. Education is no exception. Formal organizations—bureaucracies—were initially described in detail by Max Weber. He attributed to them conditions such as hierarchical arrangements of authority, specialization of tasks among employees, and specification and recording of work rules which could facilitate efficiency. Weber's ideas were significantly assisted in the early twentieth century by the "scientific management" analyses of Frederick Taylor. Taylor emphasized the utility of time and motion studies to enhance worker productivity.

Reaction to the mechanistic and technocratic formulations of Weber and Taylor contributed to the formulation in the 1920s of a human relations school of management thought which stressed the human needs of employees and pointed out the existence of a significant pattern of interaction outside the bureaucratic norms of an organization. This behavior came to be known as the informal side of organizations.

By the 1960s, a synthesis between bureaucratic and human relations views began to occur. One form this synthesis took is the "systems" approach, which stresses the relationship of the component parts of organizations and the link between an organization and its larger environment. Each of these three schools of management thought has significantly influenced school organizational structure and behavior. Schools, however, are unique organizations. They are open systems with both tight and loose coupling characteristics. In important respects schools can be viewed as a selective linkage system.

Within the school system professional bureaucratic tensions can be noted. Professionals possess a number of characteristics, such as control over a specialized body of knowledge, lengthy period of preparation, control over entry into the profession, and paramount concern for client welfare. On occasion, professional principles conflict with bureaucratic organizational norms. Education, though more of a "quasi" or "semi" profession than a full profession, nevertheless faces the continued prospect of conflict between professional and organizational goals. The conflict can be relieved in part by educators adopting more of the characteristics of professionals.

SELECTED READINGS

Benveniste, Guy, *Bureaucracy*. San Francisco: Boyd and Fraser, 1977.

Bidwell, Charles E., "The School As a Formal Organization," *Handbook of Organizations*, ed. James G. March. Chicago: Rand McNally & Company, 1965.

Blau, Peter M., and W. Richard Scott, *Formal Organizations*. San Francisco: Chandler Publishing Co., 1962.

Etzioni, Amitai, *Modern Organizations*. Englewood Cliffs, N.J.: Prentice-Hall, 1964.

Lawrence, Paul R., and Jay W. Lorsch, *Organization and Environment. Managing Differentiation and Integration*. Homewood, Ill.: Richard D. Irvin, Inc., 1969.

Meyer, Marshall W., and others, eds., *Environments and Organizations*. San Francisco: Jossey-Bass, 1978.

Mitchell, Terence R., *People in Organizations: Understanding Their Behavior*. New York: McGraw-Hill Book Company, 1978.

Scott, W. Richard, *Organizations. Rational, Natural, and Open Systems*. Englewood Cliffs, N.J.: Prentice-Hall, Inc., 1981.

CURRICULAR
AND INSTRUCTIONAL
POLICIES

chapter 8

The content of what is taught, *curriculum,* and how it is to be taught, *instruction,* are operational components of schooling to which educational leaders must pay attention. Curriculum policies particularly, and instructional activities on occasion, are expected to reflect public and community values, and, thus, may possess the potential to provoke intense conflict. This chapter analyzes the governmental dynamics by which school policies in these areas are developed and implemented; describes several major contemporary curricular and instructional issues; and suggests important policy and practical dimensions which administrators should continually monitor in order to enhance the performance of pupils and provide appropriate stability to school districts, schools, and other educational organizations.

CURRICULAR DYNAMICS

At its Latin roots, the word "curriculum" refers to a circular course. By extrapolation, the subject matter content of schooling has come to be known as "courses." These courses should be capable of developing a desired condition within students. The "what" of schooling should result in a state of knowledge, character, or capability that presumably was not previously or fully present prior to exposure to the curriculum course content.

In an ideal sense, if complete societal agreement existed regarding the desired outcomes of schooling, the curriculum would then be far more of a technical than political matter. Under conditions of full agreement, the subject matter of schooling could be left to professional educators to determine because they could then simply decide which subject content leads most effectively to which school outcomes.

Full agreement regarding desired outcomes of schooling is not easily obtained. A dictatorship can attempt to impose outcomes for schools. A few societies have sufficient cultural homogeneity that substantial public consensus exists regarding educational goals. Democratic societies with diverse populations typically exhibit less agreement. Political mechanisms exist in the United States for arriving at a public position about what schools in a state or a community ought to teach. Nevertheless, for reasons we will explain, these mechanisms do not eliminate controversy and do not usually result in an accurate or easy translation. The distance between public preferences and curricula offerings can be wide. There are at least four conditions which impede the ability of schools to implement public views regarding the content of schooling.

Confused and Conflicting Public Preferences

What is the purpose of schooling? This question has been debated since the time of Plato, and the answers are presently no less elusive. A 1960 publication summarized a series of opinion polls regarding the publicly preferred purposes of schooling.[1] This study uncovered substantial variation. For example, as can be seen from Figure 8.1, residents of the eastern portion of the United States held moral training and education for world citizenship to be of great importance and were less enamored of using schools for students' physical development or acquiring social acumen. By contrast, those sampled in the west held social and civic functions of schooling in high regard and thought relatively less of education for moral purposes and consumer understanding. Canadians and Southerners had different preferences. Differences in view were also found to characterize residents of suburbs compared to those in rural areas, and the latter relative to urbanites.

The larger the geographic boundaries and the more heterogeneous the population encompassed by local school districts, the greater the probability of encountering differences of view regarding functions and purposes of education. Should schools emphasize a technical, vocational curriculum or place greater stress upon college preparatory academic subjects? What should be the relative attention in an elementary setting given to developing students' self-esteem compared with time devoted to group identity or racial and ethnic tolerance, physical coordination, or

---

[1] See Lawrence W. Downey, *The Task of Public Education: The Perception of the People* (Chicago: University of Chicago Midwest Administration Center, 1960); and John Schaffarzich and Gary Sykes, eds., *Value Conflict and Curriculum Issues* (Berkeley: McCutchan, 1979). As an illustration of the conflict that can result when two value streams collide, see Franklin Parker, *The Battle of the Books: Kanawha County* (Bloomington: Phi Delta Kappa Educational Foundation, 1975).

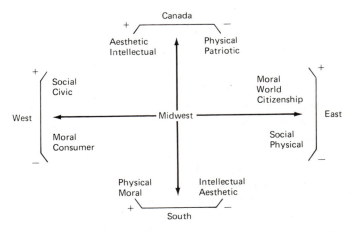

Figure 8.1   Regional Differences in Perception of the Public School's Task. Downy, *The Task of Public Education.* **Midwest Administration Center, University of Chicago Press.**

artistic understanding? Or should all the foregoing be subordinated to the development of academic skills such as reading, writing, and computation?

Educational leaders are frequently faced with questions such as these. They are not rhetorical inquiries. The answers are hard to discern, and the process is made more difficult by the diversity of views held by the clients of schooling. A frequent result is compromise and obfuscation. Political dilemmas of this nature promote platitudes such as "We educate the whole child." This can be a farcical claim. Nevertheless, such slogans may fend off parental concerns that one value or another is being overemphasized while some other function held by a parent to be important is being neglected.

Another strategy is simply for a school's "philosophy" or goals to include a long list of encompassing terms. Clients can then peruse the statement and, presumably, be satisfied if they find listed those goals of greatest concern to them. In truth, such a rainbow of purposes increases the risk that no one goal or set of related goals will receive systematic instructional attention. School resources are limited. Promising to pursue many purposes may create false expectations. Efforts to spread resources over an unreasonable spectrum can dilute effectivenss.

Professional Autonomy

Except under unusual circumstances, such as those subsequently described, translation of public preferences for schooling can also be jeopardized by the instructional isolation of many teachers. Whatever the statement of philosophy adopted by a school board and regardless of statutory and judicial mandates, a classroom teacher has substantial autonomy in instruction. Even when observation and evaluation by administrators is systematic, many teachers have great discretion regarding the topics, sequence, and duration of their instruction. Their individual classrooms have substantial sanctity.

This is not to assert that teachers systematically subvert curriculum policies. Indeed, it is often the case that individual teachers, by their instructional acumen, impute far more integrity to the curriculum than might otherwise occur if district curriculum guides and state policies were relied upon exclusively. Nevertheless, a teacher having individual instructional responsibility for a semester or a year over a group of students has virtually complete control when it comes to selecting instructional content. The supervision of classroom teachers and the assessment of their performance is infrequent. Such autonomy contributes to the sociological "loose coupling" of the school bureaucracy described in Chapter Seven.[2]

Haphazard and Inappropriate Measurement

In the absence of national standardized tests which assess progress toward objectives specified in curricula policies, there is little hope of knowing the true curriculum of a school. Examinations developed by teachers may well appraise what transpires in their individual classrooms. However, such tests offer few guarantees that district or state content guidelines are being met. Similarly, tests developed by organizations outside a district, or even outside a state, may be standardized but may be inconsistent with district or state educational objectives. The widely used Scholastic Aptitude Test (SAT) is a prime example.

The SAT is developed and administered by the Educational Testing Service of Princeton, New Jersey, under contract to the College Entrance Examination Board (CEEB). This test is intended to provide institutions of higher education with an objective appraisal of an applicant's likelihood of college success. Whereas the test is generally judged successful for such purposes, it is not necessarily aligned with the curriculum objectives of any particular school, district, or state. The purpose of the SAT is to predict future performance, not assess acquisition of subject matter knowledge taught in a particular school setting.

The SAT is said to be "norm referenced"—that is, it is deliberately constructed to distribute respondents' scores over a bell-shaped "normal curve." Questions easily answered by all test takers and those which virtually no one can answer are deliberately eliminated from the examination. Such questions have little ability to discriminate among students and consequently possess no predictive power. Test questions which are consistent with the content of classroom instruction offer a better appraisal of the degree to which students are comprehending what is being taught. Such questions constitute so-called "criterion referenced" tests.

Despite possible incongruity between SAT coverage and what it is that schools may be attempting to teach, much of the American public takes national average SAT scores to be a barometer of the United States system of education.

[2] Karl Weick, "Education Organizations as Loosely Coupled Systems," *Administrative Science Quarterly*, 21 (1976), 1–14.

Education is badly in need of a better "Dow Jones Index." In time, the National Assessment of Educational Progress (NAEP), a federally funded ETS operated testing program which samples student achievement throughout the United States, may evolve into a better understood and more widely accepted indicator of educational "productivity." Meanwhile, only with a so-called "criterion referenced" test can a district or state accurately assess the extent to which students are learning what is intended to be taught by curriculum policies.

The "Hidden" Curriculum[3]

The formal content of courses may not constitute the only knowledge conveyed by schools. Some social scientists contend that the overall school environment presents a powerful instructional message, a message which may not always be consistent with learning outcomes intended by district policy or the content conveyed by instructors in their classes. For example, it is alleged that a rigidly hierarchical school climate, where students are permitted little discretion and are seldom encouraged to make decisions, eviscerates formal course content extolling the virtues of democracy. Similarly, students observing what may be unfair segregation of their peers into ability tracks may be "learning more" (acquiring a cynicism regarding equal opportunity and the "American Dream" of social mobility) than from the abstract ideals they are being taught in history and civic courses.

In a pioneering study which revealed the underlying student status structure of a school, Coleman found that students accorded greater prestige to extracurricular conditions, such as sociability and athletic prowess, than to academic performance.[4] Schools sponsoring interscholastic sports events, but offering relatively few rewards for intellectual achievement, only reinforce such conditions.

Administrators should be conscious of the possibility that the total school environment may itself be a powerful curricular element and one about which they should be cognizant. In a subsequent section of this chapter we describe the utility for aligning the "hidden" curriculum with the formal and intended content of instruction.

STANDARDIZING INFLUENCES

Given destabilizing conditions such as conflicting public perferences, "loose coupling," ineffective assessment, and the hidden curricula, why is there not widespread curriculum anarchy? In a few schools such may be the case. However, most American schools give the appearance of being remarkably ordered and similar. What accounts for this similarity?

---

[3] For added information on this topic, see Albert I. Oliver, *Curriculum Improvement: A Guide to Problems, Principles, and Process,* 2nd ed. (New York: Harper & Row, Publishers, Inc., 1977).

[4] James S. Coleman, *The Adolescent Society: The Social Life of the Teenager and Its Impact on Education* (New York: The Free Press, 1961).

There are a number of standardizing influences, many of them operating on a national level, which move the purposes of schooling and the content of the curriculum toward uniformity. The status of the curriculum in any particular school or district will be a product of the previously described destabilizing forces vis-à-vis an array of standardizing pressures described next.

Textbooks

Whereas there are thousands of school districts and tens of thousands of schools in the United States, there are but a few dozen major publishers of instructional texts. Less than 20 percent of these may control 80 percent of the elementary and secondary market. Publishing textbooks ia a major industry. It is estimated that U.S. schools spend approximately $2 billion annually on such materials. Business dynamics dictate that large numbers of a particular volume be sold in order to recoup textbook development and production costs and realize a profit. If only a limited number of books are to be sold, then the price of each copy can be elevated. However, under such conditions the publisher risks being unable to meet price competition. In order to achieve necessary dollar volume, major publishers employ a substantial sales force that encourages states to adopt, and districts to purchase, their books. As a consequence of these dynamics, a relatively small number of texts, particularly those used for instruction in elementary school subjects such as reading, mathematics, and science, come to dominate the market.

In order to be competitive, not only are these books comparably priced, but they are also often similar in character and content. Publishers are anxious to appeal to the widest possible audience; thus, their books are aimed at a common denominator of tastes and student ability. This is particularly the case where publishers are attempting to gain statewide adoptions.[5] In such instances not only do the texts have a unifying influence, but they also begin to slide toward the bland. These widely used texts begin to exert a standardizing influence upon what is taught in schools.

In the early 1980s, the textbook adoption process was widely criticized, and efforts were made by states to agree to higher literary standards and to enforce them by forming purchasing consortia. States such as California, Florida, and New York, when operating in the aggregate, possess abundant purchasing power so that by acting in consort, they are able to influence the quality and character of texts. It is presently too early to assess the outcome of this cooperative purchasing strategy.

---

[5] Approximately one-half the states "adopt" textbooks or approve a list of textbooks which then are supplied to or can be purchased by local school districts; see Barbara Crane, "The 'California Effect' on Textbook Adoptions," *Educational Leadership,* 32 (February 1975), 283–85; Frederick M. Wirt, "The Uses of Blandness: State, Local and Professional Roles in Citizenship Education," *Teaching About American Federal Bureaucracy,* ed. Stephen L. Schechter (Philadelphia: Temple University, 1983), ch. 8; and "Watered-Down Texts Worry Educators: Books Are Boring Critics Say," *The Washington Post,* October 16, 1984, pp. A1 and A10.

College Admission Requirements

It may well be that college entry criteria are the single largest determinant of secondary school subject matter content. The evidence is substantial that the majority of American secondary schools segregate students into "tracks." The utility of this instructional practice is arguable under the best of circumstances and may be counterproductive. Regardless, it happens, and students who are perceived, sometimes incorrectly, as the least able will be placed in "general" and "vocational," or "remedial," tracks. Academically oriented students will be placed in college bound tracks. The college bound curriculum is also likely, though in dilute form, to characterize the general track. These two tracks, college and general, between them contain the overwhelming majority, probably 75 percent, of secondary students.[6]

The majority of senior high schools shape their college bound course content and graduation requirements to conform with state university admission criteria. A select few high schools, those sending a disproportionate number of graduates to prestigious universities, may orient their curriculum to the admissions criteria of Stanford, Harvard, and other elite private higher educational institutions. Under these arrangements, students may well take subjects in addition to or in an advanced form over what their local college or state university system may require.

State college and university systems tend toward their own brand of entrance requirement uniformity. Higher educational institutions are part of an informal national network which judges and ranks colleges and universities, even if impressionistically, on the rigor of their academic standards and achievement of their student body and faculty. The result, even in the absence of a national secondary curriculum, is that senior high schools offer much the same schedule of course content regardless of the geographic region in which they are located or the kinds of youngsters they enroll.[7]

National Reform Efforts

American education is remarkably sensitive to societal influences. Periodically, a set of economic, social, or international circumstances may set in motion developments which will have substantial importance for education. Such upwellings may provoke discomfort for educators expected to conform to a reform surge, even if it is not particularly applicable to their school or district. Reform movements are not easy to predict, and their implications are often difficult to foresee even while in their midst. Generally, it is only after the fact that historians are able to discern their origins and lasting consequences, if any.[8] Educational leaders may be fortified by knowing the history of past periods of great school change and thus

---

[6] California State Department of Education, *California High School Curriculum Study: PATHS Through High School* (Sacramento, Calif.: January 5, 1984).

[7] Oliver, A., *Curriculum Improvement*, p. 158.

[8] See, for example, Diane Ravitch, *The Troubled Crusade: American Education 1945–1980* (New York: Basic Books, 1983); and David Tyack, Robert Lowe, and Elisabeth Hansot, *Public Schools in Hard Times: The Great Depression and Recent Years* (Cambridge: Harvard University Press, 1984).

may be better able to buffer themselves, their staff, and clients from inappropriate demands for reform.

What pattern emerges from more than six decades of curriculum reform? Almost always initiatives for macro reform stem from the larger society and are converted by the political system into alterations in educational policy. From that point on, however, it is useful to emphasize that no one reform era repeats itself.[9] Societal conditions which trigger periods of curriculum change may have comparable components, for example, international tension or economic uncertainty. However, particulars are unlikely to be the same over time. Similarly, only in the most general outline can reforms be categorized, for example, proposals for more testing, more rigorous graduation requirements, or more student discretion. Even the leadership for these movements has not proven identical. At times business interests have trumpeted the need for reform. On other occasions it has been military leaders, prestigious academicians, university presidents, and professional educators themselves.

CURRICULUM LEADERSHIP

Systematic Review

Public expectations, state statutes, economic conditions, student demographic composition, and the state of knowledge are continually changing. These and related conditions argue for regular reviews of curricula. Indeed, such systematic reviews can be part of an organization's strategic planning processes described in Chapter Eleven. Faculty senates and parent advisory councils, or whatever their analog, can assist in an annual or biennial review at a school site. Appropriately selected employee representatives and school board appointed citizens can engage in the same activity at the district level. State boards of education and chief state school officers often profit from a parallel procedure.

The intention of such activities is not to regularly change the content of instruction. The status quo may be perfectly appropriate. Rather, what is important is to appraise what exists and recommend change if there is good reason to do so. Change or no change, systematic reviews can ensure that what is being done or being proposed is suitable for the time and clientele to be served. Results of such systematic appraisals can be included in a school or district's annual report (see Chapter Fourteen).

Articulation

This label is conventionally used among educators to describe course content and performance expectation linkages from one grade level or one school level to the next. Does the content of the fifth grade mathematics program fit logically

---

[9] "Every reform is only a mask under cover of which a more terrible reform, which dares not yet name itself, advances."—Ralph Waldo Emerson.

with what is expected to be subsequently taught in the sixth grade? Does the science program in junior high or in a middle school mesh logically with what is taught in secondary school? Ensuring that the curriculum or content expected to be conveyed at each level is logically linked is a major responsibility of the principal at the school level and an appropriately assigned district level official. One of the dimensions upon which the annual or biennial curriculum review should concentrate is "articulation."

Articulation has yet a further dimension to which administrators should be attentive. Even when the curriculum of a school or system displays appropriate sequence, it is still possible for the program of any particular student to be illogical. College preparatory students are at the least peril in this regard. Higher education entry requirements are generally arrayed in sequence, for example, algebra leads to advanced mathematics, and science courses build upon each other. However, it is too often the case that students in a "general" track are overlooked. When subjected to scrutiny, their transcripts display a careless illogicality or a curriculum of least resistance, for example, algebra followed by consumer math or shop math, or world history followed by a course in "Yearbook."[10]

It is not typically an administrator's responsibility to ensure that each student has a coherent course of study. However, it is a school or district leader's responsibility to ensure that there is a policy and chain of command which oversees curriculum coordination or "articulation" for each student.[11]

Alignment

What is expected to be taught (reflected in policy), what teachers actually convey in their classrooms, what is transmitted through the larger school environment (the "hidden curriculum"), and what tests actually assess may all be different. It is possible for all four of these curricular components to overlap, but they need not necessarily be congruent. However, the effectiveness of an educational institution depends crucially upon their proper alignment. Disjuncture dilutes the effectiveness of curriculum policies and may lead to antithetical student outcomes. In order to ensure that these components are ordered correctly, it is necessary to periodically undertake an assessment of curriculum alignment. An improper alignment is represented graphically in Figure 8.2. An effective alignment is depicted in Figure 8.3.

There are no magical shortcuts in undertaking an assessment of alignment. It involves the time and deliberation of policy makers or their representatives, administrators, instructors, those responsible for constructing standardized tests, and often students. It is crucial that agreement be reached regarding the intent and content of instruction, to ensure thereafter that the environment of the school is

---

[10] California State Dept. of Education, *PATHS*.

[11] Evidence and advice on this topic is ably provided by John Goodlad, *A Place Called School* (New York: McGraw-Hill Book Company, 1983).

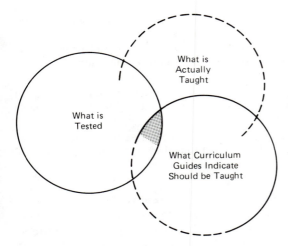

Figure 8.2   Before Curriculum Alignment.

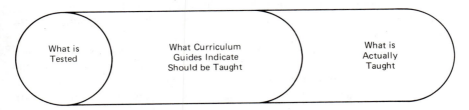

Figure 8.3   After Curriculum Alignment.

consistent with such purposes, and that tests validly assess the objectives being sought.[12]

INSTRUCTION

It is periodically proposed that school site administrators carry instructional responsibilities, even if but for one or a few hours each week, so as to better understand or remember the difficulties involved in teaching and to accord teaching higher status. If a school site administrator can arrange his or her other responsibilities to be able to undertake instruction, there appear to be several advantages:

> Administrators can model effective teaching practices (staff development literature indicates that teachers learn new teaching practices more effectively by watching others teach than by direct supervision).

[12] See Rubin Ingram, *Curriculum Implementation: Four Critical Elements* (Fountain Valley, Calif.: Fountain Valley Unified School District, 1983).

Administrators model the process of professional growth for teachers by visibly attempting to enlarge their own teaching repertoire.

Administrators, by teaching in every classroom over a period of time, create a new dimension for discussion and exchange with teachers about students, curriculum, and instruction.

Administrators, in interacting with students as instructors, gain knowledge of individual students and discipline leverage that would not be easily attainable any other way.

Administrators acting as instructors gain opportunities to diagnose school-wide problems such as noise level, classroom disruption, and student skill level.

Regardless of the utility of site administrators being directly engaged in teaching, the idea has not so far proven persuasive on a large scale. (Exceptions occur in small schools where administrative tasks may fall to a "head" teacher.) Consequently, instruction is an activity for which administrators often have responsibility but in which they are seldom direct participants. If an administrator is to be an effective "instructional leader," then he or she most often must accomplish this through the promulgation of policies and practices, and by inspiring and directing others.

Synthesis of research conducted on effective schools suggests several policy dimensions and leadership activities under the control of schools which can influence instruction and student achievement. This research strongly emphasizes the role of a school leader, the principal, in ensuring a high quality instructional staff, rigorous expectations for student and staff performance, maintenance of a supportive organizational climate within the school, effective grouping of students, allocation of time, and the provision of productive instructional strategies.[13]

Instructional Staff

Assuming that a school or district has employed a cadre of teachers which, at least on balance, is composed of able professionals, then much of instruction can be left to their discretion. Establishing the purposes of schooling or specifying, at least broadly, what the outcomes of schooling should be, can rightly be a responsibility of the public and the educational policy making system. However, selection of professional means for achieving such objectives can reside with teachers. Thus, in many dimensions, the most important instructional responsibility borne by an administrator is to ensure that only the most able available instructors are employed. Thereafter, effective leadership involves supporting the instructional staff, ensuring that their time is appropriately protected, and that they are rewarded for their efforts.

---

[13] This research is summarized by James Sweeney in "Research Synthesis of Effective School Leadership," *Educational Leadership* (February 1982), pp. 346–51.

Goal Setting and Expectations for Performance

Even within the context of a district or a single school, there are many more useful purposes to pursue than there are time and resources with which to accomplish them. To be effective, an organization as well as an individual must make choices from among a spectrum of activities competing for attention, for example, assisting students with academic preparation, personal growth, emotional security, or vocational training. Only by narrowing an organization's effort to a relatively few outcomes can resources be concentrated sufficiently to hold the prospect for success. Thus, an educational administrator has goal setting as one of his or her major duties. Seldom does this mean individually selecting one or a limited set of objectives and thereafter informing all others in the organization that they must pursue the newly announced ends. Rather, successful leaders elicit from the range of possible alternatives those which are most consistent with client expectations and, given the interests and capabilities of school staff, within reach of being accomplished. An example follows.

In 1961 President Kennedy announced that the United States would strive to place a man on the moon by the end of the decade. This was but one of many goals he could have announced. The goal could have been to end world hunger, eliminate armed international conflict, dispel unemployment, conquer cancer, or liberate all political prisoners. Presumably, all of these would have been valuable ends to achieve. However, the United States may not have had the wherewithal to succeed with some of them. Kennedy knew from his advisors that the technological ability to reach the moon was almost at hand and, with the appropriate motivation and marshalling of resources, the feat could be accomplished. In retrospect, the utility of such a goal can be questioned. How has mankind benefited as a result? The jury is still out on the issue. Nevertheless, as an act of leadership it was masterful. It was inspirational for citizens around the world; it motivated Americans and others to strive toward the goal.

Though a superintendent or principal might establish less lofty goals, the principle is the same. Individually and in the aggregate, human beings are advantaged by having agreed upon goals for which to strive. The manner in which the goals are established and the realistic prospect of their accomplishment are important. Nevertheless, to be effective, a school and district must be oriented around a sense of shared purpose, which must be conveyed to students. Research has made even more clear that high expectations for the performance of students is an important component in an effective school. It is perhaps the case that the strongest instructional instrument available to educators is the communication of high but not unreasonable achievement expectations.[14] Research on school effectiveness strongly suggests that a school's goals should stress academic achievement. Apparently, to do otherwise risks diluting the school's efforts.

[14] J. E. Brophy and T. L. Good, "Teachers' Communication of Differential Expectations of Children's Classroom Performance: Some Behavioral Data," *Journal of Educational Psychology,* 61 (1970), 365–74.

Instructional Strategies and Program Coordination

One of the means by which effective educational leaders link school personnel to the goals of their organization is by promoting encompassing instructional strategies. These strategies assist in concentrating school or district resources upon the educational objectives to be accomplished. Effective strategies involve the selection of textbooks and other instructional materials consistent with the agreed upon goals. Also, it is here that the content of each grade level and of various instructional categories of the curriculum is focused upon overall school objectives. The curriculum alignment to which we referred earlier in this chapter comes into play. When an administrator ensures that these and other components of instruction are focused and coordinated in a manner which facilitates accomplishment of previously agreed upon goals, the result can be an organization which is mobilized and motivated to achieve its purposes. The pieces of the puzzle fit together. Pupils, parents, and professional educators within the organization can all comprehend, agree with, and be committed to a sense of purpose.

Purposeful and Ordered Environment

Instructional goals for a district or school will depend upon many conditions, for example, parent expectations, state requirements, faculty and staff ability and interests, current status of student achievement, resource flexibility, and past practice. An educational administrator and his or her staff need to assess factors such as these before arriving at a relatively limited agenda of objectives—academic performance prime among them. However, once having established and gained agreement on a slate of goals, the organization can thereafter be suffused with a sense of purpose.

This sense of purpose can be accomplished by actions such as the following. Expectations for student achievement and staff performance can be clearly and consistently communicated. School resources can be oriented appropriately toward achievement of the goals. Monitoring procedures can enable members of the organization to know and understand the progress that is being made. Communication of progress can be accurate and frequent. Rewards can be public and appropriate. Assistance can be available for those having difficulty in achieving their part of the overall objective.

Student behavior needs to be consistent with the learning purposes of the school. Discipline policies appear most effective when agreed to by parents and staff, conveyed to students, and fairly and firmly enforced. The climate need not be heavy and oppressive, but simply be clearly oriented toward learning, not play or other distractions.

Goals should be structured so as to make clear that it is a team effort for which the cooperation of all portions of the school community is necessary. Periodic setbacks should be expected and, to a degree, even tolerated. On occasion, it may be necessary to revise a goal or extend a time limit. However, continued motivation toward achievement of goals is a professional responsibility of educational leaders.

Student Grouping

Students can be viewed through two sets of instructional policy lenses. On one hand, they are the recipients of instructions. As we have emphasized, the educational system is established in substantial measure for their benefit. Additionally, students can be viewed as an instructional variable. Research findings reveal that students' social and intellectual characteristics can influence instructional effectiveness. Students are themselves an instructional resource. Highly motivated students can assist in establishing a rigorous academic tone for a class or school.[15] Conversely, students who hold themselves in low regard and whose expectations for their own achievement may have been eroded over time can contribute to a classroom or schoolwide feeling of despair. This is one of the reasons why the drawing of school district lines, school attendance boundaries, and decisions regarding academic streaming and tracking of students are significant and often controversial.

There are at least three student allocation dynamics in operation. Decisions regarding who attends class with whom may be a decision about the allocation of an important instructional resource—student motivation and expectations. Second, the student composition of a class can influence the expectations, teaching style, and ultimately the effectiveness of an instructor.[16] Third, grouping students into tracks on the basis of "academic ability" may be allocating access to certain kinds of knowledge, for example, math or science, the absence of which jeopardizes a student's subsequent life chances.[17]

In addition to the qualitative consideration of students' social composition, there are considerations of quantity. What is the appropriate size for a school district, a school, or a class? Answers to the first part are quite mixed. Large districts and schools may enjoy economies of scale and may be better able to afford instructional specialization. They may give up advantages of client participation and organizational responsiveness in the process.[18]

School size is equally controversial. Informed opinion is beginning to lean more favorably toward smaller schools than was the case in prior decades when the school consolidation movement was in high gear. An evolving rule of thumb is that an elementary school should contain at least two classes per grade level so that a parent or child can always be offered the choice of another teacher should there be

[15] James S. Coleman and others, *Equal Educational Opportunity* (Washington, D.C.: U.S. Government Printing Office, 1966).

[16] J. Ide, G. D. Haertel, J. A. Parkerson, and H. J. Walberg, "Peer Group Influences on Learning: A Quantitative Synthesis," *Journal of Educational Psychology,* 73 (1981), 472–84.

[17] See John I. Goodlad, *A Place Called School* (New York: McGraw-Hill Book Company, 1983).

[18] See J. W. Guthrie, "Organizational Scale and School Success," *Educational Evaluation and Policy Analysis,* 1, no. 1 (1979), 17–27.

some irreconcilable conflict. Conversely, an elementary school in which it is impossible for the principal to know the names of every student is perhaps too large.

The greatest policy quandary may be over appropriate class size. The number of students for which an individual instructor has primary responsibility is a matter of substantial educational and financial significance. It is intuitively attractive to believe that the smaller the class the more effective instruction is likely to be. However, it rapidly becomes evident that any such analysis is confounded by variables such as the characteristics of students, subject matter being transmitted, and style and ability of the teacher. The matter becomes more of an issue by virtue of the fact that efforts to lower class size are among the most expensive instructional changes. The entire topic is generally controlled by state statutory size and is also subject to collective bargaining.

Regrettably, educational research findings regarding the consequences of class size are still in conflict.[19] What appears logical is that, one, in order to be worth doing, class size reduction probably must result in pupil groupings of twenty or fewer, depending upon subject matter and pupil characteristics. Otherwise, to spend money on reducing classes from an average of, for example, thirty-five to thirty-four, all other things being equal, may make little sense. Other instructional improvement strategies might make greater sense for the money.[20] The second logical point is that unless the teacher employs instructional techniques designed to take advantage of smaller classes, for example, more questions and less lecture, the added expense is unlikely to be to the benefit of students and their achievement.

Allocation of Time

Another major instructional policy variable over which educational administrators can exercise influence is "time." Time is a scarce resource. How much time of a student's life is to be devoted overall to schooling? Of the amount of student time schools obtain, how is it to be apportioned, throughout one's life or even in any one year? Of the amount allocated to any particular dimension or subject of schooling, how is it to be organized and used? How is the school day to be organized?

In the mid-1980s, Americans became highly conscious of the fact that U.S. students spent less time in school than their counterparts in nations such as Japan, Germany, France, and the Soviet Union.[21] It also became evident that even within

---

[19] B. S. Bloom, "The New Direction in Educational Research: Alterable Variables," *Phi Delta Kappan,* 61, no. 6 (1980), 382–85; and P. A. Cohen, J. A. Kulik, and C. C. Kulik, "Educational Outcomes of Tutoring: A Meta Analysis of Findings," *American Education Research Journal,* 19 (1982), 237–48; and Gene V. Glass, "A Meta Analysis of Research on Class Size and Achievement," *Educational Evaluation and Policy Analysis,* 1, no. 1 (1979), 2–16.

[20] Henry M. Levin, Gene V. Glass, and Gail R. Meister, *Cost Effectiveness for Four Educational Interventions* (Stanford, Calif.: Stanford University School of Education, Institute for Finance and Government), May 1984.

[21] See, for example, Thomas P. Rohlen, *Japan's High Schools* (Berkeley: University of California Press, 1983).

the United States various states required more time in school than did others. An initial reaction was to assume that more time, *ipso facto,* translates to higher achievement. Indeed, it is logical that all other conditions being equal, the longer a subject is studied, the more a pupil will learn. Most research results are consistent with this belief.[22]

As a reaction to the findings about "time," some states enacted programs offering financial incentives to local districts to extend their school year for more days and their school days for more minutes. Experts also began to suggest that the manner in which student time is spent is equally important. Simply extending school hours is by itself no guarantee that time is productively utilized. Hence, the concept of time has been refined to consider "time on task," or time in which the students are actively engaged in learning.[23]

It is probable that some subjects lend themselves to different time allocation patterns. For example, it may be that foreign language instruction is most effective when drill and reinforcement are frequent and systematic, perhaps for forty or forty-five minutes every school day. In contrast, a science class, particularly if it involves laboratory exercises, may well need a longer period of time, even if on a less frequent basis. Also, the effectiveness of instructional time can be enhanced by assignments to be completed outside of school. Homework policy can reinforce the purposes of schooling.[24]

Our purpose here is not to provide definitive answers. Rather, we wish to emphasize that "time" is among the most valuable resources and instructional policy variables at the disposal of educators. Overall length and scheduling sequence of the school year, whether or not schooling should be "year round," and when vacation periods should occur are important. Similarly, scheduling of the school day and the daily allocation of time to various components of the curriculum are significant items deserving thoughtful deliberation. Lastly, the manner in which available instructional time is used by the teacher is crucial.

In several "time" dimensions, research evidence is beginning to reach a stage where it can increasingly influence practice.[25] However, there continue to be many questions about time allocation and instruction for which there presently are no solid empirical answers. It is here that educational administrators will continue to have to pay attention to clients' tastes and the preferences and capabilities of their staffs in arriving at a schedule and time allocations which enhance instruction.

[22] For evidence on this point, see W. C. Frederick and H. J. Walberg, "Learning as a Function of Time," *Journal of Educational Research,* 73 (1980), 183–94.

[23] See Henry M. Levin, "What Time Is It?" (paper distributed by the Institute for Finance and Government, School of Education, Stanford University, Stanford, Calif., 1984). Also see Carolyn Denham and Ann Lieberman, eds., *Time to Learn* (Washington, D.C.: U.S. Dept. of Education, National Institute of Education, 1980).

[24] R. Paschal, T. Weinstein, and H. J. Walberg, "Effects of Homework: Quantitative Synthesis," *Journal of Educational Research* (in press).

[25] H. J. Walberg, "Improving the Productivity of America's Schools," *Education Leadership,* 41, no. 8 (1984), 19–27.

Evaluation

An effective school is likely to be one which engages in systematic assessment of student performance. Instructional objectives must be clear to teachers, parents, and students. Thereafter, a testing program is needed to appraise progress toward those goals. Test results are used for diagnosing impediments to individual student progress, gauging success of instructional strategies, as a means for informing parents and policy makers, as criterion measures for cost-effectiveness analyses, and possibly as outcomes by which to evaluate a principal and his or her staff.

A STRATEGY FOR STAYING ON COURSE

Dimensions of curriculum and instruction are among the most difficult policy issues with which educational administrators must deal. Few other circumstances are as intensely suffused with questions of value. Scheduling school buses, negotiating teacher contracts, and designing state school finance distribution formulae are laden with the potential for conflict. However, each is more amenable to compromise and does not strike so strongly at the core of public beliefs as do questions of what ought to be taught, who ought to be grouped with whom, who should have access to what knowledge, and how should teaching take place. Also, the fact that much of teaching remains an art and not a full-fledged science renders it difficult to acquire technical answers to many policy questions.

Given these many indeterminate conditions, what can educational administrators do to provide curriculum and instructional leadership and contribute appropriate stability to their organizations? Two strategies emerge as crucial in response to this question. One is for an administrator to regard himself or herself as a "hypothesis maker," constantly assessing what works best under what circumstances. Second, it is useful to continually assess societal conditions, educational research, student characteristics, and client and staff preferences in order to know when and in what directions change is appropriate.

By no means do we believe that a district or school leader should be a chameleon, constantly striving to have programs and practices take on the coloration of the latest public opinion nuance or faddish academic pronouncement. On the contrary, as we have emphasized elsewhere in this book, organizations cannot easily tolerate repeated change. A modicum of stability is necessary for employees and clients to be productive. Nevertheless, reasoned adaptation to change is appropriate. Such changes can be made more effectively if an organization's leader anticipates them accurately and focuses forces for change in productive channels.

One way to continually gauge the appropriateness and effectiveness of a school or school district's curricular offerings and instructional procedures is by relying on systematic assessment. Michael Kirst suggests that the following questions, if asked regularly, can assist in taking the curriculum and instructional pulse of an educational organization.[26]

Category I: Student Access and Availability of Courses

1. What courses and subjects are being offered (particularly in advanced content areas)? How and why have course offerings changed over the past five to ten years?

2. What are the trends in enrollments for courses by student subgroups over five or ten years? Why have some subjects increased or decreased in student enrollment?

3. What courses are then required for graduation? Recommended? Are these graduation standards pervaded by minimum concepts?

4. What are criteria for student access to courses? Do students and others know these? What do students see as barriers to taking particular courses?

5. When and how do students select or become assigned to courses, sequences, and tracks? Why do they take the courses they do (expecially *not* taking advanced courses)?

6. How much is course access affected by scheduling, number of periods per day, electives, and work experience programs?

7. What information is provided to students about the relationship between courses, sequences, requirements, college, and job entrance? What characterizes this student course planning process?

8. When and how is the information in 7 provided? (Prior to high school?)

9. What are sources of information and influences on student course planning? How are parents involved in this planning process? Are they aware of curricular choices and consequences?

10. Do students and parents feel well informed and confident about getting information? Are they satisfied with courses and their qualifications to choose them? How do they assess the planning process?

11. Are students tracked, laned, or otherwise grouped? How many tracks are there and what characterizes them (courses, students)? What effect does tracking have on instruction, content, student self-image, and aspirations?

12. Do courses in all tracks prepare students for advanced coursework (or is the track a barrier to advancement)?

Category II: Nature of Courses and Course Content

1. How consistent is course content across teachers and schools in terms of a) materials covered (texts, topics), b) number of assignments (writing, reading), and c) entrance and exit criteria?

[26] Questions are adapted from Michael W. Kirst, "Policy Implications of Individual Differences and the Common Curriculum," (chapter drafted for the 1983 National Society for the Study of Education Yearbook) *Individual Differences and the Common Curriculum,* ed. John Goodlad and Gary Fenstermacher (Berkeley: McCutchan, 1984).

2. How do policies or views of common curriculum or individual needs influence the outcomes in No. 1?

3. Why do teachers teach the particular courses they do?

4. How do teachers and others assess adequacy of course content, difficulty, and achievement? Is there periodic analysis of these?

5. How much do teachers modify their courses to accommodate student characteristics? What are the characteristics that most affect teacher planning?

6. Are courses sequential or otherwise articulated or coordinated? How? Why or why not? Is there an organizational structure to support this? Do students, teachers, and others see connections and continuity in sequences?

7. Do students experience instructional continuity in skills and subject matter? Do they get instruction in missing areas when needed? What barriers do they see in getting content, assistance, and good grades?

8. What are screening or entry and exit criteria for determining student mastery of content and access to appropriate instruction? Who decides what courses fit into various tracks? What specific content fits into tracks?

9. Are remediation, special assistance, and lower track courses designed to provide students with skills for more advanced work (or are they dead ends)?

Administrators as Hypothesis Makers

By "hypothesis maker," we mean a prevalent frame of mind among administrators. There is not yet a sufficient scientific base to justify rigidly prescribed instructional procedures. Educational research is increasingly of use to practitioners,[27] but the technological base of instruction needs continual expansion. Each school leader should attempt to add to that base by viewing current curricular and instructional arrangements as hypotheses, the effectiveness of which is continually to be assessed.

If a rearrangement is to take place in the school day, a different mode of grouping students to be initiated, a new textbook series to be purchased, or a new teaming of teachers to be tried, they should be viewed, in part, as "experiments" to be evaluated. It will not be possible in every instance to impose upon such experiments the rigorous canons of evaluation and scientific inquiry described in Chapter Eleven. Nevertheless, an administrator should specify (even if only to him- or herself) what it is about a new arrangement which is intended to improve student performance or enhance organizational effectiveness, and attempt in advance to note the criteria by which it will be possible to assess outcomes.

In an ideal world, each educator would be engaged in such hypothesis testing—teachers and administrators alike. When results were worth reporting, which does not necessarily mean that each "experiment" had positive outcomes, the hypothesis maker would write a short description of the procedures and consequences and submit it to a local or regional education journal for publication. In this man-

[27] B. S. Bloom, "The New Direction in Educational Research: Alterable Variables," *Phi Delta Kappan,* 61, no. 6 (1980), 382–85.

ner, practitioners could effectively contribute to the knowledge base of schooling and the entire educational enterprise could be rendered more productive and professional.

SUMMARY

The content of instruction, the curriculum, is tightly tied to the expectations for schooling held by a society generally, and the clients of a school specifically. In the United States, the school curriculum is established as an outcome of the dynamic tension existing between destabilizing forces such as conflicting public opinion, "loose coupling" of education organizations, the so-called "hidden curriculum" of schools, and inappropriate measurements procedures. Nationalizing forces such as textbook publication and selection, education reform efforts, national organizations, and college entrance requirements are also important factors. Instructional policies, though increasingly based upon scientific findings, are always subject to controversy.

Administrators are advised to assess the content of instruction on a regular basis and to pay particular attention to school goals and expectations for student performance, student instructional groupings, and use of time in schools. Lastly, the scientific base of instruction and the professional nature of education can be enhanced by school leaders who adopt the stance of hypothesis makers and thereafter begin to contribute to the systematically acquired base of knowledge regarding instruction.

SELECTED READINGS

Boyer, Ernest L., *High School: A Report on Secondary Education in America.* New York: Harper & Row, Publishers, Inc., 1983.

Flesch, Rudolf, *Why Johnny Can't Read.* New York: Harper & Row, Publishers, Inc., 1955.

Goodlad, John I., *A Place Called School.* New York: McGraw-Hill Book Company, 1983.

Kirst, Michael W., and Decker Walker, "An Analysis of Curriculum Policy Making," *Review of Educational Research,* 41 (1971), 479–509.

LEADERSHIP BEHAVIOR

chapter 9

Functions performed by education executives at school site and central office levels have expanded in scope and become extremely complex. For example, school administrators are expected to provide leadership in important educational endeavors such as goal setting, organizational planning, guiding instruction, implementing curricular changes, and evaluating personnel while simultaneously managing concrete activities such as transportation, facilities, maintenance, and food service. It may be the case that other staff will provide assistance; nevertheless, major responsibility for educational leadership and management is that of the chief administrator at either the school site or district office. Thus, school administrators not only must acquire broad knowledge concerning functions they will be expected to perform but also must possess the skills necessary to carry them out. In this chapter we concentrate particularly upon conceptualizations of the administrator's role, insights on leadership effectiveness, influences on administrative behavior and managerial thought, decision making, theories of motivation, and effective time management.

CONCEPTUALIZATIONS OF THE ADMINISTRATOR'S ROLE

Several efforts have been undertaken to conceptualize basic components of the administrator's role. What should administrators do and what do they actually do? The role of the school administrator, therefore, can be viewed through two lenses: process or universal principles and tasks or actual practices.

Administrative Principles

Among initial advocates of the universality of administrative functions or principles of management was Henri Fayol. Writing in the early 1900s, Fayol posited that essential management elements consisted of planning, organizing, commanding, coordinating, and controlling.[1] He viewed these endeavors as undergirding all managerial processes. Gulick later augmented this list and held that the administrative process consisted of planning, organizing, staffing, directing, coordinating, reporting, and budgeting.[2] Subsequent generations of administrators have relied upon the mnemonic "POSDCORB" as a means to remember these functions.

Fayol's and Gulick's conceptualizations of universal principles of administration continue to be useful. Other theorists also have contributed to our understanding of administration. For example, in 1923 Sheldon stressed that administration was both a scientific process and a philosophy.[3] Managers not only perform functions such as those listed by Fayol but also have an ethical and moral responsibility to the community. Herbert Simons[4] and Daniel Griffith[5] have written persuasively about the decision-making functions of administrators. The sum of these views is an expanded list of administrative functions: planning, leading, evaluating, decision making, coordinating, organizing, budgeting, and staffing—PLEDCOBS.

Administrative Practice

In contrast to the theoretical and normative dimensions of an administrator's role, what is it that school administrators actually do? Much of the site administrator's time is spent engaged in important but fundamentally noninstructional activities: supervising students between classes in the hallways, at lunch, at various extracurricular events, before and after school, during bus loading and unloading; responding to parental and community concerns; preparing reports and responding to central office requests; resolving conflicts between students and between students and teachers; handling student discipline; requiring and distributing particular teacher resources; scheduling classes and other school activities; supervising staff; meeting with individuals and small groups of students, teachers, and parents; and responding to any number of unexpected school emergencies that may arise during the school day. Activities that are more clearly within the purview of instructional

---

[1] Henri Fayol, *Administration Industrielle et Générale*, trans. Constance Storrs, *General and Industrial Management* (London: Sir I. Pitman and Sons, Ltd., 1949).

[2] Luther Gulick, "Notes on the Theory of Organization," *Papers on the Science of Administration* (New York: Institute of Public Administration, Columbia University, 1937.) Also, see Jesse B. Sears, *The Nature of the Administrative Process* (New York: McGraw-Hill Book Company, 1950). These concepts were tailored to education by Ordway Tead, *Art of Administration* (New York: McGraw-Hill Book Company, 1951).

[3] Oliver Sheldon, *Philosophy of Management* (London: Sir I. Pitman and Sons, Ltd., 1923).

[4] Herbert A. Simon, *Administration Behavior. A Study of Decision-Making Processes in Administrative Organization,* 2nd ed. (New York: Macmillan, Inc., 1961).

[5] Daniel E. Griffiths, *Administrative Theory* (New York: Appleton-Century-Crofts, 1959).

leadership, such as teacher supervision, classroom observation, curriculum development and evaluation, and instructional support and technical assistance for teachers, generally have not represented significant portions of the site administrator's day. The crucial instructional leadership role of the site administrator, which we observe more fully in Chapter Eight, is mitigated by routine and managerial responsibilities.

Several studies confirm the domination of noninstructional leadership functions in which site administrators engage. A national survey of high school principals revealed that their median work week was 56.5 hours. During this period the top three activities that consumed the majority of their time were school management, personnel management, and student activities.[6] In contrast, these high school principals desired to spend a major portion of their time on (1) program development; (2) personnel activities; and (3) school management. A complete listing of the activities of the principal during a typical work week ranked in order from the most time consuming activity (1) to the least (9) is displayed in Table 9.1.

Using an ethnographic approach to analyze how a single elementary school principal used his time throughout the school day, Wolcott provides an interesting account of the enormous amount of time spent interacting with others.[7] Because of these interactions, Wolcott concludes that the amount of administrator time available for other school activities is restricted.

In another ethnographic study in which twenty-four building principals were studied over a two-year period, Morris and his associates concluded that the principal's workday typically is not focused on instructional leadership activities. Rather, the principal's day is unpredictable and filled with short duration face-to-face encounters with staff, students, and parents that are encouraged through such mana-

Table 9.1   ALLOCATION OF TIME FOR A TYPICAL WORK WEEK

AREA OF RESPONSIBILITY	DO SPEND TIME	SHOULD SPEND TIME
School management	1	3
Personnel	2	2
Student activities	3	4
Student behavior	4	7
Program development	5	1
District office	6	9
Planning	7	5
Community	8	8
Professional development	9	6

Source: David R. Byrne, Susan A. Hines, and Lloyd E. McCleary, *The Senior High School Principalship,* Vol. I, The National Survey (Reston, Va.: National Association of Secondary School Principals, 1978), p. 20.

[6] David R. Byrne, Susan A. Hines, and Lloyd E. McCleary, *The Senior High School Principalship,* Vol. I, The National Survey (Reston, Va.: National Association of Secondary School Principals, 1978), p. 21.

[7] Harry F. Wolcott, *The Man in the Principal's Office. An Ethnography* (New York: Holt, Rinehart and Winston, 1973), p. 88.

gerial activities as student monitoring, disseminating information to others in and outside the school, and handling disputes and disturbances.[8] Several other studies also underscore the fact that school principals and superintendents spend a majority of their time performing tasks that have little direct relationship to instruction.[9]

School administrators must be both managers and leaders. As managers they must ensure that fiscal and human resources are used effectively in accomplishing organizational goals. As leaders they must display the vision and skills necessary to create and maintain a suitable teaching and learning environment, to develop school goals, and to inspire others to achieve these goals. It is essential to school effectiveness that both managerial and leadership functions be rank ordered and superbly performed. Simultaneously, school systems are obligated to provide sufficient administrative support so that the pressure of managerial functions does not, out of necessity, restrict the opportunity to engage in leadership activities related to teaching and learning.

LEADERSHIP EFFECTIVENESS

Throughout this volume we have referred to various functions of the school leader and to the importance of leader effectiveness. It is clear that individual school and school system effectiveness is a function of leadership. By leadership we refer to that quality which enables an individual within a given setting to motivate and inspire others to adopt, achieve, and maintain organizational and individual goals. School leaders such as principals and superintendents are legally empowered and liable for different operational aspects of the educational system. These leaders derive authority and power from their positions. Hence, one dimension of leader effectiveness is associated with the legitimate use of authority and power to accomplish organizational tasks. But leader effectiveness is also dependent on personal characteristics, interaction with followers, and the situation itself. Consequently, four basic lines of research have been pursued in an attempt to account for leader effectiveness: (1) identification of traits; (2) influence through power; (3) analyses of behaviors; and (4) the relationship of situational variables and leadership—the contingency approach. School leaders should understand these conceptualizations or approaches as they seek to enhance their effectiveness.

[8] Van Cleve Morris, Robert L. Crowson, Cynthia Porter-Gehrie, and Emanuel Hurwitz, Jr., *Principals in Action. The Reality of Managing Schools* (Columbus, Ohio: Charles E. Merrill Publishing Company, 1984).

[9] For example see Rodney J. Reed, *School Principals: Leaders or Managers* (Eugene, Oregon: ERIC Clearing House on Educational Management, University of Oregon, 1978); Kent D. Peterson, "The Principal's Tasks," *Administrator's Notebook,* 26, no. 8 (1977-78), 1-4; W. T. Martin and D. J. Willower, "The Managerial Behavior of High School Principals," *Educational Administration Quarterly,* 17, no. 1 (1981), 69-90; Donald J. Willower and H. W. Fraser, "School Superintendents on Their Work," *Administrators Notebook,* 28, no. 5 (1980), 1-4.

Leadership Traits

An insistent and vivid theme displayed in early studies was that effective leaders possess a set of innate traits and abilities that distinguish them from non-leaders. By identifying these traits and abilities, a composite picture could be constructed against which future or potential leaders could be assessed. Reviews of early leadership trait studies reveal no consistent pattern of traits for leaders exclusive of nonleaders or for effective leaders compared to ineffective leaders.[10] A different conclusion emerges, however, from more recent literature.[11] Several traits are apparently associated with effective leaders in management situations. These include high need for achievement, self-confidence, need for socialized power, desire to compete with peers, high energy level, interest in oral, persuasive activities, and relevant technical, conceptual, and interpersonal skills.[12]

Power-Influence Approach

Leaders and followers have influence over one another. Leaders exert influence through *power* (the ability of one actor to get another actor to change his or her behavior or to do something which he or she might otherwise might not do) and *authority* (the right to exert influence legitimated by follower consent or the position held). The manifestation of power by followers is associated with the extent to which leaders depend on information they generate, expertise they possess, or cooperation shown in meeting organizational goals. Leaders derive power from two sources: their position (position power) and personal characteristics (personal power) such as expertise or charisma.

Several conceptualizations and definitions of power can be noted. Weber defines power as "the probability that one actor within a social relationship will be in a position to carry out his own will despite resistance."[13] Weber distinguishes power from authority by saying that the latter encompasses legitimation, which connotes an acceptance of power because of value-congruence between the exerciser of power and those affected by it. In other words, authority is legitimated power.[14]

Weber held that legitimated power or authority is inherent in the hierarchical

---

[10] See Ralph M. Stodgill, "Personal Factors Associated with Leadership: A Survey of the Literature," *Journal of Psychology,* 25 (January 1948), 35–71; Cecil A. Gibb, "Leadership," *Handbook of Social Psychology* ed. Gardner Lindzey, (Cambridge, Mass.: Addison-Wesley Publishing Co., Inc., 1954), pp. 877–920.

[11] Ralph M. Stodgill, *Handbook of Leadership: A Survey of Theory and Research* (New York: The Free Press, 1974); Gary Yukl, *Leadership in Organizations* (Englewood Cliffs, N.J.: Prentice-Hall, Inc., 1981); Bernard M. Bass, *Stodgill's Handbook of Leadership: A Survey of Theory and Research,* rev. and expanded ed. (New York: The Free Press, 1981).

[12] Gary Yukl, "Managerial Leadership," *The Effective Principal. A Research Summary* (Reston, Va.: National Association of Secondary School Principals, 1982), p. 2.

[13] Max Weber, *The Theory of Social and Economic Organization,* ed. Talcott Parsons and trans. A. M. Henderson and Talcott Parsons (Glencoe, Ill.: Free Press & Falcon's Wing Press, 1947), p. 152.

[14] Amitai Etzioni, *Modern Organizations* (Englewood Cliffs, N.J.: Prentice-Hall, Inc., 1964), p. 51.

structure he advocated for the bureaucracy. In this structure each higher office assumes superiority over a lower office. Each office is staffed on the basis of technical expertise and competence, which presumably ensures that the office-holder willingly accepts authority vested in that position. It is not reasonable to expect that the technical competence of office-holders will always be superior to that of subordinate staff within an office. Yet the structural hierarchy of authority is viewed as essential for organizational effectiveness and for the coordination and control of goals, objectives, and standards.

Etzioni posits three types of power—coercive, remunerative, and normative. By coercive power he refers to the application (or threat) of physical sanctions. Remunerative power refers to control over material resources and rewards. Normative power is the allocation and manipulation of symbolic rewards and deprivations through employment of leaders, manipulation of mass media, allocation of esteem and prestige symbols, administration of ritual (pure normative power), and influence over the distribution of acceptance and positive response (social power). Etzioni argues further that when two kinds of power are emphasized at the same time over the same subject group they tend to neutralize each other.[15]

French and Raven provide an expanded conceptualization of power in which five sources of power are postulated.[16]

Reward power—the control and distribution of rewards valued by others.

Coercive power—the control and withholding of reward valued by others.

Legitimate power—authority vested in or assigned to a position.

Expert power—the expertise of special knowledge, skill, or experience.

Referent power—personal attractiveness or membership in someone's primary experience group. The desire to be like someone.

French and Raven's conceptualization distinguishes between power derived from the organization—reward, coercive, legitimate—and power which resides in the individual—expert, referent. Which form or forms of power used will clearly depend on the situation. There is evidence, for instance, to suggest that expert, legitimate, and referent power are preferred and more willingly accepted than reward or coercive power by college teachers and salesmen.[17]

According to Pfeffer, power in organizations may be viewed as a structural phenomenon created by the division of labor and departmentalization that occurs

[15] Amitai Etzioni, *A Comparative Analysis of Complex Organizations* (New York: The Free Press, 1961).

[16] John R. P. French, Jr., and Bertram Raven, "The Bases of Social Power," *Studies in Social Power* ed. Dorwin Cartwright (Ann Arbor, Mich.: Institute for Social Research, 1959), pp. 150–67.

[17] See Jerry G. Bachman, "Faculty Satisfaction and the Dean's Influence: An Organizational Study of Twelve Liberal Arts Colleges," *Journal of Applied Psychology,* 52, no. 1, Part 1 (1968), 55–61; and Jerry G. Bachman, C. G. Smith, and J. A. Slesinger, "Control, Performance, and Satisfaction: An Analysis of Structural and Individual Effects," *Journal of Personality and Social Psychology,* 4, no. 2 (1966), 127–36.

as task specialization is implemented.[18] As a result, some tasks will be considered more important than others. Those persons and units having the responsibility for performing more critical tasks in the organization have a natural advantage in developing and exercising power. Consequently, the power of members in an organization is determined by the importance of what they do and the skill with which they do it. Pfeffer, therefore, proposes eight sources of power within organizations: (1) dependence; (2) providing resources; (3) coping with uncertainty; (4) being irreplaceable; (5) affecting the decision process; (6) consensus as represented by easily articulated and understood positions and perspectives; (7) processes of power requisition, for example, appointments to boards; and (8) political skills.[19]

Power resides in the individual and is bestowed by the office or position within the organization. It cannot be avoided in an organization, nor should it be. It is essential for establishing and accomplishing organizational goals effectively, maintaining standards, and reducing uncertainty. Coercive and reward power, however, tend to be less acceptable or satisfactory than expert, legitimate, or referent power.[20]

Behavioral Approach

Studies of leader behavioral styles reveal that concern for the individual and for the task of the organization are important dimensions of leadership. As defined in the Ohio State University studies, these dimensions were "initiating structure" and "consideration."[21] *Initiating structure* refers to the manner in which organizational procedures and leader-follower role relationships are defined in seeking to satisfy organizational goals. *Consideration* is that capacity to foster and engender leader-follower trust, warmth, and respect.

Likert's research generated similar dimensions of leadership. He concluded that leaders could be classified as being "job-centered" or "employee-centered."[22] The former—production-oriented leaders—concern themselves with accomplishing organizational tasks. Employee-centered leaders focus on employees' individual needs for fulfillment and involvement. Likewise, Cartwright and Zander's research indicates that goal achievement and group maintenance are significant features of leadership.[23]

Concern for the task of the organization or the interpersonal needs of individuals are distinct facets of leader behavior. Some leaders manifest more of one

[18] Jeffery Pfeffer, *Power in Organizations* (Marshfield, Mass.: Pitman Publishing Co., 1981), p. 98.

[19] Pfeffer, J., *Power,* pp. 97–135.

[20] French, J. and Raven, B., "Bases of Social Power," *Studies in Social Power,* ed. Cartwright, pp. 150–67.

[21] Ralph M. Stogdill and Alvin E. Coons, eds., *Leader Behavior: Its Description and Measurement,* Research Monograph No. 88 (Columbus: Ohio State University, Bureau of Business Research, 1957).

[22] Rensis Likert, *New Patterns of Management* (New York: McGraw-Hill Book Company, 1961).

[23] Dorwin Cartwright and Alvin Zander, eds., *Group Dynamics: Research and Theory,* 2nd ed. (Evanston, Ill.: Row, Peterson & Company, 1960).

than the other, some neither. In general, leaders who frequently display high levels of individual consideration and concern for organizational goals tend to be more effective.[24] Effectiveness of leadership style, however, is contingent on the situation. It is logical to assume, therefore, that a single and inflexible leadership style is impractical, undesirable, and unwarranted.

Contingency Approach

Effective leadership, as postulated by contingency theorists, is a function of the interaction of leader behavior or style and situational variables. In this view, there is no single best leadership style. Leadership behaviors are effective or ineffective depending upon the situation in which leadership is exercised.

Fiedler, an early proponent of the contingency approach, holds that favorableness of the situation for the leader in relationship to the leader's style determines group effectiveness or how successfully tasks are accomplished. Situation favorability is measured by (1) *leader-member relations*—degree of respect and extent of support the leader is accorded by subordinates; (2) *task structure*—existence of guidelines and procedures relative to organizational tasks and job assignments; and (3) *position power*—leader's discretion and influence over hiring, evaluating, rewarding, and dismissing subordinates.[25] The most favorable situation is one in which leader-member relations are positive, the task is highly structured, and position power is strong.

In Fiedler's model, effectiveness is a function of the leader's style, which is classified as task or relationship oriented. Style is determined by measuring leader attitude through use of Fiedler's least preferred coworker scale (LPC). Leaders who score low on the LPC are thought of as task oriented and those with high scores as relationship oriented. Both facets are indicative of leader attitude or motivation. According to Fiedler, task-oriented leaders are more effective than those who are relationship oriented in situations that are either very favorable or very unfavorable to them. Conversely, relationship-oriented leaders are more effective in situations that are moderately favorable. Fiedler's contingency theory, however, has been criticized because it has low predictive ability and methodological flaws.[26]

House employs a "path-goal" theory to explain leader influence on subordinate work motivation and satisfaction.[27] According to this view, subordinate motivation and satisfaction must be seen in relationship to situational outcomes. That is,

---

[24] Andrew W. Halpin, *Theory and Research in Administration* (New York: Macmillan, Inc., 1966), pp. 97–98.

[25] Fred E. Fiedler, *A Theory of Leadership Effectiveness* (New York: McGraw-Hill Book Company, 1967).

[26] Ahmad S. Ashour, "The Contingency Model of Leadership Effectiveness: An Evaluation," *Organizational Behavior and Human Performance,* 9, no. 3 (June, 1973), 339–55; Gary Yukl, "Managerial Leadership and the Effective Principal," *The Effective Principal, A Research Summary,* p. 5; Chester A. Schriesheim and Steven Kerr, "Theories and Measures of Leadership: A Critical Analysis," *Leadership: The Cutting Edge* eds. James G. Hunt and Lars L. Lawson (Carbondale, Ill.: Southern Illinois University Press, 1977).

[27] Robert J. House, "A Path Goal Theory of Leadership Effectiveness," *Administrative Science Quarterly,* 16, no. 3 (September 1971), 321-38.

the force of an individual's motivation to act is related to perceived desirability of the outcome and the expectation that the outcome will be attained. Leader behaviors thought to influence the path-goal expectancy linkage are categorized by House and Mitchell as (1) *directive*—gives specific orders to subordinates; (2) *achievement-oriented*—sets high standards, offers challenging goals. has high expectations for subordinate performance; (3) *supportive*—concern for interpersonal needs of subordinates; and (4) *participative*—consulting with subordinates in making decisions.[28] Directive and achievement-oriented leaders can be equated with "initiating structure" while supportive and participative leaders bear a similarity to the "consideration" dimension, identified in the previously mentioned Ohio State University leadership studies. Each behavior is applicable depending on the situation. When there is role ambiguity, directive leadership increases job motivation and satisfaction. Supportive leadership increases satisfaction in situations in which tasks are narrowly defined. Achievement-oriented leader behavior enhances subordinate feelings of self-confidence in meeting challenging goals while participative leader behavior increases work satisfaction when tasks are unstructured. These behaviors are summarized in Table 9.2.

A third contingency approach is the situational leadership theory of Hersey and Blanchard. These researchers contend that leadership style should be a function of follower maturity level. Maturity is viewed on two dimensions: job ability and psychological willingness.[29] Leadership styles to be used in accordance with maturity level are categorized as telling, selling, participating, and delegating. The first two styles—telling and selling—are considered to be task behaviors in which direction and guidance are provided. The second two styles are relationship behaviors, those in which the leader provides "support, encouragement, 'psychological strokes,' and facilitating behaviors." The fit between leader style and follower maturity level is depicted in Table 9.3.

Hersey and Blanchard's model simply posits that as followers or groups mature, the style of the leader should change from task orientation to relationship orientation. While the model has some appeal, research data regarding the validity of its inherent propositions are sparse. Moreover, whether other situational variables besides follower maturity level are important in determining leadership style or whether leadership style includes a broader range than that indicated in the model are questions of continuing concern.

In summary, leader behavior is crucial to the effectiveness with which followers, subordinates, groups, and schools perform their tasks. In an attempt to understand effective leadership, research attention was originally focused on leader traits. Early studies displayed inconsistent findings. More recent studies indicate, however, that some characteristics of leaders are important, for example, high need for achievement, self-confidence, and high personal energy level. The power-influ-

---

[28] Robert J. House and Terence R. Mitchell, "Path-Goal Theory of Leadership," *Journal of Contemporary Business,* 3, no. 4 (Autumn 1974), 81–97.

[29] Paul Hersey and Kenneth A. Blanchard, *Management of Organizational Behavior: Utilizing Human Resources,* 4th ed. (Englewood Cliffs, N.J.: Prentice-Hall, Inc., 1982), p. 157.

Table 9.2 SUMMARY OF PATH-GOAL RELATIONSHIPS

LEADER BEHAVIOR AND CONTINGENCY FACTORS	CAUSE	SUBORDINATE ATTITUDES AND BEHAVIOR
1 Directive 2 Supportive 3 Achievement-Oriented 4 Participative		
1 Subordinate Characteristics 　Authoritarianism 　Locus of Control 　Ability } Influence	Personal Perceptions	1 Job Satisfaction 　Job → Rewards 2 Acceptance of Leader 　Leader → Rewards
2 Environmental Factors 　The Task 　Formal Authority System 　Primary Work Group } Influence	Motivational Stimuli Constraints Rewards	3 Motivational Behavior 　Effort → Performance 　Performance → Rewards

Source: Robert J. House and Terence R. Mitchell, "Path-Goal Theories of Leadership," *Journal of Contemporary Business*, 3, no. 4 (Autumn 1974), 89.

Table 9.3   **LEADERSHIP STYLES APPROPRIATE FOR VARIOUS MATURITY LEVELS**

MATURITY LEVEL	APPROPRIATE STYLE
M1 *Low Maturity* Unable and unwilling or insecure	S1 *Telling* High task and low relationship behavior
M2 *Low to Moderate Maturity* Unable but willing or confident	S2 *Selling* High task and high relationship behavior
M3 *Moderate to High Maturity* Able but unwilling or insecure	S3 *Participating* High relationship and low task behavior
M4 *High Maturity* Able/competent and willing/confident	S4 *Delegating* Low relationship and low task behavior

Source: Paul Hersey and Kenneth H. Blanchard, *Management of Organizational Behavior: Utilizing Human Resources,* 4th ed. (Englewood Cliffs, N.J.: Prentice-Hall, Inc., 1982), p. 154.

ence approach to leadership effectiveness posits that power resides in the position as well as in the individual. Followers or subordinates also possess power which can be a counterbalance to the excessive use of power by leaders. Legitimate, referent, and expert power tend to be more readily accepted by followers than coercive or reward power. The behavioral approach to leadership study revealed that leader behavior consists of two components which could be plotted on distinct axes: initiating structure—concern for goal attainment or organizational tasks; and consideration—concern for individual interpersonal needs. The contingency or situational leadership approach holds that leader effectiveness must be juxtaposed with situational variables. There is no one best style of leadership. Effective leaders use several styles as the situation demands.

Influences on Administrative Behavior

Current theories seek to explain interaction between leaders' styles and situational characteristics. How individuals behave in leadership positions or the styles that characterize their behavior may result from implicit and explicit assumptions they hold regarding subordinates. Such assumptions are the focal point of several management theories. One of the most compelling of these was formulated by McGregor.[30] It is his contention that the manner in which managers behave toward

[30] Douglas McGregor, *The Human Side of Enterprise* (New York: McGraw-Hill Book Company, 1960), pp. 33-34.

workers, or the management strategies they use, result from either the notion that exercise of authority and control is necessary to motivate people to accomplish organizational ends (Theory "X") or a belief that people intrinsically wish to perform well and accomplish individual goals through meeting those of the organization (Theory "Y"). The assumptions of Theory "X" are

1. The average human being has an inherent dislike of work and will avoid it if he can.

2. Because of human distaste for work, most people must be coerced, controlled, directed, or threatened in order to induce them to put forth effort toward achievement of organizational objectives.

3. The average human being prefers to be directed, wishes to avoid responsibility, has relatively little ambition, and above all wants security.

In contrast, Theory "Y" assumes

1. Expenditure of physical and mental effort in work is as natural as play or rest. The average human being does not inherently dislike work. Depending upon controllable conditions, work may be a source of satisfaction (and will be voluntarily performed or a source of punishment (and will be avoided if possible).

2. External control and threat of punishment are not the only means for bringing about effort toward organizational objectives. Humans will exercise self-direction and self-control in the service of objectives to which they are committed.

3. Commitment to objectives is a function of rewards associated with their achievement. The most significant of such rewards, for example, satisfaction of ego and self-actualization needs, can be direct products of effort directed toward organizational objectives.

4. The average human being learns, under proper conditions, not only to accept but also to seek responsibility. Avoidance of responsibility, lack of ambition, and emphasis on security are generally consequences of experience, not inherent human characteristics.

5. Capacity to exercise a relatively high degree of imagination, ingenuity, and creativity in the solution of organization problems is widely, not narrowly, distributed in the population.

6. Under conditions of modern industrial life, intellectual potentialities of average human beings are only partially utilized.

Theories "X" and "Y" might be thought of as opposite ends on a continuum. Theory "X" embraces an authoritarian model of leadership while Theory "Y" is humanitarian and assumes the utility of participatory decision making and democratic principles. Theory "X" views people as dependent and in need of control while Theory "Y" assumes a human tendency to progress toward independence and self-sufficiency. From the vantage point of Argyris, this is a movement from immaturity toward maturity.[31] It is unlikely, however, that modern administrators

[31] Chris Argyris, *Integrating the Individual and the Organization* (New York: John Wiley & Sons, Inc., 1964).

function exclusively under assumptions of either Theory "X" or Theory "Y." In practice, managers may display characteristics associated with either theory depending upon organizational and individual characteristics.

Rensis Likert also has speculated about the presumed nature of workers, which influences managerial strategy and behavior. Perceptions of the degree to which managers have confidence and trust in subordinates and thus involve them in a participatory or consultative way can be placed on a continuum that includes four belief systems. System I is analogous to McGregor's Theory "X." At this level the trust and confidence managers place in workers is virtually nil. At the other end of Likert's continuum is the System IV manager who has full confidence in workers and who consults with them and involves them in decision making. Systems II and III represent progressive movement toward IV.[32]

It is conceivable that school administrators view leadership through an authoritarian lens (Theory "X" or System I). Yet notions of "running a tight ship" depend upon assumptions about subordinates that may be dysfunctional. This dysfunctionality is illustrated in Ouchi's analysis of Japanese and American businesses.[33] It is his view that American organizations embrace principles that generally fail to involve workers and provide for their development in a fashion that demonstrates trust, confidence, and respect. Ouchi offers the following organizational contrast:

Japanese Organizations	*American Organizations*
Lifetime employment	Short term employment
Slow evaluation and promotion	Rapid evaluation and promotion
Nonspecialized career paths	Specialized career paths
Implicit control mechanisms	Explicit control mechanisms
Collective decision making	Individual decision making
Collective responsibility	Individual responsibility
Wholistic concern	Segmented concern

Leader behavior is influenced at a fundamental level by implicit and explicit assumptions regarding workers. School leaders should recognize that staff members often desire to be closely involved in decisions and may possess the potential for making significant contributions to the organization's overall effectiveness. While it may not always be possible or desirable for school administrators to avoid behaviors identified with McGregor's Theory "X" or Likert's System I, leadership assumptions associated with Theory "Y" and System IV are probably more effective in a school setting.

[32] Rensis Likert, *The Human Organization* (New York: McGraw-Hill Book Company, 1967).
[33] William G. Ouchi, *Theory Z. How American Business Can Meet the Japanese Challenge* (New York: Avon Books, 1982).

DECISION MAKING

A major function of administrators is making decisions—the process through which a plan for action is selected from at least two alternatives. Decision making involves several steps: specifying the problem, analyzing its components, developing strategies or alternatives for resolving the problem, selecting the best alternative, developing and implementing an action plan, evaluating effectiveness of the plan, and recycling as necessary.

The first step in the process—specifying or identifying the problem—involves determination of a disparity between an existing and a desired state. This determination may result from an assessment of organizational goals and objectives. For example, the goal of school "E" may be to produce national merit scholars. In examining the extent to which this goal has been achieved, it is determined that not one national merit scholar has been produced in the fifteen years since the organization proclaimed that goal. So the problem, at least on the surface, is a failure to produce merit scholars. Another problem might be students who are frequently sent out of a particular class for discipline. The problem in this instance may be unruly students, or perhaps inappropriate curriculum materials fail to capture the class' interest. Problems emerge from a variety of conditions. In general, however, they come into existence when there is a discrepancy between what exists and what is desired.

Once identified, the manner in which a problem is handled by those in leadership positions depends on whether the issue is routine or unique. Routine problems often can be resolved through established policies, rules, or procedures. Decisions that make use of these developed-in-advance plans for action are referred to by Simon as programmed decisions.[34] Unique problems are those for which procedures or policies have not been developed in advance. These issues require non-programmed decisions. Unique problems trigger a decision-making or problem-solving sequence which, ideally, is designed to provide the best or most rational solution to the problem. As shall become evident, rational or ideal solutions are not always possible.

The second step in the decision-making process is to analyze the problem. This necessitates careful analysis of the forces that create and maintain the problem. Using an earlier example, absence of national merit scholars may be a manifestation of other related problems. In this instance one might ask, "Is this actually a problem of inappropriate curriculum, low student or teacher morale, inadequate classroom equipment, or lack of individualized instruction?" Clearly, any or all of these reasons, and others not indicated, may contribute to the stated problem and may in fact be the more appropriate problem to address. Determining the primary cause of the problem is a matter of judgment informed by expertise. Such determination can be made individually but is sometimes more effectively made through a decision-making group (we explore this point in a later section).

---

[34] Herbert A. Simon, "The Executive As Decision Maker," *An Introduction to School Administration, Selected Readings,* ed. M. Chester Nolte (New York: Macmillan, Inc., 1966), p. 209.

In analyzing the problem through a decision-making group, the use of force-field analysis may be of great use.[35] This analytical technique provides for identification of forces which prevent, and those which serve to move toward, achievement of a desired state. Once identified, forces are placed in priority order within each of the two categories. Selection of the problem to be addressed is made on the basis of its priority listing and the degree to which it is amenable to change.

The third decision-making step is generating a series of strategies or alternatives for resolving the problem. A useful technique is brainstorming—generating as many ideas as possible within a given time frame without attempting to evaluate them specifically. "Brainstorming" involves the solicitation of ideas from group participants in an environment of positive support. The attempt is to encourage creativity, hence the absence of critical comments.

Step four in the process is to examine each alternative's pros and cons and to select, presumably, the best. Some aids that can be used here are (1) comparative analysis—placing information about each alternative (cost, availability, advantages, disadvantages and the like) into a matrix for purposes of comparison; (2) probability theory—attempting to indicate the frequency with which an occurrence might happen; (3) simulations—attempting to project programmatic options from the manipulation of input variables; and (4) cost-effectiveness analysis—an analysis of inputs which are subject to market pricing, and outputs which are not.

Developing a plan for implementing the preferred alternative is the fifth step in the decision-making process. At this point, an action plan is devised and internal and external arrangements necessary to accommodate and implement the alternative are indicated. These include matters such as physical, psychological, and economic adjustments that have to be made; new equipment and materials required; and the information that must be disseminated and to whom. The plan for action also should include an implementation timeline.

The sixth step involves evaluating the effectiveness of the preferred alternative and whatever recycling proves necessary. This may mean redefining the problem or selecting or attempting a new alternative solution.

The above process represents a *rational approach* to decision making. Decisions resulting from such procedures, however, are not, and cannot be, based on the consideration of all alternatives. Because human beings are incapable of thinking about or knowing all possible alternatives, the ideal choice from among alternatives is difficult to make. Decisions reached will represent a satisfactory choice based on available knowledge. In this way administrators "satisfice." They seldom have the capacity to maximize.[36]

In attempting to achieve rationality, organizations often limit the range of directions to be taken by members by defining organizational goals and responsibilities and developing rules and procedures.[37] Through these devices, choice is re-

---

[35] Kurt Lewin, *Field Theory in Social Science* (New York: Harper & Row, Publishers, Inc., 1951).

[36] Simon, H., *Administrative Behavior*, p. xxv.

[37] Peter M. Blau and W. Richard Scott, *Formal Organizations* (San Francisco: Chandler Publishing Co., 1962), p. 37.

stricted and the number of decision alternatives reduced. Rationality is thus more closely approached even if never achieved. A rational approach to decision making also often fails to consider the reality of political accommodation. That is, various participants' interests and influence will often be resolved through negotiation or accommodation in reaching a final decision. The one best alternative to a problem or issue is thus replaced by a decision based on political reality or expediency. On another level, because problem solving and decision making in schools typically occur in brief cycles, power may be frequently used to influence selection among choices. In addition to these considerations, decisions may be bound by time, space, and search costs.[38]

In using a process model of organization decision making, involvement of appropriate individuals at appropriate times is highly desirable. In fact, some of the earlier mentioned techniques for analyzing the problem, generating and assessing alternative solutions, and selecting the most satisfactory alternative, depend upon group participation. Blau and Scott isolate the following reasons for involving others in decision making: anxieties are reduced through discussion and social approval; weaknesses in arguments and faulty logic may be detected and corrected; and, because individuals appreciate respect, their desire serves as an incentive for suggesting sound solutions and strategies for dealing with problems and for criticizing those that are weak.[39]

Participation in organization decision making by individuals who will be affected by the decision and who are knowledgeable about the area in which a decision is to be made has several advantages. Where there is group participation, feelings of satisfaction are enhanced, creativity encouraged, and participants' acceptance and commitment to the decision is strengthened. The quality of the decision also may be improved by the larger number of alternatives that can be generated and analyzed.

Participatory or shared decision making is most effective when it is not perfunctory. Groups or individuals invited to participate in the decision-making process after a decision has been reached simply to affirm the decision, or who believe adequate consideration will not be accorded their views, find little to justify their participation. When there is the potential for influence, and not merely passive involvement, participation in the decision-making process becomes valued.[40] A challenge to administrators, particularly in schools, is to develop ways in which genuine participation in the decision-making process can be appropriately encouraged.

To assist administrators in determining when teachers should be involved in decision making, Bridges proposes use of a zone of acceptance model. When decisions fall outside of teachers' zone of acceptance, participation in the decision-making process is more effective. Conversely, if decisions fall within their zone of acceptance, participation is less effective. In making such determinations, Bridges

[38] Pfeffer, J., *Power in Organizations*, pp. 27–29.

[39] Blau, P., and Scott, W., *Formal Organizations*, pp. 242–43.

[40] On this point see Daniel L. Duke, Beverly K. Showers, and Michael Imber, "Studying Shared Decision Making in Schools," *Organizational Behavior in Schools and School Districts*, ed. Samuel B. Bacharach (New York: Praeger Publishers, Inc., 1981), pp. 313–51.

proposes that a *test of relevance*—do teachers have a personal stake in the decision?—and a *test of expertise*—do teachers possess the knowledge necessary to contribute to the decision?—be applied. If the answers to these tests are yes, then, the decision falls *outside* the teacher's zone of acceptance. If the answer is yes to one of the questions and no to the other, teachers should only occasionally be involved in the decision-making process.[41]

A second model designed to assist managers in determining appropriate decision-making participation is proposed by Vroom and Yetton.[42] Though somewhat complex, the model is designed to suggest appropriate levels of employee participation for various decision problems. In the Vroom-Yetton model, participation is placed on a continuum ranging from none to full. Included along the continuum are the following designations: AI—manager makes decision alone; AII—information sought from subordinates who may or may not be cognizant of the problem, but decision is the manager's; CI—information and evaluations are solicited from subordinates after they are informed of the problem and dyadic rather than group meetings are held, but manager makes the decision; CII—problem is discussed in group meetings of the manager and subordinates, but the decision is made by manager; GII—full participation—manager and subordinates are involved in group discussion and decision making. *A* type decisions are autocratic, *C* type involve consultation, and category *G* indicates group-shared decision making.

Vroom and Yetton suggest that the amount of subordinate decision-making participation can be determined by answering the following questions about fourteen decision problem types (see Table 9.4): manager's knowledge about the problem, degree of subordinate acceptance needed, structure of the problem, degree to which organizational goals are shared by subordinates, likelihood of conflict, criterion by which a successful solution can be determined, and whether the problem can be systematically approached. The Vroom-Yetton model is depicted in Table 9.4.

Although participatory decision making is desirable, it can be criticized because (1) it increases the length of time needed to make a decision; (2) it may not be cost efficient; (3) it may perpetrate decisions by accommodation or negotiation; and (4) it may increase participant conflict in periods of budget cuts or retrenchment.

Decision making can also be hindered or helped by organizational structure. In hierarchical organizations with closely defined levels of authority, communication flow is restricted and problem solving and decision making impeded. In such organizational structures, status differences restrict participation by those low in the hierarchy, channel disproportionate amounts of communication to high-status members, discourage criticism of suggestions by high-status members, encourage rejecting correct suggestions of low-status members while simultaneously reducing their work satisfaction and their motivation to make contributions.[43]

[41] Edwin M. Bridges, "A Model for Shared Decision Making in the School Principalship," *Education Administration Quarterly*, 3, no. 1 (1967), 49–61.

[42] Victor H. Vroom and P. W. Yetton, *Leadership and Decision Making* (Pittsburgh: University of Pittsburgh Press, 1973).

[43] Blau P. and Scott, W., *Formal Organizations*, p. 243.

Table 9.4 SUMMARY OF VROOM AND YETTON MODEL

Types of Problems	QUESTIONS							SOLUTION
	1 Is There a Criterion Which Will Show that One Solution Is Better than Another?	2 Do I have Enough Information?	3 Is the Problem Structured?	4 Do I Need Subordinate Acceptance?	5 Will I Get Acceptance if I Decide Alone?	6 Do Subordinates Share the Organizational Goals?	7 Is Conflict among Subordinates Likely?	Amount of Participation
1	No			No				A I
2	No			Yes	Yes			A I
3	No			Yes	No			G II
4	Yes	Yes		No				A I
5	Yes	Yes		Yes	Yes			A I
6	Yes	Yes		Yes	No	Yes		G II
7	Yes	Yes		Yes	No	No	Yes	C II
8	Yes	Yes		Yes	No	No	No	C I
9	Yes	No	Yes	Yes	Yes			A II
10	Yes	No	Yes	No				A II
11	Yes	No	No	Yes	Yes			C II
12	Yes	No	No	Yes	No	Yes		G II
13	Yes	No	No	Yes	No	No		C II
14	Yes	No	No	No	No			C II

NOTE: Blanks in the table simply mean that the information is irrelevant due to the response to some other question.

Source: Terrence R. Mitchell, *People in Organizations: Understanding Their Behavior* (New York: McGraw-Hill, 1978), p. 272).

In contrast, Likert's link-pin model (see Figure 14.2) serves to assist shared decision making by linking members of various organizational units through a structure which ensures multiple unit membership. Although an individual member may have two superiors, communication flow and the opportunity for shared decision making is improved.

Other organizational arrangements conducive to shared or participatory decision making include task forces, *ad hoc* committees that cut across organizational levels, and management committees such as a school superintendent's cabinet or senior staff. Although the individuals involved in a management committee usually represent only a school district's highest administrative eschelon, representatives of other school or administrative units in the organization can be invited to participate as appropriate. Two participatory decision-making models that can be effectively used include school site councils and school human environment assessment groups.[44]

A final participatory decision-making model is that of *quality control circles* used in Japanese business organizations. A group of two to ten employees constitute a "circle" which analyzes production or service problems related to their work. Each circle is headed by a foreman and meets each week for one or two hours over a period of three to six months.

The fundamental purposes of the Quality Circle are to

Contribute to the improvement and development of the organization.

Respect individuals and build a pleasant, conducive workshop in which it is meaningful to work.

Provide an opportunity to capitalize on the full range of human capabilities.[45]

The quality control circle concept is not significantly different from the school human environment assessment group (SHEAG) referred to above. Both are problem-solving mechanisms to provide management with assistance in improving organizational effectiveness. They differ in that employees are the primary members of the quality control circle whereas all actors who have a stake in the school are represented on the SHEAG. Moreover, quality control circles focus on problems relating to production and service while the SHEAG is free to focus its energies on any school-related problem. The quality control circle model has been adopted to education and, like the SHEAG, is a useful approach to group problem solving and participation.[46]

---

[44] See Rodney J. Reed and others, *Improving the Human Environment of Schools: Problems and Strategies* (Sacramento, Calif.: Department of Education, Office of Intergroup Relations, 1979), p. 51.

[45] Union of Japanese Scientists and Engineers, reported in William G. Ouchi, *Theory Z*, Appendix 2, p. 226.

[46] See Larry Chase, "Quality Circles in Education," *Educational Leadership*, 40, no. 5 (February 1983), 18–26. (This article also contains a useful bibliography on Quality Circles.)

MOTIVATION

What drives individuals to satisfy certain needs? Why do individuals seek to satisfy personal and organizational goals? Why do people make choices among several possible outcomes? What conditions serve to motivate and satisfy job performance? These are but a few of the questions addressed by theories of motivation. Knowledge of these theories provides assistance and guidance for leaders and managers.

Maslow's Theory of Human Motivation

Maslow holds that individuals seek to gratify a hierarchical order of needs consisting of five levels. Lowest are physiological needs (hunger, thirst, sex) followed by safety needs (security, freedom from fear, stability). Belongingness and love needs (affectionate relationship, to belong to a group or family, caring) occupy the third level. At the fourth level are esteem needs (self-esteem—desire for achievement, for competency, for self-respect; and esteem by others—status, recognition, appreciation). The fifth and highest level in the hierarchy is the need for self-actualization (self-fulfillment, becoming fully that of which one is capable).[47] According to Maslow, human needs form a hierarchy of relative prepotency. When lower needs are sufficiently gratified, successive sets of higher level needs emerge.

Satisfaction of Maslow's basic needs requires existence of a set of preconditions. These prerequisites include freedom of speech, freedom of choice, freedom to seek information, justice, and honesty. Without such conditions it is problematic that basic needs can be satisfied. Maslow's theory provides a compelling, even if partial, explanation of human behavior. Research evidence regarding its validity, however, is mixed.[48] Moreover, the hierarchical sequence of human needs as conceptualized by Maslow differs by individuals and across cultures.[49]

To the extent that Maslow's theory is accurate, school administrators should identify ways in which to provide for higher order needs of school staff, assuming of course, that lower order needs are generally satisfied. Recognition and reward of staff members for achievement, inclusion in participatory decision making, providing opportunities for professional and personal growth, development of a school climate in which feelings of belonging are enhanced, and manifestation of respect for others are illustrative of means by which higher needs may be met.

---

[47] Abraham H. Maslow, *Motivation and Personality*, 2nd ed. (New York: Harper & Row, Publishers, Inc., 1970), pp. 35–46.

[48] See, for example, Mahmoud A. Wahba and Lawrence G. Bridwell, "Maslow Reconsidered: A Review of Research on the Need Hierarchy Theory," *Organizational Behavior and Human Performance*, 15, no. 2 (April, 1976), 212–40; Benjamin Schneider and Clayton P. Alderfer, "Three Studies of Need Satisfaction in Organizations," *Administrative Science Quarterly*, 18, no. 4 (December, 1973), 489–505; and Douglas T. Hall and Khalil E. Nongaim, "An Examination of Maslow's Need Hierarchy in an Organizational Setting," *Organizational Behavior and Human Performance*, 3, no. 1 (February, 1968), 12–35.

[49] Mason Haire, Elwin E. Ghiselli, and Lyman W. Porter, "Cultural Patterns in the Role of the Manager," *Industrial Relations*, 2, no. 2 (February, 1963), 45–47.

Herzberg's Motivation-Hygiene Theory

Based on the view that individuals seek to avoid pain from the environment and derive growth from tasks, and on research findings regarding job satisfaction, Herzberg posits a two-factor theory of motivation.[50] One set of factors is associated with job satisfaction and is labeled motivators. The second set of factors consists of job dissatisfiers referred to as "hygiene" or "maintenance."[51] Motivators are effective in stimulating personal growth, superior effort, and self-actualization. Hygienes have limited effect on positive work attitudes.

Motivators or satisfiers and hygienes or dissatisfiers are distinct and unipolar. That is, one factor is not the obverse of the other. In Herzberg's theory, the opposite of satisfaction is not dissatisfaction; it is no satisfaction. Likewise, the opposite of dissatisfaction is no dissatisfaction. Since satisfiers and dissatisfiers are distinct, enhancement or removal of factors within one category will not bring about a change in the other. Stated differently, if conditions which contribute to personal growth and satisfaction are not present, then dissatisfaction does not result. In a similar manner, absence of such factors as supervision and adequate management policy (hygienes) will create dissatisfaction, but their presence will not bring about significant levels of satisfaction or serve to motivate.

Motivators or job satisfiers consist of achievement, recognition, work itself, responsibility, and advancement. They are intrinsic and related directly to the nature of work and rewards attainable from work performance. Hygienes or dissatisfiers include company policy and administration, supervision, salary, interpersonal relations with superiors, subordinates, and peers, and working conditions. They are associated with the work environment. The strength of these factors, based on the research of Herzberg and his associates, is shown in Figure 9.1.

While a few studies serve to verify Herzberg's theory,[52] it has been criticized in several dimensions: critical incident methodology and faulty research foundations,[53] lack of corroborating evidence of the two-factor theory,[54] weak theoretical

---

[50] Frederick Herzberg, Bernard Hausner, and Barbara Snyderman, *The Motivation to Work,* 2nd ed. (New York: John Wiley & Sons, Inc., 1959).

[51] The term hygiene is intended to show that job dissatisfiers are preventative and environmental. Thus, hygiene in this sense is analogous to its medical use. See Frederick Herzberg, *Work and the Nature of Man* (Cleveland: World Publishing Co., Inc., 1966), p. 74.

[52] For example, Herzberg, F., *Work,* pp. 92–267; David A. Whitsett and Erik K. Winslow, "An Analysis of Studies Critical of the Motivator-Hygiene Theory," *Personal Psychology,* 20, no. 4 (Winter 1967), 391–416.

[53] Robert J. House and Lawrence A. Wigdor, "Herzberg's Dual-Factor Theory of Job Satisfaction and Motivation: A Review of the Evidence and a Criticism," *Personal Psychology,* 20, no. 4 (Winter 1967), 369–90; Joseph Schneider and Edwin A. Locke, "Critique of Herzberg's Incident Classification System and a Suggested Revision," *Organizational Behavior and Human Performance,* 6, no. 4 (July 1971), 441–57; and Donald P. Schwab and Larry L. Cummings, "Theories of Performance and Satisfaction: A Review," *Industrial Relations,* 9, no. 4 (October 1970), 408–30.

[54] For example, see J. Richard Hackman and Greg R. Oldham, "Motivation Through the Design of Work: Test of a Theory," *Organizational Behavior and Human Performance,* 16, no. 2 (August 1976), 250–79; and Bernard L. Hinton, "An Empirical Investigation of the Herzberg Methodology and the Two-Factor Theory," *Organizational Behavior and Human Performance,* 3, no. 3 (August 1976), 250–79.

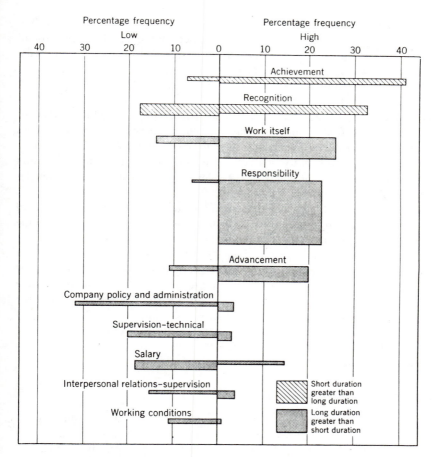

Figure 9.1 Comparison of Satisfiers and Dissatisfiers. Frederick Herzberg, Bernard Mausner, and Barbara Bloch Snyderman, *The Motivation to Work*, 2nd ed. (New York: John Wiley, 1959), p. 81.

base, and oversimplification of job satisfaction and dissatisfaction.[55] Despite its critics, the theory usefully stresses the potential importance of esteem and self-actualizing factors, or needs as postulated by Maslow, for motivation. It also serves to illustrate that much of what has been emphasized by school administrators and professional teacher groups in collective bargaining and contract negotiations—working conditions, job security, and salary—are hygienes which may prevent dissatisfaction when present but may fail by themselves to promote significant levels of satisfaction.

[55] Gerald R. Salancik and Jeffery Pfeffer, "An Examination of Need-Satisfaction Models of Job Attitudes," *Administrator Science Quarterly,* 22, no. 3 (September 1977), 427–56; and Marvin D. Dunnette, John P. Campbell, and Milton D. Hakel, "Factors Contributing to Job Satisfaction and Job Dissatisfaction in Six Occupational Groups," *Organizational Behavior and Human Performance,* 2, no. 2 (May 1967), 143–74.

Vroom's Expectancy Model of Motivation

Further insight into the nature of human behavior is provided by Vroom, who makes explicit the association between motivation and the expectation of desirable outcomes. Thus, an individual's motivation to act is a function of perceived desirability of an outcome and probability that the act will result in a particular outcome.

The conceptual model with which Vroom views human behavior attempts to explain choices made from among an array of voluntary responses, which he views as the fundamental problem for motivation theorists.[56] Thus, Vroom's motivation model states that "the probability of a person performing an act is a direct function of the algebraic sum of the products of the valence of outcomes and expectancies that they will occur given the act."[57]

Three concepts are fundamental to the model—valence, expectancy, and force. "Valence" refers to the perceived desirability or attractiveness of an outcome which may be final (primary) or conceived of as a means to attain or avoid other outcomes (secondary). In this latter sense, the primary outcome is thought of in terms of its usefulness or instrumentality in attaining or avoiding other outcomes. "Expectancy" refers to the perception of the probability that a desired outcome will be attained because of an action. "Force" is one's motivation to act and the direction of that act. It is the product of valences and expectancies. The efficacy of Vroom's model is supported by research in areas such as student occupational choice and preferences,[58] effective teaching and teacher satisfaction,[59] and job productivity and performance.[60]

EFFECTIVE TIME MANAGEMENT

In order to be an effective leader of an educational organization, one must manage time. Time is a limited and precious commodity. It can never be replaced. Given the many functions an educational executive is expected to perform, it is imperative

[56] Victor H. Vroom, *Work and Motivation* (New York: John Wiley & Sons, Inc., 1964), p. 9.

[57] Vroom, V., *Work and Motivation,* p. 276.

[58] See, for example, Victor H. Vroom, "Organizational Choice: A Study of Pre- and Post-decision Processes," *Organizational Behavior and Human Performance,* 1, no. 2 (December 1966), 212–25; Victor H. Vroom and Edward L. Deci, "The Stability of Post-Decision Dissonance: A Follow-up Study of Job Attitudes of Business School Graduates," *Organizational Behavior and Human Performance,* 6, no. 1 (January 1971), 36–49; and Terence R. Mitchel and Barrett W. Knudsen, "Instrumentality Theory Predictions of Students' Attitudes toward Business and Their Choice of Business as an Occupation," *Academy of Management Journal,* 16, no. 1 (March 1973), 41–52.

[59] Cecil Miskel, Jo Ann DeFrain, and Kay Wilcox, "A Test of Expectancy Motivation Theory in Educational Organizations," *Educational Administration Quarterly,* 16, no. 1 (Winter 1980), 70–92.

[60] For example, see Paul Goodman, Jerry H. Rose, and John E. Furcon, "Comparison of Motivational Antecedents of the Work Performance of Scientists and Engineers," *Journal of Applied Psychology,* 54, no. 6 (December 1970), 491–95; and Jay Galbraith and L. L. Cummings. "An Empirical Investigation of the Motivational Determinants of Task Performance: Interactive Effects between Instrumentality—Valence and Motivation—Ability," *Organizational Behavior and Human Performance,* 2, no. 3 (August 1967), 237–57.

that he or she use time efficiently. Prescriptions of how best to manage time will vary by individual and job position. Nevertheless, there are fundamental guidelines which can assist administrators in allocating the time necessary to accomplish the numerous tasks with which they are confronted.

Organize Yourself

Effective time management is fundamentally a matter of organizing yourself. Several activities are useful in this regard. First, it is essential to know in advance, to the extent possible, what demands will be placed on your time—meetings and conferences, reports that must be prepared, student activities, staff supervision and evaluation, and personal and professional growth activities. Second, these demands should be placed on a yearly calendar or a long-range calendar so that for any given week one will be aware of activities demanding personal attention. Third, a schedule designating blocks of time committed and time available for other activities should be prepared for such work.

Weekly schedules should include at least one hour, preferably two, to respond to priority items. Schedule this period to correspond to the time of day when you are most productive and then guard it zealously. Do not make appointments, accept telephone calls, or permit drop-in visits or other nonemergency interruptions during this priority period. During the priority period, respond only to items considered to be priority. Such items may include preparation of a beginning teacher evaluation report, preparation of a budget, a response to a letter, review of curriculum materials, and so forth. While every priority item may not be addressed or completed in a single priority period, some progress can be made toward eventual completion of all items during each period. For example, a report that must be prepared may require a commitment of time in each of several priority periods before it is completed.

Routine activities—requisitions for supplies, routine correspondence, classroom visitations for purposes of supervision and evaluation, and appointments including telephone calls—also should be scheduled weekly. Encourage individuals to make appointments. As a society we are conditioned to make appointments when desirous of another person's time. Appointments are made to see most physicians or attorneys, or to have the plumber or electrician attend to a necessary home repair. Given a tight schedule, nothing can be more disruptive than unnecessary interruptions. By scheduling appointments, such interruptions can be minimized.

This is not to suggest that all interruptions can or should be avoided. Clearly, in school situations some unscheduled events are unavoidable, particularly when there is an emergency. School site administrators are subject to particular frustration in this regard. An important component of the position of a school principal or vice-principal is responding to the requests and actions of others. An absent teacher, irate parent, and late bus simply are not predictable. Consequently, there will be unexpected intrusions upon the time schedule of even the best organized school site executive. This is simply a condition of the job. It is important to be appropriately responsive. Do not begrudge the time necessary to solve an important problem. The high probability of unexpected intrusions makes all the more significant the need to organize other components of the workday as efficiently as

Table 9.5 SCHOOL PRINCIPAL'S SCHEDULE: WEEK OF _____

TIME	MON.	TUES.	WED.	THURS.	FRI.
A.M.					
7:00– 7:30					
7:30– 8:00	Mtg. w/ Admin. Staff		Priority Block		Mtg. w/Math, Curric. Center
8:00– 8:30		Appt. w/Teacher		Appt. w/Teachers	
8:30– 9:00	School Begins—8:45 A.M.				
9:00– 9:30	Appt. w/Student & Parent	Flexible	Mtg. on/site Administrators & Supt.		Appt. w/Parent
9:30–10:00	Priority Block	Priority Block		Priority Block	Priority Block
10:00–10:30					
10:30–11:00	Classroom Visitations			Appt. w/Custodian	
11:00–11:30		Classroom Visitations	Appointments	Open	Routine Matters
11:30–12:00	Open				

P.M.

12:00–12:30 12:30– 1:00	School Lunch Period(s) (lunch meetings with groups of students or teachers)
1:00– 1:30 1:30– 2:00	Routine Matters — Classroom Visitations
2:00– 2:30 2:30– 3:00	Reserved for Appointments — Mtg. with Student Council — Appointments
3:00– 3:30	School Dismissed—3:15 P.M.
3:30– 4:00 4:00– 4:30	Mtg. w/ Parent Group — Faculty Meeting — Participate in Prof. Growth Activity — Open — Open
4:30– 5:00	Athletic Event
5:00– 5:30	
5:30– 6:00	
6:00– 6:30	
6:30– 7:00	
7:00– 7:30	
7:30– 8:00 8:00– 8:30	School Bd. Mtg.

possible. Advance appointments also ensure that visitors will receive undivided attention. An example of a weekly schedule for a school principal is on pp. 220–21.

What becomes apparent in examining Table 9.5 is that by scheduling activities for the week, all commitments can be accommodated. Importantly, however, there are available blocks of time for unanticipated time demands and flexibility. It is also apparent that evenings are unscheduled, thus permitting time for personal activities as well as the occasional spillover of school-related work that must be addressed. Obviously, this sort of schedule will change each week. What is important is that by preparing weekly schedules, available time for appointments and unanticipated meetings becomes more apparent.

Organize Your Staff

An administrator should ensure selection of competent secretarial and administrative staff, then delegate responsibilities to them. Rely on a secretary to schedule appointments and to screen school mail and telephone calls so that priority and routine items can be sorted. Delegate specific responsibilities to administrative staff—scheduling of classes, student attendance and classroom discipline problems, and extracurricular events. In addition, ensure that administrative staff participate in overall school policy formulation and are aware of your school expectations.

Organize Your Office Procedures

Develop an efficient file system. Install in-baskets for priority items, routine items (including junk mail), and professional magazines, and an out-basket. Items placed in these baskets should be handled in accord with your previously formulated schedule. After reviewing an item, respond to it, circulate it as appropriate for comments, and for information to and from others. File an item only if absolutely essential that it be retained, or discard it. Do not permit paper to accumulate. Not only does paper occupy space, but its presence also eventually becomes overwhelming and psychologically oppressive.

Dictate letters and as many other documents as possible. If at all possible use a dictating or recording machine. Write responses on memos or letters received when appropriate, and when feasible use the telephone to initiate requests, to contact others, and to respond to inquiries or letters. In using the telephone, develop a system to record incoming and outgoing calls with respect to follow-up activities required.

Time also can be more efficiently used when there are designated places for materials and equipment within your office. Attempting to locate something you remember seeing and know is there somewhere can absorb considerable time, particularly when viewed over a period of a week or month. Also, if you desire that your employees keep good records and be well organized, you had better model the behavior.

Organize Your Meetings and Appointments

Develop an agenda for meetings or appointments that you initiate and be sure to cover those items. Focus your attention and that of others with whom you are meeting on the agenda. Meetings and appointments that are well planned flow smoothly and are time effective.

Meetings intended for problem solving can be aided greatly through use of meeting facilitation.[61] Use of this technique requires a meeting facilitator (other than the administrator), a recorder, and a group memory, for example, butcher paper taped to the walls on which ideas generated by the group are placed. Meeting groups, ideally fifteen to twenty in number, form a semicircle facing the group memory. The facilitator ensures that the group stays on task, that everyone has an opportunity to participate, and that each participant's ideas are accurately recorded on the group memory. Use of meeting facilitation focuses the group's attention on a particular problem and can reduce wasted time.

Education executives can successfully surmount numerous tasks if they are organized and are able to organize their staff and their office, set priorities, have a capable staff to whom they delegate responsibilities, and plan ahead.

SUMMARY

The role of the administrator includes planning, leading, evaluating, decision making, coordinating, organizing, budgeting, and staffing. While all leaders engage in these activities for varying amounts of time, educational administrators reportedly spend more time on managerial functions than on school or instructional leadership functions. Both sets of functions are important. The challenge to educational executives is to achieve an appropriate balance between them—a matter of task priority and time management.

Leadership effectiveness, essential to meeting school goals, can be viewed from several research approaches: leader traits, power-influence, behavior, and the situation. Management theory provides a useful lens through which assumptions about employees can be examined and in turn influence leadership style. Finally, knowledge of decision making, the appropriate involvement of staff in the decision-making process, and motivational theories are also important to leader effectiveness.

SELECTED READINGS

Bass, Bernard M., *Stogdill's Handbook of Leadership: A Survey of Theory and Research*. Revised and enlarged edition. New York: The Free Press, 1981.

Hersey, Paul, and Kenneth H. Blanchard, *Management of Organizational Behavior:*

---

[61] M. Doyle and D. Strauss, *The New Interaction Method: How to Make Meetings Work* (Chicago: Playboy Press, 1976).

Utilizing Human Resources (4th ed.). Englewood Cliffs, N.J.: Prentice-Hall, Inc., 1982.

Mintzberg, Henry, *The Nature of Managerial Work.* New York: Harper & Row, Publishers, Inc., 1973.

Morris, Van Cleve, Robert L. Crowson, Cynthia Porter-Gehrie, and Emanual Hurwitz, Jr., *Principals in Action. The Reality of Managing Schools.* Columbus, Ohio: Charles E. Merrill Publishing Company, 1984.

Simon, Herbert A., *Administrative Behavior. A Study of Decision-Making Processes in Administrative Organization* (2nd ed.). New York: Macmillan Inc., 1961.

Taylor, Harold L., *Making Time Work For You.* New York: Dell Publishing Co., Inc., 1981.

Wolcott, Harry F., *The Man in the Principal's Office. An Ethnography.* New York: Holt, Rinehart and Winston, 1973.

Yukl, Gary A., *Leadership in Organizations.* Englewood Cliffs, N.J.: Prentice-Hall, Inc., 1981.

MANAGING
EDUCATIONAL
INFORMATION[1]

chapter 10

Managing and leading an organization is both a science and an art. However, no educational administrator can succeed in the absence of appropriate information. Thus, this chapter concentrates on the management of information. We begin with a description of computers and their uses in educational administration. These machines have become a crucial component of information management, and an effective administrator is required to have an understanding of their fundamental components and processes as well as be able to appreciate their capabilities and limitations. Following this description and analysis, we explain the concept of management information and describe the uses of management information systems in education.

HOW COMPUTERS WORK

Figure 10.1 is a simple representation of the basic elements of a computer's *hardware*. Hardware refers to physical devices that comprise a total system. *Input* refers to the process of entering data into a computer. The terms *data* and *information* have specific meanings when applied to computers. Data refers to bits of information, which by themselves have little or no meaning. Responses to individual items

[1] The major portion of this chapter was contributed by Richard Pratt affiliated with the Legislative Analyst Office of the state of California.

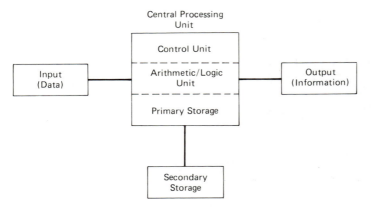

Figure 10.1 Diagram of Computer Hardware.

on a test serve as an analogy. No one can adequately interpret a student's ability by looking at a single item on a one hundred item test. However, when all items have been corrected and a composite score derived, then one has useful information on his or her ability as measured by the test. As this example suggests, the process of converting data into information (defined as a set of data that has meaning with reference to a particular problem or question) is one of aggregation—that is, gathering and organizing data. It follows that information (such as one student's score on a test) can become data in a higher level of aggregation (average score of all students in a school).

A familiar means of input is punched cards (often called "IBM cards"). Data are encoded on a card by a keypunch machine. Computers decode data and convert them into electrical impulses for storage and processing. Paper tape is used in a similar fashion. Other means of input include magnetic tape or disk, on-line terminals, and optical character recognition (OCR). Optical character recognition devices use laser beams to "read" symbols or alpha-numeric characters directly off paper. On-line input uses computer terminals or microcomputers connected to a central processing unit to enter data directly into memory.

The *central processing unit* (CPU), often called the "mainframe," is the heart of a computer. It consists of three subunits—primary storage, arithmetic-logic unit, and control unit. The storage unit, as the name implies, stores data. First generation computers had a storage capacity of approximately 1-4K bytes.[2] Current systems greatly exceed that, having capacities of up to 10^{13} bytes. As large as this is, it is insufficient for handling many computer tasks. Therefore, secondary storage devices are used. These are usually tape or disk units connected to the mainframe and accessed as needed.

The *arithmetic-logic unit* (ALU) is where arithmetic calculations or logical comparisons are made. Data are transferred between storage and the ALU for these operations several times in processing a problem. The *control unit* governs the

[2] In reference to bytes, K equals 1024, not 1000—so, for example, 4K equals 4096.

operational sequence of all computer units. Proper sequence is provided by program instructions stored in the primary storage unit and interpreted by the control unit, which signals other units regarding what to do and when to do it.

The *output unit* is a device with which information coming out of a computer is printed or displayed. Typically, this is a cathode ray tube (CRT), television monitor, or a paper printer (including on-line typewriter terminals). Other output devices include punched cards, magnetic disk or tape, and computer-output microfilm (COM). It is clear that some output devices, such as on-line terminals, are also used for input, and other devices, such as tape, disk, and punched cards, can be used either for input, storage, or output.

COMPUTER SOFTWARE (PROGRAMS)

A program is a set of instructions directing a computer what to do with data. Programming for first generation computers was done almost exclusively in machine language, which means all instructions are coded in binary form—all 0s or 1s. Machine language is the only medium computers actually "understand." Unfortunately, programming in machine language is tedious, error prone, and time consuming. To solve this high level problem, languages have been developed which permit more human-compatible programs. Computers then use a language translator to convert high level programs into a machine language program. Some of the more familiar high level languages include FORTRAN (FORmula TRANslator), BASIC (Beginner's All-purpose Symbolic Instruction Code), and COBOL (COmmon Business Oriented Language). A simple BASIC program will be presented later.

Processing

There are five basic ways in which a computer processes data: (1) batch, (2) transaction, (3) realtime, (4) timesharing, and (5) distributed processing. In *batch processing,* as the name suggests, large data sets are entered and processed at one time. Typically, punched cards are used for this type of operation. Batch processing is the fastest means for entering and processing data, thus saving valuable computer time. Its main disadvantage is that files are only as current as the latest batch and become dated between batches. Batch processing may be appropriate for analyzing standardized test results or for other applications that require periodic, rather than continual, updating.

Transaction processing allows processing of transactions as they occur. Airlines nicely illustrate this mode. When a customer buys a ticket, a sales agent enters the transaction record into the company's computer. In this way, other agents anywhere in the U.S., by referring to their computer terminal, can immediately obtain accurate information on the number of seats available for each flight.

In *realtime processing,* the computer is used to monitor and control a physical system by making automatic adjustments. An example is again provided by commercial airlines, where a computer is capable of guiding a jetliner's flight from takeoff to landing. During flight, a computer can monitor altitude, speed, wind conditions, and other factors as well as make constant course adjustments without pilot intervention.

Timesharing permits several simultaneous users. This allows users to purchase computer processing and storage from a commercial service center. This is an alternative to buying one's own computer. Many timeshare systems have programs for accounting, payroll, inventory control, and other business applications as well as simulation and forecasting programs for sophisticated planning and decision-making applications.

In *distributed processing,* computer capability in an organization is decentralized. Typically, this involves connecting minicomputers located at remote sites

Table 10.1 SAMPLE USES OF MICROCOMPUTERS

STUDENT	FINANCE
Athletic Eligibility List	Accounts Receivable/Payable
Attendance (annual)	Activity Accounting
Attendance (daily)	Financial Forecasting
Class Records	Food Service
Census (family)	General Accounting
Enrollment Projection	General Ledger
Graduate Follow-Up	Investment Accounting
Guidance Records	Vendor Reports
Instructional Management	Purchase Orders
Mark Reporting	
Scheduling Assistance	GENERAL
School Calendar	
Student Records	Activity Scheduling
Test Scoring & Analysis	Ad Hoc Reporting
	Bus Routing
PERSONNEL	Information Storage & Retrieval
	Library Circulation
Paycheck Calculation	Media Reservations
Payroll Reporting	Mailing Lists/Labels
Personnel Record	Project Planning and Budgeting
Salary Simulation	Statistical Analysis
Staff Assignments	Snow Removal Schedule
	Word Processing
FACILITIES	
Energy Management	
Facilities/Equipment Inventory	
Facilities Utilization	
Maintenance	

Source: John E. Haugo, "Management Applications of the Microcomputer: Promises and Pitfalls," *School Business Affairs* (January 1982), p. 24.

with a large central computer. Data can be processed locally by remote installations or transmitted to a central, "host" computer. Distributed processing can be especially beneficial to companies that are physically dispersed by providing each location data processing capability as well as an ability to quickly transmit and receive data from a central facility and other remote installations. The organizational structure of a typical school district makes it a prime candidate for distributed processing, with the central computer at the district office and mini or perhaps microcomputers located in each school.

Microcomputers

This is a good place to insert a comment about microcomputers. Since they can "stand alone," that is, give administrative units and personnel independent computing, microcomputers can perform many tasks once restricted to a large central system. Some of these tasks are shown in Table 10.1, which lists functions for which software has been written. These programs have been written for microcomputers with 32K of memory, though most micros now sold for business purposes have 512K or more of memory. In addition to these special purpose programs (which can perform only narrowly-defined functions), general purpose software is also available. These include programs for word processing, "electronic spreadsheets," and database management that can be adapted to a variety of uses, including those listed in Table 10.1

SAMPLE COMPUTER PROGRAM

Below is an example of a deliberately simplified computer program intended to display basic components. If we were running an actual program, we would add a few features. The explanation of each programming element follows.

```
05   INPUT N
10   INPUT A
15   LET A$ = "LIST OF STUDENTS WITH 5 OR MORE
     UNEXCUSED ABSENCES"
20   LET B$ = "LIST OF STUDENTS WITH 3 OR 4
     UNEXCUSED ABSENCES"
25   IF A > 4 THEN GO TO 40
30   IF A > 2 THEN GO TO 55
35   GO TO 65
40   PRINT A$
45   PRINT N, A
50   GO TO 65
55   PRINT B$
60   PRINT N, A
65   END
```

Assume a high school principal is concerned with a rising number of unexcused student absences. The principal desires a program that will automatically report on a regular basis names of students who exceed a certain number of unexcused absences during a specified time period. One must first establish "critical values" for unexcused absences. This provides a basis for specific actions. In this example, the principal decides that if a student has three or four unexcused absences a month, a letter addressing the problem will be sent home to parents. If a student has five or more unexcused absences, school counselors will be instructed to meet personally with both the parents and student. A computer program could be devised to handle this problem.

We have chosen to illustrate programming with the BASIC language. Note that each line of the program is numbered. A computer executes a program line by line, in the sequence in which lines are numbered, unless it is specifically instructed to bypass lines or return to an earlier line. Programmers customarily number lines in increments of five or ten to provide space for additional lines at a later time if needed.

Lines 5 and 10 are input statements. They instruct the computer to assign specific values to variables N and A. In this example, N stands for the student number, and A is the number of unexcused absences. In actual practice these values would have been taken from an attendance record (also on computer) that a previous instruction told the computer to "read." N and A are numeric variables that can only assume the value of numbers.

Lines 15 and 20 deal with "string variables," designated by a letter followed by the dollar sign ($). String variables can designate any combination of numbers and letters. In this way, a computer can employ words and phrases as well as numbers. Lines 15 and 20 are "let" statements that simply set the value for a variable. From now on (unless otherwise instructed) the computer will interpret the variable, A$, to mean "list of students with 5 or more unexcused absences" and B$ as meaning "list of students with 3 or 4 unexcused absences."

Lines 25 and 30 are referred to as "if-then" statements. These are used when the next step to be taken depends on a condition being satisfied. In this case, line 25 says that if student number N has an unexcused absence amount (A) that exceeds 4, then go to line 40. Note that this is a case where the computer is instructed to bypass a line, rather than executing all lines sequentially. If this condition is not met, for example, if A equals 3, then the computer ignores the "then" part of the statement and simply proceeds to the next line. To gain insight into the nature of some of the problems programmers face, study what would happen if lines 25 and 30 were reversed. Line 35 is a GO TO statement that jumps to the end of the program if the number of unexcused absences is less than three.

Lines 40 through 60, with the exception of 50, are "print" statements. Lines 40 and 45 will be executed only if the value of A exceeds 4, and lines 55 and 60 will be printed only if the value of A exceeds 2, but is not greater than 4. If a student has, for example, five unexcused absences, his or her number and number of absences will be printed (either on a screen or on paper) under a heading that reads, "list of students with 5 or more unexcused absences." Lines 55 and 60 operate in a similar fashion for students with three or four unexcused absences. Note that if a student has zero, one, or two unexcused absences, nothing happens.

Line 50 simply instructs the computer that it is finished, and must go to the end (line 65). It should be clear, however, that this is a highly simplified program and that an actual program would not stop after processing one student. Instead, additional commands would instruct the computer to "loop," return to the beginning and process the next student's attendance record, and to continue this process until all student records were analyzed. Still more commands would shape the format of the information into a presentable report. Such a program would result in two lists, one for students with more than four, and one for students with three or four unexcused absences. These procedures, and a few others, have been omitted from the sample for the sake of simplicity, but the essential nature of programming has been captured.

This program illustrates advantages, as well as some problems, of computers. Advantages should be obvious—computers can process more information in a shorter period of time more accurately than humans. The alternative to the program in this example would be for someone manually to read through the entire attendance file each month and record names of students meeting established criteria. This could be a minor inconvenience in a small school. For a school with several hundred or thousand students, however, the computerized process has a distinct advantage.

Computers can be a mixed blessing. A program like this assumes, or compels the user to assume, that the "critical" number of unexcused absences is the same for everyone. This may not in fact be the case. Suppose each of two students has one unexcused absence. It is easy to think of many circumstances in which that occurrence would signify or pose a greater problem for one student than the other. The computer does not know this. It cannot evaluate data; it only performs mathematical operations. It is theoretically possible, of course, to compile a complete file on each student so that an "objective" calculation of the individual critical value can be made, but that would be unduly expensive. Moreover, translation of impressionistic knowledge about a student into data that a computer can handle is itself a subjective process and reduces the apparent objectivity of the computer program.

This example illustrates the necessity of standardizing a decision-making process or activity. In order to make the process amenable to computerization, many of the factors that go into decision making by humans must be eliminated. This is usually thought to be an advantage of computers in that eliminated factors are ones involving subjectivity and irrationality. However, as this example displays, there is a place for individual judgment in management, and attempting to eliminate it for the sake of administrative convenience may have negative consequences.

This example also illustrates a point that will be made throughout the remainder of this book—the computer represents a powerful technology and can be a valuable administrative tool. Using a computer, however, does not automatically make administration rational, nor does it necessarily make it better. Little-understood questions regarding the "interface" between humans and computers, and organizations and computer systems, may be more important than actual technology in determining the utility of computers to organizations. Material is presented later in this chapter that provides insight into these issues.

ADMINISTRATIVE USES OF COMPUTERS

Administrative uses of computers are often divided into two broad categories—electronic data processing (EDP) and decision support systems (DSS). EDP uses a computer to process data electronically and DSS uses a computer to process data and produce information for use by decision makers. Here we explain EDP functions. Later we describe decision support systems utilizing computers. In Chapter Eleven, on planning, budgeting, and evaluation, we explain particular techniques, for example, PERT and SIMULATIONS, which depend heavily upon computers.

Typical EDP applications include payroll, general ledger, purchasing, activity scheduling, and attendance control. These functions require standard processing of data even in the absence of computerization. A payroll department, for example, must record each employee's rate of pay, hours worked, and fringe benefits. Time cards, employee files, and other standardized forms are used to collect and store needed data in an appropriate format. In other words, payroll activities are standardized, routinized, and programmed even before a computer enters the picture. This greatly facilitates the transfer from a manual system to a computer-based one. If computer introduction involves automating routines that previously were accomplished manually, then little has occurred regarding job content and work relationships. The major change, faster, more accurate processing of data, is seen as positive.

Computer conversions are rarely simple. However, there are several characteristics of successful implementation. The first distinguishing characteristic of successful EDP installations is that data needs are known and relatively stable over time. This means that simply the needed data—no more, no less—can be collected and that routines and formats for data collection are not subject to frequent or major change. Second, information (or output) the system is expected to produce is well defined and agreed upon. In the payroll example, the system is expected to produce a correct check, for the correct amount, to the correct person, at the correct time. Deviations from these expectations are easily recognized, measured, and corrected. Third, there is knowledge of the relationship between data and information (or between input and output) so that the manner in which data are processed to produce the desired output can be established. Fourth, there is little or no conflict or disagreement over system goals—everyone wants a paycheck and will be happy with a system that delivers it. Fifth, output has a well-defined and accepted use. These characteristics are deceptively simple and easy to achieve, but many systems do not have them, and they often perform poorly as a consequence. This is especially true of decision support systems, to which we now turn.

Decision Support Systems

Whereas EDP systems automate record keeping and transaction processing, decision support systems (DSS) are designed to aid administrators in decision making and implementation. Electronic data processing systems and DSS may share a common data base, but the data are used for different purposes and therefore are usually aggregated in different ways. For example, a computer system may have a personnel data base that contains information on hours worked, rate of pay, benefits, and so forth for each employee. In the above EDP example, the payroll department used this to issue paychecks. However, these same data can be aggregated in ways to display, for example, trends in employee turnover or absenteeism. Or it can be combined with other information to ascertain instructional costs per student.

In general, DSS involve collapsing data into information that administrators find useful in helping them implement and evaluate decisions. Decision support systems can perform this task in several ways. Some systems, for example, simply allow direct access to the data base, providing administrators with the capability to acquire data as needed. Other systems may proceed further by allowing manipulation of data in several ways to reveal more useful information. Still others provide models that can project consequences of specific decisions or calculate optimal decisions within given constraints. Four major computer applications for planning and decision making are described in Chapter Eleven—PERT, linear programming, queuing theory, and computer simulation.

MANAGEMENT INFORMATION SYSTEMS

Electronic data processing systems and DSS are often employed to accomplish specific functions in organizations. Management information systems (MIS), on the other hand, involve a more "organic" integration between managerial activity and an information system. Furthermore, an MIS usually encompasses and serves an entire organization, not simply individual units or segments. Experience suggests, however, that subunits of an organization are not homogeneous with respect to what they require from an MIS. That is, different units have different information needs. Much of the current literature on the "architecture" of MIS makes use of Robert Anthony's view of the organization as a three-tiered, pyramidal hierarchy (Figure 10.2).[3] Those at the "operational level" are most concerned with an organization's day-to-day functions. These are operations that are performed on a routine basis, for example, taking student attendance and completing employee time cards.

Those at the "managerial level" are concerned with efficient and effective utilization of organizational resources. Their job is to monitor and evaluate activities under their control to ensure that organizational goals are achieved and resources used efficiently. Teacher supervision and evaluation is an example of a managerial function.

At the "strategic level," members are concerned primarily with setting and evaluating broad organizational goals. In school systems, this takes place at the district superintendent level, at the school board level, at the state department of

---

[3] Robert Anthony, *Planning and Control Systems: A Framework for Analysis* (Cambridge, Mass.: Harvard University Press, 1965).

Figure 10.2   Organizational Hierarchy.

education level, and at the level of the state legislature. It includes activities such as establishing curricula and setting budgetary priorities.

This view of the organization is helpful to MIS planners in designing systems that meet information needs of members at different organizational levels. Consider, for example, information on student achievement. At the operational level, teachers use this information to evaluate student progress and plan lessons. A teacher must monitor each student's progress in order to provide feedback, diagnose individual strengths and weaknesses, and plan appropriate action.

At the managerial level, a principal uses information on student achievement as an aid in evaluating teachers and assessing the school's instructional program. Here, the concern is not the performance of individual students, but with overall student achievement in the school. Information such as average achievement and measures of dispersion from this average will be useful.

At the strategic level, decision makers and planners will be concerned with performance measures for an entire school district or perhaps a state. At this level, information on events external to the organization also becomes more important, for example, information concerning graduates or public attitudes toward education. We illustrate strategic planning further in Chapter Eleven.

Notice that the further up an organizational hierarchy one ascends, the higher the level of data aggregation. Information on individual students is used by the operational level. School-wide measures are used at the managerial level. System or state-wide measures are used at the strategic level. While superfluous, it is of course technically possible to design a system that would supply strategic level planners with information on individual students. This point serves to illustrate, however, that an important function of MIS is not to supply decision makers with as much information as possible, which could be overwhelming, but to supply that which is needed to filter out the rest. Recognizing different information needs at different organizational levels is helpful in designing the "filter" for MIS.

The concept of a *system* is fundamental to the definition of management information systems. Management information systems represent a systems approach to management, with the organization being a special type of system within which the MIS constitutes a subsystem. Systems theory is derived from our understanding of biological systems. An organism, such as a human being, is a complex system comprised of several subsystems—cardiovascular system, central nervous system, digestive system, respiratory system, and others—that function together and contribute to the health and vitality of the total system.

Three basic systems concepts are input, output, and feedback. A school receives input from its environment in the form of students, financial support, and information; output consists primarily of graduates. The role of information, obviously, is a special concern of MIS. A school receives information on, for example, legal requirements and community expectations with regard to its instructional program. This information is taken into account as that program is planned and delivered. Graduates constitute the major form of output, and are prime sources of information regarding the school's performance. Other forms of output, such as auditors' reports, may depict school performance in specific areas. Feedback is information that is derived from output and then returned. This allows a system to monitor its own effectiveness and make necessary adjustments.

Organizations may be viewed as information processing entities, whether or not they have formal MIS. A model of an information processing system is presented in Figure 10.3. The collection, organization, and transformation of data into information is related to the information requirements of managers for decision making. This model illustrates the manner in which subsystems are related to other subsystems in an organization. In this case, linkage points are provided by data collection. It is here that data produced by other subsystems within the organization,

Figure 10.3 MIS for Strategic, Tactical, and Operational Levels. Bonita J. Campbell, *Understanding Information Systems,* Cambridge, Mass. (Winthrop Publishers, 1977), p. 52.

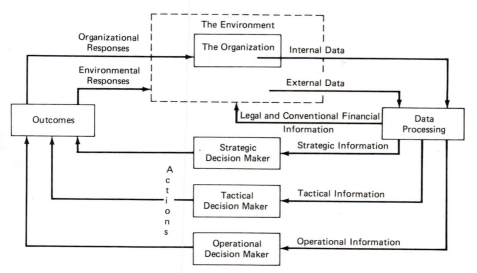

as well as data from an organization's environment, are entered into the MIS. Management information systems also have linkages with clients, in this case managers, who receive and use the information produced.

The value of the systems approach in designing information systems is that it assists planners in identifying discrete yet interrelated subsystems that comprise organizations and focuses attention on critical relationships between them. The input of one subsystem is the output of another, and vice versa. Management information systems output must be tailored to the needs of subsystems that use it. Similarly, data produced by other subsystems must be in a format that fits MIS data collection requirements. Clearly, communication and coordination between subsystems is essential.

Problems with MIS

Management information systems have not enjoyed unmitigated success since making their appearance in the 1970s. To the contrary, there have been serious problems with the performance of MIS in organizations. In general, an MIS can be considered a failure if any of three conditions persist: (1) it produces incorrect information; (2) data are inappropriately aggregated; or (3) information is not produced and delivered on a timely basis.

Incorrect information. At first glance, it would seem that one of the strengths of an MIS is freedom from error. It is easy to succumb to the myth that "computers never make a mistake," and since computers are the dominant technology of MIS, we often think of the latter as equally infallible. However, we should remember that MIS are people- as well as computer-based. People do the data collection, entry, and programming, and it is in these areas that errors can and do occur. Errors can never be eliminated completely, but are easily corrected if the system provides adequate mechanisms for detection and correction.

Improper aggregation. This refers to transformation of data into information in a manner unsuitable for users. It may be too detailed, in which case decision makers must sift through extraneous data in order to arrive at needed information, or it may be too general, in which case important facts are concealed. For example, gross projected enrollment figures may be helpful in calculating expected revenues, but a demographic breakdown of that figure is necessary for allocating staff, establishing school boundaries, and planning for pupil transportation.

Another misaggregation is insufficient filtering. In this case, too much data are transmitted, data that could and should have been filtered by the MIS. In order to insulate users from information overload, MIS must incorporate ideas on what information users do and do not need.

Untimely delivery. If MIS output is to be used for decision making, it must be delivered at an appropriate time. Tardy information may lack utility for obvious reasons. Information that is available too early may be less useful if it becomes dated or, in the case of paper printouts, simply gets "lost in the shuffle."

A number of factors can contribute to the persistence of these three conditions. Only a few will be considered here. One is uncertainty over what kind of information the system should provide. If managerial needs are ill defined, then an MIS is unlikely to achieve maximum effectiveness. Uncertainty over which data to collect often leads to a situation in which all data are collected in the hope that nothing important will be missed. This results in information overload, which is an expression of the common, but mistaken, view that "more is better." There is an inherent conflict between the most efficient use of information technology—which is in the direction of greater data manipulation and increased output—and the most efficient use of a manager's time, of which only a portion can be allocated to the assimilation of MIS output.

If an MIS spans most or all of an organization, it will require cooperation and coordination among units that previously may have been relatively autonomous. All formats for collecting and reporting data will have to conform to central processing needs as will the timetable for data collection. This may result in considerable organizational conflict and tension, especially if a data collecting unit sees little relationship between its responsibilities and its regular functions. In education, as in other endeavors, this is best exemplified by the attitude toward "unnecessary paperwork" that is compiled for a distant bureaucracy. This can result in carelessness (error), procrastination (untimely delivery of data), or both.

As stated previously, an MIS fails if these three conditions—error, misaggregation, and untimeliness—persist. Reasonable allowance must be made for occasional problems; one simply cannot expect any system to be perfect. However, it is also reasonable to expect a system to have mechanisms for making necessary corrections. It may well be that the difference between a successful and unsuccessful MIS resides in the existence of corrective mechanisms. Three such mechanisms are redundancy, feedback, and flexibility.

Redundancy.   A synonym for *redundant* is *superfluous*. This illustrates the connotation of "excessive," or "unnecessary" that *redundant* normally carries. However, redundancy can have benefits, for example, multiple control systems on airplanes; if one fails, there is another. Similarly, dual brake systems on cars are redundant, but few consider them excessive. In MIS, redundancy is useful in correcting or compensating for errors. Systems designers desire to "streamline" operations. However, they should not completely eliminate redundancy and thereby reduce the probability of detecting error. Redundancy is not costless, and how much is desired will depend on the degree to which an organization can tolerate error.

Feedback.   Once an error or other problem is detected, information must be fed back to the source so that corrective measures can be taken. Feedback is a critical link between error detection and correction. Accomplishing effective feedback in an organization is often difficult because there are normally few, if any, rewards for focusing attention on problems. Examples of this condition occur occasionally when government officials are dismissed or demoted for reporting cost overruns or other forms of waste or possible malfeasance. Thus, while it is possible to design a system that has appropriate channels, whether or not feedback actually occurs depends primarily on organizational incentives.

Flexibility.   A system is flexible if it can adapt to changing needs. This capability is important because even with the most thorough planning all needs cannot be foreseen, and many needs change over time. An inflexible system that fails to keep pace with needs will simply not be used by clients. For several years the Richmond, Virginia, school system shared computing services with the city. As a consequence of sharing facilities with other users with diverse needs, the schools were often unable to obtain needed program changes. Often the needs of other city departments, such as police or health, were accorded higher priority than schools. In order to gain needed flexibility, the Richmond Public Schools eventually developed their own computing system. However, similar problems can exist within an organization where the MIS may be more responsive to some subunits than others. Care must be taken to ensure that the allocation of flexibility within an organization is fair and functional. In order to meet this goal, many school systems rely upon a "users committee" which meets regularly to assess the need for computer program and system design changes.

Management Information Systems in Schools

While computers are now used for many school data processing applications, examples of MIS in school systems are rare. Most literature on computers in education consists of anecdotal accounts of the manner in which a school uses computers for a particular purpose. The Chapter Fifteen reprint of an article on one school's use of computers for bus route planning is typical. Lack of literature, as well as casual observation, leads to the conclusion that most schools do not have an MIS. There are reasonable explanations for this condition including high costs, lack of incentives (no competitors to beat or profits to gain), and uncertainty over relationships between data and decisions. This last point deserves clarification. For any school district, data on items such as student achievement, pupil-teacher ratios, and instructional costs per student are relatively easy to obtain. These data will be helpful in making decisions about establishing and maintaining a high quality instructional program. We know, for example, that classes should not be too large, and we can compare instructional costs with other school districts acknowledged as "good." Beyond this, however, knowledge of relationships between educational inputs and student achievement is imprecise. Thus, there exists a gap between the ability to collect, store, and refine data and the substantially more limited ability to make sense of it. Uncertainty regarding data organization for effective decision making is one of the major problems facing MIS.

History, however, is not always the best guide to the future. There is reason to believe that, despite past problems and obstacles, MIS may become more prevalent in education. One reason is an increasing concern with educational "production." This can have two effects: First, if MIS are seen as an aid to more efficient and effective management, then they are likely to find favor among those striving to reduce costs. Second, if a concern for efficiency leads to more research on and understanding of education "production functions" (a term defined more fully in Chapter Eleven), then managers can more effectively interpret and utilize data in their decision making.

In addition, MIS technology—both hardware and software—is becoming less expensive. At the same time, computer capability is increasing. Reduced costs and increased benefits will undoubtedly make MIS more attractive to many schools.

A third reason for believing MIS will become more prevalent in schools is the increased educational use of microcomputers. One of the advantages of microcomputers is that they provide users with independent computing capability. There is little doubt that they will continue to be used in this way. However, it is also to be expected that micros will gradually be used to transmit and receive data from central computing facilities as well as other micros in a distributed processing arrangement. This eventually will be the most efficient way to collect system-wide data. Microcomputers may become more important as links in a district-wide MIS than as stand-alone computing devices.

SUMMARY

We have come a long way from the abacus. Computers can perform feats that were undreamed of even a generation ago. However, there is a growing awareness that there is much that computers can do *to* as well as *for* organizations. On the one hand, computers are mechanical marvels that can process vast amounts of data and produce voluminous reports, graphs, charts, maps, and other printouts at the push of a button. On the other hand, they can be unmanageable beasts that do not perform as expected (or as needed), causing dissension, uncertainty, and conflict. This chapter has attempted to convey some sense of this paradox. The purpose is not to underplay the value or utility of computers, but to emphasize that only by understanding their organizational contexts and consequences can we hope to design and manage systems that make maximum use of the computer's potential.

SELECTED READINGS

Burch, John G., Jr., Felix R. Strater, and Gary Grudnitski, *Information Systems: Theory and Practice* (2nd ed). New York: John Wiley & Sons, Inc., 1979.

Geisert, Gene, "The Last Thing You Want To Do Is Buy a Computer," *Journal of Education Finance*, 9 (Fall 1983), 241–44.

Gustafson, Thomas J., *Microcomputers and Educational Administration.* Englewood Cliffs, N.J.: Prentice-Hall, Inc., 1985.

Northwest Regional Educational Laboratory, *The Computer in Educational Decision Making.* Hanover, N.H.: Time Share, 1978.

Pogrow, Stanley, *Education in the Computer Age: Issues of Policy, Practice, and Reform.* Beverly Hills: Sage, 1983.

Slotnick, David L., and Joan K. Slotnick, *Computers, Their Structure, Use, and Influence.* Englewood Cliffs, N.J.: Prentice-Hall, Inc., 1979.

EDUCATIONAL PLANNING, BUDGETING, AND EVALUATION[1]

chapter 11

American education can benefit substantially from greater managerial attention to planning and program evaluation. Schooling directly effects the lives of millions of individuals and annually absorbs hundreds of billions in dollar resources. An undertaking of such magnitude is deserving of careful planning regarding future endeavors and assessments of past performances. This chapter explains the purposes and utility of educational planning, outlines planning processes, illustrates planning techniques useful for education executives, explains budgeting procedures and their relation to planning and evaluation, and describes and illustrates important program evaluation concepts.

Planning and evaluation represent obverse sides of a chronological coin, or complimentary points in a cycle of organizational activities. Planning is a process for systematically determining future allocation of resources. Planning shares many features with the rational decision-making model described in Chapter Nine, but differs in three ways.

> The planner may not in fact be the individual or team of individuals responsible for implementing a plan. In short, planners may not be the executive or decision maker.
>
> Planning is oriented toward a time horizon beyond the immediate present.

[1] The authors wish to acknowledge the assistance of Richard Pratt in the preparation of this chapter.

Planning involves systematic efforts to reduce uncertainty, to convert unknowns to statements of probability. A decision maker concerned with an immediate condition may not have the luxury of being able to assign reasoned estimates to alternative scenarios. Planning can mitigate the risks in having to make instant decisions.

Evaluation is more concerned than planning with the immediate present or, even more likely, with events that occurred in the past. Evaluation involves assessing outcomes of one or more events, making judgments regarding effectiveness, and providing information which thereafter can shape future decisions.

Taken together, planning and evaluation are two major stages in a cycle of events aimed at enhancing an educational organization's ability to serve its clients—pupils, parents, and the public. The full cycle involves planning for future events, implementing or executing the plan, and evaluating outcomes.

Budgeting is a practical bridge between planning and evaluation. Figure 11.1 graphically illustrates relationships between planning, budgeting, and evaluation.

Figure 11.1 Planning-Budgeting-Evaluation Cycle.

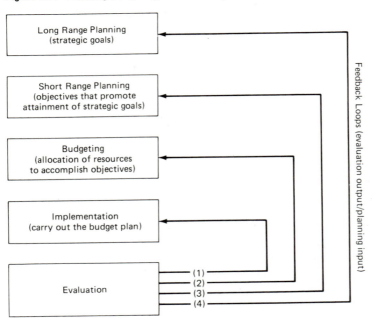

Types of Evaluation:

(1) Program and budget auditing. (Has the budget been implemented as planned?)
(2) Economic analysis. (Were resources sufficient and appropriately allocated to allow achievement of objectives?)
(3) Program evaluation. (Are objectives appropriate? Were there any unforeseen consequences?)
(4) Forecasting. (Are long range goals appropriate and realistic? Are environmental changes necessitating changes in strategic goals?)

Budgeting is an important component of the planning and evaluation process. Budgets represent the financial crystallization of an organization's intentions. It is through the budgeting process that a school or school district can arrive at decisions about the allocation of resources for achieving organizational goals. Ideally, resources are expended consistent with the organization's overall plans, and evaluations of programs and activities subsequently inform the next cycle of planning and budgeting. We do not wish to convey the misimpression that budgeting is a technocratic process which is always rational and devoid of political considerations. Such is not the case. However, a planning and evaluation process is empty of meaning unless it can influence an organization's resource allocation. Budgeting is the process of allocating an organization's resources. Thus, in this chapter we describe budgeting processes and their places in the planning and evaluation process.

PLANNING

Planning is a management function which should occur at all levels within an educational system. As decentralized as education is in the United States, even federal officials should concern themselves with broad trends and provision of incentives for states and local districts to act in the national interest. State officials should be concerned with matters such as enrollment projections, teacher supply and demand, and capital needs. Local officials, in addition to having state concerns, are regularly engaged in planning for matters such as a new building, alterations in the curriculum, changes in attendance boundaries or bus routes, implementing new student grading policies, or launching school site parent advisory councils.

Some anticipated undertakings may occur with sufficient frequency as to obviate planning. An elementary principal with twenty years of administrative experience in a stable enrollment district may have opened school successfully for so many fall semesters as to have reduced the matter to a set of routine operations. Experience can substantially inform future activities, and such a principal may have need only to review previously developed lists in order to refresh his or her memory regarding necessary steps. We do not advocate formation of elaborate procedures in anticipation of future events if the undertaking is already covered by routine—planning at this level can become trivial. At the opposite end of the spectrum, undertaking racial desegregation in a large school district can involve complexity akin to a major construction project's deployment of personnel and supplies. Success will be difficult under any circumstances, but the absence of systematic long range planning for an undertaking of such complexity virtually assures its failure. What is the educational planning process?

The planning process. The purpose of planning is not simply to institute change. Change will occur whether or not there is a plan. Rather, a prime purpose of planning is to reduce uncertainty and focus organizational activities so as to utilize resources efficiently. Through systematic long-range planning it may be possible for an organization to reduce the amount of time involved in delivering a service, produce greater pupil achievement or parent satisfaction, induce greater client participation, and so on for a number of goals. There is not one comprehensive planning process or set of techniques which, if pursued, universally guarantees efficiency and effectiveness. Rather, depending upon the goals sought and the organization involved, one or another planning mode may be appropriate. National level manpower, industrial, agricultural, and educational planning is favored by some socialist governments. American values do not generally include such a degree of centralization. Hence, planning undertaken by private sector organizations and subunits of government is favored. Thus, this process can become highly disaggregated. Indeed, much planning is left to households or even to individual citizens. However, capitalism and freedom are not arguments against planning. The question is the appropriate level of planning and decision making, not planning versus no planning.

Planning can be conceived as *strategic* or *managerial.* The distinction here is one of abstraction. A strategic plan for one level of operation may be regarded as managerial by another. Regardless, we can illustrate the general meaning of the terms by example.

Strategic planning. A nonprofit hospital increasingly loses patients. Rising medical costs and competition from outpatient and neighborhood surgical clinics have reduced revenues. The board of directors requests top level administrators to prepare a strategic plan for recapturing the hospital's share of the medical market. After examining available demographic and medical service information, the conclusion is reached that several patient populations in the region are underserved. The hospital's board of directors adopts a strategic plan to enhance its client population—that is, increase its market share by providing new services to the elderly as well as open new weight loss and sports medicine programs. Once having settled upon such a strategy for becoming more competitive, the board instructs management to undertake the detailed planning necessary to implement such a strategy.

An education-related example might involve a school board becoming uncomfortably aware of an increasing proportion of district students choosing nonpublic schools. In this case, the board directs the superintendent to assess the situation and develop a strategic plan for becoming more competitive. Market surveys reveal that new nonpublic school families are upper income professionals who can afford private school tuition and who believe that public schools are insufficiently rigorous academically, too lenient regarding discipline, and have classes which are too large. The superintendent contends that these parental perceptions are only partially correct. He concedes that the school district's classes are large and that student discipline has become more lenient than the standard with which he is comfortable. On the other hand, he believes the district's academic standards are high and that there is evidence in support of his position, for example, statewide reading scores, high school SAT averages, and percent of secondary students gaining entry to selective colleges. He concludes that the district has not informed its potential clients well regarding its academic successes. The goal is to recapture as much of the lost clientele as possible. Three strategic objectives are agreed upon: (1) to reduce class size over a period of time; (2) to strengthen district policy regarding student absenteeism and discipline; and (3) to publicize the district's academic success. The board then turns to the administration to undertake the managerial planning and operational procedures necessary to implement these objectives.

Whether strategic or managerial, whether done by a school district or another organization, planning processes are remarkably similar. A problem must be identified. In the above two examples, it is the loss of clientele or market share. Subsequent analyses must be undertaken to identify possible causes of the problem. Efforts must then be expended to generate possible solutions. An assessment of likely costs and effects of solutions should be made. Where a solution depends upon events or actions outside an organization's immediate control, an effort should be made to judge the probability of such events taking place. Finally, having assessed alternatives and their associated probabilities, a ranking of solutions should take place. Once agreement regarding a solution is reached, detailed planning necessary for its implementation can occur. Planning follows a paradigm similar to problem solving or decision making. However, there are planning techniques which can assist in rationalizing the process and reducing uncertainty.

Planning Techniques

There are many useful planning techniques. We present four examples here: PERT, linear programming, queuing theory, and computer simulation. In the subsequent section on evaluation we discuss cost-benefit analyses.

PERT is an acronym which stands for planning, evaluation, and review technique. It was initially developed for use with the Polaris missile program in the 1950s as a technique for managing large-scale, multistage projects. Stages of a large project are interdependent so that, for example, completion of step B may first require completion of step A. Development of a PERT chart requires an analysis of each of the steps required for project completion. This means more than simply identifying necessary steps and putting them in sequential order. It also means assessing resources needed for each step. Resources translate to three things: money, knowledge, and time. An important component of PERT is the *critical path*. This is the sequence of activities that has the least room for delay and that therefore requires special attention. The critical path determines the minimum amount of time necessary for project completion.

Figure 11.2 is a simplified PERT chart displaying the activity sequence involved in planning and implementing a management information system. The first step is a needs assessment. The goal of this step is to establish the information the system should produce, when it should produce it, and to whom it should be sent. The second step is to review the system (by computer or manually) currently supplying management information. As the chart indicates, steps one and two are per-

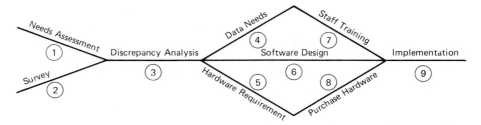

Figure 11.2   PERT Chart.

formed concurrently and are related, since one way to identify information needs is to examine currently used information. The first two steps lead to step three, which is an analysis of the discrepancy between needs and current practice. The expectation, of course, is that the management information system (MIS) will be an improvement over current practice—the discrepancy analysis identifies goals for the system and areas where improvement is needed. A fourth step is to ascertain what data should be collected in order to produce desired information. Step five is to identify the system's hardware requirements. This involves determining needed storage capacity, processing speed, and peripheral equipment. The sixth step is software design (programming) that will transform data into information with the given hardware. The final three steps involve purchasing hardware, training staff in the system's use, and actual implementation of the system.

The chart is highly simplified and each component could be further broken down into smaller steps. For example, step one could be divided into designing questionnaires and conducting surveys and interviews. In addition, a basic function of PERT is to estimate the time needed to complete each component activity, and thus for the entire project. For projects involving a large number of steps, computers are used to generate the total sequence of activities and to identify the critical path.

Advocates of PERT claim it can be used for a variety of purposes in administration, including budget preparation, feasibility studies, and curriculum evaluation. However, PERT is rarely used for these or other purposes in education. We examine some of the reasons why this may be true in Chapter Ten.

Linear programming is used in planning resource allocation where one factor is to be optimized (made as large or small as possible) while other factors are held constant or maintained within certain limits. Suppose, for example, that a school district decides to purchase computers for instructional use. This district would like to minimize costs (that is, optimize savings). Suppose, further, that the district has narrowed its choice to two computers. Computer A costs $10,000 and will support as many as ten terminals simultaneously. Computer B costs $12,000 and will support up to fifteen terminals at one time. The problem can be expressed as the following linear equation:

$$C = 10,000A + 12,000B$$

where C is total cost, which is to be minimized. Suppose an additional requirement is that the district will have up to 200 student users at one time. This constraint can be stated as

$$10A + 15B \geqslant 200.$$

This means that any combination of computers A and B must be able to accommodate 200 users (terminals) at any one time. If the district invests all its resources in the less expensive computer, A, then it will need to purchase twenty, so that

$$10(20) + 15(0) = 200.$$

The cost would be

$$\$10,000(20) + \$12,000(0) = \$200,000.$$

On the other hand, the district could acquire all computer Bs. In this case, it would need fourteen computers, since

$$10(0) + 15(14) \geqslant 200.$$

Fourteen is the smallest integer that satisfies this condition. Now the cost would be

$$\$10,000(0) + \$12,000(14) = \$168,000.$$

This is clearly less than $200,000, but has C been minimized? With further calculation we find that if the district purchases two computer As and twelve computer Bs, then the cost is

$$\$10,000(2) + \$12,000(12) = \$164,000.$$

At the same time, the constraint of $10A + 15B \geqslant 200$ is met. This is the lowest possible value of C, given the constraint.

These calculations can be performed in about fifteen minutes with a pocket calculator. It is easy to see, however, that this process would become unwieldy if more constraints were added, which is usually the case, or if constraints were not specified as a set value but rather as a range of values. A decision maker may want to compare costs of a system that could serve 200 simultaneous users with a system that could serve 150 simultaneous users, for example. In such cases, a computer is an enormous asset.

While linear programming has the advantage of bringing a rational, systematic process to bear on a decision, it does not follow that the planning decision itself has been made rational. Decisions still must rest heavily on underlying assumptions—such as that a computer system should serve 200 users at the same time—that may defy quantitative justification. Moreover, linear programming utility suffers from the fact that most real world problems do not lend themselves to mathematical formulation. There are a number of conditions that schools would like to optimize—student learning, resource utilization, use of teachers' time, to name a few. However, there are no universally accepted measures of optimality in these areas, nor is there agreement on what contributes to optimality. Thus, we cannot easily plan resource mixes in pure quantitative terms.

Queuing theory. A queue is a waiting line. It can be comprised of either people—such as people waiting at a bus stop, or students in line at a cafeteria—or things, such as equipment waiting for repair or "jobs" waiting for a computer run. Queuing theory addresses the question of whether lines are too long or waiting periods are excessive. It applies to situations in which the following conditions are present: (1) elements in the queue arrive at random time intervals and arrival of each element is independent of the arrival of all other elements; (2) service time for each element in the queue is independent of service time for any other element and is not affected by length of the queue; (3) the queuing system is in equilibrium (that is, it has been in operation a sufficient time to allow laws of probability on which the theory is based to take effect); (4) elements in the queue are served on a "first-come, first-serve" basis; (5) elements in the queue do not leave until they have received service; and (6) the average number of elements arriving in the queue during a unit of time is less than the average number of elements that can be serviced during the same unit.

To illustrate queuing theory, we return to the example involving purchase of computers for instruction and ask how it may have been decided that there should be terminals to accommodate 200 users simultaneously. Suppose the school district operates on a five-hour day, would like its computers to serve 1900 students daily, and would like to restrict average waiting time to gain access to the computer to less than four minutes. The following calculations illustrate that these conditions are met by the solution to the linear programming problem.

First, assume the average length of a computer session is one-half hour. This means that 200 terminals, at one-half hour per session, and five hours per day have an average service capacity of 2000 students per day. This capacity exceeds the expected use of 1900 students per day, thus satisfying condition six above. Now, if students were allocated to specific time periods on the computer, there would be no waiting and queuing theory would not apply. Remember that one of the assumptions is that each person's arrival at the queue is random and independent of any other person's arrival. If students choose their own times to use the computer, then we must expect that occasionally there will be excess demand (that is, users will outnumber terminals) and that some students will have to wait their turn. We can calculate average waiting line length with the following formula:

$$E(W) = \frac{A^2}{S(S-A)}$$

where "$E(W)$" is expected waiting time, "A" is arrival rate of students per day, and "S" is service rate, or number of students per day the system is able to accommodate. Thus, we have

$$E(W) = \frac{1900^2}{2000(2000-1900)} = 18.05 \text{ students.}$$

This formula is based on probability theory and has no simple, intuitive explanation. It is not necessary to go into its derivation for our purposes here.

If the average queue length is 18.05 persons, then those who join it must, on average, wait until 18.05 persons ahead of them have been served before getting their turn. Therefore, average waiting time—"E(T)"—is

$$E(T) = \frac{E(W)}{A} = \frac{18.05}{1900} = .012 \text{ days} = 3.6 \text{ minutes}$$

at five hours per day.

Thus, we have established that 200 terminals will serve 1900 students per day with the desired average waiting time of less than four minutes. Notice that the decision makers in our example would have started with the desired value for "E(T)" and worked backwards to obtain the needed number of terminals.

We have again used a simple example that required only manual calculation. In fact, many queuing problems can be solved by hand. The computer can be an advantage, however, in more complex problems, such as those involving more than one service center, or if decision makers would like to solve problems using different values. For instance, the problem in our example would be solved by recognizing each school as a service center with its own expected arrival rate. In addition, decision makers may want to analyze how much money they could save (by purchasing fewer computers) if average waiting time were extended to ten minutes.

Queuing theory can be used in a number of situations in a school setting, but it has limitations. Perhaps its most serious drawback is that it deals only in averages. It cannot determine expected waiting times in individual cases, or even maximum waiting times, which may be more important in some cases. For example, queuing theory may tell us that the average wait in a cafeteria line is ten minutes (with a thirty minute lunch period). This may seem fine, until experience shows that the maximum wait is twenty-five minutes, giving some virtually no time to eat.

Queuing theory is another planning technique that can inform decision making, but should not be misunderstood as actually making decisions. Its utility extends beyond supplying "objective" data—it also uncovers basic assumptions not directly amenable to quantification about which executives can make decisions. One assumption in our present example is that the average waiting time should be less than four minutes. As queuing theory yields more precise information regarding relationships between number of terminals and waiting time, decision makers can make fairly accurate cost estimates for reducing waiting time or the savings that could be made by lengthening it. This process involves placing a dollar value on waiting time, which, in the absence of a market system, must be established arbitrarily. In this case, then, monetary value of student time is an assumption that queuing theory assists to identify in quantitative terms.

Computer simulation. Models impute order to reality by positing relationships between things and events. They need not be complex or sophisticated. Most humans have mental models that allow them to give meaning to everyday experiences and to make predictions about future events. When negotiating a teacher pay scale with the school board, one might use a mental model of school board characteristics, past behavior, and current budget constraints to predict the achievable and plot strategy accordingly.

Computer simulation attempts to accrue information about a process or phenomenon through use of models. A model may be representative, in which case it reflects reality and allows a user to learn about and understand the phenomenon under study. An example of a representative model is a computer-simulated cockpit, which allows a pilot trainee to learn how to fly under realistic conditions without ever leaving the ground. Other models may be predictive. These must also be representative, in the sense that they resemble actual processes, but they are programmed to provide users information regarding possible outcomes given different circumstances. The atomic chart is a representative model, but it has also served as a predictive model in that it has allowed scientists to project characteristics of undiscovered elements (and, in fact, even to predict that such elements exist). The field of economics utilizes many predictive models. Policy makers use economic models to predict the effect of a tax increase on consumer demand and its consequences for inflation and employment.

Models may be *deterministic* or *stochastic.* In a deterministic model, similar inputs always produce similar outputs. In the simulated cockpit, if the pilot follows correct procedures, and if equipment is functioning properly, a smooth landing will always result. In a stochastic model static relationships between inputs and outputs do not hold, because random events are present. Policy makers cannot predict with absolute accuracy the effect of a tax increase because too many random events that can possibly affect the outcome are present. Stochastic models incorporate statistical procedures that simulate these random events. Most models in education, such as educational production functions, are stochastic.

Because models incorporate large numbers of variables and relationships, simulations are almost always done by computer. Computer simulation cannot be described in terms of simple formulas or processes, and its complexities are beyond the scope of this chapter. However, there is one issue regarding simulations that is central—that is the relationship between models and theories. Simply put, theories attempt to explain relationships between phenomena. Physics theories explain revolution of planets around the sun or release of energy from a split atom. In anthropology, theories explain human evolution. In education, we have no generally accepted theories. We have no definitive explanation, for example, of the relationship between teaching and learning. Though substantial progress is being made, no one can explain completely for humans the manner in which knowledge is acquired and accumulated. Nor is there even agreement on the precise nature of intelligence. In order to construct a representative or predictive model that translates inputs into outputs, it is necessary to have a theory that specifically relates outputs to inputs. Since such theories do not yet fully exist in education, modeling and simulating are hampered.

Modeling, nevertheless, is attempted. For example, researchers have constructed models relating student achievement to a variety of factors including family background, school quality, intelligence measures, and ethnicity. To the extent these models are successful in measuring the relative influence of each factor on student achievement, policy makers can understand and perhaps "control" (improve) students' achievement levels, even if in a limited way.

More successful uses of computer simulation exist in education. These can be found in areas such as revenue projections and enrollment trends. An example of using computer simulation to plan school bus routes is provided in Chapter Fifteen.

BUDGETING

It is through budgeting that an organization aligns its resources with its purposes. Also, the budget process is the concrete, practical link between planning, the forward looking portion of an organization's management activities, and *evaluation*, activities which focus systematically upon past performance.

It is common in textbooks to describe budgeting in the context of school finance and business practices. We eschew such a convention for three reasons. First, as we have mentioned in the above paragraph, budgeting is more usefully viewed as a component of management's planning and evaluation activities. In addition, a budget should represent a plan for the direction of an organization's total discretionary resources—time, personnel, and physical resources—not simply money.

The budget process must also be understood as a political activity. Resource allocation is not simply a technocratic undertaking. Once resource decisions have been made regarding matters such as goals, personnel, salary levels, and supplies, keeping accurate records, though by no means simple, is a technical activity. However, prior to that point, budget decisions may involve "bargaining." Depending upon their value orientation—equality, efficiency, or freedom—various school constituencies may desire different organizational outcomes. Parents may prefer smaller classes, teachers may reasonably prefer higher salaries. Science cannot easily be invoked to solve such conflict. Bargaining, hopefully conducted in good faith with the purposes and welfare of the organization in mind, may have to be the mechanism for resolving such differences. Once a bargain has been struck, then its fiscal consequences should be represented in the budget. In this sense, a budget is a political document. It is the concrete representation of the political compromises that have been made.

BUDGETING'S FUNDAMENTAL ASSUMPTIONS

In order for "budgeting" to be a fact and not an organizational fiction, three critical conditions must exist. Budgets must meet the tests of annualarity, comprehensiveness, and balance.[2]

---

[2] The authors are grateful for the explanations of Aaron Wildavsky in arriving at an understanding of these assumptions.

Annualarity

A budget—an organization's resource allocation plan—is intended to cover a fixed time period, generally a year. This need not be a calendar year beginning January 1 and ending the subsequent December 31. Indeed, few school districts utilize a calendar year. The budget year is generally known as a "fiscal year." The fiscal year for the majority of U.S. school districts begins July 1 and concludes at the end of the following June, in the next calendar year. However, there are districts that utilize a fiscal year coinciding with the academic year (beginning when school opens in autumn) or with their state's legislative appropriations cycle.[3]

Regardless of the precise time period involved, or even if it is a two-year period, the important principle is that there is a previously agreed upon span of time over which resource allocation and financial administration occur. Also, in order to be maximally useful, the budget time period—fiscal year—should not be altered frequently. Select a fiscal year and stay with the decision. Otherwise, public confidence, record keeping, and fiscal analyses are jeopardized.

Comprehensiveness

An organization's budget must encompass all fiscally related activity, both on the resource and expenditure side. The budget may contain a variety of funds and accounts, for example, instruction, administration, maintenance, and transportation. It may well keep track of expenditures in more than one way—that is, by function (for example, physical education), as well as object of expenditure (for example, instructional salaries). What is important is that all the revenues received by the organization, regardless of source or purpose, and all that the organization spends, regardless of source or purpose, be encompassed by the budget and the budget process. If a budget is not comprehensive, then organizational resources may be accrued or utilized for purposes outside the control of its leaders. This may or may not be illegal, depending upon specifics. It certainly is inefficient.

Balance

This is the third critical budget assumption. What is received by way of resources must not exceed what is spent. This is not to assert that all organizations must always live within their immediately available resources. Certainly resources can be borrowed and paid back at a later time. We have already illustrated such conditions in Chapter Five; borrowing money to construct a long-lasting building makes sense. What is being emphasized is that a budget assumes explicit organizational acknowledgement of resources and obligations, and the two must match. If they are out of balance, it is again the case that the organization is out of control.

---

[3] The federal government's fiscal year begins October 1 of any given calendar year and concludes September 30 of the subsequent year.

COMPONENTS OF BUDGETING

Budgeting contains four important sequentially occurring components. The first, *budget development,* is oriented toward the future, a concern for what will or should be. Another dimension, *budget administration,* is concerned with the immediate present and focuses upon proper procedures and approvals. A third dimension, *accounting* (or *bookkeeping*), is oriented toward the immediate past—what happened and to what degree was it consistent with the expected projection? The fourth component, *cost effectiveness analysis,* takes a longer view of the past and makes an assessment of past actions and appraises their effectiveness relative to costs.

The first of these, budget development, should be aligned with an organization's planning cycle. The fourth, cost effectiveness analysis, should be aligned with the evaluation portion of the cycle. In what follows we concentrate on the extremes, budget development and cost effectiveness analysis, pausing only to explain in broad terms the purposes and operation of budget administration and accounting. Before turning to each of these components, we wish to explain their distribution over time by referring to what conventionally is labeled the "budget cycle."

THE BUDGET CYCLE

Reference to a "cycle" for budgeting makes it clear that there is a repetitive pattern to the activities of organizations and the life of its constituents. Such a pattern facilitates looking toward the future and assessing the past. An organization's budget cycle has a beginning and an end, and then, as is the nature of cycles, begins again. The four components of budgeting—development, administration, accounting, and analysis—are arrayed sequentially in this cycle, but they exhibit substantial overlap. All four activities may be, indeed should be, occurring simultaneously, though each may well be focused upon a different fiscal year.

For example, in August or September of any particular year, a school district's staff might well be engaged in current fiscal year budget administration activities such as preparing payrolls and approving purchase orders for the forthcoming spring semester's instructional supplies. This is budget administration. Accounting staff might well be closing the books on the recently completed school year. They would be summing expenditures for different categories and setting records in order for the annual audit. This is bookkeeping. Evaluation staff members might well be engaged in the collection of data and analytic procedures involved in appraising results of an instructional innovation that was tried during the school year just ended. They might be undertaking these cost-effectiveness analyses in order to inform the superintendent whether or not the innovation should be continued or terminated. Lastly, officials may be engaged in developing the budget for the school year beginning the following September.

Even though all four phases of budgeting may be transpiring simultaneously, we will focus upon each one individually and do so in order of its appearance in the cycle for any particular fiscal year. Thus, we begin with "budget development."

Budget Development

This is the forward-looking planning phase of budgeting. This is the time during which decision makers reach agreement, even if only implicit, regarding an organization's mission and the objectives to be accomplished for the forthcoming fiscal year. They must also agree regarding assumptions crucial to budgeting. For example, what will average class size be, how many days during the year will the school district operate, what will be the average size of schools, and, thus, how many school buildings will the district operate? Will there be a need to open new schools or close old ones? What will district revenues be from various sources—local, state, federal, and philanthropic? These and dozens of related decisions must be made in as orderly and reasonable a fashion as the political process permits. It is often the case that educational decision makers neglect formal discussion of such important topics. Under such circumstances, decisions are made by default and inertia prevails. This is a pity. When appropriately conducted, decisions regarding such important preconditions are described in a "budget assumption letter." This document is distributed to appropriate budget process participants and guides the framing of their budget proposals.

In order to facilitate budget planning, organizations generally design a so-called "budget development calendar." (An example of such a calendar is displayed in Table 11.1.) It typically is the responsibility of the district's budget officer to develop the calendar and gain its approval by the superintendent and school board. Thereafter, the budget officer is responsible for seeing that factual items and necessary analyses are supplied in sufficient time to mesh with appropriate calendar target dates.

A complete budget development calendar is guided by chronological events such as state legislated approval dates, actions by the legislature on appropriations, expiration of collective bargaining agreements with employees, and the school academic calendar. Such important dates are specified in the left hand column of the sample calendar.

In addition to critical dates, a complete budget development schedule makes clear crucial items of information, or assumptions about crucial information. Examples are projected enrollments for the forthcoming school year, expected revenues, salary increases for employees as a consequence of bargaining, and the size of the teacher workforce. Often, these informational items will be contained in the previously mentioned "budget assumption letter."

The budget development schedule should also specify participants in the decision process. These are listed in the right hand column of the sample development calendar. The district being illustrated here has a highly centralized budget development process. To be sure, principals and other employees participate in budget

Table 11.1   BUDGET DEVELOPMENT

PRELIMINARY BUDGET PLANNING CALENDAR

Wed. 1/19 Board Room	Preliminary budget development discussion with Board	Superintendent Business Office
Mon. 1/24 3:30–5:00	General Orientation Meeting. Preliminary budget development discussions.	Budget Committee Principals Union Reps
Wed. 1/26 1:00–5:00	Workshop to review base budget parameters (Revenue, Expenditures, Staffing, etc.). Begin to develop and balance preliminary budget.	Committee
Fri. 1/28 1:30–5:00	Continue 1/26 session.	Committee
Mon. 2/7 3:30–7:30	Review/discuss preliminary budget recommendations.	Committee Principals
Tues. 2/8 3:30–7:30	Review/discuss preliminary budget recommendations.	Committee Union Reps
Wed. 2/16 Board Room	Presentation of balanced preliminary budget with Board.	Board Superintendent
Wed. 2/23 Board Room	Continue 2/16 regular board meeting. NOTE: LAST DATE FOR ACTION ON LAYOFFS, if necessary (to effect notice by 3/15).	Board Superintendent
March–April	General Group and Board Workshop/discussion sessions on program budget planning, e.g., Special Education; Elementary and Secondary Instruction; Operations and Maintenance; Instructional Support Services; others. Dates and specific bedgets for review to be determined.	All Board

IF PRIOR LAYOFF ACTION, TAKEN, FOLLOW-UP WOULD BE

Thurs. 4/7 2:00–8:00	Refine preliminary budget—develop tentative budget. Review recommendation regarding layoffs.	Committee
Mon. 4/11 3:30–7:30	Review/discuss refined preliminary budget.	Committee Principals
Tues. 4/12 3:30–7:30	Review/discuss refined preliminary budget.	Committee Union Reps
Wed. 4/20 Board Room	Board action on final layoff notification (by 5/15); if necessary.	Board Superintendent
Wed. 4/27 Board Room	DATE FOR BOARD ACTION ON LAYOFF (to effective notice by 5/15); if necessary.	Board Superintendent

Table 11.1 (cont.)

IF NO PRIOR LAY-OFF ACTION TAKEN, THEN CONTINUE HERE

Tues. 5/17 and Tues. 5/24 2:00–8:00	Tentative Budget workshop. Finalize Education Plan and Tentative Budget Recommendations for Board approval	Committee
Thurs. 6/2 3:30–7:30	Review/discuss Tentative Budget Recommendations.	Committee Union Reps
Mon. 6/6 3:30–7:30	Review/discuss Tentative Budget Recommendations.	Committee Principals
Wed. 6/8 Board Room	Board Workshop/discussion of Tentative Budget Recommendations	Board Superintendent
Wed. 6/15 Board Room	Board to Adopt Tentative Budget.	Board Superintendent

Fri. 7/1	LAST DAY TO FILE ADOPTED TENTATIVE BUDGET
	      WITH COUNTY. Must indicate date, time, and location
	      of public hearing on Final Budget.
		Business Office

Thurs. 7/7 9:30–2:30	Review, discuss, finalize Final Budget Recommendation. Group effort.	Committee Principals Union Reps
Wed. 7/13 and Wed. 7/27 Board Room	Board workshop/discussion sessions on Final Budget Recommendations.	Board Superintendent

On or before
8/1
	County shall review and return filed Tentative Budget.
	      County may accept changes in the date, time, and
	      location of public hearing on Final Budget.
		Business Office

Wed. 8/3 Board Room	Board to hold public hearing and adopt Final Budget.	Board Superintendent
Wed. 9/7	LAST DATE TO HOLD PUBLIC HEARING, ADOPT, AND FILE FINAL BUDGET.	Board Superintendent Business Office

decisions. Indeed, the "committee" to which frequent references appear on the calendar is comprised of representative employees. However, even though employees participate in developing the budget, the result is still a centralized school district plan. It is possible to allocate substantially greater budgetary discretion to school sites—to have a decentralized budget. We describe the dynamics of this arrangement later in this chapter.

It is during the budget development phase that the results of prior analyses should be taken into account. Planning techniques such as those illustrated earlier in this chapter can inform this part of the budget cycle. It is also at this point in planning the next year's resources that a decision should be reached regarding the expansion of what has been appraised and found effective and the termination of that which is judged ineffective. This is where the evaluation portion of the planning cycle begins to feed back into the planning cycle.

Budget Administration

Once having reached agreement among various components of an organization regarding planned resource allocation for the forthcoming fiscal year, it then becomes crucial to ensure that resources are indeed allocated in accord with the agreement—that is, expenditures are consistent with the budget. This is the function of those members in the organization responsible for "budget administration." Here are found employees with titles such as "Comptroller," "Bursar," and "Business Manager." Regardless of label, the overall responsibility is to approve or to see that approval has been obtained for requests for spending. The purpose is to ensure that spending requests are consistent with previously agreed upon budget plans. For example, payroll departments, purchasing officers, maintenance supervisors, and shipping and receiving departments as well as line administrators all have a role to play in seeing that resources are received and distributed in keeping with the district's overall resource allocation plan—its budget.

Accounting

Assuming that resources are allocated in an approved manner, it still is necessary to maintain records of such transactions. This is done for three reasons. First, to see that over time any particular function is not receiving more resources than was intended for it. Here, accounting procedures can keep track of accrued actual expenditures by budget category as well as "encumbrances," resources not yet spent but already obligated.

The second reason records are kept is to be able, after the fact, to ensure compliance with the spending plan. To do this, bookkeeping records are utilized by "auditors." They review spending actions to report compliance, or lack thereof, with the budget. An organization, if sufficiently large, may have both internal and external auditors. Most states require school districts to have an external audit of their books at least annually to ensure that spending is in compliance not only with district budgets, but also with state and federal regulations.

The third reason for financial record keeping is to be able to use the information as the basis for subsequent analyses, such as cost-effectiveness analysis or appraisals of equity. These analytic endeavors depend crucially upon records being kept accurately and in a useful form. Generally, the more abstract the level of aggregation, the less useful the data. For example, to conduct analyses it typically is of little use to have a single record entry such as "salaries." How many individuals were being paid how much to do what for how long? These latter questions imply the kinds of bookkeeping categories which more likely permit studies of efficiency and equity.

School districts generally adhere to a uniform accounting code. In 1957, what was then known as the United States Office of Education published *Financial Accounting for Local and State School Systems: Standard Receipt and Expenditure Accounts.* This was intended as a guide to state and local education agencies in keeping their financial records. This document and its successors have had a widely beneficial influence. By encouraging local and state agencies to adopt a standard form of record keeping, research across geographic boundaries as well as over time has been facilitated. Each state now has a uniform accounting manual patterned much like the federal government model.

Budget approvals and accounting are typically considered together as budget administration. We have separated them here simply for purposes of explanation. However, each of them differs substantially from the fourth component of the budget cycle, evaluation.

Cost-Effectiveness Analysis

Cost-effectiveness analysis is a special case of cost-benefit analysis. In the latter, costs and benefits are both expressed in monetary terms and compared to identify the program or programs that yield the greatest monetary benefit relative to costs. Cost-effectiveness analysis is employed when benefits are not easily expressed in monetary terms, but are otherwise measurable, such as achievement test scores or student school retention rates. Cost-effectiveness analysis, then, relates costs, expressed in dollar terms, with program objectives, expressed in nonmonetary terms.

The objective of cost-effectiveness analysis is to identify programs that can accomplish a given level of objectives at the lowest cost. Thus, cost-effectiveness analysis looks both at the past and toward the future. It glances backward in time in order to assess actual costs incurred relative to objectives that have been achieved. This analysis of past experience, plus evaluations of possible alternative programs to accomplish the same objectives, can identify strategies to enhance effectiveness in the future.

To understand cost-effectiveness analysis, it is helpful to view the budget as a statement of relationships between educational resources and objectives. To be sure, a budget is many other things as well, but a rational budget will always imply a theory (or at least an educated guess) regarding which combination of schooling resources will most effectively produce cognitive achievement and other desired outcomes.

In order to achieve an optimal allocation of resources, it is useful to have information regarding how much each resource contributes to the desired outcomes. Economists refer to this as the *marginal productivity* of inputs. This is the amount of additional output associated with an added unit of input. A model of productivity that incorporates the concept of marginal productivity is called an *educational production function.* Ideally, additional amounts of each input will be acquired (with budget constraints, this will mean correspondingly less amounts of other inputs) until the marginal productivity of that input is equal to the marginal productivity of all other inputs. If the marginal productivity of an input is greater than that of other inputs, then more output could be produced by allocating additional resources to it. On the other hand, if the marginal productivity of an input is less than that of other inputs, then fewer resources should be allocated to that input. These are the principles underlying cost-effectiveness analysis.

Levin provides an early example of cost-effectiveness analysis that assessed the relative contribution of teacher experience and teacher verbal ability to verbal learning of students.[4] The educational production function was estimated via a statistical technique known as *multiple regression analysis.* This yields estimates of the marginal productivity of each of the inputs included in the analysis. Levin found that teacher experience costs five times as much as teacher verbal ability because teachers receive greater pay increments for added years of teacher experience than for added verbal ability. At the same time, however, teacher experience was found to be only one tenth as effective as verbal ability with respect to the verbal learning of Black students. The conclusion of this study is that school budgets would be more cost-effective (with respect to verbal learning) by spending less money to acquire teachers with more experience and more money to acquire teachers with greater verbal ability.

A more recent study by Wolfe[5] used a technique similar to Levin's with data on students in Philadelphia. Her data set was superior to Levin's in that it was more pupil specific. In other words, student learning could be related to inputs actually received by each student rather than to a school-wide average of pupil inputs. Wolfe was concerned with the problem of funding reductions and attempted to identify areas where budget cuts could be made with the least detrimental impact on effectiveness. By estimating an educational production function with the Philadelphia data and relating this to the school district's budget constraint, Wolfe found that average pupil achievement could be increased by up to 9 percent, not by adding resources, but by reallocating existing resources. If spending must be reduced, an important implication of this is that systematic, rather than across-the-board budget cuts would be more effective. In fact, even in the face of declining resources, Wolfe found that employing additional resources to reduce class size would be an effective expenditure for low-achieving students.

The cost-effectiveness analyses employed by Levin and Wolfe require a capacity for research that most school districts do not possess. In addition, due to statistical limitations, this technique becomes less satisfactory when more than one output is considered. In practice, then, cost-effectiveness analysis, to the extent it is performed, usually concentrates on identifying least-cost programs relative to a given level of achievement. (A more expensive program may be desirable if the gain in effectiveness exceeds the added cost, that is, if the ratio of benefit to cost is

[4] Henry M. Levin, "A Cost-Effectiveness Analysis of Teacher Selection," *Journal of Human Resources,* 5(1) (Winter 1970), 24–33.

[5] Barbara Wolfe, "A Cost-Effectiveness Analysis of Reduction in School Expenditures: An Application of an Educational Production Function," *Journal of Educational Finance,* 2(4) (Spring 1977), 407–18.

greater.) In this case, the object of study becomes the differences in total cost be-tween alternative programs rather than the allocation of resources within programs. Performing such analysis may result in substantial savings for school districts, how-ever, as more is learned about educational production functions. As school districts acquire a greater capacity for more sophisticated research, cost-effectiveness studies like those of Levin and Wolfe may have an even greater impact on increasing school effectiveness.

BUDGETING, DECISION MAKING, AND POWER

The individuals empowered to make decisions regarding the allocation of resources have the potential to determine the organization's direction. Frankly, budget con-trol is power. The appropriate conventional phrase is "power of the purse." The budget process can be used to concentrate power in the hands of a relatively small number of individuals or distribute it to an expanded number of actors. In order to illustrate this maxim, we describe the principles involved in program budgeting and zero based budgeting, budget development strategies which concentrate power, and school site budgeting, a strategy which decentralizes decision-making discretion.

Program Budgeting and Zero Based Budgeting[6]

Budgeting in most organizations is said to be "incremental." This is particu-larly the case in public sector institutions such as schools. "Incremental" in this context refers to the tendency to make resource allocation changes only at the "margin." The vast bulk of expenditures continue year after year, budget cycle after budget cycle. The "base" changes little. The major reason this is the case is because of the political influence of individuals and groups who gain advantage by maintaining the *status quo.* For example, current employees, and the parent clients they serve, should there be any added resources, are anxious to derive the benefits themselves. Teachers, for example, might well lobby or bargain intensely for higher salaries and smaller classes should the school district have the prospect of increasing its revenues. For a variety of reasons, parents might side with teachers on these issues. Consequently, a school board and administration might be sub-jected to political pressure to accord added resources to those already employed because the employees believe they are entitled to at least as much as they received last year and a "fair share" of any addition.

In this scenario, the best that can be hoped for is to gain control over a por-tion of any anticipated increase and direct such resources toward new goals. When resources are declining, entrenched interests, if anything, are more adamant in their protection of the "base."

---

[6] See Joseph S. Wholey, *Zero Base: Budgeting and Program Evaluation* (Lexington: Lexington Books, 1979); and I. Carl Candoli and others, *School Business Administration: A Planning Approach* (Boston: Allyn & Bacon, Inc., 1973).

To the extent that such organizational dynamics are present in schools, they render it difficult to make decisions about total revenues. It is only an increment to the base that typically can be redirected. Often this can occur only after successful negotiations.

Program budgeting and zero based budgeting are efforts to gain greater central control over an organization's resources. Each of these strategies calls for resources to be aligned with organizational purposes, programs, or objectives instead of with actual objects to be purchased, personnel, or materials. If a purpose is agreed to by decision makers, then whatever expenditure is necessary to accomplish the purpose is permitted. If a purpose or program is no longer thought to be important or necessary by decision makers, then its expenditure base is reduced or eliminated. An old purpose or program may be replaced by a new one. Individuals employed to conduct the old program might be released and new personnel employed who possess the qualifications necessary to perform the new functions. Program budgeting assumes that each program, or at least a significant number of an organization's programs, will be assessed periodically to determine their usefulness and effectiveness. Those judged wanting can be improved or eliminated. Similarly, zero based budgeting assumes that annually, or at least with regularity, the entire budget can be built from the ground up with no assumption of existing obligations. Collective bargaining contracts, the existence of tenure for teachers, and the large capital cost already sunk into school building typically militate against a school district's undertaking a true form of zero based budgeting. Even program budgeting is unusual. Periodically, districts attempt such efforts, but generally revert to incremental budget behavior, attempting to spend added monies as wisely as possible and phasing out old programs if there is evidence of their ineffectiveness or lack of political constituency.[7]

School Site Budgeting[8]

In order to enfranchise a larger set of actors, some districts utilize a budgeting mechanism whereby a portion of a district's revenues are allocated by formula to school sites. School level decision makers, usually the principal assisted by a site advisory council of teachers and parents, can then decide allocation patterns. Such systems must be carefully designed to work in tandem with central districts' collective bargaining contracts. However, well developed technical mechanisms exist for budgeting and accounting for revenues school by school. School site budgeting ap-

[7] The difficulties involved in implementing PPBS are described by Jay Chambers and Thomas Parrish in *The Legacy of Rational Budgeting Models in Education and a Proposal for the Future,* publication of the Institute for Finance and Governance (Stanford, Calif.: Stanford University Press, 1984).

[8] See John Greenhalgh, "School Site Budgeting: Decentralized School Management" (Lanham, Md.: University Press of America, 1984); James W. Guthrie, *School Budgeting: The Relative Advantages of Centralized and School Site Budget Development* (San Francisco Public Schools Commission, 1975); and Lawrence C. Pierce, *School Based Management,* Eugene, Oregon, School Study Council, 23, no. 10 (1980).

pears to be an idea which is increasingly popular in circumstances where state-level decision making is increasing.

PROGRAM EVALUATION

Program evaluation involves systematic assessment of an endeavor in order to determine its effects. Once the effects in several selected dimensions are known, then evaluation usually entails a judgment of the endeavor's relative success or failure. Such a judgment may involve measuring project results against a predetermined goal. Did reading achievement scores increase? Were student absenteeism and vandalism reduced? Was parent satisfaction enhanced? These are the kinds of questions evaluators pose. Their objective is to determine whether or not or to what degree a desired outcome occurred, to suggest the manner in which the undertaking might be rendered more effective, and to influence the allocation of organizational resources as a result.

In this section we describe evaluation purposes and concepts important for educational executives. We explain cost-benefit analysis in order to illustrate the manner in which evaluation procedures can be utilized to influence resource allocation—budgeting decisions. We also describe a range of data items and procedures that can be used to collect, compile, and display information about the effectiveness of a school's or district's educational programs. This is not a textbook on methodologies; consequently no effort is undertaken to explain technical evaluation details. Personnel evaluation is described in Chapter Thirteen on *Human Resources Administration*.

Purposes of Program Evaluation

The purpose of a program evaluation may be *formative* or *summative*. The former is an assessment undertaken to assist an on-course or in-progress correction. A statement regarding such an assessment might say, for example, "We are anxious to continue the after school intensive remedial reading program, but we want to ensure that it is as effective as possible. Hence we are evaluating it now in hopes that our results can reshape whatever components are found to be ineffective." A summative evaluation is undertaken to render a judgment regarding the value of a program or project. An experimental or pilot project may be evaluated at its conclusion to determine whether or not it is worth continuing, or if it is sufficiently effective to justify implementing on a broader scale. At least in concept, the fate of an endeavor may depend upon the outcome of a summative evaluation. As with many definitions, however, it is possible to identify evaluations which blur the distinction between formative and summative.

The Evaluation Process

As with the formal procedures or stages involved in decision making, problem solving, and long-range planning, program evaluation is a systematic and rational process. There may be other avenues through which humans can arrive at knowledge, for instance, intuition or revelation. However, formal evaluation is rooted in a scientific paradigm which involves the following sequence of steps.

Identification of objectives. In order to conduct a systematic educational program evaluation, it is imperative that project or program purposes be known explicitly. Purposes or objectives constitute the criteria against which an undertaking's effectiveness can be judged. Under the healthiest of circumstances, a program's purposes were specified at the time of inauguration or implementation. As unlikely as it may initially seem, however, programs are sometimes enacted without a clear idea of their expected outcomes. For example, policy enactment procedures sometimes render obfuscation useful in order to gain greater political support. In 1965 when the Elementary and Secondary Education Act was passed it was heralded as a bill which would "break the cycle of poverty." This was an admirable objective; numerous supporters sought to cluster under such a humanitarian banner. However, were the federal government compensatory education funds authorized by the bill intended to dispel poverty by elevating students' academic achievement, ensuring better nutrition and adequate health care, or expanding out-of-school educational opportunities? Such specificity, should it have been included in the bill, ran the risk of alienating potential supporters. Thus, the bill's advocates responded by listing all such good and possible purposes as the program's equally valuable objectives.

Evaluators of ESEA Title I subsequently had to infer specific purposes in order to assess whether or not local district compensatory educational programs were effective. If evaluators imputed motives to a particular school's program coincident with the operators' intent, then the evaluation possessed at least the potential for being valid. However, if the program operators at schools believed that provision of proper nutrition and health care would remove impediments to academic motivation, and evaluators incorrectly judged that the program's intent was enhancement of reading skills and administered a reading test, then the evaluation was probably invalid.

The point, simply, is that care must be taken initially in specifying a program's purposes, and the purposes must possess sufficient specificity to enable progress toward them to be measured. An evaluation team may well assess the extent to which a program is meeting two or more sets of objectives, for example, those held for it by policy makers and those held by operators or clients.

Design and methodology. Useful evaluation almost always involves comparison. The program or project to be assessed can be viewed as a "treatment." This involves deliberate manipulation of an "independent variable" to determne its consequences for one or more "dependent variables." In order to determine effectiveness, either a before and after comparison or a comparison with a "control group" which did not have the "treatment" must be made. The comparison of those receiving the treatment in at least two points in time, a so-called times series comparison, necessitates advance consideration. A baseline measure, a pretest of some sort, must be undertaken prior to implementing the "treatment." In the absence of such a baseline, comparison with another group is the only avenue of "control" possible. This too is greatly facilitated if thought is given to the matter in advance of implementing the new program, the "treatment." Detailed technical considerations for selecting a sample for measurement and comparison is a matter better explained elsewhere. The point for administrators is that evaluation is not an undertaking to be left until last and then hastily conducted. Rather, systematic program assessment demands prior consideration not only of program purposes and their specification, but also of the populations with whom the treatment group will be compared.

Measurement. Once having agreed upon program purposes and the design by which an evaluation will be conducted, it is also necessary to identify means for measuring potential outcomes. If the program is designed explicitly to elevate student achievement, then some form of test is likely to be in order. Similarly, specific efforts to increase parent participation, enrollment in extracurricular activities, attention to personal health and hygiene, or to reduce truancy, class cutting, tardies, dropout rates, or vandalism lend themselves to explicit outcome measures.

There are two additional categories of outcome measures which tend to be overlooked by educational executives—"unobtrusive measures," and "downstream measures." The social psychologist, Eugene Webb, advocates greater attention to outcome measures, which by virtue of their subtlety interfere minimally if at all with the program itself.[9] In Chapter Seven we explain the so-called Hawthorne Effect wherein subjects of an experiment, regardless of the "treatment," tend to alter their behavior because of the added attention focused upon them. Such an interaction with an experimental program can distort validity of the evaluation. Webb reasonably contends that unobtrusive measures render an evaluation more neutral and precise. If a program is intended to encourage reading among students, count the users of the library or the number of books checked out in a specified time period. If funds are being spent to upgrade science achievement, then observe the wear on floor tiles in front of display cases or dioramas. If physical fitness or strength is the focus for improvement, observe the paint-wear pattern where the Nautilus or Universal weights are adjusted. The search for useful, unobtrusive measures is another point at which creativity is to be applauded.

Downstream measures refer to lagged effects—outcomes likely to occur later in time. Schools are notably deficient in undertaking follow-up studies of program participants or graduates. What occurs at a subsequent stage can provide useful insight regarding a program. How do students in Ms. Smith's third grade class perform in subsequent years? How do students from Washington Elementary School perform when they attend junior high and high school? How do graduates of school district "X" compare with graduates of other districts in their freshman and upper class courses at universities? What are the occupational patterns of graduates? Edu-

---

[9] Eugene J. Webb, Donald T. Campbell, Richard D. Schwartz, and Lee Sechrest, *Unobtrusive Measures: Nonreactive Research in the Social Sciences* (Chicago: Rand McNally & Company, 1971).

cators correctly claim that there is much about schooling which does not lend itself to immediate measurement. This is all the more reason for a school or district to inaugurate a systematic effort to measure the performance of students "downstream."

Pitfalls of Evaluation

Experiments in education possess the potential to be uncommonly complicated. The range of intervening variables is broad; ability to control for outside influences is slender. Often, many parties have a high investment in the new program, and jobs and other resources can ride on an evaluation's outcome. For these and other reasons, appropriate design of a valid educational program evaluation is difficult. Experts in methodology have identified several sources of invalidity in evaluations. Whether conducting evaluations personally or simply absorbing the results of evaluation research, educational executives are well advised to be aware of these common sources of invalidity.

Assessing "non-events." Charters and Jones write persuasively of the circumstances in which an "experimental treatment" in education differs so little from standard procedures as to be insignificant. Regardless of the label attached, if a treatment is to be effective, something different must occur. "If the differences between what the research regards as 'experimental' and 'control' programs is fictional, the findings of the study will be fundamentally misleading irrespective of their nature."[10] Charters and Jones propose using four criteria to ensure that in fact, not simply in rhetoric, an experimental treatment was implemented. The tests involve (1) an official specification of what it is that is to be altered; (2) some structural change or alteration which is observable, for example, a new teacher was employed, a new set of books purchased, or the school day rearranged; (3) behavior actually changed—for example, teachers utilized a new instructional technique; and (4) respondent activities are altered—for example, students engage in different learning drills.

Sources of internal invalidity. Assuming that there is sufficient evidence that an "experimental treatment" is actually occurring, there nevertheless exist conditions which can invalidate evaluation results. Donald T. Campbell and Julian C. Stanley list eight such sources of invalidity.[11]

History

This refers to the specific events which occurred between first and last measures taken of a program's effectiveness. For example, a school district undertook an intense effort in its hygiene classes to reduce cigarette smoking

---

[10] W. W. Charters, Jr., and John E. Jones, "On the Risk of Appraising Non-events in Program Evaluation," *Education Researcher,* 2, no. 11 (November 1973), 5.

[11] Donald T. Campbell and Julian C. Stanley, "Experimental and Quasi Experimental Designs for Research on Teaching," *Handbook of Research on Teaching,* ed. N. L. Gage (Chicago: Rand McNally College Publishing Company, 1963).

among students. At the conclusion of the pilot curriculum project, a reduction in smoking was noted, both in the students' self reports and in the number of packages sold in vending machines available to students. It appeared that, at least for a short term, the program was successful in reducing smoking. However, The United States Surgeon General issued a major report on the relationship of smoking to cancer during the two week curriculum unit. Student cigarette smoking may have diminished, but a highly publicized report by an eminent authority offers an alternative explanation for the results. Also, the package price of cigarettes was increased in vending machines, which may have dampened demand.

Maturation

Processes independent of the "experimental treatment" may operate within the subjects to confound results. For example, a six-month preschool program intended to enhance student physical coordination would almost inevitably be confounded by the children's natural physical maturation.

Testing

It is sometimes the case that the effort to obtain a baseline measure of pupil peformance prior to initiating an "experimental treatment" may itself enhance pupil performance. Students can learn from taking a pretest, which may add to their post test score aside from whatever other instruction they receive. This is known as pretest-post test interaction.

Instrumentation

Alterations in the measuring instruments or errors in pre and post observation can bias evaluation results. For example, an inaccurate counter on a secondary school library turnstile undercounted the number of library patrons and led school administrators incorrectly to conclude that a new reading enhancement program was ineffective.

Statistical Regression

There is a tendency for extremes to gravitate to a mean. All other conditions being equal, the offspring of extremely tall or short parents will be closer to average height. If a sample is populated by too many individuals possessed of an extreme trait, e.g., scored at the lowest point on a test, regardless of treatment they can be expected to score closer toward the mean on subsequent administrations. This could lead to the erroneous conclusion that a new program was effective.

Differential Selection of Comparison

Errors in selecting a control group with which to compare experimental program subjects can bias evaluation results. If the control group is not matched properly on appropriate dimensions, then comparisons with experimental subjects will reveal more or less progress than accurately should be attributed to the "treatment."

Experimental Mortality

Differential attrition of respondents either from a control or treatment group can bias evaluation results.

Selection-Maturation Interaction

This is a potential difficulty when an evaluation project involves multiple groups and bias develops because one or more control groups is selected in which maturation occurs at a rate different from experimental groups.

The above-listed conditions can prevent program evaluation results from possessing *internal validity*. Other conditions can impede program evaluation results from being generalizable to other populations—that is, jeopardize *external validity*. An illustration may assist in understanding this latter difficulty. Behavior quite common to one culture may not characterize another. Thus, a "treatment" which might be judged effective in enhancing reading achievement among students in Japanese schools might not prove effective for American students drawn not simply from a different culture but perhaps from many different cultures. Educational executives involved with program evaluation should be concerned with both internal and external validity, but it is the latter which most frequently plagues school-related experiments.[12] Being able to generalize from the experimental subjects to a regular school setting is important. Otherwise results of the experimental program have been for naught.

Politics and Evaluation

Evaluations can determine continued existence of a program and possibly the allocation of scarce resources, for example, jobs. The more that is at risk as a consequence of an evaluation outcome, the greater the probability that efforts will be made to influence the evaluation through political means. There is also considerable client resistance to evaluation findings that fail to legitimize and reinforce clients' expected results.[13] Given these circumstances, then, it is not uncommon, for example, for those potentially affected the greatest by the outcomes to attempt to discourage an evaluation altogether. Without success in such an undertaking, a next step is to try and influence the evaluation design or the "instruments" to be used in the measurement. Determining a program's purposes may legitimately be an endeavor suited to the political process. At that juncture, potential benefactors should be consulted. Thereafter, however, evaluation is more technical than political.

If a program is ineffective, then resources are being utilized which could otherwise be expended in a beneficial manner. Conversely, an effective program discontinued because of a flawed or politically biased evaluation procedure is defrauding recipients of a service they may badly need and which the political process may have fairly allocated to them. Hence, once program purposes have been determined, an educational administrator is professionally obligated to ensure evaluations are conducted in a manner as free of unwarranted political intrusion as reasonably possible.

[12] This argument is made strongly by Lee J. Cronbach in *Designing Evaluations of Educational and Social Programs* (San Francisco: Jossey-Bass, Inc., Publishers, 1982). See Chapter Four particularly.

[13] See Reginald K. Carter, "Clients' Resistance to Negative Findings and the Latent Conservative Function of Evaluation Studies," *The American Sociologist,* 6 (May 1971), 118–24.

REPORTING SCHOOL AND SCHOOL DISTRICT PLANNING AND EVALUATION RESULTS

Principals and central office administrators should constantly be conscious of the need to assess what is currently taking place so they can be aware of what might take place in the future. This is the continuous planning-evaluation cycle to which we have referred previously. In order to facilitate the planning portion of this cycle, attention should be given at the classroom, school, district, state, and national levels to the systematic collection of data regarding pupil, teacher, school, and school system performance. For our purposes here, we exclude the ends of the continuum, classroom evaluation and the collection of national statistics, from further consideration. Teachers should be involved in assessing classroom performance so they can provide feedback to students regarding learning and evaluate their own instruction. Similarly, federal government officials should systematically collect, analyze, and distribute information about schools in order to ensure that education is fulfilling national purposes. However, it is with the evaluation responsibility of school, district, and state leaders that we are concerned here.

The Existing Evaluation Model and Its Limitations

The primary means by which U.S. schools presently are evaluated is through a process labeled "accreditation." Accreditation is conducted by regional associations of which there are six. The process is long standing and has been useful in elevating school standards in the United States.[14] This is particularly true for rural high schools. However, at least as currently practiced, school accreditation procedures need to be improved.

Current accreditation standards focus heavily upon "inputs and processes" and almost not at all on "outputs." The qualifications of teachers, the number of volumes in libraries, and the range of course offerings are all arguably important components of a school. However, it is conceivable that a secondary school could be rich in inputs and proper regard to many "processes" and still not be productive in terms of pupil performance.

In order to be more useful to professional educators, policy makers, and the public, school and school district evaluation must also include measures of "output"—indicators of pupil performance. Ideally, a system of educational evaluation is school based. The basic "production" unit is taken to be the school, and it is from this unit that data are collected. Some data elements should be unique to the school; other elements should be standard for a district; yet other data dimensions should be standard for a state.

For example, a state might reasonably require that each elementary and secondary school annually publish a performance report. The report should serve as

---

[14] For additional information see Harold Orlans, *Private Accreditation and Public Eligibility* (Lexington, Mass.: D. C. Heath & Company, 1975), ch. 1; Robert Kirkwood, "Accreditation," *Encyclopedia of Educational Research*, 5th ed., vol. 1, ed. H. E. Mitzel (New York: The Free Press, 1982); and Kent W. Leach, "History and Purposes of Accreditation," *National Elementary Principal*, 43, no. 2 (May 1964), 36–41.

the basic data collection building block in the district and as the initial step in a state data collection and evaluation system. Such a report would be intended both for lay and professional audiences. It should be made available to parents, enrolled students, and those contemplating using the school in the future. The annual report should also be published, at least in abstract form, in the appropriate local newspaper. The annual performance report should provide a summary and evaluation of a school's efforts over the past year and present a plan for its efforts over future years. It is at once a report to the school's various constituencies and a plan for the school's professional educators. An illustration of the components of such an annual report follows.

School Information

Name, location, enrollment, age of building, number of classrooms, number of specialized rooms, school site size, state of repair, amount spent on maintenance in the last year and last decade, library volumes, etc.

Staff Information

Number of staff by category, proportion in various license classifications, age, sex, ethnic background, experience, degree levels, etc.

Student Performance Information

Intellectual performance: all results of student performance in standardized tests should be reported in terms of state-established minimum standards. Relative performance of different schools in the district should also be provided. Other performance information might also be included: student turnover rate, absenteeism, library circulation, performance of past students at next level of schooling (junior high, high school, college), etc.

Areas of Strength

Here the school can describe what it considers its unique or noteworthy characteristics. The purpose is to encourage every school to have one or more areas of particular specialization and competence, or to espouse a particular educational philosophy, or employ a distinct methodology or approach. This section would inform parents about the tone or style of the school.

Areas for Improvement

This section would identify areas in which a school needed improvement and would outline its plans regarding them. These problem areas might in some schools change over the years, but in others remain the same as the schools mounted a long-term improvement project. This section should encourage schools to be self-critical, to establish specific goals, and to report on subsequent progress.

Parent, Teacher, and Student Assessment of School Performance

Responsible parents, teachers, and students should be permitted an uncensored opportunity to assess school performance. This section would permit various school constituencies to express their opinions of school success or failure with respect to such matters as actual instruction, curriculum development, racial relations, student participation in decision making, drug abuse, etc.

SUMMARY

Planning is a future-oriented organizational activity. Planning involves goal setting and determination of alternative procedures likely to result in achievement of goals. Technical planning methods, for example, PERT, linear programming, queuing theory, and computer simulation, can assist in this process by assigning probability to uncertain events or conditions and by more rapidly forecasting likely outcomes.

Evaluation is a set of procedures undertaken to assess effectiveness of a program. The intent can be either to improve the program or to make a judgment regarding its continuation. Evaluation almost always involves comparison of a group of subjects or conditions which received a "treatment" (a condition in which one independent variable has been altered), with a "control group" to which the "treatment" has not been given (an independent variable was not manipulated). Evaluation is subject to numerous technical pitfalls not the least of which is the chance that the experimental "treatment" did not differ sufficiently from control conditions to justify the label "treatment." There are additional sources of both internal and external invalidity which can jeopardize the accuracy of an evaluation effort. It is also the case that evaluations can become intensely politicized, and educational administrators are cautioned to exercise care to prevent such occurrences. Budgeting can be a practical bridge between planning and evaluation. A budget should serve as an organization's plan for the allocation of resources. It should exhibit annualarity, comprehensiveness, and balance. In the process of developing the budget, an organization should take into account its long- and short-range plans and evaluations of its current programs. Once developed, it is then necessary to ensure that resources are allocated in a manner consistent with the budget. This is known as budget administration, which involves responsible procedures for the disbursement of funds and the subsequent accounting for them. The final budgeting stage coincides with an organization's evaluation cycle.

SELECTED READINGS

Arthur Andersen and Company, *Sound Fiscal Management in the Public Sector,* 1976.

Campbell, Donald T., and Julian C. Stanley, "Experimental and Quasi Experimental Design in Education," *Handbook of Research On Teaching,* ed. Nathan L. Gage. New York: Macmillan, Inc., 1963.

Cook, T. D., and D. T. Campbell, *Quasi-Experimentation Design and Analysis Issues.* Chicago, Ill.: Rand McNally & Company, 1979.

Cronbach, Lee J., *Designing Evaluations of Educational and Social Programs.* San Francisco: Jossey-Bass, Inc., Publishers, 1982.

Cronbach, Lee J., and others, *Toward Reform of Program Evaluation.* San Francisco: Jossey-Bass, Inc., Publishers, 1980.

Gramlich, Edward M., *Benefit-Cost Analysis of Government Programs.* Englewood Cliffs, N.J.: Prentice-Hall, Inc., 1981.

Langbein, Laura Irwin, *Discovering Whether Programs Work: A Guide to Statistical Methods for Program Evaluation.* Santa Monica: Goodyear Publishing Co., Inc., 1980.

Levin, Henry M., *Cost-Effectiveness, A Primer.* Beverly Hills, Calif.: Sage Publications, Inc., 1983.

Murphy, Jerome T., *Getting the Facts: A Fieldwork Guide for Evaluators and Policy Analysts.* Santa Monica: Goodyear Publishing Co., Inc., 1980.

Sederberg, Charles H., "Budgeting," *Managing Limited Resources: New Demands on Public School Management,* eds. L. Dean Webb and Van D. Mueller. Cambridge: Ballinger Publishing Co., 1984, pp. 59–86.

Walberg, Herbert J., ed., *Evaluating Educational Performance: A Sourcebook of Methods, Instruments, and Examples.* Berkeley: McCutchan, 1974.

COLLECTIVE
BARGAINING
AND AMERICA'S
SCHOOLS
chapter 12

Collective bargaining for public school teachers is a relatively recent phenomenon.[1] Bargaining in the private sector was sanctioned legally with passage of the 1935 National Labor Relations Act (Wagner Act). It was not until almost a quarter century later, 1959, that Wisconsin became the first state to enact legislation granting collective bargaining rights to municipal employers, teachers included.

Currently, thirty-two states have some form of collective bargaining legislation covering teachers and other certificated instructional personnel (see Table 12.1). Legislation authorizing teacher collective bargaining in other states is nonexistent, yet bargaining occurs in some of them. For example, although there is no enabling legislation in Arizona, Colorado, Illinois, and Ohio, many teachers in these states are covered by agreements and contracts reached through bargaining. In the majority of states it is clear that collective bargaining is an accepted part of the public employer-employee labor relations landscape.

As of October 1980 there were more than 1.5 million instructional staff in school districts who belonged to an employee organization. This number represented 65 percent of all full- and part-time professionals in their districts. At the same time, 14,129 contractual agreements and 3826 memoranda of understanding combined for a total of 17,955 labor-management agreements between in-

---

[1] The terms collective bargaining, collective negotiations, bargaining, and negotiations are used interchangeably throughout this chapter.

Table 12.1 STATE PUBLIC EMPLOYEE COLLECTIVE BARGAINING LAWS AFFECTING EDUCATION

State	Number of Statutes[1]	Type of Laws			Professional Coverage[5]			Classified Coverage[6]			Supervisor Coverage[7]			Union Security Provisions[9]	
		Local[2]	State[3]	Omnibus[4]	K-12	CC[8]	PS	K-12	CC[8]	PS	K-12	CC[8]	PS		
Alabama															AL
Alaska	2	x		x	x		x			x	x			x	AK
Arizona															AZ
Arkansas															AR
California	3	x	PS		x	x	x	x	x	x				x	CA
Colorado															CO
Connecticut	3	x	x		x	x	x	x	x	x	x	x	x	x	CT
Delaware	2	x			x	x	x	x	x	x				x	DE
Florida	1			x	x	x	x	x	x	x				x	FL
Georgia															GA
Hawaii	1			x	x	x	x	x	x	x	x	x	x	x	HI
Idaho	1	x			x						x				ID
Illinois															IL
Indiana	1	x			x									x	IN
Iowa	1			x	x	x	x	x	x	x				x	IA
Kansas	2	x		x	x	x	x	x	x	x				x	KS
Kentucky															KY
Louisiana															LA

273

Table 12.1 (cont.)

State	Number of Statutes[1]	Type of Laws Local[2]	Type of Laws State[3]	Type of Laws Omnibus[4]	Professional Coverage[5] K-12	Professional Coverage[5] CC[a]	Professional Coverage[5] PS	Classified Coverage[6] K-12	Classified Coverage[6] CC[a]	Classified Coverage[6] PS	Supervisor Coverage[7] K-12	Supervisor Coverage[7] CC[a]	Supervisor Coverage[7] PS	Union Security Provisions[9]	
Maine	2	x	PS,CC		x	x	x	x	x	x	x			x	ME
Maryland	2	x			x			x			x			x	MD
Massachusetts	1			x	x		x	x		x	x		x	x	MA
Michigan	1			x	x		x	x		x	x		x	x	MI
Minnesota	1			x	x	x	x	x	x	x	x	x	x	x	MN
Mississippi															MS
Missouri	1			x				x			x				MO
Montana	1			x	x	x	x	x	x	x				x	MT
Nebraska	2	x		x	x	x	x	x		x					NE
Nevada	1	x			x			x			x			x	NV
New Hampshire	1			x	x		x	x		x	x		x		NH
New Jersey	1			x	x	x	x	x	x	x	x			x	NJ
New Mexico															NM
New York	1			x	x		x	x		x	x		x	x	NY
North Carolina															NC
North Dakota	1	x			x						x				ND
Ohio															OH
Oklahoma	1	x			x			x			x			x	OK
Oregon	1			x	x	x	x	x	x	x				x	OR

State	[1]													Abbr
Pennsylvania	1			x	x	x	x		x			x	x	PA
Rhode Island	3		x	x	x	x	x		x			x	x	RI
South Carolina														SC
South Dakota	1			x		x	x		x			x		SD
Tennessee	1			x		x								TN
Texas														TX
Utah														UT
Vermont	3		x	x		x	x		x			x	x	VT
Virginia														VA
Washington	4	CC	x	x	x	x	x	x	x	x		x	x	WA
West Virginia														WV
Wisconsin	2		x	x	x	x	x	x	x			x	x	WI
Wyoming														WY
District of Columbia	1		x	x		x	x		x			x	x	DC
TOTALS	**19**	**7**	**17**	**32**	**12**[8]	**24**	**27**	**12**[8]	**24**	**20**[8]	**5**	**13**	**26**	

[1] Represents the number of separate statutes summarized on the table for each state.

[2] Coverage for local-level employees only.

[3] Coverage for state-level employees only. California, Maine and Washington laws are specific for postsecondary and/or community colleges.

[4] Coverage for employees of more than one governmental level.

[5] Teachers or personnel with similar or higher status.

[6] Below the rank of teacher; non-administrative support personnel.

[7] Any or all levels of supervisors and administrators, in one or more laws in the state.

[8] This column is checked only if community colleges are noted specifically in law. State structures vary, and community colleges may be included in the K-12 system, in the postsecondary system, or may be a separate system.

[9] This column is checked if union security provisions are present in one or more of the state laws.

Source: Doris Ross and Patricia Flakus-Mosqueda, *Cuebook II, State Education Collective Bargaining Laws* (Denver, Colo.: Education Commission of the States, 1980), pp. 12–14.

structional staff and school districts. These agreements represented 52 percent of the total number of agreements entered into by all state and local government employees.[2]

Contractual agreements, or memoranda, between instructional staff and school districts encompass a wide array of conditions of employment that vary by state and by school districts within states. However, basic collective bargaining concepts, the collective bargaining process, and principles of contract administration are similar across state lines. These collective bargaining dimensions are the focus of this chapter. We describe the evolution of collective bargaining, offer a comparison of bargaining in the private and public sectors, explain fundamental components and issues associated with the bargaining process, and conclude with an assessment of the effects of bargaining in education.

EVOLUTION OF COLLECTIVE BARGAINING

Private Sector

Collective bargaining in the United States is rooted mainly in private industry. Rights currently enjoyed by labor to bargain for wages, hours, and other conditions of employment have been shaped by an evolution of federal legislation dating back to the Sherman Antitrust Act of 1890. This law encouraged open business competition by voiding formation of business cartels or conspiracies. Courts construed this reasoning to include union activity, such as strikes, as a restraint on trade.

The Clayton Act of 1914 and the Norris-La Guardia Act of 1932 aided unions by restricting the role of courts in labor disputes. It was not until the 1933 passage of the National Recovery Act, however, that the concept of collective bargaining was legally embraced. Though more sympathetic to labor, this law still contained no penalties for management which refused to bargain. Congress subsequently enacted, and the U.S. Supreme Court upheld, the National Labor Relations Act (Wagner Act) of 1935. This legislation provided a legal basis for employees to organize and bargain through their selected representatives.[3]

Additional federal legislation affecting labor-management relations was not enacted until 1947 with the passage of the Labor-Management Relations Act (Taft-Hartley Act). This was a response to the public concern that the power of labor, as manifested in strikes, had become too great. The Taft-Hartley Act generally provided employers with rights against unfair practices by unions, such as closed shop agreements and illegal strikes.

The last significant federal legislation pertaining to labor-management rela-

---

[2] These statistics are reported in U.S. Bureau of the Census, *Labor-Management Relations in State and Local Governments: 1980,* series GGS no. 102 (Washington, D.C.: U.S. Government Printing Office, 1980), p. 7.

[3] *National Labor Relations Board* v. *Jones and Laughlin Steel Corporation,* 301 U.S. 1, 57 S. Ct. 615 (1937).

tions in the private sector was the Landrum-Griffin Act of 1959, also known as the Labor-Management Reporting and Disclosure Act. This law was designed to curb abuses in the internal affairs of unions. It addressed issues related to union governance, fiscal matters, requirement for membership, and reporting and disclosure. Further, it restricted employers from making contributions to labor organizations or their officials.

Public Sector

Public sector collective bargaining activity did not become significant until the 1960s. In 1962, President Kennedy signed Executive Order 10988, which granted federal employees the right to join unions of their choice, to have three forms of recognition—informal, formal, and exclusive—depending on the proportion of members of a particular unit belonging to the union, and which permitted advisory arbitration in grievance procedures. Through exclusive recognition, unions could meet and confer with management on personnel policies and working conditions within the legal sphere of management responsibility and the law. These later provisions were significantly strengthened by a series of subsequent executive orders signed by Presidents Nixon and Ford.[4]

Executive orders regarding labor-management practices in the federal government have been a major influence in the growth of bargaining in state, county, and local governmental agencies.[5] Public sector bargaining has also grown as a result of discrepancies in pay between private and public employees, success of private sector unions, substantial growth of employees in the public sector, an increase in percentage of white collar workers,[6] and the rivalry between the National Education Association and the American Federation of Teachers. Also important has been the court finding that the right of an individual to form and join a union is protected by the First Amendment.[7] An Illinois court ruling that the Chicago Board of Edu-

---

[4] See F. J. Loevi, Jr., *Collective Bargaining Under E.O. 11491,* Personnel Pamphlet Series no. 2 (Washington, D.C.: Department of Health, Education and Welfare, 1973).

[5] A comprehensive discussion of the growth of bargaining, private as well as public sector, and labor relations at federal, state, and local levels is contained in Marvin J. Levine and Eugene C. Hagburg, *Public Sector Labor Relations* (St. Paul, Minn.: West Publishing Co., 1979), pp. 12–100.

[6] The total number of white collar workers in 1960 was 28.5 million or 43.4 percent of the total number of employed persons 16 years and over (65.8 million). For blue collar workers in 1960, excluding farm workers, 24 million (36.6 percent) were employed. In 1975, the total civilian labor force sixteen years and above was 84.7 million. Of that number, 42 million were white collar employees (49.8 percent) and 28 million (33 percent) blue collar. By 1979, of the total work force of 97 million employed persons sixteen years and over, 49 million (50.9 percent) were white collar workers and 32 million (33.1 percent) blue collar workers. While these figures are not strictly comparable for years prior to 1975 because of reclassification of some occupations, they are nevertheless indicative of the increase in white collar workers. See "Employed Persons, By Major Occupation Group and Sex: 1960 to 1979," U.S. Bureau of Census, *Statistical Abstract of the United States: 1980,* 101st ed. (Washington, D.C.: U.S. Government Printing Office, 1980), p. 418.

[7] *McLaughlin* v. *Tilendis,* 398 F. 2d 287 (7th Cir. 1968).

cation could voluntarily bargain with its teachers despite the absence of state legislative authority has also had significant impact.[8]

Bargaining in the public sector is widespread and growing. In 1980, there were almost 80,000 state and local governments. Approximately 18 percent of these (14,302) had a labor relations policy and engaged in collective negotiations or had discussions with employees.[9] Moreover, as of October 1980, 32 percent of all full-time and part-time employees in state and local governments, including school districts, were covered by labor-management agreements. This represented an increase of 6.8 percent over those in effect a year earlier.[10]

Bargaining in Public Education

Growth of bargaining in public education generally parallels the growth of public sector bargaining. In fact, teachers' gains in securing bargaining agreements cannot be overlooked as a significant contributor to the general escalation of public sector bargaining.

Much of the overall increase in public education bargaining can be attributed to the rivalry between two major teacher organizations, the National Education Association (NEA) and the American Federation of Teachers (AFT). The NEA, organized in 1857 as the National Teachers' Association, and the older of the two organizations, initially stated as its purpose: "To elevate the character and advance the interests of the profession of teaching and to promote the cause of popular education in the United States."[11] In 1870, the name of the organization was changed to the National Education Association, and when it was incorporated in 1907 the word "popular" was eliminated in the statement of purpose.[12] The preamble of the Constitution of the NEA, which has guided its objectives and actions, states:

> We, the members of the National Education Association of the United States, in order that the Association may serve as the national voice for education, advance the cause of education for all individuals, promote professional excellence among educators, gain recognition of the basic importance of the teachers in the learning process, protect the rights of educators and advance their interests and welfare, secure professional autonomy, unite educators for

[8] *Chicago Division of the Illinois Education Association* v. *Board of Education of the City of Chicago,* 222 N.E. 2d 243 (Ill. 1966). In contrast, a Virginia Court ruled that unless specifically imposed by state statute there is no duty compelling a public agency to bargain with an exclusive agent. See *Commonwealth* v. *City School Board of Arlington,* 232 S.E. 2d 30 (Va. 1976).

[9] U.S. Bureau of the Census, *Labor-Management Relations in State and Local Governments: 1980,* pp. 2–3.

[10] U.S. Bureau of the Census, *Labor-Management Relations,* p. 3.

[11] National Educational Association, *NEA Handbook 1981–82* (Washington, D.C.: National Educational Association, 1981), p. 133. For a history of the NEA see, Edgar B. Wesley, *NEA: The First Hundred Years. The Building of the Teaching Profession* (New York: Harper and Brothers Publishers, 1957).

[12] NEA, *NEA Handbook 1981–82,* p. 133.

effective citizenship, promote and protect human and civil rights, and obtain for its members the benefits of an independent, united teaching profession do hereby adopt this constitution.[13]

The AFT came into being in 1916 as an affiliate of the American Federation of Labor.[14] Its objectives are

1. To bring associations of teachers into relations of mutual assistance and cooperation.

2. To obtain for them all the rights to which they are entitled.

3. To raise the standards of the teaching profession by securing the conditions essential to the best professional service.

4. To promote such a democratization of the schools as will enable them better to equip their pupils to take their places in the industrial, social, and political life of the community.

5. To promote the welfare of the childhood of the nation by providing progressively better educational opportunity for all.[15]

An an affiliate of organized labor, the AFT has traditionally sought to achieve its aims through collective bargaining. It was not until 1944, however, that one of its locals, Cicero, Illinois, entered into a contract achieved through bargaining with the Cicero Board of Education. In contrast, the NEA traditionally sought to achieve its objectives through lobbying and cooperative action.

The intent of each organization was to attract teacher members and become their primary representative. Competition for representational rights became heated following the 1960 victorious effort of the United Federation of Teachers, an AFT local, to become the exclusive representative of New York City teachers. Success of the AFT in bargaining for New York teachers and its willingness to strike to achieve bargaining ends were attractive to teachers who were becoming more militant and assertive in voicing demands for improvements in wages and conditions of employment. Thus, membership in the AFT increased, and it was initially successful in being elected the exclusive representative of teachers in large cities such as Chicago, Detroit, Philadelphia, Washington, D.C., and San Francisco.

Success of the AFT motivated the NEA. Although maintaining its stance as an independent organization free from affiliation with organized labor or any particular segment of the population, the NEA became more active in seeking to attract members and negotiate teacher contracts. In this process, it endorsed use of sanctions, professional negotiations, and strikes.

---

[13] NEA, *NEA Handbook 1981-82*, p. 138.

[14] William Edward Eaton, *The American Federation of Teachers, 1916-1961. A History of the Movement* (Carbondale, Ill.: Southern Illinois University Press, 1975), p. 15.

[15] "Constitution of the American Federation of Teachers" (Chicago: American Federation of Teachers, October, 1964), p. 3, reported in Myron Lieberman and Michael H. Moskow, *Collective Negotiations for Teachers. An Approach to School Administration* (Chicago: Rand McNally & Company, 1966), p. 34.

It is significant that although both organizations presently endorse use of strikes, neither did so initially. At its 1947 convention, the AFT reaffirmed its opposition to strikes in adopting a statement which in part stated "[t]he use of the strike is rejected as an instrument of policy. . . ."[16] This official policy remained until 1962, following the New York UFT strike.[17] The NEA also had a clear no-strike policy for many years. In fact, it was not until 1967 that it embraced use of mediation, fact-finding, arbitration, political action, and sanctions to achieve teacher agreements with boards of education. Use of strikes, however, did not become official NEA policy until 1973. In that year the NEA passed a resolution consistent with part of its purpose—"to protect the rights of educators and advance their interests and welfare"[18]—recommending strikes as one of several procedures to be used "if conditions make it impossible for teachers to provide quality education."[19]

At issue in the use of strikes and contributing to the reluctance of teacher organizations to adopt an official policy condoning strikes is the fact that historically public sector strikes have been illegal. This was forcefully noted by the Connecticut Supreme Court in its ruling in the case of the Norwalk Teachers Association, an independent union, and the city of Norwalk. Although it did hold that the Association could bargain with the board, the Court stated:

> In the American system, sovereignty is inherent in the people. They can delegate it to a government which they create and operate by law. They can give to that government the power and authority to perform certain duties and furnish certain services. The government so created and empowered must employ people to carry on its task. Those people are agents of the government. They exercise some part of the sovereignty entrusted to it. They occupy a status entirely different from those who carry on a private enterprise. They serve the public welfare and not a private purpose. To say that they can strike is the equivalent of saying that they can deny the authority of government and contravene the public welfare. . . .[20]

Despite the sovereignty doctrine, teachers and their organizations witnessed private sector gains where strikes had been legal since the Wagner Act of 1935 and

[16] The Commission on Education Reconstruction, *Organizing the Teaching Profession. The Story of the American Federation of Teachers* (Glencoe, Ill.: The Free Press, 1955), p. 272.

[17] Although the AFT had a no-strike policy prior to 1962, several strikes were engaged in by various of its local affiliates. As early as 1947, AFT teachers in Buffalo, N.Y., struck for higher salaries. In 1948 the Men's and Women's Federation of Minneapolis went on strike; in 1949 teachers in Oglesby, Illinois, picketed the board of education, and in 1951 teachers in Pawtucket, Rhode Island, engaged in a strike. See William Edward Eaton, *The American Federation of Teachers, 1916–1961*, pp. 143–151.

[18] From the preamble to its constitution, see National Education Association, *NEA Handbook*, p. 133.

[19] National Education Association, *NEA Handbook* (Washington, D.C.: National Education Association, 1973), p. 77.

[20] *Norwalk Teachers* v. *City of Norwalk*, 138 Conn. 269, 83 A. 2d 482 (1951).

began to utilize this weapon themselves.[21] The legal right of teachers to engage in strikes has been granted by several states. As of 1980, Alaska, Hawaii, Minnesota, Montana, Oregon, Pennsylvania, Vermont, and Wisconsin permitted strikes by teachers after other impasse resolution procedures had been exhausted.[22]

Willingness to fight for better wages, participation in school policy formulation, and overall working conditions through bargaining and use of work stoppages to enforce demands characterize both the NEA and the AFT. While the AFT was initially the more aggressive of the two organizations, and more willing to use conventional labor tactics, both the NEA and AFT are now quite similar in this dimension. Yet competition for members and the right to represent teachers for purposes of contract negotiations in a given school district persists. Both organizations have grown dramatically. The NEA remains the larger of the two. In 1968, NEA membership was slightly in excess of one million. By 1978 it had grown to more than 1.6 million.[23] Corresponding membership figures for the AFT are as follows: 1968—165,000; 1978—500,000.[24]

COMPONENTS IN THE COLLECTIVE BARGAINING PROCESS

Collective bargaining is a process in which employee and employer representatives negotiate in good faith a written and time-bound agreement covering at its most fundamental level "wages, hours, and other terms and conditions of employment."[25] In the private sector, bargaining is legitimated by the National Labor Relations Act of 1935. In the public sector, the legal framework for bargaining is provided by state statute. Bargaining is also permissible when state statutes are silent in this regard but impermissible if statutory provisions specifically deny it.

In the private sector, bargaining occurs through use of a bilateral model in which negotiators assume an adversary relationship and in which conflict is thought to be inevitable. Basic elements of this model, which follow, have been adopted for general use in public education where bargaining is permitted.

---

[21] In 1979, according to the U.S. Labor Department, there were 181 work stoppages involving approximately 59,000 teachers and constituting 836,000 idle worker days. U.S. Department of Labor, *Analysis of Work Stoppages, 1979,* Bulletin 2092 (Washington, D.C.: Government Printing Office, Bureau of Labor Statistics, 1981), pp. 36–37.

[22] Doris Ross and Patricia Flakus-Mosqueda, *Cuebook II, State Education Collective Bargaining Laws,* Report no. F80-5 (Denver, Colo.: Education Commission of the States), pp. 16–47.

[23] National Education Association, *NEA Handbook* (Washington, D.C.: National Education Association, 1981), p. 132.

[24] U.S. Bureau of the Census, *Statistical Abstract of the United States: 1980,* 101st ed., p. 428.

[25] These bargainable items are specified in the National Labor Relations Act of 1935.

Representation

A primary element in the bargaining model is for employees to request formal recognition. Election and certification procedures for an exclusive bargaining representative must conform to state guidelines or those of the National Labor Relations Board. The exclusive bargaining representative must represent all appropriate employees within the boundary of a contract whether they are members of the organization selected to bargain or not. Stated differently, if the NEA is selected as the exclusive representative in a given school district, it must bargain for all teachers in that district whether they are members of the union or not.

Unit Determination

In general, the bargaining unit is based on a community of interests related to areas of work, wages, and terms and conditions of employment. Past collective bargaining practice may be considered in unit determination as well as employee desire. Managerial, supervisory, and confidential employees are usually excluded from employee bargaining units.

Appropriateness of a bargaining unit in education, and in the public sector, is determined in most instances by a state level employment relations board. In the private sector, unit determination is adjudicated by the National Labor Relations Board (NLRB). In the federal sector this is accomplished by the Assistant-Secretary of Labor-Management Relations.

Scope of Bargaining

In the private sector, mandatory bargainable items are specified by the NLRB and include wages, hours, and terms and conditions of employment. In public education, the scope of bargaining varies by state and is determined by state statute and judicial decree. In most states an employment relations board assumes a major role in determining the scope of bargaining. According to one study, however, local politics and school district-teacher organization relationships are aspects that affect teacher contract strength and scope in bargaining more significantly than state statutes.[26] Bargainable items may be mandatory, as prescribed by federal or state action, or permissible, as agreed upon by mutual consent. Some items, such as delegation of power by an agency in the public sector, are illegal for purposes of bargaining.

A number of noneconomic items have emerged in teacher bargaining. Such provisions in teacher contracts include grievances, teacher evaluation, school hours, pupil exclusion, classroom assignment refusal, class size, promotion rules, transfer criteria, instructional committee membership, reduction in force procedures, and teacher aides.[27]

[26] Lorraine McDonnell and Anthony Pascal, *Organized Teachers in American Schools* (Santa Monica, Calif.: The Rand Corporation, 1979), p. 55.

[27] McDonnell, L., and Pascal, A., *Organized Teachers,* p. 12.

Union Security

Unions that become bargaining representatives typically seek to strengthen their ranks and secure assistance from employers in the collection of dues from the members and nonmembers they represent. Several arrangements may be used to accomplish these purposes—union shop, agency shop, dues checkoff, and maintenance-of-membership. Selection of any arrangement may be subject to negotiation depending on whether union organizational security provisions are permitted by state statute.

In the *union shop,* employees are required to join the union within a specified period of time after employment. An *agency shop* arrangement provides for dues collection from bargaining unit or union members and fees from nonmembers for bargaining services. A *dues checkoff* provision permits the employer to collect dues through payroll deduction and forward such monies to the union. Generally, there is no charge for this service. A *maintenance-of-membership* arrangement requires that employees who join a union will maintain membership in that union as a condition of employment throughout the life of the contract. The most prevalent form of union or organizational security in education, and in the public sector generally, is the dues checkoff arrangement.

Grievance Procedures

Grievance procedures attempt to ensure a systematic and peaceful manner by which disputes are resolved in the interpretation and implementation of the negotiated contract and other employment-related disputes. In both the private and public sectors, grievance procedures help to gain adherence to terms of the collective bargaining agreement. Additionally, they provide a safety valve which, when the final step in resolving grievances is binding arbitration, becomes a mechanism for avoiding work stoppages.

Generally, elements contained in a grievance procedure include definition of a grievance, an indication of who may file a grievance and how, and steps to be followed. The procedure typically calls first for an informal resolution attempt between the aggrieved party (teacher) and the immediate supervisor (principal). Failing satisfactory resolution at that level, a formal grievance may be filed in writing at the lowest applicable level in the organizational hierarchy and proceed through a series of predetermined, successively higher levels until the dispute is settled. For example, if within a designated number of days a grievance is not informally resolved, a formal grievance is filed in writing by the grievant to the supervisor, who must respond in writing within a specified time period. Failing resolution of the grievance at the school-building level, the grievance may proceed up the school hierarchical ladder through three or more steps. These levels may include director of personnel, assistant superintendent, and superintendent. If the grievance has not been resolved at these levels, it may be submitted to a third party for settlement through binding or advisory arbitration. School board or judicial review may be sought if arbitration is advisory. Time limits are generally imposed for response by either party at each step in the grievance resolution process.

In the grievance procedures in one school district the following definition of a grievance for certificated personnel is used: "A grievance is a formal, written allegation by a teacher that he or she has been adversely affected by a violation or a dispute regarding the meaning, application of interpretation of a specific provision of [the teacher-school district negotiated agreement]."[28] In this district a grievant is defined as "any teacher covered by the terms of [the negotiated teacher-school district agreement]." Moreover, "the Union may grieve any of the Union's rights included in the Agreement."[29]

Impasse Resolution

Failure to reach an agreement between contract negotiating parties in the public sector generally leads to the use of third party resolution procedures—mediation, fact finding, and arbitration. These procedures may be voluntary or imposed by law.

Mediation. Mediation involves use of a neutral third party (mediator) who attempts to persuade the parties to continue an open dialogue that may lead to dispute settlement. The mediator may make suggestions to alleviate the stalemate and foster resolution of the obstruction to negotiation. In both the private and public sectors, mediators are authorized for use through the Federal Mediation and Conciliation Service (FMCS). In addition to services of the FMCS, states may provide mediation services through a public employees relation board. Mediators are appointed upon request of the parties of the dispute.

Fact finding. This procedure calls for either a neutral single individual or panel, agreed to by both parties of the negotiation impasse, to collect and review facts surrounding the dispute. It is hoped that facts will uncover information that can be used to resolve differences. Fact finding may be with or without recommendations, and reported either privately to the parties or to the public. Generally, however, fact-finder recommendations are made public.

Arbitration. This procedure is sometimes referred to as *interest arbitration,* that which is used to ameliorate a contract negotiation impasse, in contrast to *rights arbitration,* which focuses on the interpretation of provisions of an existing contract to resolve a grievance. Interest arbitration is usually binding on negotiating parties and is used when authorized by state law. In interest arbitration, resolution of contract negotiation impasse becomes the function of a neutral third party arbi-

[28] Board of Education, Berkeley (Calif.) Unified School District and the Berkeley Federation of Teachers, AFT Local 1078, AFL-CI0, *Agreement,* July 1, 1982–June 30, 1985.

[29] Board of Education, Berkeley, and the Berkeley Federation of Teachers, *Agreement,* July 1, 1982–June 30, 1985.

trator or arbitration panel. Use of interest arbitration provides an alternative to the strike, which in the public sector is illegal in most states.

Impasse resolution through interest arbitration may require that the arbitrator select the final offer of either employer or employees, which then becomes binding on the negotiating parties. Alternatively, this last best-offer procedure may require that a mixture of last offers from both sides of the bargaining table be selected by the arbitrator. That is, some offers of management and some of labor should be chosen. Whether or not a final-offer arbitration procedure is used, the arbitrator is expected to deliver a final decision in regard to the negotiation stalemate.

Strikes. This activity is used to pressure employers or school boards to resolve contract negotiation disputes when other impasse resolution procedures have failed. Through use of a strike, employees engage in concerted action to withhold their services. For teachers and other public employees, the legal right to strike issues from state statutory provisions. Without such provisions, teacher strikes are illegal and may be subject to penalty. For example, in New York, teachers who participate in an illegal strike can be penalized economically at a level which is twice their daily rate of pay for each day they are on strike.[30] School districts may also seek an injunction through the courts against illegal teacher strikes. Should teachers fail to observe an injunction, they or their union leaders can be held in contempt of court and fined or arrested.[31] Ultimately they may be dismissed or fired for engaging in illegal strikes.[32] Teacher action short of a strike may include work slowdowns, "sick-ins," and working absolutely by the rule book.

Lockout. This tactic is used by employers or school boards to prevent employees or teachers from working. It is management's version of the strike and may be used to exert pressure on employees to accept an economic package offered. Lockouts are illegal in several states, particularly if used as a means of refusing to bargain or to prevent unions from organizing.

Unfair Labor Practices

Neither employers nor employees may engage in procedures that thwart the purposes of negotiation or the resolution of impasses. In teacher bargaining these procedures may be specified by state law[33] or may be derived from the private sector. Examples of unfair employer labor practices include impeding selection of

[30] *Lawson v. Board of Education,* 307 N.Y.S. 2d 333 (1970); also, *Wilson v. Board of Education, Union Free School District,* 333 N.Y.S. 2d 828 (1972).

[31] *In re Block,* 236 A. 2d 589 (N.J., 1967); also, *Joint School District No. 1, City of Wisconsin Rapids v. City of Wisconsin Rapids Education Association,* 234 N.W. 2d 289 (Wis. 1976).

[32] See *Hortonville Joint School District No. 1 v. Hortonville Education Association,* 426 U.S. 482, 96 S. Ct. 2308, 49 L.ed. 1 (1976).

[33] For example see *California Senate Bill No. 160,* Chapter 961, section 3543.5 (1976).

an exclusive bargaining representative, giving preference to a particular employee organization, or union, conducting antiunion campaigns, coercing or questioning employees in an unusual manner with respect to their voting intentions, or threatening employees with reprisals for engaging in union activity. Further, where bargaining is permissible by state law, employers may not refuse to bargain or to engage in impasse resolution in good faith.

In a similar view, a union may not use or threaten to use violence or coercion against employees in an attempt to influence their vote in exclusive representation elections. Unions must also bargain with employers and participate in impasse resolution procedures in good faith.

Private sector unfair labor practices are resolved through use of National Labor Relations Board prescribed procedures. In the public sector such procedures vary by state.

CONTRACT ADMINISTRATION

The negotiated contract specifies terms and conditions of employment that will govern working relationships between employer and employees for a designated period of time. The effect of a final contract, however, is not felt until it is implemented in the work setting. Here, procedures that may have been painted in broad strokes in the contract are refined and ambiguities made lucid. Thus, practical administration of the negotiated contract is crucial to its effectiveness.

In the work setting, supervisors, employees, and union representative(s) must become familiar with the contract's terms. In the school setting this translates to the site principal, teachers, and the union building representative, for it is at the school that the contract will have its greatest effect. Even with complete familiarity with terms of the contract, differences between the supervisor (principal) and employees (teachers) will exist regarding interpretation and implementation. Moreover, not every facet of the work arrangement will be covered within the scope of the contract. These differences of opinions must be resolved and areas of omission tested through use of grievance procedures.

Grievance procedures were discussed in an earlier section. Such procedures are essential for effective contract administration because they provide a mechanism for resolving conflict, clarifying the contract, and delineating rights of supervisors and employees. In addition, availability of reasonable grievance procedures enhances communication between labor and management.

ISSUES IN EDUCATION AND BARGAINING

Collective bargaining in schools has grown dramatically since it was first authorized in Wisconsin. Undoubtedly, it has caused a shift in the relationship between teachers and school boards and school administrators. Through collective bargaining teachers have become more assertive participants in decisions affecting terms and conditions of their employment and, in many instances, in the development of educational policy. These dimensions are significant, albeit partial, evidence of the impact bargaining has had upon public schools. Bargaining as it is presently practiced in public education gives rise to several issues. Six are discussed: (1) appropriateness of the existing bargaining model; (2) citizen participation; (3) bargaining, public confidence, and school support; (4) effect of bargaining on management-union relations; (5) bargaining and school principal representation; and (6) the effect of bargaining on student educational outcomes.

Appropriateness of the Bargaining Model

At issue here is not the efficacy of collective bargaining, but the model through which bargaining is currently accomplished. Public school bargaining uses a model adopted from the private sector. This model assumes a bilateral, adversarial relationship between labor and management. It is a model in which the demands of employers and employees are moderated by economic constraints of the marketplace. The underlying principle here is that consumer-good prices must be kept low enough to remain competitive while maximizing profit. Excessive demands for increases in economic benefits will cause prices to escalate beyond the consumers' willingness to purchase the companies' products. As a consequence, profits fall, income for wages is restricted, and jobs may be lost.

The private sector bargaining model is one in which the bargaining strategy has been described as "quasi distributive" and "game playing." As such, its characteristics are

1. A series of specific demands and offers on a package of bargaining issues.
2. Deferral of formal commitments on issues until they can be supported by reference to an impending test of power.
3. Controlled and distorted private communication designed to disguise true costs and goals and permit favorable trade-offs of concessions for demands.
4. Withholding of concessions on all major issues until the last possible moment when they can be used as the final 'buy-out' to avoid the impending test of power.[34]

Suitability of the private sector model for teacher collective bargaining is criticized because teachers are accorded a number of rights not provided private sector employees, for example, teacher influence in determining who is management and tenure rights they enjoy without a collective bargaining agreement.[35] Further, teachers' demands generally are in their own interest and not necessarily

[34] Charles R. Perry and Wesley A. Wildman, *The Impact of Negotiations in Public Education* (Worthington, Ohio: Charles A. Jones Publishing Company, 1970), p. 63.

[35] Myron Lieberman, "Eggs That I Have Laid: Teacher Bargaining Reconsidered," *Phi Delta Kappan,* 60, no. 6 (February 1979), 415.

in the interest of students. As a consequence of conditions such as these, it has been suggested that representational rights of teachers should be less than private sector employee rights.[36]

Use of the bilateral private sector bargaining model in public education comes under additional criticism because final decisions regarding policy and economic considerations are not the exclusive province of management. Consequently, it is proposed that multilateral models involving use of political pressure and public opinion as sources of bargaining power,[37] trilateral practices in which the bargaining process is subject to examination by third party interest groups,[38] and collective bargaining which relies on mutual problem solving and cooperation[39] become alternatives to the private sector model. These models are predicated on the assumption that the bargaining process should be opened to include others who may have a vested interest in the process, a point which we explore in the next section. While the effectiveness of such models is relatively unknown, their intent is to ensure a bargaining process in education in which less emphasis is placed on an adversarial relationship between administrators and teachers and more on cooperative problem solving and participatory decision making in the best educational interests of students.

Citizen Participation

It has been argued that direct participation of citizens in the public education bargaining process will provide a greater degree of control and an opportunity to influence the formulation of educational policy by consumers who have legitimate vested interests.[40] It is argued further that citizen participation will moderate demands for economic resources to be used primarily for personnel costs. Such arguments have borne fruit in California, Florida, Idaho, Iowa, Kansas, Maine, Minnesota, North Dakota, and Wisconsin where citizen participation in some form has been legislated.[41]

[36] Lieberman, M., *Bargaining Reconsidered,* pp. 415-19.

[37] Kenneth McLennon and Michael W. Moskow, "Multilateral Bargaining in the Public Sector," *Industrial Relations Research Association, 21st Annual Proceedings* (Madison, Wis.: The Association, 1968), pp. 31-40.

[38] John R. Pisapia, "The Open Bargaining Model," *Journal of Law and Education,* 10, no. 1 (January 1981), 65-76.

[39] Wayne Buidens, Margaret Martin, and Arthur J. Jones, "Collective Gaining: A Bargaining Alternative," *Phi Delta Kappan,* 63, no. 4 (December 1981), 244-45; also, Jeanne Kolar, Leo Croce, and Justin M. Bardellini, "Integrative Bargaining in One California School District," *Phi Delta Kappan,* 63, no. 4 (December 1981), 246-47.

[40] See, for example, Lawrence Pierce, "Teachers' Organizations and Bargaining: Power Imbalance in the Public Sphere," in National Committee for Citizens in Education, Commission on Educational Governance, *Public Testimony on Public Schools* (Berkeley, Calif.: McCutchan Publishing Corporation, 1975), pp. 122-59; Charles W. Cheng, *Altering Collective Bargaining: Participation in Educational Decision Making* (New York: Praeger Publishers, Inc., 1976); Pisapia, J., "Open Bargaining Model," *Journal of Law and Education*; James W. Guthrie, "Public Control of Public Schools: Can We Get It Back?" *Public Affairs Report,* 15, no. 3 (1974).

[41] Ross, D., and Flakus-Mosqueda, P., *Cuebook II, State Education Collective Bargaining Laws,* pp. 48-50.

Whatever the logical merits of arguments for citizen participation, McDonnell's and Pascal's comprehensive study of the noneconomic effects of collective bargaining led them to conclude that citizens are generally less than enthusiastic about such participation. They state

> Despite the significant effect of collective bargaining on school costs and tax rates, the general public shows little sustained interest in teacher bargaining except during times of crisis. Citizens may simply assume that their elected representatives on school boards take an active part in negotiations, but we have seen that this rarely happens. In any case, community participation advocates appear to lead a phantom army. However, general public attitudes toward organized labor and collective bargaining do affect the very broad parameters of contracts, probably through election of sympathetic board members who then appoint like-minded school executives.[42]

Bargaining, Public Confidence, and School Support

Through collective bargaining teachers have gained considerable authority in shaping policies that affect their work conditions and work functions. These gains are significant. At issue, however, is whether public confidence and support, which public education needs, is being eroded as a consequence of negotiating practices and teacher gains in the face of declining student academic performance. Stated differently, are teacher negotiated gains consistent with improved schooling and student performance?

Teacher bargaining has focused on salaries, work hours, and other conditions of employment such as grievance procedures, due process, and job security with its attendant relationship to teacher evaluation procedures. Whereas much attention has centered on the issue of salaries, it is in the latter two areas that more significant negotiated gains can be noted.[43]

Teacher unions have been rather successful in negotiating contracts that redefine their work hours and subsequently their availability for school-related activities. Negotiated personal and sick leave time and fewer hours for extracurricular activity supervision and after school meetings have had the net effect of reducing teacher-student contact hours. Work slowdowns and strikes, when they occur, further limit student contact hours. Although the recommendations of national reports call for lengthening the school day and school year,[44] whether increasing classroom or student-teacher contact hours will result in improved student school performance is debatable. Nevertheless, teacher-negotiated contracts that limit school-related services they render and reduce teacher-student contact hours are

[42] McDonnell, L., and Pascal, A., *Organized Teachers,* pp. 87–88.

[43] One study which spanned two decades finds no evidence to support a positive collective bargaining influence on teacher salaries. See Richard Wynn, "The Relationship of Collective Bargaining and Teacher Salaries 1960 to 1980," *Phi Delta Kappan,* 63, no. 4 (December 1980), 237–42.

[44] For example, see The National Commission on Excellence in Education, *A Nation at Risk: The Imperative for Educational Reform. A Report to the Nation* (Washington, D.C.: U.S. Department of Education, 1983).

often perceived negatively by the public. It is likely, therefore, that such agreements place a significant strain on public support for schools.

Negotiated procedures regarding teacher evaluation may serve to standardize this important function and protect teachers from arbitrary evaluation judgments. Yet such procedures signal an additional degree of teacher authority. To the extent that the public perceives negotiated teacher evaluation procedures as protecting incompetent teachers, public confidence in the schools is diminished.

Teacher-school district bargaining practices cannot be viewed simply as occurring between teachers and district administrators or the school board. The manner in which negotiations are conducted and the cost of agreements reached have political and economic consequences that reverberate throughout the community served by a school district. Particularly germane here is the fact that student performance as measured by national tests and other standardized indices generally have declined over the past decade. Although it is rather difficult to show a causal relationship between teacher-negotiated contracts which call for fewer student-teacher contact hours and standardized teacher evaluation procedures on the one hand, and decreasing student academic performance levels on the other, the issue is one that is politically potent and one not easily dismissed. If parents and community members believe they are being asked to provide more to schools, via teacher demands, while corresponding student benefits are not visible, then public confidence and support for public schools will wane.[45] Teacher unions and school administrations must develop strategies to enhance public confidence in, and increase public support for, public schools while simultaneously responding positively to legitimate teacher demands.

Effect of Bargaining on Management-Union Relations

It is clear that bargaining has had a profound effect on school management, particularly middle management or principals. Much of the principal's authority in areas such as teacher classroom assignment, frequency of faculty meetings, evaluation of teachers, and extracurricular activity assignments has been complicated by contract agreements. In addition, because of contractual grievance procedures, decisions that once were final with the principal may now be challenged, thereby further undermining his or her authority. The role of the principal has become more exacting in dealing with teachers as contractual agreements place restrictions on once-enjoyed positional power. What emerges is a more formalized set of administrator-teacher procedures that require more attention to work relationships and greater adherence to contract stipulations. The challenge to school site administrators is to develop ways to work with teachers to better serve the educational needs of students and the school.

[45] One scholar argues that public sector bargaining is leading to the abdication of public support and a diminution of public confidence in public education. He further predicts that public sector bargaining will cease to exist by the early twenty-first century. See Myron Lieberman, "Teacher Bargaining: An Autopsy," *Phi Delta Kappan,* 63, no. 4 (December 1981), 231–34. Opposition to Lieberman's view is provided by Albert Shanker, "After 20 Years, Lieberman's Vision Is Failing," *Phi Delta Kappan,* 63, no. 4 (December 1981), 236 and 278.

At the school district level, management-union relations provide a forum for voicing teacher job-related demands and the district's willingness to support those demands. Given the reality of economic resources, this exercise is more political and the issues more organizational than economic.[46] If this bargaining relationship is adversarial, feelings of distrust and apprehension are likely to develop. What must be considered, therefore, are negotiating strategies and models through which co-operation and compromise produce benefits for teachers *and* improvement in the quality of schooling.

Bargaining and School Principal Representation

Representation of principals in the bargaining process is not always apparent. Principals are not included in teacher bargaining units nor are they considered exclusively top management. To this extent their representational rights are not clear. In some instances principals have formed their own unions to address this condition. States in which more than one administrator union exists include Alaska, California, Connecticut, Florida, Illinois, Kansas, Maine, Maryland, Massachusetts, Michigan, Minnesota, Missouri, New Jersey, New York, Ohio, Pennsylvania, and Washington.[47] One problem associated with independent principal groups at the local level, however, is that they are too small to exercise significant leverage in all but very large urban districts. The future interests of principals, therefore, may be best served by their inclusion with district-level management. The dilemma of this arrangement is that affiliation at that level may have the dysfunctional effect of fostering a "we-they" attitude at the school site. In other words, principals not only may be viewed as contract administrators, but also as contract negotiators, or representatives of the school board and school district management. Resolution of principals' role ambiguity resulting from collective bargaining remains a challenge. Principal unions may be a viable solution to ensure their representational rights.[48]

Effect of Bargaining on Student Educational Outcomes

Do the gains teachers derive from collective bargaining and bargaining in general have an effect on student academic performance? What differences can be observed in student performance as a result of negotiations which almost uniformly include teacher requests such as reduced class size and fewer working hours?

In the opinion of several informed observers, bargaining as presently practiced

---

[46] On this point, see Douglas E. Mitchell, and others, "The Impact of Collective Bargaining on School Management and Policy," *American Journal of Education,* 89, no. 2 (February 1981), 147–88.

[47] Bruce S. Cooper, "The Future of Middle Management in Education," *The Principal in Metropolitan Schools,* eds. Donald A. Erickson and Theodore L. Reller (Berkeley, Calif.: McCutchan Publishing Corporation, 1979), p. 285.

[48] Cooper argues that principals, as middle managers whose authority has been weakened because of collective bargaining, may need to affiliate with the community, with top management, as members of the management team, with teachers, as head teachers, and with administrator unions. Cooper, B., *Future of Middle Management,* pp. 272–79.

has not influenced student achievement positively. Clark, for example, posits that collective bargaining has had a negative influence on student achievement for the following reasons:

1. Delivery of educational services, which requires a close working relationship between administrators and teachers, is jeopardized by the negotiations process. It leads to a breakdown in the cooperation and communication necessary to deliver high quality services.

2. Teacher strikes disrupt the continuity of instruction and result in loss of instructional days.

3. Cultivation and establishment of a trade-union mindset on the part of bargaining union members tends to bring pressure on those teachers who give extra effort, thus discouraging them from so doing.

4. The extent and degree of parental involvement is reduced because teacher attendance at school open houses is voluntary and limitations are placed on the number of parent-teacher meetings.[49]

The matter of classroom instructional time as a result of collective bargaining and student achievement is also called into question. One survey of over 3000 elementary school teachers revealed that instructional time was reduced by an equivalent of five school days over the period of a school year or 3 percent during a typical school day.[50] While generalizations from this single study are inappropriate, to the extent that length of the school day and length of the school year are positively associated with student achievement, then collective bargaining may have had a negative effect on achievement.[51] It should be noted, however, that this study was conducted at a point in history when teachers' salaries were falling far behind rates of inflation, and reduction in work time may have been a means of compensation for low salary. The question of whether or not collective bargaining can have an influence on student achievement has not been resolved.

SUMMARY

Collective bargaining, long present in the private sector, is a recent phenomenon in public education. However, since enactment of the first bargaining legislation in Wisconsin (1959), bargaining for teachers is now authorized in most states. Major

---

[49] R. Theodore Clark, Jr., "Commentary," in *Faculty and Teacher Bargaining. The Impact of Unions on Education,* ed. George W. Angell (Lexington, Mass.: Lexington Books, D.C. Heath & Co., 1981), pp. 89–91.

[50] R. W. Eberts and Lawrence C. Pierce, *Time in the Classroom: The Effect of Collective Bargaining on the Allocation of Teacher Time* (Eugene, Oreg.: University of Oregon, Center for Educational Policy and Management, 1982).

[51] The negative effect of the reduction of classroom instructional time on student achievement also is posited by Doherty. See Robert E. Doherty, "Does Teacher Bargaining Affect Student Achievement?" *Faculty and Teacher Bargaining. The Impact of Unions on Education,* ed. George W. Angell, pp. 63–76.

bargaining issues are economic, and it is generally only after these have been negotiated that noneconomic concerns come to the surface. Where bargaining is legally authorized, employees and employers are required to negotiate in good faith. In the event contract negotiating practices reach an impasse, resolution techniques— mediation, fact finding, arbitration, and in some states, strikes—are used. The heart of most negotiated contracts is a grievance procedure which may rely on arbitration for final resolution. Although some gains for teachers can be observed as a result of collective bargaining, several issues emerge regarding its utility: appropriateness of the private sector model in education; lack of citizen participation; bargaining, public confidence, and school support; the effect of bargaining on management-union relations; bargaining and school principal representation; and the effect of bargaining on student educational outcomes.

SELECTED READINGS

Cheng, Charles W., *Altering Collective Bargaining: Citizen Participation in Educational Decision Making.* New York: Praeger Publishers, Inc., 1976.

Cresswell, Anthony M., Michael J. Murphy, and Charles T. Kerchner, *Teachers, Unions, and Collective Bargaining in Public Education.* Berkeley, Calif.: McCutchan Publishing Corporation, 1980.

Elam, Stanley M., Myron Lieberman, and Michael H. Moskow, *Readings on Collective Negotiations in Public Education.* Chicago: Rand McNally & Company, 1967.

Johnson, Susan Moore, *Teacher Unions in Schools.* Philadelphia: Temple University Press, 1984.

Levine, Marvin J., and Eugene C. Hagburg, *Public Sector Labor Relations.* St. Paul, Minn.: West Publishing Co., 1979.

Lieberman, Myron, and Michael H. Moskow, *Collective Negotiations for Teachers: An Approach to School Administration.* Chicago: Rand McNally & Co., 1966.

McDonnell, Lorraine, and Anthony Pascal, *Organized Teachers in American Schools.* Santa Monica, Calif.: The Rand Corporation, 1979.

Mitchell, Douglas E., and others, "The Impact of Collective Bargaining on School Management and Policy," *American Journal of Education,* 89, no. 2 (February 1981), 147–88.

Perry, Charles R., and Wesley A. Wildman, *The Impact of Negotiations in Public Education: The Evidence from the Schools.* Worthington, Ohio: Charles A. Jones Publishing Co., 1970.

Ross, Doris, and Patricia Flakus-Mosqueda, *Cuebook II, State Education Collective Bargaining Laws,* report no. F80-5. Denver, Colo.: Education Commission of the States, 1980.

Walton, Richard E., and Robert B. McKersie, *A Behavioral Theory of Labor Negotiations: An Analysis of a Social Interaction System.* New York: McGraw-Hill Book Company, 1965.

HUMAN RESOURCES ADMINISTRATION

chapter 13

Schools are labor intensive, they are people oriented. They are concerned with educating students through a process that relies almost exclusively on human resources consisting of administrators, teachers, counselors, librarians, support, and service staff. Not surprisingly, 85 to 90 percent of a typical school district's operating budget is absorbed by personnel costs, thus reflecting the importance of certificated and noncertificated staff.

School human resources administration is concerned with securing appropriate school staff and managing the general conditions of employment from initial appointment to termination. It includes staff recruitment, selection, induction, supervision, appraisal, and development; administration of economic and noneconomic reward and incentive systems; employee record keeping; and collective bargaining, which we discussed in Chapter Twelve.

In medium- to large-size school districts, human resources administration is usually assigned to a separate office headed by a director having appropriate staff. In small districts it may be included in the school business manager's or even the superintendent's portfolio. Regardless of district size, the human resources director tends to be a staff officer who functions in an advisory and supportive capacity to central office and school site line officers—those having direct responsibility and authority over instructional programs and staff.

Since the vast majority of school personnel are assigned to individual schools, human resources administration must be coordinated carefully with school site administrators. Whereas general personnel policies and programs may be planned, developed, and implemented at a school district's central office, management of face-to-face personnel practices is a fundamental concern of the school site administrator. In this regard, the primary responsibility for staff recruitment may reside in the central office while the major responsibility for staff selection, induction, supervision, appraisal and development, and implementation of noneconomic reward or incentive programs may be vested in the principal. In this chapter, therefore, we discuss the administration of these human resources functions with particular attention given to district office and school site responsibilities.

RECRUITMENT AND SELECTION

The linkage between staff quality and organizational success is well established. In large measure, school effectiveness is intimately associated with quality of school leadership and teacher skill and ability.[1] Thus, recruitment and selection of talented and able staff is an extremely important function. Personnel recruitment strategies are designed to generate a large pool of applicants possessing desired job qualifications and selection procedures structured to choose and employ the best applicant for a particular position. Well managed recruitment and selection procedures are part of sound personnel administrative practice. Before addressing such procedures, however, we examine briefly the potential teacher applicant pool and the overall academic quality of that pool.

It is expected that teacher shortages will occur in many academic and geographical areas by the end of the 1980s.[2] In bilingual education,[3] mathematics, and science,[4] shortages have long existed and may become worse. In addition to these conditions, the number of college education majors has declined as students turn to fields of study—computer science, accounting, and engineering—that hold the promise of better economic rewards.

[1] See, for example, Eigil Pedersen, Therese Annette Faucher, and William W. Eaton, "A New Perspective on the Effects of First-Grade Teachers on Children's Subsequent Adult Status," *Harvard Educational Review,* 48, no. 1 (February 1978), 1–31.

[2] See Gary Sykes, "Teacher Preparation and the Teacher Work Force: Problems and Prospects for the 80s," *American Education,* 19, no. 2 (March 1983), 23–30; Timothy W. Weaver, "Educators in Supply and Demand: Effects and Quality," *School Review,* 86, no. 4 (August 1978), 552–93; National Education Association, *Teacher Supply and Demand in Public Schools, 1980–81* (Washington, D.C.: NEA, 1981); Gary Sykes, "The Schools, The Teachers, and Excellence in Education," testimony presented before the National Commission on Excellence in Education (Atlanta, Ga., May 12, 1982).

[3] California Commission for Teacher Preparation and Licensing, *Status Report on Bilingual-Cross Cultural Teacher Preparation in Accordance with California Education Code. Section 10101* (Sacramento: The Commission, 1981).

[4] James W. Guthrie and Ami Zusman, "Teacher Supply and Demand in Mathematics and Science," *Phi Delta Kappan,* 64, no. 1 (September 1982), 28–33.

Annual salaries for individuals entering education are low in comparison to other academic or professional fields. As displayed in Table 13.1, in 1984 the average annual salary for graduates in electrical engineering was $28,086 and only $17,082 for education graduates. For computer science graduates, annual salary averaged $26,690 and for accounting graduates it was $19,262. The attraction of education as a career is obviously affected by the potential for economic rewards.

At another level, according to data compiled by the National Education Association, demand will exceed the supply of new teachers beginning in the late 1980s. For example, in 1985–86 the NEA projects that nationally 112,000 estimated new graduates will apply for 122,000 teaching positions. The balance of teachers needed in that year may be supplied, however, by graduates of previous years (see Table 13.2 on p. 298–299).

Table 13.1 SALARIES BY ACADEMIC FIELD

	Average Expected Starting Salary	Change From 1984
BACHELOR'S DEGREE IN—		
Electrical engineering. .	$28,086	+3.7%
Metallurgy, materials . .	$28,012	+2.7%
Mechanical engineering.	$28,004	+3.4%
Chemical engineering . .	$27,827	+2.7%
Computer science	$26,690	+3.5%
Physics	$25,411	+2.6%
Packaging	$23,358	+1.7%
Civil engineering.	$22,789	+2.6%
Mathematics	$20,630	+2.7%
Financial administration	$19,506	+2.3%
Accounting	$19,262	+2.7%
Marketing, sales	$19,157	+2.6%
Business administration	$17,782	+2.2%
Social science	$17,640	+2.3%
Personnel administration.	$17,181	+2.2%
Education	$17,082	+2.6%
Hotel, restaurant management.	$16,871	+2.1%
Agriculture.	$16,658	+1.7%
Communications	$16,299	+1.9%
Liberal arts.	$15,124	+2.3%
Human ecology	$14,827	+2.2%

USN&WR—Basic data Michigan State University

Source: Reprinted from *U.S. News & World Report* issue of Dec. 17, 1984. Copyright, 1984, U.S. News & World Report, Inc.

Teacher recruitment and selection also will be affected by the academic quality of education majors. On the basis of scores on tests associated with academic ability—Scholastic Aptitude Test (SAT), Graduate Record Examination (GRE)—and data from the National Longitudinal Study of the High School Class of 1972,[5] the least able students consider teaching as a career and are likely to become teachers.[6] Moreover, there is evidence to suggest that the most academically qualified teachers do not remain in teaching.[7]

Because of the aforementioned circumstances, recruitment and selection of able individuals may be quite difficult. Well designed and executed plans become all the more essential to secure the services of the best candidates from among the shrinking pool of potentially able teachers.

Recruitment

Policy setting. Before the recruitment process actually begins, it is necessary that a set of written policies be formulated and adopted at the highest level of school governance. Typically, this will be the school board in local school districts and the state board of education, or the designated representative body of the state legislature, for state departments of education. Such policies are guides to action and ensure consistency of recruitment procedures throughout an organization. They include, for example, affirmative action considerations—the degree to which there is commitment to attracting and employing minorities and nonminority women, whether recruitment for other than beginning teachers' positions will be conducted within or outside the organization, and initial salary scale placement given training and experience considerations. After such policies are enacted, employment targets must be determined and position descriptions developed.

Planning. Projections of employment targets or needs will emerge from long-(five to ten years) and short-range (one to four years) planning and will be indicated through a comprehensive employee record keeping system. The fundamental planning question to be answered is how many certificated and classified staff persons are likely to be needed for a specified time frame given (1) staff turnover statistics—resignations, retirements, deaths, transfers, promotions, dismissals, layoffs, leaves of absence; (2) programmatic needs, for example, an expanded reading or mathematics program requiring teachers with special training; (3) staffing ratio goals, for example, a predetermined or negotiated reduction in the teacher pupil ratio; and (4) fiscal constraints?

[5] National Center for Education Statistics, *National Longitudinal Study of the High School Class of 1972* (Washington, D.C.: U.S. Department of Education, 1983).

[6] See Timothy W. Weaver, "Educators in Supply and Demand: Effects on Quality," *School Review,* 86, no. 4 (August 1978), pp. 552–93; and Timothy W. Weaver, "The Talent Pool in Teacher Education," *Journal of Education,* 32, no. 3 (May/June 1981), 32–36.

[7] Phillip C. Schlechty and Victor S. Vance, "Do Academically Able Teachers Leave Education? The North Carolina Case," *Phi Delta Kappan,* 63, no. 2 (October 1981), 106–12.

Table 13.2   **TRENDS IN TEACHER SUPPLY AND DEMAND**

Session	PREVIOUS YEAR'S GRADUATES PREPARED TO ENTER TEACHING (IN THOUSANDS)		ESTIMATED NUMBERS OF NEW GRADUATES (IN THOUSANDS)		Supply as Percent of Demand
	Actual and Projected	Estimated from 1967 Proportion	Applying for Teaching Jobs	Receiving Teaching Jobs	
1	2	3	4	5	6
1967–68 ..	220	220	164	164	100.0
1968–69 ..	233	248	175	183	95.6
1969–70 ..	264	284	199	184	108.2
1970–71 ..	284	308	213	152	140.1
1971–72 ..	314	326	236	121	195.0
1972–73 ..	317	346	244	131	186.3
1973–74 ..	313	362	242	128	189.1
1974–75 ..	279	372	215	121	177.1
1975–76 ..	238	364	184	126	146.0
1976–77 ..	222	368	171	87	196.6
1977–78 ..	194	366	149	119	125.2
1978–79 ..	181	367	139	87	159.8
1979–80 ..	163	372	126	67	188.1
1980–81 ..	159	378	123	71*	173.2
Projected					
1981–82 ..	160	380	124	67	185.1
1982–83 ..	163	385	125	70	178.6
1983–84 ..	161	382	124	85	145.9
1984–85 ..	159	377	123	98	125.5
1985–86 ..	156	370	120	110	109.1
1986–87 ..	156	369	120	120	100.0
1987–88 ..	152	361	117	123	95.1
1988–89 ..	152	360	117	125	93.6
1989–90 ..	152	359	117	. . .	. . .

*Estimate based upon a lower reduction in total number of teachers than is projected by NCES, and upon a lower net percent of teachers employed the preceding year (3.9 percent) as the turnover-based component of demand for beginning teachers than is used for preceding and subsequent years.

PERCENT OF PREVIOUS YEAR'S TEACHER EDUCATION
GRADUATES ON NOVEMBER 1

Employed as Teachers	Seeking a Teaching Job	Otherwise Gainfully Employed	Status Unknown	With Follow-up Information Reported
7	8	9	10	11
70.0	0.9	4.2	15.5	83.8
70.5	1.6	3.8	14.8	79.2
67.3	2.5	4.3	16.8	81.0
60.1	4.6	5.8	18.8	88.0
53.3	7.6	6.4	22.5	82.0
50.9	10.1	9.7	20.6	81.2
49.8	9.4	9.5	23.1	77.3
47.8	9.1	10.3	24.0	84.7
45.7	10.6	10.1	25.3	86.4
47.4	11.7	11.0	21.4	67.3
49.4	9.1	11.8	21.1	69.3
50.1	7.6	11.6	22.7	72.7
54.2	5.9	11.5	20.4	72.0

Source: National Education Association, *Teacher Supply and Demand in the Public Schools, 1980–81,* p. 19.

Information regarding employment targets requires planning projections at both central office and school site levels. While staff turnover data should be readily available through central office records, forecasts of programmatic needs are best determined at the school site. That is, replacement and program expansion needs with respect to skills and abilities needed for a given position can be more effectively accomplished at the school site.

Position descriptions. Once staff needs have been projected, job descriptions for each position to be filled provide a communication link between the organization and those it seeks to attract. Job descriptions are statements which indicate (1) the nature of the position—what is required, duties and responsibilities, to whom position holder reports; (2) a brief description of the employment setting—school district size, goals and philosophy, general characteristics of the employment site; (3) minimum professional and personal qualifications within legal parameters; (4) starting date and length of employment; (5) application procedures—what material is to be submitted, to whom, and when; and (6) how applications will be processed.

The intent of the job description is to furnish prospective applicants sufficient information to assess their qualifications for the position and to determine whether the position offers a possibility of self-satisfaction, career development, and growth. From the district's point of view the job description represents a carefully drawn document against which to assess applicant qualifications, a set of standards to be used in evaluating performance, and a specification of predetermined supervisory relationships between a prospective employee and managerial staff. An example of a job description is displayed in Table 13.3.

Table 13.3 SAMPLE JOB DESCRIPTION

10TH GRADE BIOLOGY TEACHER
EQUITY HIGH SCHOOL, PROGRESS, CALIFORNIA

Position	Progress Unified School District of Progress, California, invites applicants for the position of 10th grade Biology Teacher.
Description of School District	Progress Unified School District is located in the beautiful city of Progress which boasts a stable population of 250,000 citizens, and a solid industrial and technological base. The city of Progress is a financial center in the west, is the home of the nationally acclaimed Progress Pirates football team, the Progress Opera Company and Progress University. The Progress Unified School District serves 45,000 ethnically, culturally, and economically diverse students from kindergarten to twelfth grade in thirty K–6 elementary schools, fifteen 7–9 junior high schools, six 10–12 comprehensive senior highs, and two continuation high schools. Equity High School serves 1100 students representative of those found throughout the district.

Table 13.3 SAMPLE JOB DESCRIPTION (cont.)

10TH GRADE BIOLOGY TEACHER
EQUITY HIGH SCHOOL, PROGRESS, CALIFORNIA

It is the policy of the district to provide for the educational needs of all students and to respect the individual dignity and worth of all individuals associated with the schools. High expectations are held for students and staff performance. All school personnel are encouraged and supported in professional and personal growth activities.

Duties and Responsibilities	Teach 10th grade general biology and supervise biology laboratory using state-mandated curriculum. Provide for individual differences in student learning styles, and maintain high expectations for student performance. Create and maintain a stimulating learning environment and establish clear student learning goals and objectives. Evaluate student performance and communicate with students and their parents in that regard. Maintain accurate attendance records, order necessary supplies and equipment. Maintain safe classroom conditions.
Reporting and Supervisory Arrangements	Reports to the chairman of the Equity High School Science Department. All instructional and noninstructional staff are under the supervision of the principal.
Minimum Qualifications	B.A. degree from an accredited college in Biology. Possession of a general high school science teaching credential or the ability to obtain one. Ability to work effectively with ethnically, culturally, and economically diverse students.
Terms of Employment	Nine month contract renewable subject to regular performance evaluation. New teachers in the district serve a three year probationary period. Annual salary level with B.A. degree—$18,500. Additional compensation given for masters, earned doctorate, or designated academic units beyond the masters degree, and experience up to five years.
Starting Date	September 1, 1986.
Contract	Submit letter of application, the names of three references and transcripts to: Director of Personnel Progress Unified School District 3238 Pacemaker Street Progress, California 94798
Application Deadline	March 15, 1986.

The Progress Unified School District believes in and practices equality of opportunity for all individuals irrespective of ethnicity, religion, sex, or physical handicap. All individuals meeting minimum qualifications for this position are urged to apply.

Announcement of employment openings.   Job announcement dissemination, recruitment field trips, and application processing are logical next steps in a recruitment process and are coordinated by the personnel administrator. How widely job announcements will be disseminated is a function of the difficulty perceived in filling the position and district policy regarding hiring from within or outside the organization. Assuming the policy for a given position, for example, school principal, is to recruit both within and outside the school district, job announcements must be posted and disseminated among district staff and advertised through appropriate publications in order to attract a large applicant pool. Additionally, personal letters and job announcements to professors and placement centers in colleges and universities, professional teacher and administrator organizations, recruiting firms, colleagues, individuals previously inquiring about positions on file, recruiting trips, professional meetings and conferences, and so forth, can be used to advantage in developing an applicant pool.

To be effective, job advertising also must be accomplished over a reasonable period of time. That is, a job announcement ought to be posted and publicized over a sufficiently long time period to ensure that it will come to the attention of a large number of potential applicants. While such time periods may vary given the nature of the position and its geographical location, usually four to six weeks from initial posting and public advertisement to application closing date is adequate.

Recruitment records.   Success of the recruitment effort can be gauged by the number of applicants meeting minimum qualifications applying for an announced position. Through systematic record keeping and applicant inquiry—what was your source of information about this position?—the most productive and cost-effective recruitment means can be determined. At a fundamental level, total recruitment cost including staff hours, printing, mailing, telephoning, travel, and advertising, divided by the number of qualified applicants will provide cost per applicant data. An analysis of the primary source of applicants as a function of cost will provide an estimate of cost effectiveness. Such assessment data are useful in specifying future recruitment budgets and in identifying the most useful recruitment sources.

Application procedures.   It is crucial that applications be acknowledged promptly and a thorough filing system of applications maintained. A preliminary review of each applicant's materials is made for completeness, and requests for additional information including letters of reference made as necessary. When completion of application forms is required, they are mailed to each applicant with a return date specified. Procedures for handling telephone inquiries and applicants who walk in must also be established.

In sum, recruitment requires careful planning and organization. Although the process is coordinated by the personnel administrator, advice from line officers is essential in developing job descriptions. Overall recruitment policy guides recruitment efforts and is enacted at the highest level of local school governance. The intent of the recruitment effort is to attract an appropriate applicant pool. Internal processing of applications, records, and inquiries are essential to overall success. Finally, the respect and courtesy with which applicants are treated, the manner in which applications are acknowledged, and responses made to verbal inquiries and written correspondence does much to project a favorable organizational image and to influence prospective employees.

Selection

Ample information must be solicited and reviewed regarding each candidate to enable a well reasoned judgment to be made. Given sufficient data, reasoned prediction can be made regarding probable success of one candidate over another for the position advertised. Having generated a large applicant pool, an employer is faced with the inevitable question of how to select the best applicant for a particular position. As a first step, assuming a carefully developed job description, data for preliminary screening are provided by the candidate's application or résumé. Minimum advertised professional qualifications, such as academic training, experience, credentials, and personal characteristics can be used to determine applicant eligibility. Since résumé formats vary by individual, however, application forms, when used, provide desired information in an easily reviewed format.

Application blanks are convenient for obtaining information regarding applicant educational background, experience or employment data, teaching, administrative, and special credentials held, particular skills or interests related to the position sought, awards or other forms of special recognition, publications, if any, and names of individuals who can be contacted as references. One caution to be observed is that questions regarding personal characteristics unrelated to the job should not be included on the application form. Inquiries such as marital status or number of children have been ruled illegal and are prohibited by federal legislation (we discuss such legislation in a later section of this chapter).

Completed applications represent a single set of applicant data. Such applications may be used to elicit basic unweighted information or weighted data—questions thought to predict success accorded higher value than others. Individuals receiving more points are viewed more favorably than others. What is not always clear in using a weighted application form is how accurately certain characteristics predict job success. The advantage of an application blank is that it provides readily accessible basic data about each applicant that are useful in preliminary screening and follow-up activities. When used with other sources of information, application data are valuable selection devices, but total reliance on weighted applications could eliminate excellent candidates. Moreover, it has been estimated that approximately one-fourth of applicant data are inaccurate.[8]

Personnel tests also yield applicant data that may be efficacious in selection procedures. Perhaps more widely used in industry than in education, selection tests

---

[8] Robert Hershey, "The Application Form," *Personnel,* 48, no. 1 (January-February 1971), 36–39.

may be of several types: achievement, aptitude, vocational interest, personality, or general ability. Tests may be used for hiring, promotion, or transfer, provided they are job related,[9] have been validated, and do not discriminate unfairly against minority groups.[10]

Depending on circumstances, any of three test validation methods satisfies federal guidelines. First, *criterion-related validity*—the test will predict a criterion measure such as job success. Stated differently, if there is a high correlation between what the test measures and some criterion such as job success, then the test has criterion-related validity. A second validation method advocated by federal guidelines is *content validity*—a determination usually by a panel of experts of the congruence between test questions and actual subject material being measured. This is a nonstatistical procedure that attempts to judge whether test questions coincide with job requirements or content. A final validation method is *construct validation*, which provides a statistical estimate of a measure or construct being studied. A construct is a characteristic, an ability or an aptitude thought to explain a facet of human behavior, for example, manual dexterity. Construct validity seeks to determine the relationship between a test and a particular theory or hypothesis. While these validation methods are important and required when validation studies are conducted, employers are encouraged to consider available alternatives to accomplish legitimate organizational goals while minimizing adverse effects of selection procedures.[11]

Use of tests in personnel selection is an attempt to provide objective information about applicants.[12] For example, many states use the National Teacher Examination (NTE) to determine eligibility for a teaching credential and have enacted legislation requiring teachers, administrators, and other school staff to pass newly developed competency tests as a condition of licensing.[13] However, the relationship of teacher scores on the NTE with the classroom performance of students they teach has not been clearly established. Further, the extent to which competency tests meet criterion-related or construct validity standards remains to be deter-

---

[9] Tests that were judged to be nonjob related and racially discriminatory have been ruled illegal by the U.S. Supreme Court. See *Griggs* v. *Duke Power Co.,* 401 U.S. 424 (1971).

[10] "Uniform Guidelines on Employee Selection Procedures (1978)," Part 60-3, Title 41— Public Contracts and Property Management, *Federal Register,* 43, no. 166 (August 25, 1978).

[11] "Uniform Guidelines," *Federal Register,* sec. V.

[12] For a succinct discussion of the use of personnel selection tests generally, see Paul Mali, "Testing and the Employment Procedure," *Handbook of Modern Personnel Administration,* ed. Joseph J. Famularo (New York: McGraw-Hill Book Company, 1972), pp. 14-1 to 14-18. Descriptions of specific tests are contained in John Smith, "Psychological Tests: Clerical, Mechanical, Dexterity, and Vocational Interest," *Modern Personnel Administration,* pp. 15-1 to 15-16 and J. B. Stone, "Psychological Tests: Mental and Personality," *Modern Personnel Administration,* pp. 16-1 to 16-10.

[13] Twenty states require passage of some form of basic skill or competency test as a condition of teacher certification. See Lisa Berland, "Teachers: A Question of Competence," *State Legislatures,* 9, no. 2 (February 1983), 11-15.

mined.[14] Given these circumstances, it is inadvisable to rely exclusively on test data in making selection decisions.

In addition, or as an alternative to data collected through application forms and selection tests, selection interviews are frequently utilized to obtain applicant data. In fact, interviews provide, perhaps, the most relied upon personal data used in selection and hiring. Depending on the position for which an applicant is being considered, selection interviews may be originated at several levels. A preliminary interview may be conducted by a personnel administrator. This may be followed by an interview at the district level, where a team may participate in the interview. Further interviewing by the school site administrator and by the superintendent or assistant superintendent often follows.

Interviews may be structured or unstructured. The former are planned and embrace a predetermined set of questions. Unstructured interviews include random questions. In general, structured interviews are more desirable for several reasons. Inter-rater reliability tends to be higher with structured rather than unstructured interviews.[15] In unstructured settings interviewers talk more than interviewees and tend to make decisions regarding the applicant early in the interview.[16] Because the same set of questions is used for all applicants for a given position, structured interviews permit a more systematic comparison. In either structured or unstructured interviews, nonjob-related and discriminatory questions are prohibited—a point amplified later in this chapter.

Interviewers should be selected on the basis of their knowledge of the school system, the position for which interviews are being held, and other personal qualities and skills that facilitate effective interviewing. These qualities and skills include being concerned, open, sensitive, and receptive rather than cold, distant, and unconcerned; having good listening skills and the wisdom not to talk excessively; and having the ability to avoid overreacting or being influenced by interviewee responses, physical characteristics, or personality. In addition, interviewers are advantaged if they possess excellent question-asking skills. Here the ability of interviewers to ask questions that are open-ended—why, how, what, tell me—rather than closed-ended—yes or no—is of immense importance. Concomitantly, effective interviewers avoid asking leading questions that forecast the desired response, such as "You wouldn't yell at a student in your classroom, would you?" To ensure that interviewers exemplify desired skills and abilities, training sessions conducted particularly for persons who are inexperienced are advised.

---

[14] Several court cases have addressed the legality of minimum scores on the National Teacher's Examination as a condition of certification, particularly with respect to its discriminatory effect on minority groups. In upholding use of this test, courts relied heavily on content validity rather than criterion-referenced validity. Future challenges may result in different decisions. See *United States* v. *State of South Carolina*, 434 U.S. 1026, 1978; and *U.S.* v. *State of North Carolina*, 11 Fair Employment Practices Cases 257 (E.D. N.C., 1975).

[15] Eugene C. Mayfield, "The Selection Interview—A Re-evaluation of Published Research," *Personnel Psychology*, 17, no. 3 (Autumn 1964), 42.

[16] Mayfield, E., "The Selection Interview," p. 93.

Interviewee performance and interview session effectiveness can be assessed using a predetermined rating scale or scoring system. Summary notes compiled following the interview and aided by brief notes taken during the interview are of tremendous assistance in this regard. A scoring system is particularly important when a panel or group of interviewers is used so that interviewee rating scores can be averaged. It also is important to have a scoring system when one-on-one interviews are conducted so that interviewees can be rated.

Although a degree of subjectivity is inevitable, selection interviews provide an opportunity to gauge applicants' verbal skills, thought processes, energy level, enthusiasm, poise, and general knowledge about job-related phenomena. The opportunity to probe questions in depth, to furnish the interviewee with pertinent job-related information and general information concerning the school organization, to answer his or her questions, to instill a degree of performance expectation and position importance, and to estimate the fit between the interviewee and the individual(s) with whom he or she will be working are additional selection interview benefits.

There are additional applicant data sources that are important: academic transcripts, letters of reference, and, in the case of teachers, demonstration of a mini teaching lesson using a group of students from or similar to those in the school in which the teaching position exists. Potential administrators may be rated in assessment centers in which in-basket exercises and other administrative tasks are performed by the candidate. While no single applicant data source will predict total job success, data variability increases overall confidence in selecting the most appropriate candidate for a given position.[17] Selection criteria weighting can be determined after careful longitudinal analyses of job performance and selection criteria.

Affirmative Action Requirements

Affirmative action policies are designed to eliminate employment discrimination and to ensure that minorities and nonminority women who have suffered because of past employment discriminatory practices are actively recruited and selected for all employment opportunities. Although arguments abound regarding their necessity,[18] effective affirmative action programs aid in bringing about a full utilization of human resources.

Under certain conditions, recruitment and selection procedures, as well as promotions, transfers, and placement are subject to affirmative action rules and regulations, civil rights laws, and U.S. constitutional guarantees. Several legal man-

[17]For a discussion of general models of personnel selection in the business and industrial setting using statistical techniques, see Abraham K. Korman, *Industrial and Organizational Psychology* (Englewood Cliffs, N.J., Prentice-Hall, Inc., 1971), pp. 178-221.

[18]See, for example, Marshall Cohen, Thomas Nagel, and Thomas Scanlon, eds., *Equality and Preferential Treatment* (Princeton, N.J.: Princeton University Press, 1977); and Daniel C. Maguire, *A New American Justice: Ending the White Male Monopolies* (Garden City, N.Y.: Doubleday & Co., Inc., 1980).

dates were discussed in Chapter Six. Here we re-emphasize specific laws, rules, and regulations which have a direct impact on personnel recruitment and selection procedures. They include the following.

Civil Rights Act of 1964, Title VI, 42 U.S.C., sec. 2000 (D)

Section 601—No person in the United States shall, on the ground of race, color, or national origin, be excluded from participation in, be denied the benefits of, or be subjected to discrimination under any program or activity receiving Federal financial assistance.

Civil Rights Act of 1964, Title VII, 42 U.S.C., sec. 2000

Section 702—permits religious corporations, associations, educational institutions, or societies to consider religion in employing individuals.

Section 703(a)—bans discrimination in compensation, terms, conditions, or privileges of employment because of race, color, religion, sex, or national origin, or to limit, segregate, or classify employees such that they would be deprived of employment opportunities or have their status as an employee affected adversely.

Section 703(e)—provides for consideration of religion, sex, or national origin in employment under certain conditions.

Section 703(h)—sanctions differences in compensation, terms, conditions, or privileges of employment because of a seniority or merit system provided there is no intent to discriminate on the basis of race, color, religion, sex, or national origin.

Equal Education Opportunity Act of 1972, 20 U.S.C., sec. 1703

Prohibits states from denying equal educational opportunity to individuals because of race, color, sex, or national origin by education agency in regard to—(d) discrimination in the employment, employment conditions, or assignment to schools of faculty or staff except in certain circumstances.

Title VII, as amended and strengthened by the Equal Education Opportunity Act of 1972, applies to all public and private educational institutions, all private employers of fifteen or more employees, labor unions with fifteen or more members, state and local governments, public and private employment agencies, and joint labor-management committees for apprenticeship and training.

Executive Order 11246, 30 Fed. Reg. 12319. Amended by Executive Order 11375, 32 Fed. Reg. 14303

Similar to Title VII of the Civil Rights Act but applies to contractors and subcontractors, including educational institutions and medical facilities, receiving federal government contracts. Executive Order 11246 prohibits discrimination because of race, color, religion, or national origin. Executive Order 11375 adds sex to that list. Contracts must provide for equal employment opportunity and contractors must file compliance reports annually. The U.S. Department of Labor has responsibility for administering these Executive Orders.

Revised Order No. 4, 41 C.F.R. Part 60-2, amended in 1977 by 42 Fed. Reg. 3454

In conjunction with Executive Orders 11246 and 11375 the Department of Labor requires contractors and subcontractors employing fifty or more employees and receiving federal contracts of $50,000 or more to develop and implement affirmative action programs. These programs must include goals and timetables to correct deficiencies in the employment of minority groups and nonminority women throughout the organization. Efforts to meet these goals and timetables must be made in good faith. Contract termination or cancellation and prohibitions against future contracts may result from noncompliance.

Age Discrimination in Employment Act Amendments of 1978, 29 U.S.C.A., sec. 621 et seq.

Section 623—makes it unlawful for employers to discriminate unreasonably on the basis of age or for labor organizations to exclude or expel individuals because of age, with some exceptions, "in programs or activities receiving Federal financial assistance."

Education Amendments of 1972, Title IX, 20 U.S.C., sec. 1681

Section 901—prohibits discrimination on the basis of sex in educational programs or activities receiving Federal funds with some exceptions.

Rehabilitation Act of 1973, 29 U.S.C., sec. 794

Section 504—prohibits discrimination against otherwise qualified handicapped individuals in programs or activities receiving Federal funds.

Equal Pay Act of 1966, 29 U.S.C.A. sec. 206

Employers covered under the Fair Labor Standards Act are required to provide equal pay for men and women performing similar work. Since 1972, executive, administrative, and professional employees and outside salespeople are included under the requirement of this Act.

Other legislation that has been used to enforce antidiscriminatory employment practices include:

AMENDMENT XIV [1868], U.S. Constitution

Section 1. All persons born or naturalized in the United States, and subject to the jurisdiction thereof, are citizens of the United States and of the State wherein they reside. No State shall make or enforce any law which shall abridge the privileges or immunities of citizens of the United States; nor shall any State deprive any person of life, liberty, or property, without due process of law; nor deny to any person within its jurisdiction the equal protection of the laws.

Civil Rights Act of 1866, 42 U.S.C., sec. 1982

grants all citizens the right to own, sell, and lease real and personal property.

Civil Rights Act of 1870, 42 U.S.C., sec. 1981, 18 U.S.C. sec 241 and 242

specifies that all persons can make and enforce contracts, be a party to litigation, and have the full and equal benefit of all laws pertaining to security of person and property.

Civil Rights Act of 1871, 42 U.S.C., sec. 1983

grants redress to any person injured by being deprived of any rights, privileges, or immunities secured by the Constitution and laws by another person acting under the color of any statute, ordinance, custom, or usage.

In addition to the above legislation, state and local laws also embody employment discrimination prohibitions. Administrators are exhorted to become familiar with those appropriate to their employment location.

Within the scope of affirmative action policy, during the process of recruitment and selection including interviewing, several non job-related, preemployment questions are proscribed.[19] These questions pertain to

1. Race, national origin, religion (although such questions are not specifically prohibited by Title VII, and may be necessary for affirmative action records, their use must be shown to be neutral or nondiscriminatory.)

2. Sex, marital, and family status (such questions may discriminate against women and seldom relate to job performance).

3. Age, date of birth (may violate provisions of the Age Discrimination Act).

4. Physical requirements (height, weight or other physical requirements may be irrelevant for job performance).

5. Availability for work on Saturday or Sunday (may violate religious needs of applicant which must be accommodated by employers under the provisions of Title VII).

6. Arrest record (not an indication of guilt).

7. Credit rating (unless business necessity).

Failure to adhere to affirmative action laws and regulations may result in termination of federal contracts and court-mandated financial remuneration to employees for past discrimination. Moreover, hiring and promotion targets may be set by a court if patterns of discrimination are found.

INDUCTION

Newly certificated and classified personnel, no matter how well qualified, will be unfamiliar with organizational policies, procedures and practices. They also will be unknown, generally, to most existing personnel. Thus, the implementation of well

[19] For a comprehensive discussion of discriminatory questions that pertain to preemployment practices generally, see Evelyn M. Idelson, *Affirmative Action and Equal Employment. A Guidebook for Employers,* Vol. 1 (Washington, D.C.: U.S. Equal Employment Opportunity Commission, 1974), pp. 40-44.

planned and systematic new employee induction or orientation sessions are pre-scribed first, to alleviate problems resulting from this inevitable unfamiliarity and, second, to integrate the individual into the work setting. Through the induction process, necessary information is disseminated to new employees, they begin to de-velop a sense of organizational belonging, are given support and assistance, and are provided tangible evidence that they are valued by the school district, individual school, and community. In addition, expectations held for them, typically dis-cussed prior to hiring, are reinforced. Further, questions that they may have per-taining to the position and to the organization are answered. In the absence of induction procedures, new employees will receive information from a variety of sources that may be inconsistent, inaccurate, and confusing. As a consequence, organizational goals, objectives, and expectations will be unclear. Additionally, a new employee's decision to affiliate with the organization may be questioned and may lead to an inappropriate early decision to resign.

Induction begins with recruitment and continues until there is assurance that school goals, policies, and practices are known and understood by the new em-ployee. The process may extend over several weeks or months. Regardless of the time, the process is guided by goals accompanied by a clear indication of leadership responsibilities.

Ideally, both district and school site personnel are involved in planning and implementing employee induction programs. Consequently, the director of person-nel, central office line officers, as well as teachers, parents, students, and adminis-trators at the school site should become active participants in the planning process. These groups plan what is to be included in the program, when sessions will be held, and specify individuals responsible for conducting sessions. In addition to school goals and policies, session content may be determined by past staff grievances filed in the district, employee exit interviews, and staff suggestions.

Induction sessions are best conducted by individuals who are factually knowl-edgeable, good speakers, and able representatives of various segments of the school community. This is a marvelous opportunity to expose new employees to key cen-tral office administrators—superintendent, business manager, assistant superinten-dent of instruction, representatives in legal matters, and school board members—and school site personnel—the principal, assistant principal, attendance clerk, nurse, custodian, school secretary, teachers, parents, and student leaders.

In addition to session presentations, a staff mentor can be assigned to a new employee for several months to a full year. The advantage of this arrangement is that a new employee will have a readily available resource for advice and counsel whenever necessary. This person, well informed and sensitive, also may reinforce basic information disseminated in organized formal sessions.

As indicated previously, induction begins with recruitment. Here, position announcements contain basic information regarding school district, employment site, and employee duties and responsibilities. More information in these areas is provided during the selection process. Such information at these initial steps is im-portant, and part of the overall induction process. However, a more extensive and well orchestrated sequence of information immediately following employment is highly desirable.

Although not so obvious, for purposes of induction and simply as common courtesy, new employees should receive letters of welcome to the school organization from the chair of the school board, superintendent, principal (if assigned to a school site), and chair of the local school parent or community organization. Through welcome letters a level of job expectancy can be subtly indicated, morale enhanced, and anxieties allayed.

Since the purposes of induction are to familiarize new employees with school and school district conditions of employment and to develop a sense of belonging, the program or process may include, for example, sessions in the following areas, as appropriate.

I. School district
   A. Overall philosophy
      1. Goals and objectives.
      2. Staff and student expectations.
      3. Curriculum and educational program.
   B. General policies and procedures: staff
      1. School assignment, transfer and promotion.
      2. Probationary period, contract renewal, and security of employment.
      3. Leaves of absence: maternity, personal, jury duty, death in family, sickness, vacation, sabbatical.
      4. Benefits
         a. economic: salary, dates of payment, adjustments, payroll deductions.
         b. fringe: retirement, insurance, tax sheltered annuities, health and dental plans.
      5. School calendar and holidays.
      6. Professional development including financial assistance.
      7. Teacher and staff liability.
      8. Supervision and appraisal.
      9. Causes for dismissal.
    10. Grievance procedures.
   C. Student policies
      1. Required course of study and options.
      2. Proficiency examinations and graduation requirements.
      3. Grade retention; grade acceleration.
      4. Grading.
      5. Programs for students with special needs.
      6. School and classroom assignment.
      7. Required textbooks and supplemental material.
      8. Suspensions and expulsions.
      9. Maternity, marriage, motherhood.
    10. Dress codes, smoking, use of drugs, violence, vandalism.
II. School site
   A. Overall philosophy
      1. Goals and objectives.
      2. Staff and student expectations.
      3. Curriculum and educational programs.

   B. Administrative concerns and procedures
      1. Class assignments and schedule.
      2. School calendar.
      3. School resources.
      4. Lunch and preparation periods.
      5. Faculty meetings.
      6. Lesson plans.
      7. Supervision and appraisal.
      8. Extra duties.
      9. Time off job, leaves.
      10. Secretarial assistance: phone calls, appointments, typing, xeroxing.
      11. Ordering supplies and equipment.
      12. Parent conferences.
      13. Health and safety procedures.
      14. Field trips.
      15. Extracurricular activities.
   C. Dealing with students
      1. Attendance and record keeping.
      2. Tardiness and class cutting.
      3. Discipline and office referrals.
      4. Homework and class assignments.
      5. Opportunities for growth and recognition outside the regular classroom.
      6. Counseling and referrals.
      7. Records and confidentiality.
III. Community
   A. Composition
   B. School-community relations
   C. Resources.

In sum, induction is that process or program in which information is provided to assist newly certificated or noncertificated staff become familiar with organizational goals, policies, and practices. The fundamental intent of the process is to effectively integrate new employees into the organization. It is more efficient when planned and coordinated at district and school site levels.

Induction sessions become more relevant when organized and conducted by representatives from throughout the organization over a period of several weeks or months. What is covered, when, and by whom are included in a checklist signed by the new employee to indicate that session topics were covered and understood. Signed checklists are retained in personnel files. Topics covered, how, and by whom are reviewed periodically to ensure they meet organizational and employee needs.

SUPERVISION

A major theme in human resources management is employee supervision. The general concern here is with coordinating, directing, organizing, and developing employee performance so that organizational goals and objectives can be met. The focus of school supervision is the improvement of instruction and, it is hoped, the subsequent maximization of student academic performance. Thus, supervision can be viewed on two levels: (1) providing for instructional effectiveness; and (2) enhancing employee performance. Although these two levels are not neatly separated, within the human resources context our attention is drawn to teacher supervision and its relationship to teacher effectiveness.

Teacher supervision is that function of leadership concerned with improving, enhancing, and reinforcing classroom or teaching effectiveness. At the school site, supervision is a function of the principal, although it may be delegated to an assistant principal, department chair in a large secondary school, or a central office subject-matter specialist or supervisor.

In recent years, supervisory practices have been influenced heavily by the concept of clinical supervision which emphasizes improvement of classroom teaching and instruction.[20] Clinical supervision is predicated on teacher-supervisor mutual trust and close interaction, a presumed desire of teachers to improve, and a systematic approach to the observation and analysis of teaching behavior. It is a model based upon a set of sequential steps or phases.

As originally conceived by Cogan and his associates, the clinical supervision model consists of an eight-step cycle. In the first phase, supervisor-teacher trust is established, and purposes of clinical supervision are explained. Phase two focuses on lesson planning, including teaching goals and objectives, teaching techniques and materials, anticipated problems, general concerns, and kinds of teacher feedback desired. While the supervisor may make suggestions, these facets are teacher centered. That is, they emerge from the teacher not the supervisor. Phase three of the cycle is used to determine what classroom observational techniques will be used and how specific data will be collected. The activity of phase four is actual classroom observation and data collection from the teaching session.[21] Here, such techniques as video and audio taping, verbal interaction analysis,[22] or student-time-on-task analy-

---

[20] The concept of clinical supervision was developed by Morris Cogan and his associates at Harvard University in the late 1950s and early 60s. It emerged from efforts to assist students engaged in practice teaching, typically a requirement in preservice teaching programs. Clinical supervision also is an effective in-service method for instructional improvement and teacher development. See Morris Cogan, *Clinical Supervision* (Boston: Houghton Mifflin Company, 1973); Robert Goldhammer, Robert H. Anderson, and Robert J. Krajewski, *Clinical Supervision: Special Methods for the Supervision of Teachers,* 2nd ed., (New York: Holt, Rinehart & Winston, 1980); Keith Acheson and Meredith D. Gall, *Techniques in the Clinical Supervision of Teachers. Preservice and Inservice Applications* (New York: Longman, Inc., 1980); and Cheryl Granade Sullivan, *Clinical Supervision. A State of the Art Review* (Alexandria, Va.: Association for Supervision and Curriculum Development, 1980).

[21] An excellent and practical description of several classroom observational techniques and other data collection instruments is contained in Acheson, K., and Gall, M., *Techniques in the Clinical Supervision of Teachers. Preservice and Inservice Applications,* pp. 97–163.

[22] Perhaps the most widely used classroom verbal interaction analysis system is that developed by Flanders. See Ned Flanders, *Analyzing Teaching Behavior* (Reading, Mass.: Addison-Wesley Publishing Co., Inc., 1970). Other classroom observational and interaction systems are contained in Anita Simon and E. Gil Boyer, *Mirrors for Behavior III. An Anthology of Observation Instruments* (Wyncote, Penn.: Communication Material Center, 1974); and Gary D. Borich and Susan K. Madden, *Evaluating Classroom Instruction: A Sourcebook of Instruments* (Reading, Mass.: Addison-Wesley Publishing Co., Inc., 1977).

sis[23] may be used. Phase five of the process is the analysis of classroom observational data by both teacher and supervisor, done independently or jointly. The specific analysis techniques used will be determined by the observational techniques employed as well as teacher goals and objectives. Generally, the analysis will reveal patterns of teacher and student classroom behavior, amount and quality of student classroom involvement and interaction, and teacher effectiveness in achieving desired teaching goals and objectives. Phase six focuses on planning the teacher-supervisor feedback conference. This involves arranging the time and place of the conference, establishing objectives, and conference strategies.

The feedback conference is phase seven in the process. Previously analyzed classroom observational data are interpreted by the teacher with assistance from the supervisor as necessary. Decisions about teaching techniques with respect to classroom outcomes are tentatively made by the teacher. Reinforcement and guidance may be provided by the supervisor. The conference is designed so that the teacher will assess his or her effectiveness in meeting desired objectives or outcomes based on data collected by the supervisor. Teacher inferences pertaining to what did or did not happen are drawn. The final phase of the cycle is renewed planning, using new targets for classroom outcomes or teaching behaviors. The cycle is thus repeated beginning at phase three.

A diagrammatic representation of the clinical supervision cycle is displayed below in Table 13.4.

Clinical supervision is a type of supervision designed to improve teaching effectiveness and classroom instruction. It enables individual teachers to assume a major responsibility for improvement based on collected classroom observational data. In this model, the supervisor-teacher relationship is one of trust, mutual respect, and face-to-face interaction. Cogan refers to this relationship as colleagueship.[24]

Although some assessment of teaching effectiveness is invariably made, teacher evaluation for purposes of retention and promotion is not the function of the clinical supervisor. Feelings of trust, essential to the clinical supervision process, are jeopardized when the clinical supervisor is required to evaluate teachers. Thus, evaluation and supervision are more effective when performed by different individuals.

The success of clinical supervision need not depend on the appointment of an exclusive clinical supervisor. In addition to site administrators and department chairs, other teachers may be used as clinical supervisors. Individuals temporarily assuming the clinical supervisor's role, and, of course, regular clinical supervisors, must be knowledgeable about effective teaching techniques, skilled in using classroom observational systems, and possess the ability to establish supportive non-threatening relations with colleagues. When other teachers are used as clinical

[23] For a description of research findings and implications of a major study on academic learning time and student learning, see Carolyn Denham and Ann Lieberman, eds., *Time to Learn* (Washington, D.C.: U.S. Department of Education, National Institute of Education, 1980).

[24] Cogan, M., *Clinical Supervision,* pp. 67–69.

Table 13.4 CLINICAL SUPERVISION CYCLE

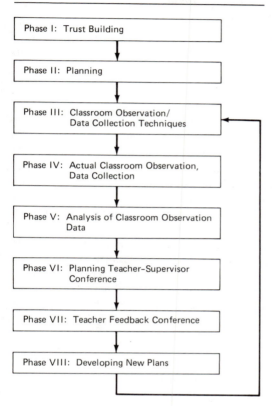

Phase I: Trust Building

Phase II: Planning

Phase III: Classroom Observation/
Data Collection Techniques

Phase IV: Actual Classroom Observation,
Data Collection

Phase V: Analysis of Classroom Observation
Data

Phase VI: Planning Teacher–Supervisor
Conference

Phase VII: Teacher Feedback Conference

Phase VIII: Developing New Plans

Source: Based on Morris Cogan, *Clinical Supervision,*
(Boston: Houghton Mifflin Company, 1973).

supervisors, benefits may accrue not only to the teacher being supervised but also to the person assuming the clinical supervisor's role. Over time, every teacher in an individual school could conceivably engage in clinical supervision as a supervisor. The key to the effectiveness in this arrangement is the principal, who must initiate the clinical supervision process and provide substantial support for it. Of no less importance is that teachers experience tangible benefits from the process.

APPRAISAL

Organizational effectiveness is closely tied to individual effectiveness. Systematically assessing or evaluating individual performance serves not only as a barometer of individual performance but also as an indicator of organizational effectiveness. To evaluate is to make a judgment with respect to established criteria. In every organization or school system a formal personnel evaluation or appraisal system is highly desirable. Implementation of such a system is a major administrative function. Given that assertion, fundamental performance evaluation questions should be addressed: Why evaluate? How will evaluation be accomplished? What will be evaluated? Who will evaluate? When will evaluation take place? What will be its consequences?

Purpose

The purposes of performance appraisal or evaluation are manifold. They include, for example, the following: to determine the effectiveness with which individual employees or position holders are meeting expected goals and objectives; to identify areas of strength and weakness; to improve performance; to reinforce performance expectations; to provide an intrinsic reward to employees when performance is perceived by others as being good or outstanding; to make administrative decisions regarding, for example, awarding tenure to probationary teachers, teacher or staff transfer, promotion, demotion, or termination. In addition to these reasons, regular performance appraisal may be mandated by the state. For example, California law requires "a uniform system of evaluation and assessment of the performance of certificated personnel of the state."[25] The California legislation further specifies that the governing board of each school district shall develop and adopt specific evaluation and assessment guidelines which shall include but shall not necessarily be limited in content to the following elements:

1. Establishment of standards of expected student progress in each area of study and of techniques for assessment of that progress.

2. Assessment of certificated personnel competence as related to established standards.

3. Assessment of other duties normally required to be performed by certificated employees as an adjunct to their regular assignments.

4. Establishment of procedures and techniques for ascertaining that a certified employee is maintaining proper control and is preserving a suitable learning environment.[26]

At the time of its enactment, this California legislation was far reaching. Its intent was to institute a system of certificated staff accountability. While its effectiveness in achieving the results envisioned are questionable, we make reference to it as another example of how performance evaluation serves many purposes.

Policies

Undergirding a performance evaluation system are several assumptions regarding employee evaluations. At one level, these assumptions might address the basic purposes of employee evaluation in the district—for example, the evaluation process

[25] California's Tenure and Evaluation Law, Assembly Bill 293, Article 5.5, Section 13485 (1972).
[26] *California's Tenure and Evaluation Law,* Section 13487.

should assist in the identification of individual strengths and weaknesses in relation to organizational and personal goals; or the evaluation system should be designed to make judgments in relation to established objectives rather than on the personal worth of the individual. At another level, assumptions may reflect the school district's philosophy regarding the nature of its employees. In this instance, such statements as all individuals desire to perform to the best of their abilities, or respect for the individual is of paramount importance in this district, exemplify a basic belief in the inherent goodness of employees, thereby reducing probable employee anxiety. At yet another level, assumptions or policies might indicate general procedures to be followed—performance objectives and evaluation strategies shall be determined jointly by the employee and evaluator; or evaluation designs are more effective when self-appraisals as well as appraisals by others are included. At still another level, a district may indicate who is responsible for evaluating employees. However, at the school site ultimate evaluation responsibility should reside with the principal.

The list of fundamental employee evaluation system assumptions, policies, and procedures will vary by district. Yet it is essential that whatever beliefs a district holds in this regard are formalized and made known to all personnel within the district. Formalization requires school board adoption of written assumptions, policies, and procedures which are subsequently placed in the district's personnel manual and widely disseminated.

Criteria

Often, what is to be evaluated is specified by a job description in which employee duties, responsibilities, and expectations are broadly stated. More precise objectives indicating targets to be attained within a given time period are written during employee-administrator evaluation planning conferences and subsequently used as benchmarks for purposes of evaluation. It is important at this preevaluation stage to have a clear notion of the district's responsibility in providing necessary resources. No person can be expected to perform at maximum levels if necessary support and resources are not provided.

Evidence

What data will be collected and how are also agreed to during employee-administrator or evaluator planning conferences. Attention must be given to the practicality of collecting data, amount of time involved, and, of course, whether the data to be collected will adequately assess employee performance.

Performance evaluation data for teachers typically tends to be linked to student performance. We hasten to add that in this regard pupil performance on standardized achievement tests or nationally published norm-referenced tests should be used cautiously. These tests are not necessarily synchronized with local learning objectives, may correlate more highly with general intelligence than classroom subject matter or school experiences, and, because of norming procedures, may fail to include enough items to adequately measure essential areas of pupil performance. Elimination of these items can be attributed to the lack of variance in responses—

that is, students answer many of them correctly.[27] Norm-referenced tests provide a relative indication of the standing of pupils against a defined group of learners, but they do not reliably assess pupil learning within the school year. If teacher performance is to be assessed in relation to student performance, then criterion-referenced tests are infinitely more desirable. Such tests compare or measure individual or group performance with respect to agreed upon performance or absolute standards in contrast to the individual's performance relative to other persons. The latter is the case for norm-referenced tests.

Performance data for personnel also may be obtained through rating scales completed by the individual employee (self-rating), peers, administrators, and students. Rating scales are economical and easy to use. Typically, questions or statements regarding some facet of performance are presented and a rating scale or response set which requires checking one category ranging from positive to negative follows. For example, for the statement "displays respect for students," the following rating scales might be used:

Yes——No
True——False
Always——Sometimes——Never
Strongly agree, agree, uncertain, disagree, strongly disagree

Other types of rating scales may include semantic differentials—for example, important ____: ____: ____: ____: ____: ____: ____ unimportant; self-assessment ratings—for example, of very great importance, of great importance, of some importance, of no importance. Ranking—placing in some order according to a common denominator—also may be used. Ranking may be guided by assigning phenomena or individuals to classes of importance or perceptions of worth—for example, superior, above average, average, below average, inferior.

While generally convenient to use, rating scales are inappropriate for use with young students when assessing teaching performance. Such scales fail to provide a common response standard and thus inhibit comparability. Respondents may have insufficient data to assess some dimensions under consideration and may use different standards when responding. The tendency to avoid giving low ratings is a further characteristic associated with the use rating scales.

Observations also are frequently used to evaluate performance. Systematically done over time, and for appropriate time lengths in contrast to infrequent once or twice a year class drop-ins by the evaluator, observations can be a rich source of performance data. Systematic observations enable teachers and others to isolate performance dimensions of concern. Moreover, such systems permit examination of teaching techniques and behaviors which may have a relationship to classroom effectiveness.[28]

---

[27] W. James Popham, *Educational Evaluation* (Englewood Cliffs, N.J.: Prentice-Hall, Inc., 1975), pp. 106–9.

[28] References regarding classroom observational systems are cited in footnote 22.

Alternate Strategies

One alternate classroom evaluation strategy is represented by contract plans. Here, a teacher or administrator negotiates a contract with the evaluator indicating objectives to be met as a consequence of teaching or administrative action. Performance tests during which teachers are assessed on their ability to meet a set of predetermined objectives in teaching a mini lesson to students or peers is another alternate evaluation technique. As discussed previously, administrators may also be judged in an assessment center where their responses to in-basket items are appraised. Teacher or administrator effectiveness may be determined further through use of unobtrusive measures such as the number and kind of students referred to the office for discipline; unexcused student tardies in class; number of employee grievances filed against an administrator; and parental complaints regarding teachers or administrators.

Performance evaluation is imprecise at best. Effective performance behaviors and characteristics vary by individual and by situation. No single instrument or technique will reveal the full range of behaviors that may or may not account for performance effectiveness. Thus, several strategies should be used systematically and continuously. In some instances, the state legal requirement is to evaluate beginning or probationary teachers once every year, and tenured teachers biennially.[29] Ideally, teachers and administrators should be evaluated at least twice a year.

Regardless of specific techniques or strategies used to evaluate performance, they should be employed by knowledgeable and competent evaluators or administrators. At the school site, the major responsibility for performance evaluation resides with the principal, although he or she may delegate responsibility to assistant principals, department heads, or rely on supervisors. When evaluators are permanently assigned to the same school there is the danger that friendship patterns may influence evaluation objectivity and a *quid pro quo* may exist between evaluator and evaluatee. Moreover, individuals may be evaluated on personality factors, for example, they are friendly or a good social mixer, rather than on performance.

It is not surprising, then, that Bridges could identify only eighty-six appellate court cases in the United States between 1939 and 1982 in which tenured teachers were dismissed for incompetence.[30] This may be due to friendship patterns, administrator lack of knowledge regarding performance evaluation, the overly detailed evaluation records that most dismissal procedures require, or it may be due to the vagueness of terms such as incompetence. For whatever reason, administrators have been reluctant to assess teacher performance critically and objectively. Thus, knowledgeable and sensitive external evaluators may be required for the objective assessment of teacher or administrator performance.

If performance evaluation is to be useful in assisting individuals to improve,

[29] See California Teacher Tenure and Evaluation Law, Assembly Bill 293.

[30] Edwin M. Bridges, "The Management of Incompetence" (paper presented at the conference of Research and Thought in Educational Administration, Rutgers University, April 7–8, 1983, p. 19). Quoted with permission of the author. See also Harry J. Finlayson, "Incompetence and Teacher Dismissal," *Phi Delta Kappan*, 61, no. 1 (September 1979), 69.

then formative rather than summative evaluations are more appropriate. Formative evaluations generate information regarding performance or program strengths and weaknesses. Such information becomes a basis for staff development activities and program alterations or changes. Summative evaluation provides a final assessment of overall effectiveness and its applicability is most pronounced in administrative decisions regarding, for example, retention, promotion, or demotion (see Chapter Eleven).

In either formative or summative evaluations, a feedback conference between evaluator and evaluatee customarily is held within a ten day period following evaluation. Written evaluation reports are prepared for this conference and related specifically to predetermined goals and objectives. Feedback conferences provide an opportunity to reinforce employee strengths, to plan tactics for improving weaknesses, and, in the case of formative evaluations, to establish targets for subsequent evaluations. If an evaluatee disagrees with ratings, then the basis of disagreement can be examined and discussed in a conference setting. Disagreements that fail to be resolved at that time can be addressed through district grievance procedures.

Evaluation system effectiveness depends upon the quality of evaluators and the care and thoroughness with which district policies and procedures have been developed. Policies must be examined frequently and revised as appropriate. Of particular concern is the reasonableness of data collected to assess performance. A basic question here is the correspondence between performance data collected and, say, individual student progress. Additional questions may exist regarding matters such as the suitability of performance data and district goals, whether evaluations are conducted in a timely fashion, the extent to which personnel morale is affected by the evaluation system, the practicality of collecting certain data, what outcomes or improvements in performance result from the evaluation system, and evaluation cost.

STAFF DEVELOPMENT

School effectiveness ultimately depends upon the skills and abilities of instructional and noninstructional staff. While careful selection procedures more likely will ensure that excellent staff are initially secured, knowledge expansion, changes in district operating procedures, and the importance of self-renewal for morale, personal, and professional growth mandates school system provisions for staff development. School systems that fail to provide opportunities for staff development jeopardize their ability to meet organizational goals.

Staff development and in-service education are frequently used interchangeably, but a logical distinction can be made between them. Staff development refers to a continuing developmental program focused on a wide range of skills, abilities, and group needs. It can be defined further as a formal, systematic program designed to foster personal and professional growth. In-service education is concerned with the acquisition of a specific skill or knowledge of a certain procedure. In-service training may be a building block within the broader context of staff development. Obviously, both staff development and in-service education are important and enhance organizational effectiveness.

A prerequisite for staff development success is organizational commitment and adequate budgetary and time allocations. All staff must know that personal and professional growth is expected and will be encouraged by the organization through well planned efforts rather than one to three hour sessions twice a year. In addition to organizational commitment, staff development must address staff members' professional needs, which can be deduced from regular staff evaluations.[31] Program effectiveness is further enhanced when planned with participants and when systematic program appraisal is used as a basis for future planning and program adjustments.[32]

An often neglected but salient feature of effective staff development programs is the conceptual base upon which they are built. Basic principles or assumptions regarding the intent of staff development programs bring into focus why programs are mounted, considerations for their implementation, and what results are expected.[33] Developmentally, adults in the work force may seek to satisfy what Maslow refers to as esteem and self-actualization needs.[34] Opportunities to meet these needs, therefore, may be a central theme in staff development programs as organizational and professional goals are addressed. Moreover, since the needs of adults as learners can be at variance with those of younger students, differences in learning arrangements are suggested. For example, adult learning is presumed to be enhanced when life and professional experiences are recognized and become the fulcrum of staff development programs.[35]

Many staff development formats are possible. They include workshops, classes, demonstrations, stimulations, role playing, and retreats.[36] Regardless of the

---

[31] A discussion of needs assessment techniques is contained in Fenwick W. English and Roger A. Kaufman, *Needs Assessment: A Focus for Curriculum Development* (Washington, D.C.: Association for Supervision and Curriculum Development, 1975).

[32] These points also are discussed in Leonard C. Burrello and Tim Orbaugh, "Reducing the Discrepancy between The Known and The Unknown in In-service Education," *Phi Delta Kappan*, 63, no. 6 (February 1982), 385-88; Fred H. Wood, Steven R. Thompson and Sister Francis Russell, "Designing Effective Staff Development Programs," Chapter 4, ASCD 1981 Yearbook, *Staff Development/Organization Development,* ed. Betty Dillon-Peterson (Alexandria, Va.: Association for Supervision and Curriculum Development, 1981), pp. 59-91.

[33] An example of a staff development program utilizing motivation theory and adult learning concepts is Rodney J. Reed, *The Administrators Institute: A Program for Professional and Personal Growth* (Eugene, Oreg.: ERIC Clearinghouse on Educational Management, 1985).

[34] Abraham H. Maslow, *Motivation and Personality* (New York: Harper & Row, Publishers, Inc., 1970).

[35] On this point see Malcolm S. Knowles, *The Adult Learner: A Neglected Species* (Houston, Tex.: Gulf Publishers, 1978); and Richard H. Bents and Kenneth R. Howey, "Staff Development—Change in the Individual," Chapter 2, *Staff Development/Organization Development,* ed. Betty Dillon-Peterson, pp. 11-36.

[36] For a discussion of additional formats see Robert N. Bush, Curriculum-Proof Teachers," *Improving In-Service Education: Proposals and Procedures for Change,* ed. Louis J. Rubin (Boston, Mass.: Allyn and Bacon, Inc., 1971), pp. 58-60; and ERS Report, *Inservice Programs for Educational Administrators and Supervisors* (Arlington, Va.: Educational Research Service, Inc., 1974).

format used, psychological support, physical comfort and attractiveness, variability in session pacing, and interaction among and between participants and presenters or resource personnel are powerful reinforcement agents that can only make the program more effective. In addition, Joyce and Showers contend that training satisfaction and transferability into the professional work setting require adherence to the following elements in training sessions:

1. Presentation of theory or description of skill or strategy.
2. Modeling or demonstration of skills or models of teaching.
3. Practice in simulated and classroom settings.
4. Structured and open-ended feedback (provision of information about performance).
5. Coaching for application (hands-on, in-classroom assistance with the transfer of skills and strategies to the classroom).[37]

Responsibility for planning, implementation, and assessment of staff development programs resides with the personnel administrator or a designated representative. As suggested earlier, collaborative planning involving participants, central office, and building representatives leads to overall commitment to staff development efforts. Staff development programs for all certificated and noncertificated school staff can be viewed as investments in human capital. The dividends derived will be in greater school effectiveness and subsequently improved student performance, higher staff morale, and greater community satisfaction.

PERSONNEL INCENTIVES

Economic rewards such as salaries, bonuses, merit increases, cost of living adjustments, and fringe benefits are deeply ingrained in the personnel incentives of American organizations, and no amount of wishful thinking is about to eliminate them. In addition, employees in education, as well as those in almost every other line of work, are motivated also by noneconomic incentives. Working conditions, collegial support, personal friendships, public respect, admiration from employers, and reinforcement from clients for effectively rendered services are all noneconomic components of the spectrum of incentives which influences human activities in organizations. An able administrator will always be aware of and attempt to fairly utilize these noneconomic incentive conditions. Education as a whole, however, currently suffers from the opposite of such incentives—a perverse set of disincentives.

Disincentives to Teach

Schools are established primarily for the transmission of knowledge, using instruction as a fundamental strategy. By this reasoning, teaching is one of education's most vital components. Regrettably, schools too often treat teaching as if it

---

[37] Bruce R. Joyce and Beverly Showers, "Improving In-Service Training: The Messages of Research," *Educational Leadership,* 37, no. 5 (February 1980), 379–85.

were among the less important undertakings in education. The clear-cut hierarchical path out of classroom instruction betrays organizational values. Becoming a teaching specialist, counselor, vice principal, or occupying a central office position are looked upon as favorable rungs on a career ladder which leads away from classroom teaching. Each step up this ladder typically involves greater discretion over one's time, greater interaction with other adults, greater prestige, and often the opportunity to earn a higher salary or be employed for a longer work year. In such circumstances, the message is clear—to get ahead in education, get out of teaching.

Economic incentives reinforce this upside down organizational career chain. Teacher salary schedules often peak after a relatively short time of twelve to fifteen years. Thus, classroom teachers may find themselves at approximately age thirty-five faced with a situation in which they have little hope for added purchasing power. This occurs at a point in life when their college peers who pursued other occupations often find their income curves beginning to rise most steeply. Career ladders and merit pay offer some hope for increased economic rewards (we discuss these in Chapter Sixteen).

Working Conditions

Incentives also include work surroundings, both physical and social, in which one is employed. During the 1970s when the American economy was subject to uncommonly high inflation and public sector spending stagnated, school facilities were often permitted to fall into disappointing disrepair. Thus, many school buildings today are badly in need of updating and maintenance. It is probably the case that few other professions would be willing routinely to report for work in the shabby environment which many teachers must tolerate.

However, it is not simply tawdry physical surroundings which cloud teacher working conditions. It is also often the case that the school instructional environment is not operated with sufficient professionalism. Classroom interruptions are a prime example. Collecting money for charitable causes, extra band and drama rehearsals, student government, senior photographs, and so on for a long list of other endeavors may all be laudable. However, their effect upon the environment for instruction must be carefully assessed. To permit noninstructional activities to regularly puncture scheduled classroom teaching is not only to dilute the effectiveness of a school's academic program, but it also contributes to a perception among both students and teachers that academic activities can be rearranged at will to assume second place to other social undertakings. Within reason, a school's academic program should be protected from intrusion, and school administrators and teachers should cooperate to ensure that such is the case.

BUILDING AN EDUCATION PROFESSION

Education is and is likely for the foreseeable future to remain an extraordinarily labor-intensive undertaking. As important as new technologies may become, human interaction between instructor and pupil is likely to be a vital component of knowledge transmission. Consequently, the most significant lever that can be used to improve school effectiveness is to recruit, properly prepare, and continually motivate able educators. Education is not now attracting and retaining sufficient numbers of able individuals. To do better requires that education become far more of a profession than is presently the case. This will necessitate heretofore virtually unprecedented cooperation between teachers, administrators, and other public officials. A part of such cooperation is the creation of school human resources systems which reward able instruction and assist school employees in achieving it. In addition, school administrators are obligated to cooperate with teacher unions, institutions of higher education, public officials, and the public to insist on higher standards of educator preparation and licensing, and higher rewards for education practitioners. Only in this way can a true profession eventuate.

SUMMARY

Human resources administration is devoted to securing and maintaining staff consistent with school organizational needs and goals. It is concerned with activities such as staff recruitment, selection, induction, supervision, appraisal, development, and incentives. Personnel goals, policies, and procedures should be developed and adopted at the highest level of school governance and disseminated widely throughout the school or educational system. Policies and procedures regarding recruitment and initial selection, transfer, or promotion are subject to federal and state affirmative action and personnel selection legislation. The human resources director is usually considered a central office administrator who functions in an advisory and supportive capacity to line administrators within the school system and who coordinates human resources functions. The effectiveness of the personnel function is dependent upon a close working relationship between the human resources director and central office and school site administrators.

SELECTED READINGS

Bolton, **Dale L.**, *Evaluating Administrative Personnel in School Systems.* New York: Teachers College Press, 1980.

Castetter, **William B.**, *The Personnel Function in Educational Administration* (3rd ed.). New York: Macmillan, Inc., 1982.

Famularo, **Joseph J., ed.**, *Handbook of Modern Personnel Administration.* New York: McGraw-Hill Book Company, 1972.

Idelson, **Evelyn M.**, *Affirmative Action and Equal Employment: A Guidebook for Employers,* Vols. I and II. Washington, D.C.: U.S. Equal Employment Opportunity Commission, 1974.

Millman, **James, ed.**, *Handbook of Teacher Evaluation.* Beverly Hills, Calif.: Sage Publications, Inc., 1981.

COMMUNICATING

chapter 14

Communication is a process by which ideas, thoughts, opinions, information, and feelings are transmitted from one individual to others through a common language or set of behaviors. The means may be verbal, nonverbal, or written. Effective communication is an essential ingredient in interpersonal relations and is crucial for organizational success. Communication links individuals, creates and maintains individual and organizational images or perceptions, and motivates, assuages, and persuades others. From the vantage point of the administrator, an important purpose of communication is persuasion.[1] This is not to imply a pejorative or manipulative use of persuasion. Rather, it is to emphasize that communication must frequently be used to change attitudes or engender support for school programs and policies.

Since almost all administrative actions or decisions must eventually be communicated, the extent to which administrators are capable in this regard is ultimately associated with their overall effectiveness. Clearly, the ability of school executives to communicate with various constituencies associated with schools—students, instructional and noninstructional staff, parents, and a diverse school community—is vital for school success. An understanding of communication processes and arrangements under which they can usefully be employed is a requisite

---

[1] For a discussion of communication and persuasion, see Leslie W. Kindred, Don Bagin, and Donald R. Gallagher, *The School and Community Relations* (Englewood Cliffs, N.J.: Prentice-Hall, Inc., 1976), pp. 78–84.

for the effective school administrator. Thus, in this chapter we discuss communication process, organizational communication, organizational structures which facilitate communication, and means for communicating with the public.

COMMUNICATION PROCESS

At an individual level, communication is a process in which a sender transmits a message that is understood by an intended receiver. Whether the message is in fact received and understood is related to the perception, attitudes, mental set, training and experiential background of the sender and the receiver, and to the channel and medium by which it is sent.

The communication process involves a sender who must first encode a message to be sent. Encoding refers to the transformation of ideas or thoughts into a form that will, conceivably, convey those ideas or thoughts to an intended receiver. Following encoding, a sender transmits the message—written, verbal, or nonverbal— through a formal or informal channel. Next, the receiver must decode the message within his or her mental and attitudinal frame of reference. To ensure that the message has been received, feedback ought to be provided to the sender. The communication process is depicted in Figure 14.1 below.

Diagrammatically, communication is deceptively simple. In reality, it is a process made complex by interference which may distort the intent of messages, ideas, or thoughts at each stage of transmission.

Whether the intended message is written, verbal, or nonverbal, the effectiveness with which the sender encodes the message will affect how well the intended receiver will understand it. Thus, the sender represents the first point at which interference can distort a message. For example, if an orchestra conductor wishes to inform musicians that a symphonic passage is to be played gradually louder with certain tones emphasized, he or she might say to the group, "Please crescendo from measures twenty-four to thirty while ensuring that the third of the chord is heard." In this case, it is assumed that the training, experience, and mental set of the conductor and orchestra members are sufficiently close to ensure that the message will be understood. If, on the other hand, the conductor is addressing a group with only a rudimentary musical background, then the same statement would probably not

Figure 14.1 The Communication Process.

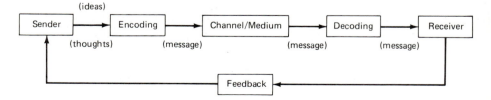

be understood. Thus, the sender will have failed to encode the message in a manner which permits the receiver to understand it. It is also clear that if messages can be incorrectly encoded by a sender, they may subsequently be incorrectly decoded by a receiver.

The channel through which messages travel provides another potential point of interference or distortion. Whether verbal, written, or nonverbal, a question remains of how communication should be transmitted. Should television, films, individual or conference telephone calls, personal letters, newspapers, or demonstrations be used? Each has advantages and disadvantages. Each potentially provides a basis for distortion. Selection of the most effective channel or medium will depend on the speed with which the message is to be transmitted, the amount of feedback desired, and a perception of how effectively received the message will be.

Interference or distortion is inevitable. It can be reduced, however, if the communication process has a feedback loop and clarifying techniques are used. These techniques or skills are designed to ensure that verbal messages are understood. According to Schmuck and Runkel such techniques include

Paraphrasing: Making an inquiry of the other person to be sure you understand the idea or suggestion as intended. This has the potential for increasing communication accuracy because it allows a speaker to assess the listener's understanding. Example, "Did I understand that you do not agree with the current plan?"

Perception Checking: Checking to ensure you understand the other person's feelings. Understanding feelings of others is a difficult task. Emotional states express themselves simultaneously in words and in nonverbal behaviors such as body movements and physiological states. Example, "You appear to feel very strongly about the point you are making."

Describing Own Feelings: This helps others to understand how you feel so that they can respond to you with greater efficacy. Dissatisfaction and hostile feelings often indicate that faulty communication and misunderstanding have occurred. Example, "I felt antagonistic about your laughing."

Describing Behavior: Describing specific observable behaviors of the other without evaluating them and without making inferences about the person's motives, attitudes, or personality. The objective in describing another's actions is to provide the person with a clean picture of the specific behavior to which you are responding. Example, "This is the third time you've asked that. Can you say more about your question?"[2]

These skills provide assistance at an individual level in helping others to understand you, and you others. They are useful in providing feedback to ensure that messages are received with accuracy and understanding.

[2] Explication of these skills is attributed to John Wallen and is reported in Richard A. Schmuck, and others, *Handbook of Organizational Development in Schools* (Eugene, Ore.: Center for the Advanced Study of Educational Administration, University of Oregon and National Press Books, 1972), pp. 39–42.

ORGANIZATIONAL COMMUNICATION

Communication is essential to organizational vitality and coordination: It is the process through which information is transmitted to large numbers of people. Within organizations, the flow of communication is classified as "formal" or "informal," each with identifiable functions.

Formal Organizational Communication

Formal communication within an organization assists in reinforcing authority structures, defines and clarifies purposes, and coordinates staff efforts. Succinctly stated by Barnard, "All communication relates to the formulation of purpose and the transmission of coordinating prescriptions for action and so rests upon the ability to communicate with those willing to cooperate."[3]

Formal communication is both assisted and impeded by an organization's hierarchical structure. It is assisted by the rapidity with which it is capable of flowing from higher to lower levels of the structure. It is impeded by the interference and distortion that can be expected as it flows from one level to another. Communication which flows from the top down is referred to as *one way,* or *downward communication.* In this configuration, there is little opportunity for the sender to be certain that the message has been understood through the feedback techniques described earlier. Written memoranda, reports, letters, announcements between superior and subordinates, instructions, procedures, and policies generally flow one way. Although such one-way communication enhances coordination, it impedes the interaction necessary for clarification and participation. This point is amplified by Blau and Scott:

> A hierarchical organization, in part precisely because it restricts the free flow of communication, improves coordination; indeed, it seems to be essential for effective coordination of group effort. This is the dilemma posed by hierarchical differentiation: while it is necessary for coordination, it blocks the communication processes that are vital for stimulating initiative and facilitating decision making. Moreover, even if there were no formal hierarchy in the organization, communication among peers would be likely to give rise to informal differentiation of status, which also creates obstacles to communication.[4]

Communication also may flow upward in the organization from subordinates to superiors. *Upward communication,* like its downward counterpart, encounters varying perceptions as it moves through organizational levels, and may not be understood by those for whom it is intended. Such communication may further be thwarted by individuals who must process the information—secretaries, assistants,

---

[3] Chester I. Barnard, *The Functions of the Executive* (Cambridge, Mass.: Harvard University Press, 1968), p. 184.

[4] Peter M. Blau and W. Richard Scott, *Formal Organizations: A Comparative Approach* (San Francisco: Chandler Publishing Company, 1962), p. 139.

or superiors. Other factors which serve to inhibit upward flow of communication are pointed out by Simon who holds that

> . . . information tends to be transmitted upward in the organization only if (1) its transmission will not have unpleasant consequences for the transmitter, or (2) the superior will hear of it anyway from other channels, and it is better to tell him [or her] dealing with his [or her] own superiors. . . . In addition, there is often failure to transmit information upward simply because the subordinate cannot visualize accurately what information his [or her] superior needs in order to make . . . a decision.[5]

Finally, formal communication may occur between administrators, between others holding comparable positions, and between the organization and external bodies, for example, governmental regulatory agencies and parent and community groups. Communication of this type is referred to as *horizontal,* in contrast to vertical, communication.

Informal Organizational Communication

Because of social relationships among members, considerable communication occurs outside official or formal organizational communication channels. Such communication is labeled informal and may serve valuable purposes. For example, informal communication networks or channels may (1) clarify formal communications; (2) provide a vehicle for obtaining reactions to ideas that are being considered for organizational policy; and (3) be used as a gauge for employee concerns and dissatisfactions. On the other hand, informal communication networks, also referred to as the "grapevine," may serve to circulate or perpetuate rumors which typically are based on incomplete and inaccurate information. This, of course, is the primary disadvantage of the "grapevine." Moreover, as Simon points out, the grapevine discourages honesty or frankness since confidential remarks may be transmitted throughout the organization.[6]

ORGANIZATIONAL STRUCTURES FOR COMMUNICATING

The preceding discussion on formal and informal communication is based on a presumed hierarchical organizational structure. Other organizational structures have been designed and assessed which enhance organizational communication and coordination. One set of structures has been formulated by Likert. Known as linking-pin structures, they assume vertical, horizontal, or cross-departmental arrangements (see Figure 14.2).

Figure 14.2 shows that *vertical linkages* or interlocking groups are created when superiors become the link between the unit with which he or she is associated

---

[5] Herbert A. Simon, *Administrative Behavior* (New York: Macmillan, Inc., 1961), p. 163.
[6] Simon, H., *Administrative Behavior,* p. 162.

ORGANIZATION DESIGN

(a) Vertical linkages

From: To:

(b) Horizontal linkages

From: To:

(c) Cross–departmental linkages

And finally to:

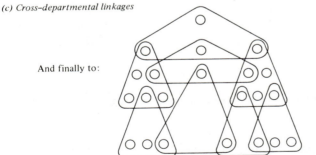

Figure 14.2   Likert's Linking-Pin Structure. From Miles, *Theories of Management,*
© **1975 as adapted from Likert,** *The Human Organization* © **1967. With
permission of McGraw-Hill Book Company.**

and the unit immediately higher in the organization. In the *horizontal link-pin* arrangement more than one member may become members of more than one group. *Cross-departmental* linkages provide for a variety of interactions and flexibility and combine vertical and horizontal linkages. The linking-pin concept blurs unit division levels and thereby enhances communication and coordination as well as shared decision making and problem solving.

Implications for other structural arrangements that may enhance communication within organizations can be gleaned from research conducted by Cohen and Bennis.[7] These analysts sought to determine communication efficiency in three communication networks. Each network consisted of five people who were given a simple task to perform—distributing twenty-five cards, each singularly coded with five of six possible colors or symbols so that each of five subjects have an equal number of cards but with one, and only one, color or symbol in common. The subjects in each communication network were permitted to communicate with each other through written messages transmitted only through the lines indicated in Figure 14.3. They were not to speak nor could they see each other.

Seven measures of communication efficiency were employed to assess the effectiveness of these networks. Using a three-point scale (1 = high; 3 = low), rankings of the three networks were determined as displayed in Table 14.1.

It is instructive to note that overall satisfaction, creativity, and adaptability were highest in the communication network labeled "circle," while speed, accuracy, cost, and role clarity were highest in the wheel arrangement. This study also revealed that the most satisfied single person in these communication networks or arrangements was the person in the hub of the wheel; the most dissatisfied were individuals in the middle of the chain.

If these communication networks are linked to organizational structure, it suggests that pyramidal, chain-like structures inhibit creativity and satisfaction. On the other hand, the communication network labeled circle provides for free information flow, but it is obvious that coordination is less efficient. Likert's model of cross-departmental linkages also provides a structure which enhances the free flow

Figure 14.3 Communication Networks. R.K. Ready, *The Administrator's Job: Issues and Dilemmas,* (New York: McGraw-Hill, 1967), p. 32.

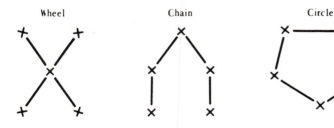

Wheel   Chain   Circle

[7] Arthur M. Cohen and Warren G. Bennis, "Predicting Organization in Changed Communication Networks," *Journal of Psychology,* 54, (October, 1962), 391–416; Arthur M. Cohen, "Predicting Organization in Changed Communication Networks: II," *Journal of Psychology,* 57, (April, 1964), 475–99; and Arthur M. Cohen, "Predicting Organization in Changed Communication Networks: III," *Journal of Psychology,* 58, (July, 1964), 115–29. Also discussed in R. K. Ready, *The Administrator's Job: Issues and Dilemmas* (New York: McGraw-Hill Book Company, 1967), pp. 31–35.

Table 14.1   RANKINGS OF COMMUNICATION NETWORK
EFFICIENCY MEASURES

MEASURES OF EFFICIENCY	COMMUNICATION NETWORK		
	Wheel	Chain	Circle
Speed	1	2	3
Accuracy	1	2	3
Cost (least)	1	2	3
Role clarity	1	2	3
Satisfaction	2	3	1
Creativity	3	2	1
Adaptability	3	2	1

Source: R. K. Ready, *The Administrator's Job. Issues and Dilemmas*
(New York: McGraw-Hill Book Company, 1967), p. 34.

of ideas and creative problem solving. Yet it is likely that coordination will be impeded if we can generalize from the communication network research.

The structure of organization, patterns of communication, and the effect upon employee productivity are becoming increasingly better understood. For example, Thomas Peters conducted comprehensive analyses of organizations noted for their uncommonly effective management and arrived at a number of conclusions regarding the relationship of communication to creativity. He contends that innovation is fostered in environments which are not organizationally tidy. Almost always a creative product or idea needs a sponsor or "champion" to be successful. Somebody has to take risk in order to launch an idea. Moreover, such creative undertakings are likely to violate or cross over almost all formal lines of communication.[8] Peters and Waterman also find that excellent companies use a vast network of informal, open communications which includes the use of first names, an open door management policy handling complaints from anyone, continuing face-to-face interaction outside of the office, and a variety of physical arrangements and configurations that promote physical contact and interaction.[9]

It is apparent that the structure of the organization is important for communication flow and coordination. As noted in the communication network study, structure can be a significant determinant of employee satisfaction and creativity or role clarity, cost, speed, and accuracy. If improved communication and coordination are desired within the organization, then organization structure should be consistent with organizational purposes. In addition to structure considerations, the quality and quantity of communication is also important for effectiveness within the organization and external to it. Communication is enhanced when clear, simple

---

[8] Thomas J. Peters, "The Mythology of Innovation, or a Skunkworks Tale, Part II," *Stanford Magazine* (Stanford University Alumni Association, Fall 1983), pp. 11–19.

[9] Thomas J. Peters and Robert H. Waterman, Jr., *In Search of Excellence. Lessons from America's Best-Run Companies* (New York: Harper & Row, Publishers, Inc., 1982), pp. 119–25, 218–23.

language is used, when it is face-to-face, when informal and open interactions are encouraged and supported, when feedback is constant and exchange intense, and when good listening skills are used. Such listening skills include making the speaker as comfortable as possible, tuning in to what the other person is saying, giving undivided attention to the speaker, asking clarifying questions, and avoiding excessive talking.

COMMUNICATING WITH THE PUBLIC

Despite many excellent public school programs and accomplishments, public perception of school quality remains low. Hodgkinson, for example, provides compelling evidence to support his conclusion:

> The U.S. public education system is a remarkably successful institution. It is designed for every student, and yet its very best students are as good as those of any nation in the world. It provides a high return on dollars invested. The future of America depends on investment in human resources. American public schools are obviously the best place to find the highest return on that investment.[10]

Yet when Gallup asked U.S. citizens in the 1984 sixteenth annual national poll on education, the questions "How about the public schools in the nation as a whole? What grade would you give the public school nationally—A, B, C, D, or Fail?" The response was: 2 percent, A; 23 percent B; 49 percent, C; 15 percent, D; 4 percent, F.[11] How were such opinions developed?

Perhaps the most profound and influential indictment of public schools is that rendered in 1983 by the National Commission on Excellence in Education. They stated

> We report to the American people that while we can take justifiable pride in what our schools and colleges have historically accomplished and contributed to the United States and the well-being of its people, the educational foundations of our society are presently being eroded by a rising tide of mediocrity that threatens our very future as a nation and a people.
>
> If an unfriendly foreign power had attempted to impose on America the mediocre educational performance that exists today, we might well have viewed it as an act of war.[12]

Nearly every major print and broadcast news media in the country highlighted the commission's report. It is probable that this report, and others similar,

---

[10] Harold L. Hodgkinson, "What's Still Right with Education," *Phi Delta Kappan,* 64, no. 4 (December 1982), 235.

[11] George H. Gallup, "The 16th Annual Gallup Poll of the Public's Attitudes Toward the Public Schools," *Phi Delta Kappan,* 66, no. 1 (September 1984), 26.

[12] The National Commission on Excellence in Education, *A Nation at Risk: The Imperative for Educational Reform,* A Report to the Nation (Washington, D.C.: U.S. Department of Education, 1983), p. 5.

will result in increased public support for schools. It has resulted in a reexamination of curriculum standards and a significant quest for improvement in school administration, teachers, and teaching. Yet it is possible that the report will reinforce the views of those critical of the public schools, sway negatively the opinions of the undecided, and lower the opinions of those who had formerly given the schools high marks.

This is not to suggest that areas of public education are not in need of improvement. But much is right with public education and exemplary programs can be identified throughout the nation. What often captures the attention of news media, however, are not positive features of public schools or other agencies but those that are negative. Why? Simply because the general public is attracted by the unusual, the sensational, the scandal, the controversial. Such news sells newspapers and attracts TV viewers.

The educational community itself must accept much of the blame for the public's low perception of public schools. It has not generally attempted to communicate with the broader community to determine and address public concerns. Nor has it endeavored systematically to inform citizens of school successes and problems.

School-community communication is important not only for informational purposes but also for closing the social distance between the school and community.[13] School-community communication is enhanced when community characteristics are known and appropriate mechanisms are used to transmit messages. Included among them are individual face-to-face contact, informational meetings, and the mass media. Selection of the appropriate mechanism will depend on whether the purpose is to reduce selective listening or retention, to provide expert feedback, or to maximize communication scope.[14]

From another vantage point, Miles and Bowles argue that successful home-school-community relations programs focus on the child. Moreover, it is of great value to identify influential community leaders and garner their support in order to increase the probability of the successful development and implementation of new or innovative school programs.[15]

Schools have recognized that most states require students to attend school until they reach age sixteen. Thus, in substantial measure schools have had a captive audience. The necessity of "selling" the school or maintaining a public relations program has been a low priority. Fortunately, this view is changing. More schools are beginning to recognize the importance of well planned public relations.

---

[13] For a conceptual framework that is useful in examining needed school-community communication linkages, see Eugene Litwak and Henry J. Meyer, *School, Family and Neighborhood: The Theory and Practice of School-Community Relations* (New York: Columbia University Press, 1974).

[14] Litwak, E., and Meyer, H., *Theory and Practice of School-Community Relations,* pp. 20–21.

[15] See William R. Miles and D. Dean Bowles, *Home-School-Community Relations as a Political Process: Four Exploratory Studies* (Madison: Wisconsin University, Research and Development Center for Cognitive Learning, April, 1975). ERIC ED 111106.

Definition and Purpose of Public Relations

Effective school public relations is a concerted and well orchestrated, two-way communication system. It is designed to bring about citizen awareness and understanding of school strengths, problems, and needs. It also serves to inform the school about community concerns and desires. Ultimately, its purpose is to build confidence in, and support for, schools. Public schools are supported by public tax dollars. The public has a need and right to know what is occurring in its schools. Schools have an obligation to inform them regularly.

In the past, school public relations efforts have often been unorganized, uncoordinated, and relatively ineffective. They have consisted primarily of local school site activities such as parent teacher association teas and fund raisers, and once-a-year back-to-school nights. These activities generally involve a relatively small number of students' parents who participate in greater numbers with the lower grades than with the higher ones.

School board meetings also provide a forum having the potential of attracting districtwide community representation and enhancing public relations. Yet relatively few citizens participate in board meetings, communicate in private with board officials, or have any success at influencing board decisions.[16] Board members are generally unrepresentative of the total community and are accused of being out of touch with community interests.[17] The future must remedy past mistakes if greater public awareness and support is to become evident.

Establishing the Public Relations Program

Three preconditions are important in initiating a school district public relations program: (1) clear school board policy; (2) understanding of public relations responsibilities; and (3) knowledge about the community.

School board policy. Effective school public relations programs begin with written school board policy. Such policy should make clear the board's intent to create an effective public relations program through which open two-way communication is maintained between the school and the various constituencies it serves. Program goals and objectives might advantageously include the board's commitment to: keep the public informed about school operation, strengths, weaknesses, and needs; elicit public opinion about community needs and how those needs can best be met; respond to public concerns honestly and with dispatch; designate district and school site responsibilities for public relations; specify (broadly) what and

[16] Harvey J. Tucker and L. Harmon Zeigler, *Professionals Versus the Public: Attitudes, Communication, and Response in School Districts* (New York: Longman, Inc., 1980), pp. 229–30.

[17] Shelly Weinstein and Douglas E. Mitchell, *Public Testimony on Public Schools,* National Committee for Citizens in Education, Commission on Educational Governance (Berkeley, Calif.: McCutchan Publishing Corporation, 1975), pp. 53–64; and Rodney J. Reed, "School Boards, the Community, and School Desegregation," *Journal of Black Studies,* 10, no. 2 (December 1982), 189–206.

how information will be collected and disseminated within and outside the school district; and appraise public relations efforts.

Public relations responsibilities. All school personnel have an active role in the public relations program. As elected officials, school board members have an obligation to maintain relationships with representative groups of the entire community, establish open school board meetings, and implement procedures whereby public concerns can be brought to their direct attention.

One of the most important functions of the school superintendent is to establish and maintain relations with the public. More than any other school official, he or she represents the local school system. It is to the superintendent that questions pertaining to every facet of school operation program and quality will ultimately be addressed. It is essential, therefore, that two-way communication exists between the superintendent and all segments of the community and representatives of the mass communication media.

Assuming a medium- to large-size district, day-to-day operation and coordination of public relations programs are inefficient without an office of public relations. Minimally, this office is staffed by a coordinator or director and a secretary. Working closely with the school superintendent, this office, for example, is responsible for conducting public polls or surveys, preparing and disseminating news releases, and maintaining direct contact with reporters of the news media. In addition, the office has a responsibility to ferret out news from throughout the school district that is worthy of exposure. Without question, it is mandatory that the director of public relations be knowledgeable about education, skilled in communication techniques, and informed regarding use of mass communication media. A small district may not be able to justify such a specialized operation. In such instances, responsibility falls even more heavily upon the superintendent.

The most immediate and direct contact with the school system, for most parents of school-age children, is the local school. Thus, a school principal assumes an important role in public relations. Immediate parental and community concerns regarding, for example, student classroom placement, school discipline, school curricular and extracurricular activities will be directed to the principal. Consistent with school board policy, it is highly desirable that the principal solicit and maintain honest and open relations with all segments of the school's community, respond to public concerns, and coordinate staff public relations efforts. Providing feedback to the central administration regarding local public relations problems and successes is a further important activity of the principal, if the overall school district's public relations efforts are to be viable. It is also incumbent upon the principal to transmit newsworthy items and activities to the district public relations office for wide dissemination.

Instructional and noninstructional staff have a special role in public relations. They, perhaps more than others, are in direct contact with students who carry the message of school conditions and practices to parents and relatives. Not only do school staff members interact with students, but each also associates with and conveys messages about the school to friends, neighbors, and members of various civic, professional, and social organizations to which they belong. Clear public relations procedures for school staff ought to be established at the school site. The intent of the district to maintain and foster good public relations must be well known, and staff techniques for effective relations with students and the public must be developed and understood. Staff, whom parents and the public may encounter in contacting the school via telephone or in person—for example, receptionists and secretaries—require particular attention.

Survey the community.   Before the school can communicate effectively with the public it will find community analysis to be extremely useful. In so doing, answers to questions such as the following are sought: What school issues are important? What educational needs exist? What school perceptions are held? What are community population characteristics? What organized and representative community groups exist? What are the centers of community power? Who are community leaders? What are existing print, radio, television, and organizational communications media? What publication philosophy or policy do they embrace? What is the publication schedule and circulation of each?

Answers to such questions can be acquired through use of periodic community surveys or polls and coordinated by the public relations office or district public relations designee. External resources may be used to conduct the survey. School staff or a school parent advisory group may also be used. Community surveys provide a wealth of information essential to the success of the public relations effort.

Public Relations Communications Media

If schools are to provide information to the community and its staff as well as reduce community concerns, then the use of a variety of communication media increases the probability of reaching a wide audience. These include but are not limited to newspapers, radio, television, and school publications.

Newspapers.   Newspapers are the major source of information about public schools. Information used to judge the quality of public schools by a majority of respondents in the fifteenth, and very likely the sixteenth, national Gallup poll on the public's attitudes toward public schools came from newspapers.[18] Using the newspaper effectively, then, is essential to the success of the public relations program. Several points are instructive.

Have a story that is newsworthy. School information that coincides with the expressed needs and interests of the community, as revealed in surveys, can provide the basis for a news release. Other school activities that are important may serve that purpose. These might include school closures, curtailment of school pro-

---

[18] George H. Gallup, "The 15th Annual Gallup Poll of the Public's Attitudes Toward the Public Schools," *Phi Delta Kappan*, 65, no. 1 (September 1983), 42–43.

grams, changes in graduation requirements, awards received for exemplary school programs, and truly outstanding and recognized student achievement.

Prepare a news release of current information or coming events, and be cognizant of the particular newspaper's philosophy. Know the audience for whom the release is intended. Use clear, direct, and concise language. Answer the basic who, what, where, when, and why questions early in the release. Provide glossy 5 × 7 inch black and white photographs, which are clearly identified. If an important speech or report is to be given, then attach an advance copy. Include the name and telephone number of a contact person. Other considerations for writing a news release are displayed in Table 14.2.

Mere submission of a news release to a newspaper will not automatically ensure publication. Timeliness of the release, its importance, and available space are conditions considered by news editors. The likelihood of publication may be enhanced when a close relationship is established with newspaper reporters, when honest and reliable information is provided the newspaper, and when the public relations office is available to answer, or secure the answer to, questions pertaining to the schools or news release.

Radio and television. Radio and television stations have a community responsibility. Public service announcements are made daily. In addition, both media provide current local and national news. Both use pretaping, remote and live broadcasting procedures. School news that is timely, important, and about which stations receive well-written news releases may result in coverage of the school event. Radio is less expensive than television news coverage and, thus, may be somewhat easier to use to convey school news or programs.

Radio stations have a more targeted audience than television. Know what audience the radio station serves and the format used. Prepare the news release or announcement accordingly. Many radio stations have call-in shows which provide an excellent opportunity for the public to discuss school issues with, say, the school superintendent. Local television stations also may have round table discussions pertaining to important school issues. Some TV programs may provide an opportunity for telephone calls or advance written questions to be answered. Other television and radio program formats useful to schools are interviews, sportcasts, cultural programs, and demonstrations.

Be aware of radio and television station policies and procedures in requesting air time or submitting news items. Checklists for preparing a public service announcement for radio or television are presented in Table 14.3. Types of broadcasts available to schools are shown in Table 14.4. Guidelines for writing a radio or television broadcast are provided in Table 14.5.

School publications. For both internal information and external public relations purposes, a variety of school publications are useful. These include newspapers, superintendent bulletins, employee news, individual handbooks for parents, students, and faculty, annual reports, school district descriptive brochures, and student yearbooks.

Table 14.2 HOW TO WRITE A NEWS RELEASE

News writing is an art but it is also a skill that can be learned. Most school publicists can be assumed to have had a good basic training in the use of English. The fundamentals of composition learned in the usual school courses apply here. To write a good news release you need an outline, an introduction, a body and a conclusion. The essence of good writing for the press is brevity and conciseness. Read the stories in any good newspaper—particularly the papers published in your own town. Note how they put the meat of the story in the opening paragraph and follow it with less important details. Note the economy of words with which the stories are written. See how a general style of writing seems to be common to the better papers.

RULES FOR EDITORIAL CONTENT

Keep the story simple—don't try to *pad* it.

Use short sentences and short paragraphs.

Try to write as though you were talking to a single person.

Use only the ideas and the vocabulary that will be understood by the average newspaper reader. Keep away from professional terms such as "frame of reference," "core curriculum," "implementation," "homogenous grouping" and similar phrases.

Stick to facts—don't editorialize. If you must have an opinion expressed, quote somebody in direct authority.

Avoid "a spokesman for the board" or "an informed source." Use names.

Use specific dates, not "yesterday," "today," or "tomorrow."

Avoid glowing adjectives and superlatives. They belong to the commercial advertisers.

Check your story to see if it answers the editor's inevitable questions, "who, what, when, how and why."

Read your story again. Can you cut it?

The first paragraph should focus attention on the time, nature, and extent of the event.

MECHANICAL STANDARDS

Use department stationery for all copies on letter size paper (8½ × 11).

Use one side only.

Type your release, using double spacing to provide room for editorial changes.

Start your story about one third of the way down the page to leave room for the editor to write in a headline or other directions; include your own descriptive headline above the article.

Leave a fair margin on each side of the copy.

Number each page, if more than one is used.

Don't break a paragraph at the bottom of a page.

At the end of each page of a multiple-page story type "MORE." At the end of the story type —30—. All newspaper offices know what these symbols mean.

Type an original and three copies of each page used.

Staple each complete article together; submit all three to the Department Chairman.

Source: The Public Information Department of the Port Jefferson, New York, schools. Reproduced in Gloria Dapper, *Public Relations for Educators* (New York: Macmillan, Inc., 1964), pp. 59–61.

Again, know the audience for which the publication is intended. Target the information and the level of language. Concise and understandable language should be used. Strive for an attractive and appealing format. Use photographs, graphs, charts, and illustrations as appropriate. The adage "one picture is worth a thousand words" still holds. Edit, reedit, and edit again. School publications reflect the quality of the school and provide a link with the public—ensure that the link is positive.

Table 14.3 CHECKLISTS FOR PREPARING A RADIO OR TELEVISION PUBLIC SERVICE ANNOUNCEMENT

Radio

1. What format does the station require? Live, interview spots? Prerecorded messages? Scripts for their personnel to read?
2. How long should the PSAs last? Ten, 20, 30, 40, or 60 seconds?
3. Who will write the copy? Should you just submit the information, or attempt to write a script that producers will then edit?
4. Will the station provide production services, such as sound effects or background music? Should you bring tapes?
5. How much lead time (time between first notice and requested air date) do they require? Two weeks or longer?

TV

1. Who will appear on screen—you or a station announcer?
2. Do you need to prepare a script or will the station take your information and do the writing?
3. Will the station want to dramatize your message?
4. Can they use background video footage of your activity?
5. Will the station provide production services such as remote film crews, studio effects, graphics?
6. If you are providing videotape, what size do they need: ¾", 1", 2"?
7. Can they use 35mm color slides, or 8x10 matte (dull) finish photographs? Should you restrict pictures to horizontal images?

Talk Show or Interview Guests (Radio and TV)

1. How long will you be on the air?
2. Does the host/interviewer need preparatory material, such as info sheets, biographic sketch, copy of book or pamphlet, list of questions and answers?

Source: Jane Freundel Levey, *If You Want Air Time* (Washington, D.C.: National Association of Broadcasters, 1983), p. 13.

Table 14.4 TYPES OF BROADCASTS AVAILABLE TO SCHOOLS

TYPE	PURPOSE	ADVANTAGE	PRODUCTION
Mention of schools on other programs	Maintain awareness of educational services and benefits	Utilizes audience already built for that program	Provide program master of ceremonies with facts
Items in newscasts	To inform about school events, actions, or achievements	Newscast audience is large, news copy is relatively easy to prepare and distribute	Items must "sell themselves" because of their news value. Reporters appreciate additional information. Use film clips for TV.
Spot announcements	To inform public of current school events	Copy is relatively easy to write and distribute. Most stations will use spots	Prepare written copy for 10, 20, or 30 second announcements. Some stations will use recorded announcements. Visual essential for TV
Occasional programs in established series	To acquaint public with a service, benefit, or need	Benefits from continuing audience for the series. Does not commit district to continued production	Requires moderate to considerable production time
Program series	To enlarge public understanding of school functions and accomplishments	High-quality programs build audience as the series continues	Major undertaking, practical only after working relationships are well established and school personnel are prepared to expend substantial amounts of effort

Source: Gordon McCloskey, *Education and Public Understanding,* 2nd ed. (New York: Harper & Row, Publishers, Inc., 1967).

Table 14.5 WRITING FOR RADIO AND TELEVISION BROADCASTING: GUIDELINES

- KISS—that's an acronym for the first rule: Keep It Simple, Stupid (or sweetheart, or silly, or . . .). That only means omit the jargon, long sentences, and ten dollar words. Words for broadcasting are to be spoken, and few of us speak in mile-long sentences, let alone pay attention to them.

- Grab the listener's attention right away. Don't back into the point of your message with a long preamble. Listeners will tune out before you get to the point.

- Use the active voice. Nothing sounds flatter and more boring than a message filled with passive verbs: Write: "Visit the Hometown Boys Club and see how new lighting improves night games," rather than "If you are to visit Hometown Boys Club you may get to see the improvements that were effected in the night games as a result of the installation of new lighting equipment.

- Keep verbs in the present tense if at all possible.

- Watch out for cliches.

- Vary the lengths of your sentences. Long sentences need not be avoided completely, if they're relieved occasionally by short sentences. Very short sentences.

- Minimize the number of prepositional phrases (why not say "my aunt's pen" instead of "the pen of my aunt), and compound sentences (those linked with "and"). One idea per sentence is plenty.

- Vary the way you start sentences. A simple check for "pet words or phrases" after you finish writing will reveal tiresome repetitions.

- Don't embroider unnecessarily. If he "said" it, that's fine. Few subjects "confide" or "share" when interviewed, and these two words are misleading and overused.

- Be informal. If you say "don't" then why write "do not"?

- Include phonetic spellings of any names or foreign words that may be unfamiliar to the broadcaster.

- Localize. If you are part of a national organization, try to refer to your hometown often.

- Don't abbreviate. Except for Mr., Mrs., and Ms., abbreviations slow down the reader. Spell out Doctor, Street, Boulevard, Highway, August, et cetera.

Source: Jane Freundel Levey, *If You Want Air Time* (Washington, D.C.: National Association of Broadcasters, 1983), pp. 14–15.

Other communication media. Several other opportunities to communicate with the public exist in most school districts. Exhibits of student work (such as art) provide an excellent public communication opportunity. Students' artwork may be displayed in the lobbies of frequently used buildings, airport waiting rooms, and corporate headquarters. Church bulletins and civic and professional organizational newsletters also provide excellent opportunities to communicate with the public. Letters to the editor of local newspapers, local magazines, and weekly or monthly publications in a foreign language aimed at limited English-speaking individuals are other communications media that should not be overlooked.

A CURRENT EFFORT

Schools increasingly recognize the importance of public relations programs.[19] An example of a countywide program is to be found in Los Angeles County, California. That county recently initiated a public relations campaign entitled "Public Education: A Sound Investment in America." It is aimed at making school successes, needs, and problems known to local citizens and politicians in order to enhance school confidence. Specifically, the campaign is a two-way effort designed "to (1) identify the information needs of the many different kinds of people in Los Angeles County; and (2) attempt to meet those needs."[20] Local boards of education within Los Angeles County may endorse the campaign and contribute to the following campaign objectives:

1. Encourage schools to improve programs and instruction for students and citizens.

2. Help citizens understand the value of education in our democratic society.

3. Increase the personal experiences parents and nonparents have with the schools.

4. Increase educators' public relations awareness and skills.

5. Increase opportunities for the media to present a balanced view of the nation's schools.

6. Encourage and enable educators to become effective leaders for education in their communities.[21]

Several major educational organizations participated in the development of the campaign theme and its objectives. They included the American Association of School Administrators, National School Boards Association, the National Education Association, and the American Federation of Teachers. These groups have endorsed the campaign and encouraged participation of their members.

[19] For an overview of several school public relations efforts, see Anne Bridgman, "Schools Wooing Public with Media Campaigns," *Education Week*, IV, no. 6 (October 10, 1984), 1, 21.

[20] Bob Grossman, "Regionalized Communications in Action: Los Angeles County's Public Confidence Campaign," *Thrust for Educational Leadership*, 13, no. 1 (September 1983), 11.

[21] Grossman, B., "Regionalized Communications," p. 13.

SUMMARY

Communication is necessary to make our thoughts and feelings known to others. Messages may be verbal, nonverbal, or written. Communication is most effective when it is two way. That is, the message from the sender is encoded and then transmitted through an appropriate medium to a receiver who decodes it and responds. Feedback is used to ensure the accuracy of messages sent and received.

Internal communication in organizations assumes formal and informal dimensions. Formal communications are necessary for direction and control. Informal communications emerge from personal needs among organizational staff. The latter is frequently referred to as the "grapevine," and may contribute to message clarification and provide an opportunity to gauge worker reaction to proposed policies. Unfortunately, it also may contribute to the perpetuation of rumors.

External school communications can be viewed as public relations, which is an important communication device for building school support. It is a two-way process that seeks to inform the public and elicit information concerning community desire for information and needs. Public relations campaigns are not last minute episodes intended to gloss over school or school district weaknesses and mistakes. Rather, they are systematic, sustained, and honest communication efforts.

SELECTED READINGS

Goldhaber, Gerald M., *Organizational Communication*. Dubuque, Iowa: William C. Brown Co., Publishers, 1974.

Kinder, Jack A., *School Public Relations: Communicating to the Community*. Fastback 182 Bloomington, Ind.: The Phi Delta Kappa Educational Foundation, 1982.

Kindred, Leslie W., Don Bagin, and Donald R. Gallagher, *The School and Community Relations*. Englewood Cliffs, N.J.; Prentice-Hall, Inc., 1976.

Lesly, Philip, *How We Discommunicate*. New York: AMACOM, A Division of American Management Associations, 1979.

Litwak, Eugene, and Henry J. Meyer, *School, Family and Neighborhood: The Theory and Practice of School-Community Relations*. New York: Columbia University Press, 1974.

National School Public Relations Association, *Building Confidence for Your Schools*. Arlington, Va.: NSPRA, 1978.

National School Public Relations Association, *Basic School PR Kit*. Arlington, Va.: NSPRA, 1980.

Tucker, Harvey J., and L. Harmon Ziegler, *Professionals Versus the Public: Attitudes, Communication, and Response in School Districts*. New York: Longman, Inc., 1980.

LEADERSHIP FOR NONINSTRUCTIONAL SCHOOL FUNCTIONS
chapter 15

In the day-to-day operation of schools, a number of services designed for student welfare and safety are essential. They are adjuncts to the instructional program and include student personnel services—guidance and counseling, individual and group testing, maintenance of student records and information services, educational and vocational placement, follow-up assessment—school transportation, health, and food services. In addition to these services, appropriate educational facilities must be procured and maintained to ensure that students have a supportive learning environment. Responsibility for these noninstructional areas resides with administrators at both school district and site levels. Policy direction, however, is established by the school board. This chapter discusses these noninstructional but important school functions.

STUDENT PERSONNEL SERVICES

Providing for student welfare, accounting for their attendance, and maintaining and reporting information regarding their school performance to parents (and other individuals and agencies as appropriate) are essential school administrative functions referred to as student personnel services. Within the boundaries of the student personnel function are activities such as (1) guidance; (2) health services; (3) food service programs; and (4) student transportation. Taken together, these noninstructional services contribute to students' well-being and success.

Guidance Programs

Guidance is a broad concept embracing a variety of planned and specialized student services aimed at better integrating the student in the school setting. Guidance supplements instructional programs through counseling services—including individual and group testing for diagnostic and placement purposes—monitoring and documenting student attendance and school performance for purposes of assistance and reporting, educational and vocational placement, and student follow-up activities.

Counseling services. Educational, personal, social, career and vocational counseling is a major component of the guidance program in most school districts. While a few large elementary schools may use counselors, they are usually assigned to secondary schools. Ideally, the major duties and responsibilities of counselors are

1. To be knowledgeable of and sensitive to individual and group differences associated with cultural, ethnic, or socioeconomic background.
2. To discuss appropriate student-related concerns with knowledgeable and relevant school staff and parents.
3. To provide academic advising and assistance with educational placement or course selection.
4. To assist students with vocational and career planning.
5. To work with students and staff to create and maintain a suitable school environment for learning and growth.
6. To provide personal and social counseling and training to student, school staff, parents, and community groups.

Whether counselors perform these duties and responsibilities is contingent on several factors. Chief among them is the number of students assigned to a single full-time counselor. The student–counselor ratio recommended by the American School Counselor Association is 250 students for each full-time counselor.[1] In many school districts, however, as many as 500 students may be assigned to a single full-time counselor.

Another factor that affects a counselor's ability to provide comprehensive services is the program support received from school administrators. It is a site administrator's responsibility to maintain a supportive school environment in which a counseling program can thrive. Student–counselor ratios must be reasonable. The organization of the counseling program must ensure that each student has a counselor with sufficient time for consultation. Administrators have a duty to recog-

---

[1] "American School Counselor Association Policy Statement," in George E. Hill, *Management and Improvement of Guidance* (New York: Appleton-Century-Crofts, 1965), p. 122.

nize the importance of the counselor's role and further ensure adequate facilities, finance, and scheduling for counseling activities.

The success of a counseling program is closely related to the skills and abilities of counselors. Obviously, counselors must be well trained in the use of counseling techniques. In addition, and very important, counselor selection and assignment to compatible schools and students may serve to increase their success. Not only must counselors understand and appreciate student values, life experiences, cultural and ethnic backgrounds, but they must also be able to translate these background factors into effective counseling practices.[2]

In addition to the school counselor, counseling services are performed by school psychologists, psychiatrists, psychometrists, social workers, and classroom teachers. Services of specialists, however, supplement ongoing counseling activities and beneficially occur on a student-referral basis.

School psychologists specialize in diagnosing learning and school difficulties resulting from students' emotional or personality problems. They analyze and make judgments regarding student performance and school adjustment through use of aptitude, achievement, personality and other diagnostic inventories, students' cumulative records, interviews, and anecdotal data. They also engage in individual and group therapy and provide guidance to school staff and parents working with students experiencing emotional or personality difficulty.

Psychiatrists may be retained by school districts to provide mental health services to students. *Psychometrists* provide leadership and assistance to counselors in understanding individual and group testing and measurement. Test and measurement data are used variously for purposes of student placement, diagnosis, aptitude and interest determination, and to assess student performance and progress. Psychometrists additionally interpret test and measurement results for use by counselors and other appropriate school staff.

The counseling referral staff may also include *school social workers*. These individuals work closely with parents to assist them, generally, in establishing supportive educational and social home environments for students. They coordinate school and community resources to ameliorate student problems that affect school performance. In addition, school social workers may provide assistance to single parents who must work and, therefore, are unavailable to provide adequate student home supervision or who are unable to arrange for an educationally and socially supportive home environment. Given the escalation in the number of single parent families and the comparatively low school performance of children in these families, it may be that the role of social workers in the school setting will become increasingly more important.[3]

---

[2] For discussions of the importance of understanding student cultural backgrounds and life experiences for effective counseling practices, see Derald W. Sue, *Counseling the Culturally Different: Theory and Practice* (New York: John Wiley, 1981).

[3] Single parent families grew from 11 percent in 1970 to 19 percent in 1979. Evidence indicates that children in single parent families have more discipline problems and lower academic performance scores than children from families in which both parents are present. See National Elementary Schools Staff Report, "One-parent families and their children: the school's most significant minority." *Principal,* 60, no. 1 (September 1980), 31–37.

Considerable student counseling is accomplished by *classroom teachers*. In fact, they are often the most effective counselors. By virtue of the fact that teachers generally are in closer regular contact with students than any other school staff member, it is logical that a certain amount of educational, vocational, and personal counseling occurs. This is particularly the case with students who are interested in the teachers' area of specialization and those who respond to the teachers' warmth, friendship, and concern. Students seek out such teachers for advice, counsel, and support. Teachers are in a position to refer students to counselors for more specialized assistance and may work closely with the school counselor in enhancing student welfare. Teachers can and do establish natural links with students' parents; also they may work closely with parents in addressing student needs or problems.

Student records and information services.   From the time students register in the public school and until their departure, information regarding school performance, progress, attendance, accomplishments, difficulties, general parent and personal data, health, aptitude and interests, and school difficulties experienced is collected and maintained at the school site. Such information may be used to assist school staff in providing appropriate classroom placement, experiences, and supportive services to students. It is used to provide information to parents, educational and social agencies, and employers. Attendance information is used to determine school facilities and staffing needs, and state funding levels.

Student information typically is retained in a cumulative record folder or system. Types of records maintained here may include the following: permanent record card—name, date of birth, sex, home address and telephone number, name of parents, their occupation, work address and telephone number, date of school entry, date of graduation or termination; health information—immunizations, physical and medical examinations, special health conditions; test data—aptitude and interest, achievement; awards received in and out of school; educational and career plans; anecdotal information submitted by school staff; and school attendance.

An important use of student records is to convey to parents their children's school performance. This may take the form of teacher- or administrator-parent face-to-face or telephone conferences, or letters. With respect to course grades, however, parents are informed periodically through use of report cards, which may be mailed directly to them or given to students to deliver. When transmitted through students, some feedback to the school is desirable—that the parent has reviewed the child's school performance (as indicated through grades or marks and teacher comments).

School academic, social, and test performance data are important for classroom placement and classification within the school, or when transferring to another school. Such data are also important for grade promotion and graduation, and are necessary for consideration for entry into higher educational institutions and for employment purposes.

As stated earlier, student attendance monitoring and accountability are important school functions. Public school funding is based on student attendance

(Chapter Five). In states using average daily attendance (ADA),[4] schools must compile accurate attendance statistics daily. In addition to this function, attendance monitoring is important because student absences and tardiness may mask more fundamental personal, home, or school problems.

Recording student attendance is typically a responsibility of classroom teachers. Day-to-day classroom attendance procedures, however, can be facilitated through use of an automated system.[5] In addition to the teacher checking attendance, many large school districts employ clerks and attendance officers to monitor student attendance, verify absences, assess causes of unexcused absences, strive for the eradication of these causes, and generally assist in enforcing school attendance laws as appropriate. A related component of student attendance is the collection of school registration and enrollment data. Compilation of these data is essential in planning for adequate school plant utilization, staffing, and student transportation.

In compiling and releasing information from student records, administrators and school staff must be cognizant of the provisions of the Family Right to Privacy Act.[6] As discussed in Chapter Six, this act provides parents of students under eighteen years of age and students eighteen and over the right to inspect school records and challenge information contained in those records. Further, except under certain specific circumstances, student information may not be released to outside agencies or individuals without written permission from the parent or student, whomever is appropriate.

Finally, a question naturally arises regarding how long records should be kept following student's high school graduation or termination, and for what purposes. In answering this question there is the obvious consideration of space and file maintenance. Files consume space and staff must be assigned to maintain them. This problem can be alleviated considerably through use of microfilming. Several advantages are evident in using this technique: microfilmed records occupy little space, can be kept indefinitely, and require little maintenance. Initial costs are offset by long-term advantages.

Student records can be kept for six or seven years and then destroyed. They may be kept for legitimate employment or educational reference requests, research, and follow-up studies. Information contained in stored student records should include only information considered to be important—for example, date of gradua-

---

[4] Average daily attendance is computed as follows:

$$\text{ADA} = \frac{\text{Total Student Days in Attendance} \times 100}{\text{Total Student Days Enrolled}}.$$

[5] Developed by Jet Propulsion Laboratory, California Institute of Technology, Pasadena, California, for use in John F. Kennedy High School, Sacramento, California, the Automated Attendance Accounting System permits teachers to punch into small remote terminals located in their classrooms absences by student identification number. This information is received by a central minicomputer. Printouts of student absences are subsequently produced. See William N. McGowan, "Crime Control in Public Schools: Space Age Solutions," *NASSP Bulletin,* 67, no. 372 (April 1973), 43–48; refer also to the Attendance Program developed by Specialized Data Systems, Oak Park, Ill., 1983.

[6] The Family Educational Rights and Privacy Act of 1974, 20 U.S.C. Sec. 1232g.

tion or schooling termination, curriculum studied, final grades, awards received, curricular and extracurricular activities.

Educational and vocational placement. The intent of educational and vocational placement is to assist students in making careful and judicious choices from among educational and vocational alternatives. Teachers, counselors, and administrators individually and collectively provide opportunities and participate in what should be well planned and carefully orchestrated activities designed for student educational and vocational exploration.

Educational and vocational placement activities are typically more pronounced in secondary than in elementary schools. Career and vocational exploration, however, may begin in elementary schools. At the high school level, the availability of centrally located college catalogs for student use is essential. Current and pertinent information pertaining to technical and vocational schools, other postsecondary educational opportunities, apprenticeship opportunities in vocational areas, financial aid, scholarships, grants, and awards available for further study are important for student academic and career planning. Further, data on careers and vocational fields as well as a collection of attention-getting biographies, descriptions, or even fiction that imaginatively captures the essence of a career or occupation should be conscientiously assembled and periodically updated so that students will have additional information on which to base decisions. They may even be inspired by such works.

Counselors assume primary responsibility for coordinating educational and vocational information-dissemination activities. These activities include career days, field trips to business and postsecondary educational institutions, and arranging for student work experiences. Further, they may conduct workshops and lead discussions on applying to colleges and universities and for employment, behavior during interviews, and résumé preparation. Acquainting school staff and students with educational and vocational information maintained at the school site and how to use it is a continuing counselor responsibility.

Teachers ideally cooperate closely with counselors in providing students with educational and vocational information and requirements. They may also assist students in exploring educational and career possibilities. In this regard, classroom bulletin boards may be used to display information on educational and vocational fields. Class projects focused on educational and vocational opportunities can provide significant information. Additionally, teachers may integrate educational and vocational perspectives into class discussions.

Support for educational and vocational information and placement activities is the site administrator's responsibility. He or she must allocate school space, equipment, and staff, and arrange school schedules to encourage and permit student participation in these vital activities. Site administrators have the additional responsibility of identifying and soliciting community participation and locating educational and vocational resources necessary to augment the school program.

Maintaining current and comprehensive information on career and vocational options, as well as assisting students in making choices, consumes considerable staff time. Assistance in this area, however, can be provided through several computer-based guidance and counseling systems. These include: the Experimental Education and Career Exploration System (ECES), sponsored by International Business Machines Corporation's Advanced Systems Development Division;[7] the Counseling Information System (CIS), marketed by Follett Systems;[8] Program for Learning According to Needs (PLAN) developed by John C. Flanagan in cooperation with the American Institutes of Research, Westinghouse Learning Corporation, and twelve school districts located throughout the United States;[9] the System of Interactive Guidance and Information (SIGI), designed by Educational Testing Service;[10] the Career Information System (CIS), developed at the University of Oregon;[11] and DISCOVER, developed by the American College Testing Program.[12]

Follow-up studies. Guidance program effectiveness can be determined through student follow-up studies. Such studies enable judgments to be made regarding appropriateness of students' educational and vocational experiences. They inform school or staff about decisions that affect students individually or collectively. They also provide a basis for examining students' educational and vocational postsecondary school choices in relation to in-school experiences. Finally, they support school program and guidance services change, moderation, or stability.

Data collected through student, faculty, parent, and employer surveys constitute an unparalleled source of information for assessing the appropriateness of school experiences and actions. Questionnaire and interview data from postsecondary educational institutions serve to gauge the adequacy of school curriculum offerings and subject matter coverage. These data are useful not only for school site program assessment but also for school district planning and budget cycles described in Chapter Eleven.

STUDENT TRANSPORTATION SERVICES

Providing transportation services for students can be a necessary and expensive school function. It is a function that, for some districts, may become even more important for several reasons. First, where enrollments continue to decline, there

[7] Frank J. Minor, Roger A. Myers, and Donald E. Super, "An Experimental Computer-Based Educational and Career Exploration System," in *Perspectives on Vocational Development,* ed. John M. Whitley and Arthur Resnikoff (Washington, D.C.: American Personnel and Guidance Association, 1972), pp. 173–81.

[8] The Follett Educational Corporation, to which Follett Systems is attached, is located in Millbrae, California. For a description of the Counseling Information System, see John W. Loughary, Murray Tondow, and Calvert W. Bowman, "The Counseling Information System 9/10," *Personnel and Guidance Journal,* 49, no. 3 (1970), 145–46.

[9] Westinghouse Learning Corporation. *PLAN: An Overview* (Palo Alto, Calif.: Westinghouse Learning Corporation, 1972).

[10] Educational Testing Service, (Princeton, N.J.: ETS, 1983). This program is designed for two and four year college students. It is also available at any ETS Regional Office.

[11] Career Counseling Center (Eugene, Oreg.: University of Oregon, 1983).

[12] DISCOVER CENTER (Hunt Valley, Md.: American College Testing Program, 1983). This program is designed for college students.

will be fewer schools. School closing and consolidations will occur more frequently and hence, many students will have to travel further to attend school. Second, school desegregation mandates frequently require student busing across neighborhood lines. Third, many states have mandatory or discretionary legislative provisions requiring transportation services for private and parochial schools at public expense.[13]

Transportation costs have escalated. Fuel costs rose over 200 percent between 1978 and 1982. Bus purchase, rental, and maintenance costs have increased dramatically. Insurance rates continue to climb. Bus driver salaries and fringe benefits have become larger.[14] These costs can be expected to rise as inflation grows and material and labor costs multiply.

A school district's transportation system is shaped by several policy dimensions. As an initial step, boards should indicate their intent to provide transportation consistent with state statutes. Such statutes may make transportation mandatory, discretionary, or both.[15] For example, board policy may mandate transportation for elementary school children but make high school level transportation service optional.[16]

Distance Considerations

Board policy establishes distance from a student's home to the school site as a requisite for transportation service coverage. How distance from home to school is measured is an important consideration. For instance, measurement may be made using the nearest public road, passable highway, or road usually traveled. The importance of measurement procedure becomes apparent when viewed in relationship to district policy regarding maximum distances students are required to walk to school. Beyond this established distance, transportation is to be provided. Depending on the manner in which measurement is made, additional mileage may be added or subtracted from home to school routes.

Two additional transportation distance matters fall into the province of board policy. First, maximum distance from students' homes to school, for which transportation will be provided, is a crucial policy matter. Second, it is imperative that boards enact policy regarding how far students should walk from home to a school bus stop and in what weather conditions. In each instance of distance determination a measure of reasonableness should prevail.

[13] Mandatory statutory provisions for parochial pupil transportation exist in Delaware, Illinois, Indiana, Kansas, Maryland, Massachusetts, Michigan, Montana, New Hampshire, New Jersey, New York, Ohio, Oregon, Pennsylvania, Rhode Island, and Wisconsin. Permissive legislation can be found in California, Connecticut, Kentucky, Louisiana, Maine, New Mexico, North Dakota, and West Virginia. See *Law and the School Superintendent*, 2d ed. (Cincinnati, Ohio: National Organization on Legal Problems of Education, 1971), p. 127.

[14] See Kent Halstead, *Inflation Measures for Schools and Colleges.* (Washington, D.C.: National Institute of Education, 1983).

[15] Leroy J. Peterson, Richard A. Rossmiller, and Marlin M. Volz, *The Law and Pupil School Operation*, 2d ed. (New York: Harper & Row, Publishers, 1978), p. 376.

[16] *Japs v. Board of Education of Jefferson County, Ky.*, 291 S.W. 2d 825 (1956).

Establishing Bus Routes

Where school transportation is provided, bus routes, stops, and time schedules must be developed and communicated to pupils expected to use school transportation services—this can be time consuming. Fortunately, data processing systems provide valuable assistance. One such system, designed by Ecosystems, a division of Ecotran Corporation, Cleveland, Ohio, is used in the Richmond, Virginia, public schools. This on-line system provides for the following:

Maintaining an accurate data base

Assigning new students to the transportation program

Modifying the initial transportation program

Maintaining administrative control of the transportation program[17]

This system also allows for general route and program maintenance. Thus, new routes can be added, bus assignments for routes changed, and route arrival and departure times to and from school shifted forward or backward to allow for better coordination.[18] The system further permits bus routes to be displayed and printed for distribution.

Another data processing system is the Vehicle Scheduling Program developed by the International Business Machines Corporation. This system permits an analysis of distances between road and street points in a geographic area and provides printouts of bus routes. Bus travel time is calculated, bus stops indicated, number of students per bus furnished, and other pertinent information provided.[19]

Uses of Transportation Service

Transportation supplied by school districts is generally used to convey students to and from schools within prescribed limits. This includes transportation for school desegregation purposes, to special emphasis or magnet schools, and transportation for field trips and extra or cocurricular activities—for example, transporting a high school band to performance sites. State statutes may indicate the extent to which public monies can be used to defray extracurricular activity transportation costs.

School boards may be authorized to provide transportation for school attendance in another school district. Statutory provisions are necessary to establish such authorization. Out-of-district transportation has been sanctioned when schools in

---

[17] "Richmond Public Schools' Transportation Department Goes On-Line," *School Business Affairs,* 48, no. 8 (July 1982), 38–39.

[18] *Ibid.*

[19] IBM Vehicle Scheduling Program No. 5734 X M5 (Armonk, N.Y.: International Business Machines, Inc., available through IBM Branch Offices, 1983); also, see James C. Edwards, "California's Computerized Pupil Transportation Systems," *School Business Affairs,* 49, no. 7 (July 1983), 48–49.

another district are more accessible,[20] and when the quality of education was believed to be better and in a student's best interest in a nearby district.[21]

When Transportation Is Not Provided

Districts may be required to reimburse parents for transporting their child to schools in outside districts if local transportation is not provided.[22] Where state statutes so indicate, school boards may elect to reimburse parents or supply money for transporting students who qualify under board policy rather than provide school bus service.[23] In some instances, parents may be required to pay part of the transportation cost.[24] However, when parents have to transport their children to nearby districts because district schools have been closed due to a lack of students, under state statute, boards may be compelled to provide a transportation allowance.[25]

Responsibilities of School Bus Drivers

Bus drivers are responsible for the safety and conduct of students during bus entry, exit, and transit. Drivers have a further duty to be familiar with and to observe all traffic safety laws. Awareness and understanding of these laws can be demonstrated through written and driving tests.

Administrative Responsibilities

Purchase and maintenance of school buses or entering into contractual agreements for student transportation services are responsibilities of district level administrators.[26] Additional district responsibilities include hiring bus drivers and implementing a transportation data processing system. Overall transportation system coordination and control may be assigned to a director of transportation services or to an assistant superintendent. General policy regarding student behavior on buses and handling student, parent, or driver complaints should be formulated at the district level.

District level administrators have a duty to maintain the school's transportation system in compliance with federal Highway Safety Program No. 17. This legislation requires each state, in concert with its school districts, to establish a

---

[20] *Fitzpatrick* v. *Johnson,* 163 S.E. 908 (Ga. 1932).

[21] *Herman* v. *Medicine Lodge School District No. 8,* 71 N.W. 2d 323 (N.D. 1955).

[22] *Ibid.*; also, *Rysden* v. *School District No. 67 of Union County,* 58 P.2d 614 (Ore. 1936).

[23] See *Hopkins* v. *Yellow Cab Company,* 250 P.2d 330 (Cal. 1952); *Reich* v. *Dietz School District No. 16 of Grant County,* 55 N.W. 2d 638 (N.D. 1952).

[24] *Seiler* v. *Gelhar,* 209 N.W. 376 (N.D. 1926).

[25] See *Bender* v. *Palmer,* 48 N.W. 2d 65 (Neb. 1951).

[26] Guidelines and a sample contract for contracting with an outside firm for student transportation services can be obtained from the National School Transportation Association, P.O. Box 2639, Springfield, Va. 22152.

comprehensive pupil transportation safety program, and includes provisions regarding bus identification, transportation personnel training, and administrative practices. Highway Safety Program No. 17 is designed to reduce the occurrence of student injury and death while being transported in a school vehicle.[27]

At the school site, principals are primarily accountable for student transportation. He or she must ensure that students safely and efficiently enter and exit school vehicles, and that policies regarding student behavior on the bus are observed and enforced. Principals are the arbiters of student or driver complaints and should encourage productive use of student travel time on school vehicles, particularly when travel time is extended. Individual school administrators also are responsible for distributing bus schedules and routes to all appropriate students and parents.

STUDENT HEALTH EDUCATION AND SERVICES

Increasingly, a total health program including student health assessments, teaching of good health practices, and opportunities for student participation in a variety of contact and noncontact sports, as well as general physical education classes, is viewed as an integral part of the school program. Typically, the school health program is characterized by three foci: student health assessment, health education, and the school health environment. Given these three areas, a school health program should:

Assist student physical, social, and emotional growth

Assess student health and identify handicaps that may impede learning and healthy living

Assist in ameliorating health deficiencies

Reduce or eliminate communicable diseases in the school

Maintain and provide services for emergency illness and injury

Ensure adequate health facilities, supplies, and equipment in the school

Assist in establishing and maintaining a healthful school environment

Provide sex education programs

Provide drug, alcohol, and substance abuse educational programs

Provide medical referrals as appropriate

Provide information concerning health services available in the school and the community

Encourage good health habits and healthy living

In implementing these goals, school boards must decide whether a health staff will be provided by the school district or whether major health services will be con-

---

[27] U.S. Department of Transportation, National Highway Traffic Safety Administration, "Highway Safety Program Standard No. 17," *Federal Register,* 37, no. 89 (May 6, 1972). This legislation became effective in June 1972.

tracted for through outside providers. At a minimum level, it is desirable that a central office health administrator coordinate district health services. In addition, by assigning school nurses to individual sites to coordinate school health educational activities and to provide basic health services, many student health needs can be met.

School health education and services staff include: physicians, dentists, health educators, nurses, principals, teachers, school psychologists, school social workers, guidance counselors, parents, and community representatives. These individuals may constitute a health council for each school and provide guidance for the school's health program.

An integral component of school health services is students' routine medical examinations. These examinations consist of the following basic components: health history, including a record of immunizations, physical examination, vision screening, screening for hearing disorders, speech appraisal, dental health examination, growth records, posture appraisal, and special procedures—that is, use of laboratory tests and other special services for health appraisal.[28]

Another school health service function is rendering emergency aid for injury and illness. In this regard it is essential that the school principal and school nurse develop and disseminate to staff a well-organized set of health emergency procedures. Likewise, it is important that school staff know basic first aid and emergency care procedures. These procedures should include signed parental statements regarding pupil care in event of an emergency injury or illness. Such statements are invaluable and typically include name, address, and telephone number of family physician, hospitalization or health plan, parents' telephone number, names of other individuals to be contacted in an emergency situation, and any other essential health information. Effective emergency care procedures depend on having basic first aid supplies, equipment, and adequate facilities at the school site.

The intent of the schools' health education program is to furnish information that will assist students in making wise choices about their physical, emotional, and social well-being. Emphasis is placed on preventive health care. Although coordinated by the school nurse, a comprehensive health education program involves teachers and health care professionals. A complete health education curriculum is one that is coordinated with the district's director of health and the school health council described earlier.

Not to be minimized in the health education program is health safety. In this area it is critical that students and staff be instructed in the correct use and handling of chemicals in science laboratories, other school areas, and in storage rooms. Further, students must understand the safe use of equipment in gymnasiums, athletic programs and physical education, science laboratories, and vocational education shops.

Additionally, school health programs are concerned with environmental safety and sanitation. The maintenance of sanitary conditions in school restrooms, showers, swimming pools, cafeterias, and kitchens merits particular attention.

[28] Oliver E. Byrd, *School Health Administration* (Philadelphia, Pa.: W. B. Saunders Company, 1964), pp. 205–9.

FOOD SERVICES

A cornerstone of good health is proper diet and nutrition. Thus, food service provisions for students exist in virtually every public school. Food service policy, planning, and budgeting are generally coordinated at the district level. Food served in school cafeterias, however, may be prepared at the school site, in central kitchens and delivered to school sites, or food preparation, delivery, and service may be contracted for with outside catering firms. In some instances, a combination of these arrangements is desirable. Many school districts have found it more economical to engage outside catering firms to provide food to school sites than to do so themselves. Specialized institutional food preparation firms are often more efficient and may possess a level of food service management expertise difficult for a school district to match.

The purpose of the food service program is to provide economically feasible nutritious and well-prepared food for students. Recognizing the importance of food and student nutrition and the harsh reality that many students are unable to purchase lunch and may leave home for school attendance without breakfast, several federal assistance programs have been implemented. These include the National School Lunch Act of 1946[29] and the Child Nutrition Act of 1966.[30] Through these federal programs, economically disadvantaged students are provided breakfast, lunch, and nutritional snacks during the school day.

Whether food is prepared at the school site, only served there, or both, the principal assumes a major responsibility for general overview of the food service program. He or she may delegate administrative responsibility to a food supervisor who supervises other food service employees and shares a major responsibility for cafeteria and kitchen sanitation. Nevertheless, the principal is ultimately responsible for school sanitation and for supervising all school staff. Scheduling breakfast, lunch, and snack periods of sufficient duration and at times in which students can be comfortably and safely accommodated is a further principal responsibility. Student supervision during these periods is an important additional administrative requirement.

At the district level, a manager or director of food services provides overall food service coordination, budget preparation, and administration. Menu planning, ordering of food, cafeteria equipment, and supplies are additional expectations. This person also works closely with individual schools in food service planning and staffing. Where outside caterers are used, the district food coordinator, with assistance of the school business manager, prepares bid specifications. Whereas selection of an outside caterer is within the jurisdiction of the school board, critiques of bid submissions may be prepared for board review by the district food supervisor. Four additional food supervisor responsibilities are to be noted: (1) collection of pertinent student data; (2) preparation of federal grant materials; (3) recruiting and selecting food service personnel; and (4) conducting or arranging for their in-service training.

[29] National School Lunch Act, 42 U.S.C.A., sec. 1751-1769a.
[30] Child Nutrition Act of 1966, 42 U.S.C.A., sec. 1771-1787.

SCHOOL FACILITIES PLANNING

Building new school facilities and remodeling existing facilities are normal school district occurrences during periods of student enrollment growth or decline. Existing facilities become obsolete because of location and design; they become physically unsafe because of deterioration and age. Consequently, they must be replaced or remodeled. In either case a series of planning steps precedes actual construction.

Determining Needs

At the behest of the school board, immediate and long-range district building needs are determined. This is accomplished through annual surveys of existing buildings and facilities. Such surveys permit examination of structural and equipment wear, building and equipment operational efficiency, and student and educational program adequacy. Wear and tear on equipment and building materials are inevitable. Normal life expectancy of equipment and materials based on length of use can be calculated from manufacturers' specifications and engineering studies. This information serves as a replacement guide and as a basis for long-range planning. Visual inspection, however, by knowledgeable individuals is essential in making final building and equipment need determinations.

Building adequacy for students and the educational program are additional considerations in need determination. Student enrollment projections provide a basis for estimating space requirements with respect to both building size and location. A district's educational philosophy regarding class size and instructional arrangements also affects space needs. For example, open classrooms and open plan school concepts, if viewed as educationally desirable, create specific space needs which traditional classroom structures may not accommodate. Moreover, traditional school design may impede desired implementation of computer and foreign language learning laboratories. Finally, building adequacy is assessed in light of access and safety for handicapped students. Entry and exit arrangements—for wheelchair students or those on crutches—are important moral, policy, and legal considerations. Locker, restroom, water fountains, door styles, movement between floors, food and cafeteria service, and storage space for equipment used by handicapped students are other building adequacy concerns.

On the basis of periodic building need surveys, long-range plans can be prepared and capital outlay estimates made. School board action is required to adopt long- and short-range plans for building replacement, remodeling, and rehabilitation. Once plans are completed, the board must make a budgetary commitment and endeavor to secure and allocate necessary capital outlay funds. This may mean obtaining state funds or passing a bond issue to raise funds.[31] In both instances, but particularly in the latter case, public support is essential.

---

[31] Technical details regarding the financing of school capital outlay are provided in Walter I. Garms, James W. Guthrie, and Lawrence C. Pierce, *School Finance: The Economics and Politics of Education* (Englewood Cliffs, N.J.: Prentice-Hall, 1978).

Securing Public Support

Perhaps the most important ingredient in developing a successful school facilities program is securing public support. How this is accomplished will vary by school district. It is desirable that a broad-based citizens' group be established to review facilities' needs, provide planning advice, and interact continuously with school staff and the community as a whole.

Schools are supported by tax dollars. The quality of school facilities is in part a reflection of community desire. Where local board issues are required for building facilities, "selling" the public is not easy. Many citizens with and without public school children resist additional taxes for school facilities. A broad-based community group can assist in debating the issue of need and in generating community awareness and support.

Planning school facilities provides an excellent opportunity for school administrators, especially superintendents, and board members to engage the public in discussions about educational programs and physical arrangements necessary for program implementation. Here, agreement can be sought for school program goals and objectives. Alternatives can be explored. Staff needs can be specified. Facilities planning provides a marvelous vehicle for school community involvement.

Development of School Building Plans

Transformation of ideas into plans requires the services of an architect. It is desirable that this individual or firm be competent, creative, and of the temperament necessary to cooperate with a variety of school staff and public representatives. When a new school site is necessary, the architect can be helpful in determining its adequacy in relation to building desires. With or without an architect's assistance, new school site considerations will include size, population to be served, suitability for building, accessibility, surrounding environment, and cost.

The architect prepares preliminary plans and provides cost estimates. These estimates become the basis for a bond issue referendum or request for state funds. Final materials, equipment, design specifications, and working drawings are prepared with appropriate advice from school staff. Construction bids are obtained. A primary contractor is selected, and building initiated. Building progress and development are reviewed by the architect.

FACILITIES MAINTENANCE

Buildings and equipment must be properly maintained for efficient operation and extended wear as well as for health, safety, and psychological reasons. The schools' physical environment contributes to school climate and, subsequently, to the efficacy of teaching and learning. Several roles should be differentiated in considering school maintenance: school board, buildings and grounds supervisor or director, site administrators, and custodians.

School boards are obligated to seek sufficient funds for building maintenance and operation. This includes funds for maintenance supplies and equipment, replacement of worn and unsafe buildings and equipment, building and equipment repairs as necessary, and preventive maintenance. The board establishes maintenance personnel hiring requirements and staffing ratios. The number of maintenance staff may be determined in relationship to building square footage, number of students attending a school, grade level, number of rooms, and type of building. In addition, the board adopts a building maintenance policy to guide district action.

Determination and specification of maintenance procedures, equipment, and supplies are usually included within the portfolio of the school district supervisor or director of buildings and grounds. This individual frequently assumes responsibility for maintenance staff selection. Staff development and general supervision activities are other responsibilities.

Site administrators have authority for the overall maintenance and operation of the schools to which they are assigned. These administrators are the immediate supervisors of the building's custodial staff and are responsible for the thoroughness of their work. Custodial work schedules are planned and approved and work quality adjudicated. Maintenance supplies and equipment orders also ought to be authorized by site administrators.

Simply put, custodians and other maintenance personnel are responsible for cleaning the school and keeping the facility in good operating order. They are responsible for regular floor sweeping, mopping and waxing, furniture dusting and cleaning of windows and glass doors, walls, toilets, water fountains, and chalkboards. They are expected to dispose of trash, fix and replace window shades, make minor repairs, replace restroom supplies, and change light bulbs. Custodians must know how to operate the school's heating and ventilation system, be able to change electrical fuses, reset electrical circuit breakers, and be aware of the location of sources of electrical power, water, and major sewer lines. Custodians regularly inspect the condition of the building and its operational equipment. Repair and replacement needs should be reported to the school site administrator.

SUMMARY

There are several essential noninstructional components of the school program. These include student personnel, transportation, health, and food services. In addition, the quality of the educational facility contributes to the learning atmosphere. Thus, the school plant must be planned with care and well maintained. Primary school site responsibility for the administration of student services resides with the school principal; yet because of the nature of these services, district level directors or supervisors provide considerable assistance. School building construction, renovation, and remodeling require central office planning, and school board and community support. However, ensuring building maintenance should be a responsibility of the principal.

SELECTED READINGS

Abend, Allen C., Michael J. Bednor, Vica J. Froehlinger, and Yale Stengler, *Facilities for Special Education Services*. Reston, Va.: The Council for Exceptional Children, 1979.

American Association of School Administrators, *To Recreate a School Building— "Surplus" Space, Energy, and Other Challenges*. Arlington, Va.: American Association of School Administrators, 1976.

Byrd, Oliver E., *School Health Administration*. Philadelphia, Pa.: W. B. Saunders Company, 1964.

Castaldi, Basil, *Educational Facilities: Planning, Modernization, and Management* (2d ed.). Boston, Mass.: Allyn & Bacon, 1982.

Herr, Edwin L., *Guidance and Counseling in the Schools: The Past, Present, and Future*. Falls Church, Va.: American Personnel and Guidance Association, 1979.

Hummel, Dean L., and Charles W. Humes, *Pupil Services: Development, Coordination, Administration*. New York: Macmillan, 1984.

Sue, Derald W., *Counseling the Culturally Different: Theory and Practice*. New York: John Wiley, 1981.

THE CHALLENGE
TO THE PROFESSION

chapter 16

In the first chapter of this book, we emphasized the dynamic nature of America's systems of education. School reform movements ebb and flow in response to societal changes, and the interplay between proponents of three value streams—equity, efficiency, and liberty. At any point in time, concern for one of the three value themes may dominate public policy. However, there is seldom a time when there exists a complete absence of concern for the other two. Responding appropriately to public concern for the value then in ascendance, while not neglecting balanced consideration for the other two value dimensions, is one of the major challenges to the education profession.

The period between 1945 and 1980 was characterized by a substantial public policy effort to enhance equality of educational opportunity.[1] Progress was not always sustained and successes were not consistent throughout every region of the nation. Moreover, advocates of greater choice would periodically command attention with voucher, tuition tax credit, or alternative school proposals. Similarly, citizens concerned about efficient deployment of public resources sporadically gained headlines with tax limitation movements and efforts to impose more businesslike practices upon schools. Despite such periodic pursuit of policies intended to enhance liberty and efficiency, a measure of progress was made in extending edu-

---

[1] A description of this reform period is provided by Diane Ravitch in *The Troubled Crusade: American Education 1945–1980* (New York: Basic Books, 1983).

cational services to handicapped students, minority group populations, and non-minority women. As useful as such reforms have been, there remains a substantial unfulfilled equality agenda, and we will shortly address ourselves to it.

The 1980s have been characterized by intense public policy attention to educational efficiency. Regard for equality and liberty has not disappeared, but these two values have been eclipsed by strong public proclamations regarding the necessity for schools to become more productive and rigorous. In 1983 alone ten major national studies were conducted criticizing public schools for low academic standards, poor pupil performance, inadequate student discipline, low caliber recruitment and poor professional preparation for teachers, and insufficient attention to science, mathematics, and technological preparation.[2] A fear was repeatedly expressed that the United States was becoming a second rate economic power unable to compete successfully with other industrialized nations such as West Germany and Japan. Moreover, the labor force was thought to be inadequately prepared in reading, mathematics, and scientific subjects to perform the exacting work necessary to maintain an economy increasingly built upon complicated technological processes. In addition, it was feared that the civic fabric of the nation was threatened by the ignorance of students about government, and the inability of large numbers of students to read and speak English.

In addition to the many reports from national commissions and high level panels, prestigious public officials and almost two hundred state-initiated study groups issued numerous pronouncements regarding the need for school reform. States began to enact far-reaching plans directed at encouraging academic rigor, elevating student achievement, and inducing more effective teaching.[3] Beginning in 1983 and continuing into 1984, federal, state, and local officials as well as business and civic leaders frequently and forcefully called attention to the necessity for improving schools. "Merit pay" for teachers, more stringent student discipline, a more rigorous academic curriculum, and better prepared teachers were frequent themes. States as diverse as Florida, North Carolina, Tennessee, and California enacted omnibus bills intended to enhance the effectiveness of schools generally and teachers particularly. In many of these efforts, both at the national and state level, the rediscovery of the link between education and economic productivity often catapulted industrial and commercial leaders into an influential role in advocating reforms.

These many proposals for school reform centered around issues of efficiency and constituted then as now a substantial professional challenge for educational administrators. Sorting reform issues, determining those upon which action is warranted immediately and those of lower priority, and assessing appropriate tactical responses to strategic pronouncements comprise the practical problems which educational leaders must confront.

---

[2] See Paul E. Peterson, "Did the Education Commissions Say Anything?" *The Brookings Review,* 2, no. 2 (Winter 1983), 3–11.

[3] *Ibid.*

In the following section of this chapter we describe many efficiency challenges. However, before doing so, we wish to make clear that if educational administration is to be enhanced as a profession it must not be continually overwhelmed by pendulum swings of reform fads. The practical outcome of such an admonition is that efforts to redress problems related to equality and liberty should not be neglected while attempting to meet the demands made by current proponents of efficiency. Educational leaders must be cognizant of societal changes and the need to alter educational institutions as a consequence. However, greater professional leadership in this capacity, rather than repeatedly reacting to proposals from outsiders, is in order. It is presently necessary to alter educational policies and the flow of resources so as to grapple with the following set of efficiency challenges.

EFFICIENCY CHALLENGES TO THE PROFESSION

The Educational Workforce

The overall quality of those attracted into education positions has frequently been low relative to other professions and private sector positions. Historically, the bright spot in the educational personnel scene occurred as a consequence of societal discrimination on another level. The relative lack of professional opportunities for women and minority group members resulted in such individuals seeking education employment disproportionate to their numbers in the population. By the mid-1970s, however, other occupations began to expand their employment of nonminority women and minorities, the result being that education no longer benefited from the unfair subsidy. Thus, by the mid-1980s, profiles of women and minorities entering teaching match that of white males, and the picture is far from satisfactory. Whether measured by undergraduate grade point averages, scores on Scholastic Aptitude Tests, or Graduate Record Examinations, those being admitted to schools of education rank among the lowest nationally of those occupational categories requiring comparable academic preparation.

Several subsequent conditions render the personnel situation worse yet. Evidence suggests that administrators do not consistently select the most able from among the pool of individuals eligible to be employed as teachers.[4] The situation is compounded by the extraordinarily high turnover rate among beginning teachers. Out of every cohort of one hundred newly hired public school teachers, five years later fewer than sixty remain as classroom instructors, and those leaving are likely to be among the most able.[5]

Problems of teacher quality are magnified by the high probability that the

[4] Gary Sykes, "Public Policy and the Problem of Teacher Quality: The Need for Screens and Magnets," in *Handbook of Teaching and Policy*, ed. Lee S. Shulman and Gary Sykes (New York: Longman, 1983), p. 102.

[5] V. S. Vance and P. C. Schlechty, "The Structure of the Teaching Occupation and the Characteristics of Teachers: A Sociological Interpretation," unpublished paper submitted to the National Institute of Education under contract No. NIEP-81-0100 1982.

United States will need to employ a large number of new teachers beginning in the latter part of the 1980s and into the 1990s. Enrollment expansions coupled with the eminent retirement of instructors employed during the post World War II baby boom render it likely that, nationwide, hundreds of thousands of additional new teachers will be employed.[6] Given the unhappy profile of many current entrants described in the above paragraph, the prospect for added quality is presently a dim one.

Moreover, since 1970 the number of individuals even entering teacher training has declined so precipitously that there is reason to be concerned about the prospect of a "teacher shortage."[7] In 1970, almost one out of every four entering college freshmen held an interest in becoming a teacher. By 1982 this condition had changed dramatically in that only 4 percent had similar aspirations. At prestigious universities the figures were even more dismal.

Teaching was once held in sufficient esteem that parents were proud to think their children might enter the profession. Gallup Poll results reveal that in 1969, 75 percent of parents reported such a view. By 1983, however, teaching had sunk to the point where only 45 percent of parents reported satisfaction with the prospect that their son or daughter would take up teaching. Judging by entrance applications, parental disapproval apparently is transmitted to their offspring. Those responsible for the provision of education have no more pressing problem than enhancing the education profession so that larger numbers of more able individuals prepare themselves to be instructors.

Dysfunctional Incentive Systems

A major explanation for the shortage of more able entrants into education are the incentives which characterize the profession. We describe this condition in Chapter Thirteen and do not wish to dwell upon it here in detail. However, it should be kept in mind that teaching typically suffers from low entry level salaries, a "flat" pay scale in terms of the remuneration available to instructors reaching the top of the salary schedule, and a career ladder which has a perverse effect upon classroom teachers. Entry salaries are seldom consistent with other fields with which education competes for qualified personnel. Similarly, the topmost salaries for classroom teachers are substantially below the potential than an individual in other government or private sector endeavors can anticipate.

Even more insidious is the fact that higher salary, higher prestige, greater discretion over one's time, and more interaction with adults is available only if one leaves classroom teaching and either departs education altogether or becomes a specialist of some kind. It is clear that the way to get ahead in American education is to get out of the classroom. Schools must have able administrators, and the probability is high that the best administrators have had teaching experience.

[6] Sykes, "Problem of Teacher Quality," p. 102.

[7] National Center for Educational Statistics, *Projections of Educational Statistics 1988–89* (Washington, D.C.: National Center for Educational Statistics, 1981).

Thus, leaving classroom teaching to be a school administrator is not bad. What is dysfunctional is that so few rewards exist for those who wish to excel at classroom teaching. Until this situation is altered materially, it is unlikely that the previously described problems of workforce quality and quantity will be solved.

Removing Impediments to Professional Status

A primary deterrent to full professional status for teachers and school administrators is their relative lack of autonomy and control over entry into the field. This is followed closely by four other conditions: (1) lack of control over training; (2) reluctance to expel incompetent members; (3) inability to expel those who flagrantly violate an organization's code of ethics; and (4) the schism that often exists between teachers and boards of education and teachers and administrators.

In the first two areas, control resides with the state through certification requirements. It seems unlikely that this authority will be relinquished. Moreover, there is little agreement on what constitutes an adequate program of preparation for either teachers or administrators, although it is clear that there is a specialized body of knowledge that can be used for preparing both. The third area—expulsion of incompetent teachers—can be controlled by administrators. However, the small number of such dismissals suggest their reluctance to use this avenue. On the fourth point, there is little evidence to suggest that either teachers or administrators have attempted to expel members for flagrant violations of their respective codes of ethics.

A fifth obstacle to the professionalization of educators is the gap that exists between teachers and the board of education, central office and, to a lesser extent, site administrators. This gap has frequently been exacerbated by adversarial posturing in collective bargaining. In this sort of relationship trust is diminished between bargaining groups, and internal tensions arise between teacher organizations over who should represent teachers as the exclusive bargaining agent for purposes of contract negotiations. Moreover, site administrators and supervisory staff who are not members of the teacher groups find it necessary to develop separate ways of negotiating with local boards of education. These conditions all serve to differentiate teacher and administrative groups and obstruct professionalization. Conceivably, greater unity among teachers, and between teachers and administrators, will advance professional status.

Understandably, teachers desire to exercise control over salaries. They are frequently underpaid and thus, this matter is often a major issue in collective bargaining. However, teachers also should have greater leadership in developing educational programs and advocating matters pertaining to students' welfare. Efforts of teachers, administrators, and boards of education should be directed toward serving the best interests of the client—the student. Thus, adversarial collective bargaining should be replaced with a form of cooperative bargaining.

Purposes of Schooling
and Arrangement of Instruction

American education has not fared well when compared on selected criteria to its own record in the past or with the present performance of other nations. The commission reports and criticisms of the 1980s, to which we have alluded, exercised a harsh judgment in this regard. Pupil performance declines, increasing drop-out rates, and naiveté regarding civic matters and world affairs have been assembled as evidence for the case that American public schools are without sufficient rigor. What such critics all too seldom state is that few national systems of schooling attempt to accomplish such a spectrum of purposes for such a wide proportion of the population. The United States, whatever its other flaws, attempts to provide a higher level of education for a wider clientele than almost any other industrialized nation.

Regardless of the accuracy of such criticism, several factual deficiencies emerge. Publishers acknowledge that difficulty levels contained in standard textbooks have drifted downward over time.[8] The length of the school day and school year in many systems has attenuated and is shorter now than that required of students in the past and in other nations today. Grade inflation has been widespread. Academic performance previously accorded a "C" or "B" is now often rewarded with a "B" or an "A."[9]

The proportion of secondary school students enrolled in academically rigorous courses has declined. Analyses of secondary school student transcripts reveal program patterns which are illogical and without cohesion. Large numbers of high schools do not even offer advanced courses in science, mathematics, English, foreign language, and social studies. Evidence regarding the success of vocational preparation provides no relief.[10] Here, too, secondary schools do not appear to be performing well.

These unsatisfactory conditions are far easier to document than to correct. Given the increasing numbers of youngsters coming to school with only a limited grasp of the English language and from single parent households, the challenge is made even more difficult. Though the problems manifest themselves most clearly at the secondary level, solutions appear to be reachable with added efforts to render elementary schools more effective. Thus, no segment of educational leadership can excuse itself from seeking solutions.

[8] See Michael W. Kirst, "A New School Finance for a New Era of Fiscal Constraint," in *School Finance and School Improvement,* ed. Allan Odden and L. Dean Webb (Cambridge: Ballinger, 1983), pp. 1–16.

[9] See James W. Guthrie, Richard Pratt, and John Parsons, *Conditions of Education in California* (Berkeley: PACE, 1984).

[10] See Charles S. Benson, *Descriptive Study of the Distribution of Federal, State, and Local Funds for Vocational Education.* Project on National Vocational Education Resources, School of Education, University of California, Berkeley. September 1981.

Resource Availability

Enhancing the teaching profession and the effectiveness of instruction will necessitate alterations and improvements in many parts of the educational system. However, improvement is unlikely to occur in the absence of additional resources. The United States has made a resource commitment to schooling which no other nation can easily equal. Between 1940 and 1978, spending for schools nationwide increased fivefold in constant dollars. However, beginning in 1979, school revenues began to lag behind inflation. For example, in 1983, the United States was spending $7000 per classroom less than five years before. More money will not itself rectify all the ills besetting American schools. Moreover, even though the economy took a dramatic upturn in 1983 and 1984 and is predicted to have continued, even if modest growth, it is unlikely that educational leaders will ever have all the resources they desire. The challenge is at once to improve education, render it more productive in keeping with public preferences, and to maximize efficient use of whatever resources are available. The hope is that if schools are improved the public and its representatives can be persuaded that education continues to be a necessary and fruitful national investment justifying the infusion of additional resources.

EQUITY CHALLENGES TO THE PROFESSION

If schools can be rendered more efficient in keeping with the previously described problem dimensions, then it is possible that the public will be more satisfied, employers more pleased, and literally millions of students more productive and personally fulfilled. However, more efficient schools will not themselves solve all of America's educational problems. Despite past efforts, resource equality has not been achieved everywhere. Worse yet, it now is evident that a more subtle form of inequality also exists—uneven access to knowledge. Solutions to these problems of inequality remain as challenges to educational leaders, even if public concern about them is less than about other schooling issues.

Access to Knowledge

Too many students in the United States continue to be denied equality of educational opportunity because the schools they are directed to attend do not offer the rigorous academic training increasingly required to gain entry to post-secondary schools and the job market. Not every secondary school has expanded its offering to match the stringent English, science, and mathematics entry requirements enacted by many colleges and universities. Also, some secondary schools still do not offer or do not have arrangements with nearby schools to offer advanced courses in selected academic subject matter fields.[11] If calculus is required

---

[11] Ernest L. Boyer, *High School: A Report on Secondary Education in America* (New York: Harper & Row, Publishers, Inc., 1983).

to gain entry to a college undergraduate engineering curriculum and no such classes are offered at a secondary school, then, at best, such a career may be delayed or may even be denied an aspiring student. Such conditions raise uncomfortable questions regarding access to knowledge. If the opportunity for occupational choice and personal economic success hinges in part upon fulfilling early educational requirements, then all students should have an equal opportunity to acquire the necessary knowledge.

Educational Attainment

Not all humans are equally endowed with ability, physical prowess, or ambition. Differences in achievement are to be expected, and schooling alone cannot compensate for inequities. However, it continues to be the case that disproportionately large numbers of low income students and youngsters from selected minority group households are not performing satisfactorily in school and too often leave before high school completion. In so doing, they carry with them a handicap which impedes their ability to lead personally fulfilling and socially productive lives. These students are sometimes restricted by economically depressed living circumstances, unstable home environments, and limited English speaking ability. Solutions to such problems are not always within the grasp of educational administrators. Nevertheless, the professional obligation is to maximize available resources to assist the learning by such students and to exercise leadership in attempting to gain society's attention for whatever other resources are reasonably needed.

Resource Distribution

The school finance reform movement described in detail in Chapter Five has achieved progress in ensuring that revenues are better distributed within many states than once was the case. Nevertheless, it continues to be true in some instances that differences in local district property wealth penetrate state-legislated equalizing arrangements and result in persistent resource inequality. Also, across states there continues to be substantial revenue inequality. Even when adjusted for regional cost-of-living differences, states such as Mississippi and Arkansas do not spend for schools the equal of states such as New York and Oregon. Efforts to rectify such situations continue as a reform agenda item for educational leaders.

LIBERTY CHALLENGES TO THE PROFESSION

Those advocating greater liberty, or choice, in the context of education often do so out of a belief that America's systems of education are either lacking in responsiveness to public preferences or are oppressive in their efforts to be religiously and culturally impartial, or both. Solutions proffered to remedy these conditions range from relatively conventional reforms such as the injection of greater parent participation via the mechanisms of district or school advisory councils, to major revisions such as proposing government subsidies of nonpublic schools via mechanisms such as vouchers or tuition tax credit plans. All of these ideas have enjoyed periodic political support. Each house of Congress has at one time enacted a federal tuition tax credit plan, though both houses have not so far simultaneously enacted a similar plan. Periodically, public opinion polls report a public preference for government subsidy of nonpublic schools. Also, the 1983 U.S. Supreme Court decision in *Mueller* v. *Allen*[12] arguably could enable states or Congress more easily to overcome previously established First Amendment impediments to public subsidy.

Even assuming the validity of the many criticisms made regarding their inefficiency, inequity, and insensitivity to client preferences, America's schools have been a powerful engine promoting public purposes, social mobility, and personal success. Whereas there continues to be much about education which is in need of improvement, as a nation it probably would not be advantageous to abandon the institution altogether. The majority of radical proposals to inject greater responsiveness into public education systems risks its demise or at least would substantially impair its potential effectiveness. The dimension which is most jeopardized in these proposals is the public school role in creating and enhancing a cohesive and civil society. Thus, the challenge to educational leaders is to successfully balance the public's immediate preferences with society's long-range best interests so as at once to render schools responsive and dilute arguments for their abandonment.

THE CHALLENGING ENVIRONMENT

Exerting effective leadership is difficult even when social conditions are relatively stable. Regrettably, educational leaders are not likely, at least in the short run, to have the luxury of such stability. International tensions and the threat of nuclear war are likely to persist and periodically exert influence on domestic issues. Short of staying informed and personally advocating reasoned efforts to achieve a balance between U.S. national interests and world peace, educational administrators seldom have a direct professional role to play in the foreign policy and diplomacy arenas. However, there are two domestic dimensions which are likely to influence public school policy and practice about which educational leaders should be informed. We refer here to the nature of the economy and to changing demography.

Economic Uncertainty

The so-called "dismal science," economics, is indeed dismal from time to time in its predictions, and despite substantial gains in analytic sophistication, it is still not a complete science. We do not yet have the ability precisely to control economic activities so as to minimize conditions such as unemployment, inflation, and environmental pollution while simultaneously attempting to maximize economic growth. Economists make proposals to strike new balances between these goals,

---

[12]*Mueller* v. *Allen,* 514 F. Supp. 998.

but even when scholarly advice proves accurate there is not always a willingness among elected officials, regardless of political persuasion, to follow it. The outcome has been and is likely to continue to be greater uncertainty regarding the economy than is ideal.

By the mid-1980s, the United States had succeeded in reducing inflation from the awesome double digit levels which scarred the latter 1970s. Also, unemployment had been reduced, but it continues to persist at levels higher than almost anyone would prefer. Measures of economic growth such as the gross national product have been increasing. These conditions have been moderately favorable; however, the prospect of sustained federal budget deficits of a magnitude not heretofore experienced since World War II continues to cast an uncomfortable shadow over the national economic future. Unless remedied, high federal deficits threaten to provoke higher interest rates, make less capital available for new business and expansion, and continue to disadvantage U.S. producers in the international export market.

Who cares anyway? Are not such complicated high level issues the concern of national officials and economists? Yes and no. Reciprocal relationships between education and overall economic conditions have become sufficiently strong that the day-to-day world of an administrator at a local school or district can be affected measurably by decisions taken in Washington, D.C. or New York and events occurring in distant nations. For example, local school district revenues are increasingly drawn from state sources. One consequence is to render education much more tightly tied to national, regional, and state economic conditions than when local property taxes were the overwhelming single source of school support. States depend heavily upon such highly elastic revenue arrangements as sales and income taxes. High unemployment, natural disasters, declines in overseas markets, and shifting federal spending priorities are illustrative of economic conditions which can substantially alter a local or state economy, spelling discomfort for educational administrators. In a world which is increasingly interconnected, educational leaders are professionally obligated to become informed regarding important economic matters and offer their best advice in those areas where education and the economy are joined.

Demographic Variability

Following rapid post World War II population growth, the U.S. birthrate began to decline substantially in the 1960s. According to Rand Corporation demographers,[13] the nation is now beginning to experience effects of zero population growth. If present low fertility persists, natural population growth (number of births less deaths among native born couples) may cease by the beginning of the twenty-first century. Population-related consequences, the nature of which have

---

[13] William P. Butz, Kevin F. McCarthy, Peter A. Morrison, and Mary E. Valana, *Demographic Challenges in America's Future* (Santa Monica: The Rand Corporation, 1982); and Peter A. Morrison, *Current Demographic Trends and Federal Policy: An Overview* (Santa Monica: The Rand Corporation, 1983).

never previously occurred, are likely for the United States. Rand Corporation analysts list the following as effects which are likely to widen and deepen as the transition to zero population growth becomes more evident.

> Immigration, both legal and illegal, currently accounts for nearly one-half of U.S. population growth.

> By the year 2000, persons 65 years and over will constitute one out of every five individuals in the population. In 1985, the comparable figure was one out of every ten individuals.

> The "typical" U.S. family is now one in which both adult partners hold employment. The majority of wives, and a near majority of mothers, are now employed outside the household.

> Households continue to become more diverse; couples without children, children without parents, parents without marriage, and many more persons living alone.

These effects are accompanied by a number of other demographic trends which already have educational consequences and which may well continue. For example, there have been substantial internal population redistributions. Since 1970, a net out-migration from large cities to smaller towns has occurred. Similarly, several regions of the nation have experienced a population loss while others have grown remarkably.

What does all of this portend for educational leaders? Variations in birth rates and the probable long-run decline in births suggest that school districts in many parts of the nation will again face sinking enrollments in the late 1980s and 1990s. This condition will be exacerbated if continued population redistribution occurs from some sections of the northeast and midwest into the south and west. Also, if present conditions persist, large numbers of students will continue to present themselves for schooling without a comprehensive grasp of English. Accommodating instruction for them will be expensive.

Population fluctuations may render it difficult to sustain a stable flow of qualified individuals into teaching. Moreover, shrinking high school graduation classes after 1990 may create an overall labor shortage, inciting ever more intense employer competition for highly qualified individuals—for example, potential teachers. The increasing proportion of single parent families and households with both partners employed will make it less likely that schools can count to the same degree, as was historically the case, upon parents' time contributions for education-related endeavors. Also, higher percentage of senior citizens makes it likely that other social services will also draw heavily upon available public sector revenues, and schools will find themselves continually hard pressed for resources.

BUILDING A PROFESSION

It will require a high order of professional leadership to appropriately address the challenges facing American education and overcome the substantial environmental difficulties we have described. Regrettably, the profession presently does not consistently possess sufficient capacity to overcome these challenges. An additional task facing educational leaders is to strengthen the profession itself.

Professionals conduct services which are vital to the personal health and safety of individuals and the sustenance of society. Because of the crucial nature of their services, society grants to professions an informal "charter" which exchanges the prospect of high personal prestige and remuneration for high standards of performance and conduct. A true profession is characterized by the possession of a technical body of expertise which requires a rigorous and sustained period of study to acquire, an overriding concern with the welfare of clients, high entry level requirements, an ethic which stresses continuous self-improvement, stringent and consistently enforced standards of performance, and a code of conduct which is enforced by the profession itself.

Educational leadership is unquestionably crucial to the productive maintenance of society. It is also essential that the substantial majority of educational leaders conduct themselves in a manner consistent with high professional standards. However, more attention must be paid in several dimensions to developing a full profession. To be professional, educational administrators must be selected and promoted on the basis of their ability to perform effectively, not on the basis of friendship patterns. Professional training must embody high standards and should evidence reasonable consistency within and across state boundaries. Entry into the profession should be fairly but carefully controlled. Administrators must consistently show high concern for the long-run welfare of students and society. An ethic must be created whereby administrators continually strive to upgrade their knowledge and improve professional performance. A professional code of conduct must be agreed to and consistently enforced by members of the profession themselves. When improvement has occurred in all these dimensions, then American education will enjoy a level of leadership the likes of which few other undertakings in society can claim. In exchange, the general public quite reasonably can be expected to have high confidence in its schools. It is our hope that this book will contribute to such a goal.

SUMMARY

Educational policy and practice is often influenced by public pressures for the pursuit of reforms heavily infused with one of three values—efficiency, equality, or liberty. The period between World War II and 1980 was characterized by intense, if somewhat uneven, striving for equality. The 1980s have given evidence of an intense striving for efficiency and productivity. Educational leaders must respond professionally to such public reform movements. However, in so doing, they should not overlook a professional obligation to pursue appropriate reforms in value dimensions other than the one currently occupying the public spotlight. Toward that end this chapter described the leadership challenges now facing the educational administration profession on equality, efficiency, and liberty dimensions and proceeded to outline several demographic and economic conditions likely to influence education leaders in the future. Not the least of these challenges is enhancing the profession of educational administration itself.

SELECTED READINGS

Boyer, Ernest L., *High School.* New York: Harper & Row, Publishers, Inc., 1983.

Goodlad, John, *A Place Called School.* New York: McGraw-Hill, 1983.

Lightfoot, Sara Lawrence, *The Good High School: Portraits of Character and Culture.* New York: Basic Books, 1983.

Ravitch, Diane, *The Troubled Crusade: American Education 1945–1980.* New York: Basic Books, 1983.

Shulman, Lee S., and Gary Sykes, eds., *Handbook of Teaching and Policy.* New York: Longman, 1983.

AUTHOR INDEX

SUBJECT INDEX